PRAYING FOR THE DEFENDERS OF OUR DESTINY

The Mi Sheberach for IDF Soldiers

Edited by Aviad Hacohen and Menachem Butler

The Institute for
Jewish Research and Publications

Cambridge, MA • 2023

12/10/23

Dear Mark,

Learning from you at Harvard in Fall 2019, and interning for Becket in the pre-Covid winter of 2020 will long remain highlights of my legal career. I share this with you now in hopes that as a man of faith, you will find it inspiring and thought-provoking. I was proud to have contributed an essay to this volume, and I am glad to share it with you now.

With Warm Wishes for a very Merry Christmas!

David J. Benger

Praying for the Defenders of Our Faith

The Mi Sheberach for IDF Soldiers

Aviad Hacohen and Menachem Butler, editors

© 2023, All Rights Reserved

ISBN: 978-1-962609-02-9

Published by The Institute for Jewish Research and Publications

Cambridge, MA

www.IJRPub.org

info@IJRPub.org

Twitter @IJRPub

ספר זה מוקדש לכבוד חיילי צה"ל
וכוחות הבטחון השומרים על עם ישראל
בארץ ישראל ובכל העולם
ה' עמכם גבורי חיל

ולעלוי נשמתם של אלו שמסרו נפשם
על קדושת השם ונפלו בחרב
ה' יקום דמם

ולרפואת כל הפצועים והחולים אשר בתוכם
ישלח דברו וירפאם וימלט משחיתותם

ובתפילה להחזרת כל החטופים והשבויים
ביד בני עולה
ופדויי ה' ישובון ובאו ציון ברנה

Table of Contents

Foreword 1
    President Isaac Herzog

Preface 5
    Eric Fingerhut

Introduction – Prayers and Perspectives: Exploring the Mi Sheberach and Zionism Amidst the Turmoil of Operation Swords of Iron 7
    Aviad Hacohen and Menachem Butler

Prayers for the Welfare of Soldiers 23
    Aaron Ahrend

Soldiers of Israel 99
    Meir Bar-Ilan

Prayer for The IDF Soldiers and Liturgical Refuge 102
    Elisheva Baumgarten

On Grassroots Jewish Activism 105
    Yosef Begun

The Shield of David: Prayers as Our Binding Force 114
    David J. Benger

Public Prayers in Times of Communal Distress 118
    Yaron Ben-Naeh

On the Mitzvot of Daily Recitation of The Prayer for Israel's Soldiers and The Prayer for Hostages 123
    Saul J. Berman

Powerful Moment of Prayer and Unity: Reflections on Leading the Prayer for IDF Soldiers Before a Gathering of 300,000 134
    Chaim Dovid Berson

Reflections on the Moral Imperative of Praying for the Soldiers of the IDF 137
    Rookie Billet

Participation through Prayer in the Battle for Israel's Safety 141
    Jonathan Blass

Praying for Israel's Defenders 144
    David R. Blumenthal

Beyond Borders: A Note on Rabbi Hillel Unsdorfer's Posthumous Article on the Mi Sheberach for IDF Soldiers 147
    Menachem Butler

Introduction to Rav Shlomo Aviner's Commentary on the Mi Sheberach for IDF Soldiers 156
    Menachem Butler

Reflection on Praying for IDF Soldiers 165
    Ruth Calderon

This Could Be You 167
    Amichai Chasson

Owning the New Implications of Familiar Words 170
    Noah Cheses

Hasidim Praying for Soldiers 173
    Levi Cooper

A Parent's Greatest Pride 199
    Pini Dunner

From Yoav's Legacy to Today's Frontlines:
Israel's Resolve and the Prayer that Binds Us ... 201
   Atara Eis

The Great Story ... 204
   Emuna Elon

Prayer, Strength, and Confronting Evil ... 207
   Rachelle Sprecher Fraenkel

Prayer and Redemption:
The Commandment to Pray in Turbulent Times ... 211
   David Fuchs

Prayers in Jerusalem Amidst the War of Independence:
A Protective Booklet for IDF Soldiers ... 225
   Uziel Fuchs

The Siren-Interrupted Meditation on the IDF Soldiers' Prayer ... 229
   Tova Ganzel

Bringing Hadar to Eretz Tzvi ... 232
   Simha Goldin

God's Presence and Israel's Wars ... 239
   Alon Goshen-Gottstein

Let Dead Words Become Prayers Again ... 243
   Ithamar Gruenwald

Not Heeding the Slippery Watershed Between
Hostile Words and Their Catastrophic Consequences ... 247
   Ithamar Gruenwald

Mi Sheberach for Shluchei Mitzvah? ... 252
   Neriah Guttel

A Voice of a Proud and Concerned Father:
A Letter from Rav Aharon Lichtenstein to Soldiers in War ... 256
   Aviad Hacohen

Neither Seen nor Found: Why is the 'Mi Sheberach' Prayer for IDF Soldiers Absent in the Lithuanian Haredi Community? 265
    Aviad Hacohen

Judah Halevi on War and Morality 317
    Warren Zev Harvey

Protect Her with the Wings of Your Love 319
    Warren Zev Harvey

Faith, Vigilance, and Solidarity through Prayer 323
    Basil Herring

Uniting In Prayer 325
    Dov Huff

Prayer for the Peace of All the IDF's Soldiers 328
    Ronit Irshai

Mi Sheberach: The Musical Aspect 331
    Elli Jaffe

The Use of the Word 'Avir' in the Prayer for the Israel Defense Forces 333
    Yaakov Jaffe

A Jewish Soldier in Prayer, His Rifle Bearing Petitions 345
    Maoz Kahana

A New Thirst for Life: Bereavement and Death in Israeli Society 350
    Maoz Kahana

'They Are All Holy':
Rabbi Yisroel Zev Gustman on the Sanctity of IDF Soldiers 360
    Ari D. Kahn

Avenging Episodes of Persecution:
A Note on the Text and Origin of Av ha-Rahamim 370
    Ephraim Kanarfogel

On the Prayer for the Success of the IDF Soldiers and Policemen 386
  Yoel Katan

**Expressing Gratitude to IDF Soldiers
through the Mi Sheberach Prayer** 390
  Aaron R. Katz

Personal Reflections on the Prayer for the Israel Defense Forces 394
  Haim (Howard) Kreisel

**The Prayer for the Welfare of the Soldiers of the
IDF and the Security Forces** 398
  Chief Rabbi David Lau

Prayer for IDF Soldiers in Ultra-Orthodox Mizrahi Prayer Books 405
  Nissim Leon

**On the Recitation of the Prayer for the Israel Defense Forces During
Operation Iron Sword** 430
  Zvi Leshem

The Word חיל and its Significance 433
  Aharon Lichtenstein

"Is it time for you to come home yet?" 438
  Phillip I. Lieberman

Prayer as Adjudication 440
  Berachyahu Lifshitz

**Why, How and When We Recite מי שברך לחיילי צה"ל
The Prayer for the Soldiers of Israel** 443
  Haskel Lookstein

The Essence of the Prayer for Tzahal 448
  Leonard Matanky

Elef LaMateh, Elef LaMateh: Praying for IDF Soldiers 451
  Dovid Miller

Reflections on the Mi Sheberach for the IDF ... 454
　Elazar Muskin

'Master of Wars, Sower of Righteousness':
The Impact of the Great War upon Rav Kook ... 457
　Bezalel Naor

A Mother's Reflections to Our Father in Heaven:
Balancing Silence, Serenity, and Prayer during War ... 466
　CB Neugroschl

Words for This Time ... 469
　Elhanan Nir

'He Who Blessed Our Ancestors… May He Bless the Soldiers of the IDF',
'Like Fiery Beings… They Flew Far to Restore Human Dignity' ... 481
　Malka Puterkovsky

On the Evolution and Significance of the
Prayer for the Welfare of IDF Soldiers ... 488
　Yoel Rappel

Uniting Humanity's Mission Amidst Unprecedented Times ... 506
　Robert S. Reichmann

Prayer for Our Heroic Soldiers ... 509
　Yitzchak Avi Roness

A Frontline Soldier's Reflection on the Mi Sheberach Prayer,
One Month After October 7 ... 515
　Hananel Rosenberg

The Prayers of the Mothers and Fathers of 'hayeladim'
on Israel's Frontlines ... 519
　Elisheva Rosman-Stollman

What Good is Communal Prayer? ... 522
　Tamar Ross

A Personal Reflection on Faith, History, and the Prayer for the Peace of IDF Soldiers ... 529
  Elyakim Rubinstein

Shake Off the Dust, Arise ... 533
  Haim Sabato

The Mi Sheberach for IDF Soldiers: Division Turns to Unity ... 535
  Dov Schwartz

Psalms for a State of Vertigo ... 541
  Bacol Serlui

The Text of Rav Ezra Zion Melamed's Mi Sheberach for IDF Soldiers ... 549
  Daniel Sperber

Setting the Mi Seberach for IDF Soldiers to Music ... 553
  Yitzy Spinner

Thoughts on Praying for Israel's Soldiers ... 554
  Joseph Tabory

The Call to Return Home ... 557
  Daniel Tropper

Sociological Aspects of the Prayer on behalf of Soldiers in the Israel Defense Forces ... 559
  Chaim I. Waxman

Praying for the Refuat Ha-Nefesh of the IDF ... 564
  Jason Weiner

The Holiest Jew ... 567
  Avi Weiss

The Noble Sacrifice of IDF Soldiers ... 569
  David Yosef

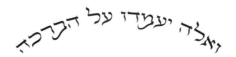

Ginzei Nistarot Society Patrons

GOLD FOUNDING PARTNER

Arielle and Donny Rosenberg

SILVER FOUNDING PARTNER

The Agus Family *(New York and Jerusalem)*

Anonymous

PATRON MEMBERS

Anonymous

Hilda and Yitz Applbaum

Nancy and Dov Friedberg

Caron and Steve Gelles

The Julis Romo Rabinowitz Family

Jennifer and Michael Kaplan

VOLUME SUPPORTERS:

Anonymous

Shedlin Outreach Foundation

In Memory of Tobias Vogelstein z"l

Marlene and Daniel Arbess

Lynn Bartner-Wiesel and Elisha Wiesel

Shani and Gavri Butler

Marnina and Jack Gottesman

Judith and David Lobel and Family

Sandy Nissel-Horowitz and Norman Horowitz

Gail and Terry Novetsky

Wendy and Larry Platt

Bonnie and Isaac Pollak

Pamela and George Rohr

Judith and Joel Schreiber

Esther and William Schulder

Sharona and Jacob Schulder

Kalman Wolchok and Family

VOLUME SUPPORTERS:

Esther and William Schulder
Sharona and Jacob Schulder
Jessica Orbach
Ruth Schulder

We offer this dedication in honor of the brave men
we are blessed to call our family currently serving in the IDF.

Their service on behalf of Jews worldwide
is the embodiment of the commitment to the future of
the Jewish people in our homeland, the Land of Israel.

It is because of the dedication and sacrifice of these brave soldiers
that we can proudly say נֵצַח יִשְׂרָאֵל, לֹא יְשַׁקֵּר.

Along with the rest of Klal Yisrael we owe them immense gratitude
for their unabated love of Torat Yisrael, Eretz Yisrael and Medinat Yisrael.

Isaac Davis, *20, Efrat*	**Sgt. Netanel Meir Kestenbaum**, *32, Rechovot*
Max Davis, *23, Efrat*	**Sgt. Mjr. Amit Nistenpover**, *34, Jerusalem*
Ori Elmakayes, *30, Jerusalem*	**First Sgt.**, Yoel Ollech, *31, Bruchin*
Rami Fischberger, *25, Jerusalem*	**First Sgt. Mordechai Ollech**, *29, Jerusalem*
First Sgt. Dvir Gamilel, *30, Bruchin*	**Sgt. Mjr. Yonatan Ollech**, *25, Jerusalem*
Itai Green, *30, Jerusalem*	**Pvt. Yehuda Ollech**, *21, Jerusalem*
Lt. Etan Kestenbaum, *30, Efrat*	**Pvt. Daniel Singer**, *20, Ramat Beit Shemesh*
First Sgt. Gilad Kestenbaum, *29, Tel Aviv*	**Daniel Shirom**, *32, Efrat*

VOLUME SUPPORTERS:

Lynn Bartner-Wiesel and Elisha Wiesel

In honor of our nephew

Yair Amikam ben Yitzchaka,

who like his father before him,

is taking up arms to defend the Jewish people.

May Hashem protect him and strengthen him in all that he does.

Patrons of The Ginzei Nistarot Society provide support to

The Institute for Jewish Research and Publications,

*directly contributing to the growth of Jewish scholarship and fostering
a deeper understanding of Judaism and its contributions to the world.*

**To join or to find out more information,
please contact info@ijrpub.org**

Foreword

President Isaac Herzog

These remarks were delivered by President Isaac Herzog on Monday, November 14, 2023, during a live broadcast address from the Western Wall in Jerusalem to the hundreds of thousands of participants in the March for Israel held in Washington, D.C. These remarks are reprinted in this volume with the permission of President Isaac Herzog.

SISTERS AND BROTHERS, I AM speaking to you from the single most sacred site in the Jewish world — the Kotel — the Western Wall in Jerusalem. The Kotel that reminds us that Am Yisrael (The people of Israel), we the people of Israel, are eternal and no one will break us.

From the Jewish symbol of fulfillment of our ancient dreams, to the American symbols of freedom, liberty and democracy. Thank you, all people of good will, friends from different communities, faiths and denominations, who have gathered today for this massive show of solidarity.

In the State of Israel's darkest moment you stood up and declared: *Hineini*, I am here. We are here. There is no greater and more just cause than this. Today we come together, as a family, one big *Mishpacha*, to march for Israel. To march for the babies, the boys and girls, women and men viciously held hostage by Hamas. To march for the right of every Jew to live proudly and safely in America, in Israel and around the world. Above all, we come together to march for good over evil, for human morality over blood thirst. We march for light over darkness.

Eighty years ago, Jews came out of Auschwitz and vowed "never again". As the blue and white flag was hoisted over our ancient homeland, we vowed "never again". Forty days ago, a terrorist army invaded the sovereign State of Israel and butchered hundreds upon hundreds of Israelis in the largest massacre since the Holocaust. Let us cry out, together: never again. Never again is now.

The Hamas savagery and crimes against humanity bring to mind, as President Biden has said, "the worst rampages of ISIS". We, the people of Israel are grateful to President Biden, his Administration, and so many Members of Congress on both sides of the aisle. The moral clarity and bold actions of our American allies, demonstrate the depth of the US-Israel alliance, which is stronger than ever before.

Since October 7th, Israeli society and the Jewish People have truly come together in unison. We feel our hearts beat as one. We hear our brothers' and sisters' blood crying out to us from the ground: "*The blood of our brothers calls out from the ground*". Once again in Jewish history we demand: Let our people go. Whilst our loved ones are held captive in Gaza, and our soldiers are fighting for our beloved Israel – Jews all over the world are assaulted for being Jewish. The hatred, the lies, the brutality, the disgraceful outburst of ancient antisemitism are an embarrassment to all civilized people and nations.

Jews in America must be safe. Jews all over the world must be safe.

I salute you, the women and men who stand up to massive hatred and pressure in the community or on campus. Just as you stand with us, we stand with you.

Dear friends, as President of the State of Israel, I vow to you from Jerusalem, from the Kotel, that we will heal, we will rise again, and we will rebuild.

To paraphrase the Prophet Zecharia: *Boys and girls shall once again play in the streets of Be'eri and Sderot and the elderly shall sit peacefully by the walkways of Nahal Oz and Ofakim.* And when the sounds of life and laughter return to the villages, the kibbutzim and the cities, our constant yearning for peace will return as well.

Together we pray for the safe return of our hostages. Together we pray for the full recovery of the wounded. And together we pray for our beloved sons and daughters in the IDF. May God bless them and keep them. Together we grieve and together we shall overcome. *Am Yisrael Chai* (The People of Israel lives). God bless Israel. God bless America.

Mr. Isaac Herzog is President of the State of Israel.

Preface

Eric Fingerhut

D URING OUR SHABBAT TEFILLAH, WHEN the Chazan begins the Mi Sheberach for the brave soldiers of the Israel Defense Forces, one can feel the mood shift in the synagogue. All talking stops as the congregants anticipate the beautiful melody and join in the call and response, voices rising in fervor and volume, until the whole room is swept up in the emotion of the moment. It is as if we are trying to physically – not just emotionally – carry our prayers up to the gates of heaven.

Why does this prayer move us so deeply here in the Diaspora?

Of course, it is always powerful to pray for the Land of Israel, for the People of Israel, and even for the State of Israel, as we do at different times throughout our services. These different prayers are recited with real kavanah and are deeply heartfelt. "To Jerusalem your city may you return in compassion… May you rebuild it rapidly in our day" we pray thrice daily in Shemoneh Esrei. "Our God in heaven, rock and redeemer of the People Israel, bless the State of Israel, the flowering of our redemption," we pray in the tefillah l'shalom medinat yisrael.

But when we sing "hu yevarech et chayalei tzvah haganah l'yisrael" – "bless those who serve in the Israel Defense Forces" – you can hear the collective pride, awe, respect and love of the entire Jewish people condensed into one powerful phrase.

Bless them, O God! Please!

For too many centuries we were powerless. Now these smart, strong, brave young men and women go into battle on behalf of the Jewish people. Bless them! For too many generations we had no land to defend. Protect them! For too many centuries, Jews were exiled, forced to leave homes and businesses of real value with no recourse. Strengthen their hands!

We who live across the ocean from the Jewish homeland know that our own existence is inextricably tied to the fortunes of these soldiers. Some of our own children choose to go and serve, lifted up as lone soldiers, but every soldier is family. They all belong to us.

This beautiful collection of essays about the Mi Sheberach for the Israel Defense Forces opens new doors to us as we recite this prayer. The authors and editors deserve our thanks. May this work enhance our understanding and strengthen us as we rise together in devotion. But mostly may it enable us to once again reflect on the light of divine providence that has enabled us to live in a time when those among the most capable Jewish men and women in history selflessly rise to our common defense, with integrity, with skill, and with total dedication.

Bless them, O God.

Eric Fingerhut is the President and CEO of The Jewish Federations of North America.

Introduction – Prayers and Perspectives: Exploring the Mi Sheberach and Zionism Amidst the Turmoil of Operation Swords of Iron

Aviad Hacohen and Menachem Butler

> *Inter arma enim silent leges*
> "For in times of war, the laws are silent."

THIS SAYING, ATTRIBUTED TO CICERO (Pro Milone, 52), was probably the source for the more popular saying in our times, according to which "when the cannons roar, the muses are silent."

Praying for the Defenders of Our Faith

Perhaps the muses of creation remain silent, but history teaches us that at least the muse of prayer also works during times of war. And not just randomly, but with determination and at an accelerated pace.

History teaches us that when a person is in situations of pressure, distress, and hardship, when we stand face to face with a war, imminent or ongoing, different prayers break through the walls of our heart, private and public prayers. Our lips murmur and articulate prayers that come from the heart – and enter it.

An expression of this can already be found in our oldest sources.

Before his meeting with his brother Esau, whom he feared and who had sought to kill him, our forefather Jacob was greatly afraid. According to our Sages, at that moment, Jacob prepared himself for three things: prayer, gifts, and war.

And specifically, prayer came first. Prayer was at the forefront.[1]

An expression of the immense power and strength of prayer during times of war, Jacob our forefather also demonstrated towards the end of his days when he sought to bless his beloved son Joseph before his passing from this world.

Among his other words, Jacob chose to mention to Joseph, out of all the events in his life, specifically his struggle with "the Amorite": "I have given to you one portion over your brothers, which I took from the hand of the Amorite with my sword and with my bow."[2]

Following the teachings of our Sages,[3] the early biblical translation and commentary, the term "sword and bow" does not mean their literal

---

1 See Rashi to Bereishit 32:9, and his source in Midrash Kohelet Rabba, Parasha 9, and Yalkut Shimoni to Genesis, Chapter 32.

2 Bereishit 58:22.

3 See Bava Batra 123a: "But is it with his sword and bow that he [David] took [the land]? Didn't it already say (Psalms 44:7), 'For I will not trust in my

meanings, but are rather to be understood as metaphors: "with my prayers and with my supplications."[4]

This teaches us the immense power of prayer during times of war.

Many expressions of this can also be found in the book of Psalms by King David, the great "man of prayer," for whom prayer was ingrained in his blood and soul, to the point where he declared, "I am prayer."[5]

In various situations of pressure and distress, King David uttered prayers with his lips. For example, when he was in the "cave," fleeing from King Saul and his men who sought to kill him, surrounded by the darkness of fear and death, hidden from the terror of his enemies and preparing for battle with them, David raised a prayer that emerged from the depths of his heart (Psalms 152):

> "A maskil of David when he was in the cave. A prayer. I cry out to the Lord; I plead for mercy to the Lord. I pour out my complaint before him; I tell my trouble before him. When my spirit faints within me, you know my way! In the path where I walk they have hidden a trap for me. Look to the right and see: there is none who takes notice of me; no refuge remains to me; no one cares for my soul. I cry to you, O Lord; I say, 'You are my

bow, and my sword will not save me'? Rather, 'my sword'—this is prayer; 'my bow'—this is request."

4 In his desire to emphasize the distinct aspect of each of these two components, the Meshech Chochmah explained: "The fixed order of prayer, as they said, 'Praise, prayer, and thanksgiving delay' (Tosefta Menachot). Whereas 'B'otai' (my times) refers to a request that a person says if he wants to add something new to his prayer."

5 Tehillim 109:4. See Rabbi Yehuda Amital's address, titled: "I Am Prayer," which was held at Yeshivat Har Etzion at the start of September 1995, and edited for publication by Aviad Hacohen, available here (https://etzion.org.il/en/philosophy/great-thinkers/harav-yehuda-amital/i-am-prayer).

refuge, my portion in the land of the living.' Attend to my cry, for I am brought very low! Deliver me from my persecutors, for they are too strong for me."

Thus, in times of trouble and in his song of hope before and after the battle (Psalms 144):

"Bow your heavens, O Lord, and come down! Touch the mountains so that they smoke! Flash forth the lightning and scatter them; send out your arrows and rout them! Stretch out your hand from on high; rescue me and deliver me from the many waters, from the hand of foreigners, whose mouths speak lies and whose right hand is a right hand of falsehood. I will sing a new song to you, O God; upon a ten-stringed harp I will play to you, who gives victory to kings, who rescues David his servant from the cruel sword. Rescue me and deliver me from the hand of foreigners, whose mouths speak lies and whose right hand is a right hand of falsehood."

The prayer that is recited in times of war is a chapter in the general order of prayer. In the world of the Jewish community, a single prayer text is established, with each congregation following its own tradition. Sages have even expressed reservations about "changing the currency of prayer."

However, Jewish history teaches us that alongside the established prayer, new prayers were added. The desire to create personal prayers, alongside communal prayer, which sometimes took on a uniform and institutionalized character, has been present since ancient times.

Even in the Bible, there is evidence of various types of prayers, such as those of Noah,[6] our forefather Jacob,[7] Moses, King Solomon, and the prophet Jonah. From those early days of Genesis to the present day, hundreds of prayers have been composed by individuals, who stood alongside the established prayers, which are traditionally fixed by the Great Assembly (Knesset HaGedolah).

It is not surprising, then, that in Jewish sources, and even in the earliest ones, man is identified not only as homo sapiens, as a thinking and intelligent being but also as "the praying man," homo liturgicus (or, in Jewish terminology, homo davenus), for whom contemplative prayer will become a core part of our religious experiences.

From here, the path is short to the establishment of the Chazal's statement that "the Patriarchs instituted the prayers." That is, the three Patriarchs of the Jewish nation, Abraham, Isaac, and Jacob, each instituted one of the three fixed Jewish prayers: Shacharit, Mincha, and Maariv.[8] The attempt to relate the institution of prayer to the Patriarchs of our Nation, even in cases where it is not explicitly mentioned and only

6   For example, consider Midrash Tanchuma, Noach, 18, which describes Noah praying using the same language as King David, who lived approximately 1,700 years after him: "When Noah was in the ark, he would constantly recite "You have brought up my soul from Sheol" (Psalm 30:4).

7   Bereishit 28:20-21.

8   See Berakhot 26b: "Rabbi Yossi, the son of Rabbi Chanina, said: The prayers of our forefathers established them… Abraham instituted the morning prayer (Shacharit), as it is said: 'And Abraham arose early in the morning to the place where he had stood before the Lord,' and 'stood' means nothing but prayer, as it is said: 'Phinehas stood and prayed.' Isaac instituted the afternoon prayer (Mincha), as it is said: 'And Isaac went out to meditate in the field toward evening,' and 'meditate' means nothing but prayer, as it is said: 'A prayer of the afflicted when he is faint and pours out his complaint before the Lord.' Jacob instituted the evening prayer (Ma'ariv), as it is said: 'And he encountered the place and spent the night there,' and 'encounter'

hinted at, reflects the significant and essential role of prayer in the Jewish heritage for generations.

As Rabbi Joseph B. Soloveitchik taught us, individuals know – and unfortunately, they must know – that despite all their achievements, they are not all-knowing geniuses. They acknowledge that despite all the theories of relativity, quantum mechanics, space exploration, and nanotechnology, there are still many areas where they remain akin to an animal.

Therefore, one must be a "person of prayer." We must know not only when to pray and what to pray but also how to pray. Tefillah means standing before God. As its etymological root teaches us, it includes both "tehilla"" in the sense of praise and gratitude, as well as "tefillah" in the sense of request, demand, and supplication.[9] The one who prays does not stand indifferently in the face of reality; rather, engages with it on an equal footing. We aspire to change it "to repair the world under the Kingdom of God."

Tell me what your prayer is, and I will tell you who you are. Every prayer, including the prayer of a person during times of war, reveals the innermost thoughts of a person, his hidden depths.

A person's prayer during wartime expresses his longing for the safe return of all the soldiers from the battle and his concern for the well-being of his brothers, sisters, friends, and relatives.

It is not surprising, then, that throughout the generations, dozens, and perhaps even hundreds of prayers for soldiers going to battle have been composed. The Mi Sheberach prayer for the Soldiers of the Israel Defense Forces is integrated into them, as another link in this long chain.

> means nothing but prayer, as it is said: 'But as for you, do not pray for this people, or lift up a cry or prayer for them, and do not intercede with Me.'"

9   See Psalms 106:30, and Sanhedrin 82b.

Indeed, Mi Sheberach is not a specific name but a family name. The diverse chapters of the book before us reveal this in a clear and fascinating manner.

Already in the Middle Ages, Ashkenazi communities had the custom of adding a section of prayer that begins with the words "Yehi Ratzon Milifnei Avinu ShebaShamayim" (May it be Your will, our Father in Heaven) which includes four short prayers. These prayers were intended to focus on the construction of the Holy Temple, to prevent destruction and plagues, to pray for the well-being of the Sages of Israel and their students, for good tidings, and for the ingathering of the exiles.

In some communities, this Yehi Ratzon prayer was recited every Monday and Thursday, immediately after the Torah reading. In others, including some Eastern communities, it was incorporated into the Shabbat Mevarchim service, close to the Birkat HaChodesh recited in anticipation of the new moon. It is interesting to note that in some of the early versions of this prayer, a section was included, apparently as the fourth part of Yehi Ratzon, that served as a prayer against enemies. Moreover, this has been preserved in several works of the Rishonim,[10] which provide indications in the order of prayer sections, where in the last of them appears the text, "May it be heard and proclaimed to destroy our enemies."

In later times, an additional section was added to these four sections of Yehi Ratzon, recited by the entire congregation as follows:

> *Our brethren, the entire House of Israel,*
>
> *who are in distress and captivity,*
>
> *standing between the sea and the dry land,*
>
> *may the Almighty have mercy on them,*

---

10 Sefer Kolbo, no. 37; Orhot Hayyim, vol. 1, Sefer Tefillat Shabbat, Shaharit.

Praying for the Defenders of Our Faith

and bring them out of distress to relief,

from darkness to light,

and from servitude to redemption,
now in haste and soon,

and let us say, Amen.

As per these dozens of essays in *Praying for the Defenders of Our Destiny: The Mi Sheberach for IDF Soldiers* that is before us, in the past two hundred years, "Prayers for the Welfare of Jewish Soldiers" have been composed and have been used in various armies around the world. These prayers were composed in different versions.

With the establishment of the State of Israel, there was a growing need to incorporate a special Mi Sheberach prayer for the well-being of the Israel Defense Forces soldiers into the prayer liturgy. This prayer was initially composed by Rabbi Shmuel Avidor Hacohen (1926-2005), the beloved uncle of Aviad Hacohen. Subsequently, it was adopted by Rabbi Shlomo Goren, the Chief Rabbi of the IDF, following Operation Kadesh in 1956. The original prayer is focused and concise, containing only 84 words in Hebrew, yet it carries great power. It quickly became widely adopted by many, both in Israel and around the world, and even integrated into the prayer books of some Jewish communities, despite their traditional tendencies.

מִי שֶׁבֵּרַךְ אֲבוֹתֵינוּ

אַבְרָהָם יִצְחָק וְיַעֲקֹב,

הוּא יְבָרֵךְ אֶת חַיָּלֵי צְבָא הַהֲגָנָה לְיִשְׂרָאֵל

[וְאַנְשֵׁי כֹּחוֹת הַבִּטָּחוֹן],

הָעוֹמְדִים עַל מִשְׁמַר אַרְצֵנוּ וְעָרֵי אֱלֹהֵינוּ,

מִגְּבוּל הַלְּבָנוֹן וְעַד מִדְבַּר מִצְרַיִם,

וּמִן הַיָּם הַגָּדוֹל עַד לְבוֹא הָעֲרָבָה

וּבְכָל מָקוֹם שֶׁהֵם,

בַּיַּבָּשָׁה בָּאֲוִיר וּבַיָּם.
יִתֵּן ה' אֶת אוֹיְבֵינוּ הַקָּמִים עָלֵינוּ נִגָּפִים לִפְנֵיהֶם!
הַקָּדוֹשׁ בָּרוּךְ הוּא יִשְׁמֹר וְיַצִּיל אֶת חַיָלֵינוּ
מִכָּל צָרָה וְצוּקָה,
וּמִכָּל נֶגַע וּמַחֲלָה,
וְיִשְׁלַח בְּרָכָה וְהַצְלָחָה בְּכָל מַעֲשֵׂה יְדֵיהֶם.
יַדְבֵּר שׂוֹנְאֵינוּ תַּחְתֵּיהֶם,
וִיעַטְרֵם בְּכֶתֶר יְשׁוּעָה וּבַעֲטֶרֶת נִצָּחוֹן.
וִיקֻיַּם בָּהֶם הַכָּתוּב
"כִּי ה' אֱלֹקֵיכֶם הַהֹלֵךְ עִמָּכֶם,
לְהִלָּחֵם לָכֶם עִם אֹיְבֵיכֶם
לְהוֹשִׁיעַ אֶתְכֶם".
וְנֹאמַר: אָמֵן

May He Who blessed our fathers, Abraham, Isaac, and Jacob, bless those who serve in the Israel Defense Forces [and its security services] who stand guard over our land and the cities of our God from the Lebanese border to the Egyptian desert, from the Mediterranean Sea to the approach of the Aravah, and wherever they are, on land, in the air, and at sea. May the Lord cause our enemies who rise against us to be struck down before them. May the Holy One, blessed is He, protect and deliver our soldiers from all trouble and distress, injury and illness and bring blessing and success upon all that they do. May those who hate us be vanquished before them, and may He crown them with deliverance and the laurels of victory. Through them may there be the fulfillment of the verse: "It is the Lord your God Who goes

Praying for the Defenders of Our Faith

with you to fight for you against your enemies, to deliver you." And let us say, Amen.[11]

Praying for the Defenders of Our Destiny: The Mi Sheberach for IDF Soldiers teaches us that the Mi Sheberach prayer for the soldiers of the Israel Defense Forces is more than just a liturgical recitation; it's also a profound expression of commitment to Zionist ideology. Its various versions express contrasting worldviews, reflecting the ongoing tension between reliance on a tangible army and the belief in Israel's security and redemption (with no inherent contradiction between the two). As such, this book includes chapters that address various aspects of the Mi Sheberach prayer for the well-being of IDF soldiers in particular, compiled in the immediate days and weeks during a time of great sadness for the Jewish people — the "Operation Swords of Iron." This war was imposed on the State of Israel on the holiday of Simchat Torah 5784, on October 7th 2023. In the past two months, this war has taken a devastating toll on the State of Israel, with the tragic loss of more than 1,200 lives on the first day alone. Among the victims were both soldiers and civilians of all backgrounds and ages, who were murdered by terrorists. Hundreds of individuals have been captured, abducted, or remain unaccounted for, while thousands more have suffered physical and emotional injuries.

Praying for the Defenders of Our Destiny: The Mi Sheberach for IDF Soldiers includes academic articles that explore the history and controversies surrounding the composition and popularity of the Mi Sheberach prayer for the soldiers of the Israel Defense Forces, details that reflect not only liturgy but also ideology, mirroring the ongoing tensions between reliance on a tangible army and the belief in Israel's

---

11 Translation adapted from *Siddur Avodat Halev*, ed. Basil Herring (New York: Rabbinical Council of America, 2018), 541-543, with permission of the Rabbinical Council of America.

security. This book also features several dozen original meditative reflections written specifically for this volume in the aftermath of the October 7th massacre, as well as previously unreleased English translations of important earlier Hebrew articles. These articles offer various aspects of the prayer of a believing individual during times of war in general, and perspectives to motivate one to encourage the recitation of the Mi Sheberach for IDF soldiers. Our book aims to achieve several interconnected goals: to demonstrate unwavering support for the State of Israel and the IDF, providing a deeper understanding of their roles and significance; to offer moral encouragement to families of soldiers serving on Israel's frontlines, sharing narratives that resonate with their experiences; and to serve as a much-needed educational resource in the face of rising global antisemitism, presented from a Jewish religious perspective that recognizes the critical importance of the State of Israel in contemporary Jewish history. Additionally, our book aims to enhance readers' understanding of Zionism within contemporary Jewish tradition and strengthen their connection with the Israel Defense Forces, especially benefiting those facing daily challenges on campus, by offering insights and perspectives from an unwavering Jewish religious viewpoint that recognizes the pivotal role of the State of Israel in contemporary Jewish history.

The dozens of contributors to *Praying for the Defenders of Our Destiny: The Mi Sheberach for IDF Soldiers*, chosen for their diverse perspectives, independently shared their insights, with each unaware of the participation of others. While the opinions expressed in each essay belong solely to the respective author and may not necessarily align with those of other contributors in this volume, this approach not only ensured an impartial collection of essays but also underscores the unity that this project strives to convey.

Praying for the Defenders of Our Faith

We were able to complete *Praying for the Defenders of Our Destiny: The Mi Sheberach for IDF Soldiers* on schedule thanks to the support and encouragement of our family, the authors who contributed their essays in a timely manner, and to the entire team at the Institute for Jewish Research and Publications, with special recognition for the production work of Rabbi David Shabtai, MD, and Ilana Landau for the cover design. The accomplishment of compiling this book in such a short time is indeed remarkable.

We would also like to express our gratitude to the patrons of the Institute for Jewish Research and Publications, as well as the additional sponsors whose names are listed at the start of the book. Their support has enabled the publication of this volume, which will be available for purchase online worldwide and in select Jewish bookstores in both America and Israel, and at an affordable price. We are also pleased to offer bulk order discounts to synagogues and schools, and we will provide complimentary copies to journalists and to Jewish students on American college campuses, all courtesy of the support of the Institute for Jewish Research and Publications, its patrons, and the donors to this volume. (If you have reflections or insights to share about this book, we invite you to send them by email to menachem@ijrpub.org.)

May this book, *Praying for the Defenders of Our Destiny: The Mi Sheberach for IDF Soldiers*, serve as both an educational and inspirational source, deepening our understanding of the vital role played by the Soldiers of the Israel Defense Forces in protecting the State of Israel. Let it rekindle our appreciation for the power of prayer. Through this book, we honor the heroes who made the ultimate sacrifice for our nation and homeland, and we extend our unwavering support to their grieving families and friends. We turn our prayers to the Holy One, Blessed Be He, seeking the safe return of captives, the missing, and the full recovery of all those among the people of Israel who are unwell. With humility, we pray to the Almighty, "Bila hamavet lanetzach umacha Hashem Elokim dim'ah me'al kol panim," beseeching the Holy One, Blessed Be He, to banish death forever and wipe away every tear from our eyes.

Aviad Hacohen and Menachem Butler

Jerusalem, Israel and Cambridge, MA

November 2023 / Kislev 5784

The 75th Year of the State of Israel

Professor Aviad Hacohen serves as the President of Sha'arei Mishpat Academic College and previously held the position of Dean at its Law School. His extensive academic research encompasses Mishpat Ivri, human rights, criminal law, civil law, and their intersections with Jewish law.

Menachem Butler, the Program Fellow for Jewish Legal Studies in the Julis-Rabinowitz Program on Jewish and Israeli Law at Harvard Law School, serves as the President of the Institute for Jewish Research and Publications.

May He Who blessed our fathers,
Abraham, Isaac, and Jacob,
bless those who serve in the Israel Defense Forces
[and its security services]
who stand guard over our land and the cities of our God
from the Lebanese border to the Egyptian desert,
from the Mediterranean Sea to the approach of the Aravah,
and wherever they are,
on land, in the air, and at sea.

May the Lord cause our enemies who rise against us
to be struck down before them.
May the Holy One, blessed is He, protect and deliver our soldiers
from all trouble and distress,
injury and illness
and bring blessing and success upon all that they do.
May those who hate us be vanquished before them,
and may He crown them with deliverance
and the laurels of victory.
Through them may there be the fulfillment of the verse:
"It is the Lord your God Who goes with you
to fight for you against your enemies,
to deliver you."
And let us say, Amen.

מִי שֶׁבֵּרַךְ אֲבוֹתֵינוּ
אַבְרָהָם יִצְחָק וְיַעֲקֹב,
הוּא יְבָרֵךְ אֶת חַיָּלֵי צְבָא הַהֲגַנָּה לְיִשְׂרָאֵל
[וְאַנְשֵׁי כֹּחוֹת הַבִּטָּחוֹן],
הָעוֹמְדִים עַל מִשְׁמַר אַרְצֵנוּ וְעָרֵי אֱלֹהֵינוּ,
מִגְּבוּל הַלְּבָנוֹן וְעַד מִדְבַּר מִצְרַיִם,
וּמִן הַיָּם הַגָּדוֹל עַד לְבוֹא הָעֲרָבָה
וּבְכָל מָקוֹם שֶׁהֵם,
בַּיַּבָּשָׁה בָּאֲוִיר וּבַיָּם.

יִתֵּן יְיָ אֶת אוֹיְבֵינוּ הַקָּמִים עָלֵינוּ
נִגָּפִים לִפְנֵיהֶם!
הַקָּדוֹשׁ בָּרוּךְ הוּא יִשְׁמֹר וְיַצִּיל אֶת חַיָּלֵינוּ
מִכָּל צָרָה וְצוּקָה,
וּמִכָּל נֶגַע וּמַחֲלָה,
וְיִשְׁלַח בְּרָכָה וְהַצְלָחָה בְּכָל מַעֲשֵׂה יְדֵיהֶם.
יַדְבֵּר שׂוֹנְאֵינוּ תַּחְתֵּיהֶם,
וִיעַטְּרֵם בְּכֶתֶר יְשׁוּעָה
וּבַעֲטֶרֶת נִצָּחוֹן.
וִיקֻיַּם בָּהֶם הַכָּתוּב
"כִּי יְיָ אֱלֹהֵיכֶם הַהֹלֵךְ עִמָּכֶם,
לְהִלָּחֵם לָכֶם עִם אֹיְבֵיכֶם
לְהוֹשִׁיעַ אֶתְכֶם".
וְנֹאמַר: "אָמֵן".

Prayers for the Welfare of Soldiers

Aaron Ahrend

IN JEWISH COMMUNITIES, IT HAS been customary for hundreds of years to say prayers and Mi Sheberach on various matters that were not included in the set prayers composed by our Sages. These prayers were dedicated to various topics: blessings for those doing good deeds, such as donors, those dealing with public needs, those fasting on BaHaB (Monday, Thursday, Monday fast days), those refraining from speaking during prayer; blessings for family joy such as birth, Bar Mitzvah; prayers for those in trouble, such as the sick and prisoners; prayers for the peace of the kingdom, and more. These prayers were said in public and had several purposes beyond asking for God's blessing: social cohesion of the community, an educational means to accustom the congregation to commandments and positive actions, and more. These prayers entered the world of prayer because their authors were rabbis. From a halachic standpoint, their status was lower than the set prayers, but they often received significant attention from the worshippers because they were usually dedicated to local community members and not to all of Israel.[1] Their recitation was usually close to the Torah reading, out of a desire to utilize both the presence of the Torah scroll, in order to give them a

---

* *Dedicated in Friendship to Major General (retired) Dr. Emanuel Sakal*
   [This chapter is an English translation of Aaron Ahrend, "Prayers for the Welfare of Soldiers," *Alei Sefer*, vol. 24-25 (2015): 297-330 (Hebrew).]

1 See Ismar Elbogen, *Prayer in Israel in its Historical Development*, third edition (Tel-Aviv: Dvir, 1988), 150-151 (Hebrew); Avraham Yaari, "The 'Mi Sheberach' Prayers: Their Evolution, Customs, and Texts," *Kiryat Sefer*, vol. 33, no. 1 (December 1957): 118-130 (Hebrew); Avraham Yaari, "The 'Mi Sheberach' Prayers: Their Evolution, Customs, and Texts," *Kiryat Sefer*, vol. 33, no. 2 (March 1958): 233-250 (Hebrew); Avraham Yaari, "Supplements to The Mi Sheberach Prayers: Their Evolution, Customs, and Texts," *Kiryat Sefer*, vol. 36, no. 1 (December 1960): 103-118 (Hebrew), with notes and supplements by Nathan Fried, "Notes to 'The Mi Sheberach Prayers: Their Evolution, Customs, and Texts', by Avraham Yaari," *Kiryat Sefer*, vol. 37, no. 4 (September 1962): 511-514 (Hebrew), and by Daniel Yaakov Cohen, "Notes and Supplements to 'The Mi Sheberach Prayers: Their Evolution, Customs, and Texts', by Avraham Yaari," *Kiryat Sefer*, vol. 40, no. 4 (September 1965): 542-559 (Hebrew). Regarding the social aspect in the world of the synagogue, see, for example, Jacob Katz, *Tradition and Crisis: Jewish Society at the End of the Middle Ages* (Jerusalem: Bialik Institute, 1958) 208-212 (Hebrew). On this aspect in the synagogue in the United States, see Samuel C. Heilman, *Synagogue Life: A Study in Symbolic Interaction* (New Jersey: Transaction, 1998). According to Eliezer Schweid, *Mahzor: A Study in Symbolic Interaction* (Tel-Aviv: Am Oved, 1996), 45 (Hebrew), the social setting in the synagogue creates a framework for addressing significant events that affect individuals, the community, and the people of Israel. Within this context, we can view these prayers and blessings, as well as the prayers for the welfare of the community, the nation, and the army. Special thanks to Dr. Haim Burgansky, Rabbi Shmuel Katz, and Dr. Rivka Raviv for their comments.

respected status, and the opportunity to say them in a central place in prayer without fear of interrupting the prayer.[2]

The military framework and wars between nations also served as a subject for a variety of prayers: prayers for peace between nations and prevention of wars, thanksgiving prayers and "HaGomel" (a blessing for deliverance) after wars, prayers for captured or missing soldiers, memorial prayers for fallen soldiers, and more. The following lines will be dedicated to examining prayers for the peace of soldiers in the last two hundred years. First, we will describe the prayers for soldiers in the Diaspora, and then we will examine the evolutions and versions of the prayers for soldiers in the Land of Israel.

Prayers for the Peace of Soldiers of Foreign Armies

A natural and common action is for people, standing on the brink of war, to turn to the Creator in prayer and outcry, seeking assistance in the battle and protection from all harm.[3] This phenomenon also exists in Judaism. In the Bible and post-biblical literature, the view is found in many places that the Holy One, Blessed be He, is with Israel during war and assists it, as the verse says (Deut. 20:4): "For it is the Lord, your God, Who goes with you to battle your enemies, for you to save you,"

---

2   See Ruth Langer, "Early Medieval Celebrations of Torah in the Synagogue: A Study of the Rituals of the Seder Rav Amram Gaon and Masekhet Soferim," *Kenishta: Studies of the Synagogue World*, vol. 2 (2003): 102 (Hebrew).

3   For example, in Islam, it is established that during times of war, some of the warriors pray while others engage in battle. See, for instance, *The Qur'an* (Hebrew Translation from the Arabic, Annotations, Appendices and Index by Uri Rubin) (Tel Aviv: Tel Aviv University Press and MAPA Publishers. 2005), Surah 4, Verse 102; and *Life and Religion in Early Islam: A Selection of Hadiths from Al-Bukhari's "Sahih"*, ed. and trans. Immanuel Koplewitz (Jerusalem: Carmel, 2011), 244 (Hebrew)

and it is told of people who prayed to God before a war and during it.[4] In later periods, Jews were accustomed, before going to war, to recite verses from Psalms and other texts whose content was a request for protection and safeguarding. Sometimes a rabbi would come to deliver words of encouragement to the soldiers and read verses. However, verses that are general and familiar did not always meet the emotional need of the soldier in these crucial moments, in which he sought to pray a special personal prayer that would express his feelings and beliefs. Due to this need, rabbis occasionally composed special prayers for soldiers to be said before a war or operational activity. These prayers incorporated verses and varied in length, style, and content. Among the contents, one can find that the soldier asks God to assist him in defeating the enemies, to return in peace, that God will forgive him for his sins, that if he dies his death will be his atonement, and the soldier's proclamation of "Shema Yisrael."[5] A special prayer for a soldier somewhat resembles, essentially,

---

4   See Jacob Shalom Licht, "War," in *Encyclopedia Mikrait*, vol. 4 (1963): 1058, 1061-1063 (Hebrew); Moshe David Herr, "War [in the Thought of the Sages]," in *Encyclopedia ha-Ivrit*, vol. 23 (1973): 644 (Hebrew); Yigael Yadin, *The Scroll of the War of the Sons of Light against the Sons of Darkness* (Jerusalem: Bialik, 1957), 190-208 (Hebrew).

5   See, for example, Yehuda Leib Bialer, "Wartime Prayers," *Shana be-Shana* (1965): 488-489 (Hebrew); Tovia Preschel, "The Prayer for the Soldiers of the Jewish Legion," in Simcha Raz, ed., *Religious Zionism in Action Essays*, vol. 5 (Jerusalem: Mizrachi World Organization, 2002), 226-233 (Hebrew). Rabbi Yitzhak Isaac Herzog composed the "Prayer for the Defenders" with the intensification of recruitment in December 1947, and it was printed in *Beit ha-Knesset*, vol. 3, no. 7 (May 1948): 311 (Hebrew). Regarding this prayer, see Yoel Rappel, "The Identity of the Author of the Prayer for the Welfare of the State," in Shulamit Eliash, et al., eds., *Masuah LeYitzhak: Rabbi Yitzhak Isaac ha-Levi Herzog Memorial Volume* (Jerusalem: Yad Ha-Rav Herzog, 2009), 614 (Hebrew). On prayers recited by IDF soldiers after the establishment of the State, see Pinchas Peli, "New Israeli Prayers,"

the special prayers composed for professionals whose hands hold the fate of human beings, such as a doctor or a judge.[6]

Beyond the prayer intended for soldiers to recite, there is another phenomenon in Judaism: a prayer for the peace of the soldiers, spoken aloud by the public envoy in the synagogue, and the congregation responds at the end with "Amen." There were rabbis in Israel who composed wartime prayers for recitation in the congregation, whose content was a request that the Holy One, Blessed be He, would protect the gentile soldiers of the kingdom in which they lived. These prayers somewhat resemble the prayers for the peace of the king and the government, such as "He who gives salvation" which has been recited every Sabbath for hundreds of years in the lands of the Diaspora.[7] The main theme in the prayer "He who gives salvation" is the peace of the ruler, but in many versions of it, his army is also hinted at or mentioned, such as in the request that

---

Mahanayim, no. 40 (Erev Rosh Hashanah 1959): 137-142 (Hebrew), and Yehiel Shemaia, *Segulot Niflaot* (Jerusalem, 1980), 22-23 (Hebrew).

6   Regarding special prayers for a physician, see Avraham Steinberg, *Halakhic Medical Encyclopedia*, vol. 1 (Jerusalem: The Dr. Falk Schlesinger Institute, 1988), 176-182 (Hebrew); and for the Prayer of a Judge, see Tzvi Tal, *Ad Bo HaShemesh* (Or Yehuda: Dvir, 2010), 143 (Hebrew).

7   On this prayer, see Barry Schwartz, "Hanoten Teshua: The Origin of the Traditional Jewish Prayer for the Government," *Hebrew Union College Annual*, vol. 57 (1986): 113-120; and Barry Schwartz, "The Jewish Prayer for the Government in America," *American Jewish History*, vol. 76, no. 3 (March 1987): 334-339; Aaron Ahrend, *Israel's Independence Day – Research Studies* (Ramat-Gan: Bar-Ilan University Press, 1998), 176-191 (Hebrew); and Jonathan D. Sarna, "Jewish Prayers for the United States Government: A Study in the Liturgy of Politics and the Politics of Liturgy," in Ruth Langer and Steven Fine, eds., *Liturgy in the Life of the Synagogue: Studies in the History of Jewish Prayer* (Winona Lake, Indiana: Eisenbrauns, 2005), 205-224.

the Holy One, Blessed be He, "cast his enemies beneath him."[8] In these prayers, for the king and the army of the gentiles, sometimes the motive was lip service, a kind of obligation of the Jews towards the gentiles. But sometimes the prayers were said sincerely, whether out of patriotic sentiment and a desire to show identification and loyalty to the state and the government and the army in their place of residence,[9] or out of fear that the fall of the regime or defeat in the war would adversely affect the Jews. Moreover, in the gentile armies of Europe, thousands of Jewish soldiers also served, especially from the end of the eighteenth-century, when the military service law was also enacted for Jews,[10] and therefore the prayer was not only for gentiles but also for Jews.[11]

Few versions of prayers for the peace of soldiers in gentile countries have been preserved, as they were mostly composed for a specific event and distributed on separate pages that were lost over time. Here are a few examples of prayers from the 19th and 20th centuries. In October 1805, shortly before the Battle of Austerlitz which took place between France and Russia and Austria, the rabbis of Prague composed a prayer

---

[8] On rare occasions, a prayer for the soldiers of the kingdom is included in the Hanoten Teshuah prayer. For example, in the prayer booklet suitable for supplication and praying to the Lord during times of distress, in Amsterdam, 5507 [1747], spanning numerous pages, there is a Hanoten Teshuah prayer that includes a prayer for the soldiers of the kingdom.

[9] For example, in Germany, see Mordechai Breuer, *Jüdische Orthodoxie im Deutschen Reich 1871–1918* (Jerusalem: Shazar, 1991), 260-267 (Hebrew). Similarly, in France, see Moshé Catane, "The Image of the Revolution in Hebrew Poetry of French Jews at the End of the 18th Century and the Beginning of the 19th Century," *Mahut*, no. 19 (1997): 37-44 (Hebrew). Regarding the protest dimension in public prayer, see Yehuda Brandes, *Torat Imekha* (Jerusalem: Sifrei Magid Beit Morasha, 1999), 510 (Hebrew).

[10] See below, "Supplications Against Enlistment in a Foreign Army."

[11] See below, footnote 21.

for the success of the Emperor of Austria in the war, which also included a prayer for the peace of his army, and set it to be said in synagogues morning and evening until the end of the war.[12] During the war between Germany and France in 1870, Rabbi Zvi Benjamin Auerbach (1808-1872), the rabbi of Halberstadt, added a prayer for the peace of Germany's soldiers to be said after "He who gives salvation."[13] Rabbi Shmuel Salant (1816-1909), the Chief Rabbi of Jerusalem, composed in 1898 a prayer for the peace of the United States Army during their war against Spain.[14] During the Russo-Japanese War in 1904, the rabbis of Jerusalem composed a prayer for the peace of Russian soldiers, which was recited by Russian Jews living in Jerusalem.[15] During World War I, rabbis in various places published prayers to be said for the peace of their

---

12   The prayer from Prague, 1806 was published in *Otzar HaTefilot*, ed. J.D. Eisenstein (Brooklyn, 1992; Hebrew). The prayer of the Jews of France and Italy from the year 1806 for the success of Napoleon and his army in his war against the armies of Prussia is presented in Yehuda Leib Bialer, "From the Archives: From the Collections of the House of the Antiquities, the Genizah of the House of Shlomo," *Shana be-Shana* (1966): 502-503 (Hebrew).

13   See the wording in Nosson Refael Auerbach, *Shomrei Mishmeres Hakodesh*, vol. 2 (Jerusalem: Feldheim, 2009), 815 (Hebrew). Two prayers from the mid-19th century for the success of the Italian army in the war against Austria can be found in Moses Avigdor Shulvass, "Hebrew Prayers for the Success of the Italian Wars of Liberation," in *Scritti in Memoria di Sally Mayer* (Jerusalem: Fondazione Sally Mayer, 1956), 208-213 (Hebrew).

14   See the wording in *The Hurvah: Six Centuries of Jewish Settlement in Jerusalem*, eds. Reuven Gafni, Arie Morgenstern, and David M. Cassuto (Jerusalem: Ben-Zvi Institute, 2010), 146 (Hebrew).

15   The prayer was printed on 25 March 1904, alongside it is the prayer HaNoten Teshuah for Emperor Nicholas II of Russia. A preserved copy is located in the National Library of Israel.

country's ruler and his army.¹⁶ At the beginning of World War II, the Chief Rabbinate of Britain composed a prayer for the peace of British soldiers participating in the war,¹⁷ and the Chief Rabbis of the Land of Israel, Rabbi Yitzhak Isaac Herzog (1888-1959) and Rabbi Ben-Zion Meir Hai Uziel (1880-1953), composed prayers for the success of the Allied powers in the war against Germany.¹⁸

In the aforementioned prayers and similar ones, sometimes alongside the request that the Holy One, Blessed be He, protect the king and his army in the war, a justification for the righteousness of that regime's war is included,¹⁹ and the righteousness and justice of the regime are

16 In the community of Adas Jisroel in Berlin, during the tenure of Rabbi Azriel Munk, a prayer for recitation in the morning service, "Shema Koleinu," was composed throughout the war. See Yehuda Leib Bialer (see above, footnote 5), 489 (Hebrew). In Jerusalem in 1915, the Hakham Bashi, Rabbi Moshe Franco, composed a prayer for recitation in all synagogues for the well-being of the Ottoman Sultan Muhammad Rashad and his army. See Benjamin Kluger, *From the Source: Old Yishuv on the Bulletin Board*, vol. 1 (Jerusalem, 1978), 37 (Hebrew).

17 See Judith Tydor Baumel, *Holocaust in Prayer* (Ramat-Gan: Bar-Ilan University Press, 1992), 135 (Hebrew).

18 Prayer dated 14 June 1940, in Rabbi Ben-Zion Meir Hai Uziel, *Mikhmannei Uziel*, vol. 3 (Jerusalem: HaVa'ad LeHotza'at Kitvei Maran, 2005), 499; Prayer dated 10 September 1940, in Ibid., p. 500; and prayer dated 12 August 1942, see Ibid., vol. 2 (Jerusalem: HaVa'ad LeHotza'at Kitvei Maran, 2004), 507 (Hebrew).

19 For instance: In the title of Rabbi Salant's prayer, it is said that it is for the success of "the sons of the United States in their obligatory war, the war of freedom for the love of man," and in the prayer itself: "This enlightened people have gone out today to wage war against a formidable enemy, not to expand their land and inherit dwellings not theirs, they went out against weapons, but in their love to proclaim liberty to the captives and to deliver a poor nation from their oppressors and to bring about eternal justice. And in the community of Adas Jisroel (mentioned above, footnote 16): "All our enemies around conspire against us to wage war." And in the prayer of the

sometimes described.[20] Some of the prayers focus on the king and his army, and others mention the king and his army but mostly consist of prayer for the local Jews and the Jewish soldiers in that army.[21] Mostly, the prayers were said by Jews, residents of the place where the soldiers

> Chief Rabbis of the Land of Israel in October 1940, it was noted that Britain and its allies are fighting "for the sake of justice and integrity, human freedom and world peace," and their enemies "are storming… to destroy and harm, to conquer and subjugate all the nations under their tyrannical rule."

[20] In the prayer for the soldiers of Russia in 1904, it is said that Russia is "a nation that fights for its existence and honor," while the Japanese people are described as "violating the laws of nations and seizing dwellings that do not belong to them." Rabbi Salant mentions the United States as "a people planted in the love of humanity and human freedom… this enlightened nation." Rabbi Franco praises the Ottoman rule extensively, stating that "Justice is her girdle, and truth and righteousness are her sash. The love of every person is always in the heart of the mighty and enlightened Ottoman Kingdom, may it be blessed, and all the races are equal in her eyes… The spirit of compassion and grace hovers over the face of all the land, and the spirit of noble freedom from our great and merciful king, the righteous and humble Sultan Mehmed V Reşâd [Sultan of the Ottoman Empire (1909-1918)], may he be blessed, is given to all the oppressed nations."

[21] The prayers of Rabbi Salant and Rabbi Franco focused on rulership and their armies. Rabbi Auerbach's prayer, on the other hand, is centered on the Jewish people and is mostly written in the first-person plural: "Our haters will flee… for with You, our enemies we will gore, in Your name we will trample our adversaries." Jewish soldiers are mentioned: "And upon our brothers and sons, the pioneers of the army… they had refuge and mighty help." In the prayers of the Chief Rabbis for the Jewish people during the Holocaust, there is a change over time. The prayer in June 1940 includes a request for the success of Britain and her alliance and a request for "our holy land" and "the remnant of Israel." This is also the case in the prayer in August 1940. However, in August 1942, when the Holocaust was at its peak, the prayer primarily includes a plea for the rescue of "the remnant of our scattered people in exile."

Praying for the Defenders of Our Faith

lived, but sometimes a prayer for the peace of soldiers was said in another country due to the worshippers' connection to it and its soldiers.[22]

Recently, the Orthodox Union in the United States composed a prayer for the peace of the US Army.[23] This prayer differs from its

---

22 The prayer for the well-being of Russian soldiers was recited in 1904 in Jerusalem because Russian Jews who had immigrated to Jerusalem were concerned about the fate of their brothers who were participating in the war, as the prayer states: "Have mercy, please, on the myriads of Israel who serve with pure hearts within the armies of mighty Russia." The prayers of the Chief Rabbis for the success of the Allied powers in World War II stemmed from concern for European Jews. Perhaps Rabbi Salant's prayer was influenced by the fact that the United States was a refuge for Jews at that time more than Spain, and therefore he prayed for the well-being of the United States as well.

23 Following the 9/11 attacks, a prayer for American soldiers was penned by Mr. Moshe Markovitz at the behest of Rabbi Fabian Schonfeld for the congregation of the Young Israel of Queens Valley in Queens, New York. Initially recited by individual congregations, this prayer was later incorporated into *The Koren Siddur* (New York: OU Press, 2009), 520-521. For insights into the history and context of this prayer, see Milton Moshe Markovitz, "Prayer for the Safety of the United States Armed Forces," in Michael J. Broyde, ed., *Contending with Catastrophe: Jewish Perspectives on September 11th* (New York: Khal Publishing, 2011), 245-248, where the author reflects: "Following the terror attacks on the morning of September 11th, 2001, and the subsequent presidential decision to launch the War on Terror, Americans maintained their resolute spirit and displayed a heightened zeal of unity and national pride. The public response to the tragic loss of nearly 3,000 innocent lives on that day was expressed through compassionate acts of loving-kindness and a determination to support the soldiers of the United States Armed Forces who were dispatched to reclaim peace around the world. The unique response by the American Orthodox Jewish community to the historical events was demonstrated via a meaningful religious medium. Shortly after the attacks of September 11th, 2001, Milton Moshe Markovitz was urged by Rabbi Fabian Schonfeld, founding rabbi of the Young Israel of Kew Gardens Hills, NY, to compose a new prayer in gratitude for the heroic sacrifice of each soldier serving in

predecessors in that it is set to be said every Sabbath and is not limited to wartime. It seems that the recitation of this prayer, more than stemming from concern for the peace of American Jews or Jewish American soldiers, stems from patriotism and a desire to express solidarity with the American nation and its army.[24]

PRAYERS FOR THE WELL-BEING OF SOLDIERS IN THE WAR OF INDEPENDENCE

For most of the first half of the 20th century, there was no actual war against the Jewish settlement in the Land of Israel, and there was no organized army of Jews fighting against the enemies. Therefore, no prayer for the well-being of soldiers in the land was composed during this period. There were severe "events" from time to time, but even then, a prayer for the well-being of soldiers was probably not composed. Rabbi Ben Zion Meir Hai Uziel composed a long prayer "For the Sake of Quiet and Peace in the Land" to be recited on the 7 July 1936, following the events that took place in the previous months. But it does not refer to the army and soldiers, but there is an appeal to God: "Go out to save your people… Fight, Lord, our fight, fight our war and avenge our revenge."[25]

> the United States Armed Forces." I thank Mr. Menachem Butler, involved in that volume's publication, for pointing me to this source.

24 Some sought to express solidarity with the American nation within the synagogue in another way: by hanging the flag of the United States and the flag of the State of Israel in the synagogue. See, however, Rabbi Moshe Feinstein, *Responsa Iggerot Moshe*, Orah Hayyim, Part 1 (New York 1959), no. 46.

25 The prayer is found within Rabbi Ben-Zion Meir Hai Uziel, *Mikhmannei Uziel*, vol. 3 (see above, footnote 18), 490 (Hebrew). In light of the danger of the invasion by the German army under the command of Erwin Rommel (1891-1944) to the Land of Israel in the Summer of 1942, special prayers were prepared, and the Chief Rabbinate of Israel formulated a special

Praying for the Defenders of Our Faith

After the UN decision on 29 November 1947, on the partition of the Land of Israel into two states, the Arabs of the land began hostile activities that led to the War of Independence. The Jewish army in the Land of Israel organized and mobilized for war against the Arabs. This war brought, probably for the first time, the formulation of prayers for the well-being of soldiers in the Land of Israel.[26]

After the United Nations decision on 29 November 1947 to divide the Land of Israel into two states, the Arabs of the land launched hostile activities that led to the War of Independence. The Jewish army in the Land of Israel organized and engaged in war against the Arabs. This war led, apparently for the first time, to the formulation of prayers for the peace of soldiers in the Land of Israel. On 6 April 1948, the "Mi Sheberach for the Recruits" was published, that is, a prayer for the Jews of the Yishuv in the Land who were conscripted for the war. In the publication, it was noted that this version was to be said every Sabbath in synagogues after the reading of the Torah. The text of the prayer goes as follows:[27]

> prayer for the upcoming Rosh Hashanah 1942. See "A Special Prayer for Rosh Hashanah from the Time of the First World War," on the website: *Israel: The Documented Story: The State Archive Blog* (2 December 2012). However, even in this case, it is not a prayer for the well-being of Israeli soldiers.

26 Regarding a prayer that was composed on the evening of the 29 November 1947 for the peace of the State of Israel, see below, "Additional Prayers," section 4.

27 See the bulletin of the Great Synagogue in Tel Aviv, called *Beit ha-Knesset*, vol. 3 (March 1948): 259 (Hebrew). The heads of this synagogue saw it as a synagogue that exceeds its local role and serves as a national and pan-Israeli symbol that influences all the synagogues in Israel. See Reuven Gafni, "'The Synagogue in Writing': On the Journal of the Great Synagogue in Tel-Aviv, 1946-1948," *Kesher*, no. 39 (2009): 138-145 (Hebrew).

"May He who blessed our fathers Abraham, Isaac, and Jacob bless all our brothers and sisters who have been conscripted for the defense of the people and the homeland and who stand guard day and night to not allow the destroyer to harm our cities and our settlements, because we pray for their peace. May the Omnipresent protect them from every injury and calamity and spread His shelter of peace over them along with all their fellow Israelites, and may they merit to see the consolation of Zion and the gathering of the exiles. And may He soon fulfill His promise to us, as written in our holy Torah: 'And I will grant peace in the land, and you shall lie down, and none shall make you afraid.' So may it be His will, and let us say, Amen."

A month later, in April 1948, this Mi Sheberach was printed in a slightly longer version to be said "every Sabbath before bringing the Torah scroll to the ark."[28] In these prayers, the expression "Israel Defense Forces" is not mentioned, but rather it speaks of "conscripts," since the IDF was established later, on 26 May 1948, and the expression "IDF" became widespread among the general public even later.[29]

---

28 See *Beit ha-Knesset*, vol. 3 (April 1948): 311 (Hebrew). The Chief Rabbinate published a notice on 28 June 1948 to recite Mi Sheberach every Sabbath before prior to the Torah reading in the synagogue. See Shmuel Katz, "Diary of the Chief Rabbinate's Activities," in Itamar Warhaftig and Shmuel Katz, eds., *Chief Rabbinate of Israel: Seventy Years Since Its Establishment*, vol. 3 (Jerusalem: Heichal Shlomo, 2002), 1316 (Hebrew).

29 Regarding this expression and the debate around it until the end of the year 1948, see Zehava Ostfeld, *An Army Is Born: Main Stages in the Buildup of the Army under the Leadership of David Ben-Gurion* (Tel Aviv: Ministry of Defense, 1994), 113-116 (Hebrew).

Praying for the Defenders of Our Faith

Who composed this Prayer for the Recruits? It appears that Rabbi Yehuda Isser Unterman (1886-1976), the then Rabbi of Tel Aviv, composed the prayer for the peace of the conscripts. In May 1948, when the Mi Sheberach was published, it was printed alongside a "Prayer for the Defenders."[30] While the latter was credited to the Chief Rabbis of the Land of Israel, no such attribution was given to the Mi Sheberach for the Recruits, suggesting they were not its authors. Interestingly, this Mi Sheberach was published in the bulletin of the Great Synagogue in Tel Aviv, where Rabbi Unterman prayed regularly. Known for composing various prayers, Rabbi Unterman often began them with the phrase Mi Sheberach. Shortly after the Mi Sheberach for the conscripts was introduced, on 14 May 1948—the day the State of Israel was declared—Rabbi Unterman composed a Mi Sheberach for the State of Israel. He ensured it was recited the following day, Shabbat, the 6th of Iyar, at the Great Synagogue in Tel Aviv.[31] At the ceremony in Tel Aviv on the day of the swearing-in of the IDF soldiers on 28 June 1948, Rabbi Unterman recited the Mi Sheberach for the recruits.[32] Thus, it's likely that Rabbi Unterman was the author of the Mi Sheberach for the recruits and ensured its recitation in the Great Synagogue.

During the summer of 1948, the Chief Rabbis of Israel composed several lengthy prayers that included many requests, including a prayer for the peace of the soldiers. For example, Rabbi Uziel composed a

---

30 See above, footnote 5.

31 See Akiva Zimmerman, "Prayers for the Peace of the State and its Government," *ha-Tsofeh* (6 May 1992): 6 (Hebrew). He also composed a prayer for the Jews of Russia, published in *ha-Tsofeh* (4 October 1967): 2 (Hebrew). See Shmuel Katz (above, footnote 28), 1390 (Hebrew).

32 Information about this in *ha-Tsofeh* (29 June 1948): 1 (Hebrew). There it is also written that this Mi Sheberach was composed by the Chief Rabbinate. It seems that the reference is to Rabbi Unterman.

prayer for the eve of Rosh Chodesh Tammuz, towards the end of the first ceasefire on 6 July 1948. This prayer describes the damage and destruction caused by the Arabs, the siege on Jerusalem, and more, and includes a plea to God to assist the Jews of the State of Israel in the war against the Arabs. Towards its end, there is a request for the soldiers: "Strengthen their force and power of your nation's pioneers and your war warriors, strengthen their spirit and enlighten them."[33] A short time later, Rabbi Ben-Zion Meir Hai Uziel composed a special prayer for Yom HaMedina, or "The Day of the State." This significant day was observed on 27 July 1948, the day of the death of Theodor Herzl. He recited the prayer at the Yeshurun Synagogue in Jerusalem, and it included gratitude for the ingathering of the exiles, the establishment of the state, and the army's stand in the war against the Arabs, words for the elevation of Herzl's soul, and a request for the peace of the State and the success of the soldiers. Here is the request for the soldiers:[34]

33 The Prayer was published in Rabbi Ben-Zion Meir Hai Uziel, *Mikhmannei Uziel*, vol. 2, p. 502 (Hebrew).

34 A facsimile of the prayer is reproduced in Chief Rabbinate of Israel (see above, footnote 28), 549 (Hebrew). Regarding Yom HaMedina, see Shmuel Katz, "The Chief Rabbinate and Independence Day," Ibid., 821-822 (Hebrew). A longer prayer has been preserved, possibly composed by Rabbi Uziel. Its title is "For the Peace of the Haganah Army and for the Peace of the People of Israel," and it was printed on a separate page. A copy is kept at the National Library of Israel. Before the prayer, there is an instruction: "A prayer to be said during the taking out of the Torah scroll." At the top of the page, handwritten is: "1948?" The content of the prayer and the expression "Haganah Army" suggest it was from a time of war and after the establishment of the state and the IDF, presumably composed in the spring of 1948. It mentions the Holocaust and the immigration to the Land of Israel and includes a plea for victory in the war against the Arabs: "Cast terror and fear upon all the Arabs, upon their kings and leaders, their counselors and their armies, and let them flee from the sword and be struck down before Your people, Israel and before our defense army... and the Lord

> "May the Lord strengthen all our armies, their commanders and officers at the forefront, who stand ready to defend our settlements and our homeland in the land of our forefathers. Empower their spirit, encourage their strength, make them wise and grant them success, and fulfill upon them Your blessed promise from Your holy Torah: 'For the Lord your God is the one who goes with you to fight for you against your enemies, to save you.' And no destructive weapon or warfare shall prevail against them, and every tongue that rises against them in judgment, You shall condemn. O Lord, show us Your salvation, and we shall rejoice in Your wonders, singing and praising Your mighty deeds for all eternity."

This passage, like other prayers for soldiers, is composed of a new prayer alongside suitable Bible verses. During the month of Elul in 1948, the Chief Rabbis of Israel published in the newspapers and in a special print a "Prayer for the Peace of the State," which was "to be said in all synagogues, in the country and in the diaspora, by the rabbi or the cantor on Sabbaths and holidays after reading the Torah."[35] This prayer includes many requests, among them also a request for the soldiers of the Land of Israel: "Strengthen the hands of the defenders of our holy land and grant them, our God, salvation, and crown them with the crown of victory, and you shall grant peace in the land and everlasting happiness

---

> will go out and fight those nations... in Saudi Arabia, Syria, Jordan, Egypt, and in all the Arab lands." The end of the prayer is dedicated to the Prime Minister, David Ben-Gurion.

[35] On this prayer, see Aaron Ahrend (above, footnote 17), 192-200 (Hebrew); Joseph Tabory, "The Piety of Politics: Jewish Prayers for the State of Israel," in Ruth Langer and Steven Fine, eds. (above, footnote 7), 225-246; and Yoel Rappel (above, footnote 5), 594-620 (Hebrew).

to its inhabitants." The prayer was published during the height of the War of Independence, and the request to strengthen the defenders and for the "crown of victory" refers to this war. Like in the "Prayer for the Defenders" mentioned above, here too the Chief Rabbis chose the expression "defenders": "defenders of our holy land," even though they could have used the expression "IDF soldiers," since the IDF already existed. It is possible that the reason is that the expression "Israel Defense Forces" was not yet commonly used by people.[36]

In the summer of 1948, the custom of saying the Mi Sheberach (a prayer/blessing) for the conscripts every Sabbath was not accepted in synagogues,[37] and therefore in the prayers for the peace of the State of Israel mentioned above, there was always also a prayer section for the soldiers.[38] After the War of Independence, there certainly was no place to say the Mi Sheberach for the conscripts, which was formulated as a prayer during war, not during calm. In contrast, the prayer for the peace of the State, which was distributed in Elul 1948 and also included a request for the soldiers, began gradually to penetrate into the Zionist synagogues in the 1950s and 1960s. It was incorporated into the prayer books for

---

36 See above footnote 29. Another possibility, though it seems less likely, is that the rabbis intended to encompass all defenders in their prayer, including the soldiers of the Palmach. The Palmach was the elite fighting force of the Haganah, the underground army of the Yishuv during the British Mandate for Palestine. It was established in May 1941 and operated independently from the IDF, only disbanding on November 7, 1948.

37 Even Rabbi Unterman did not mention it in the prayer order he composed for Independence Day 1949. See Shmuel Katz (above, footnote 34), 840 (Hebrew).

38 Also in other prayers for the well-being of the country composed by Rabbi Uziel, later mentioned is the topic of the well-being of the soldiers. See the prayer for Independence Day 1950, *Mikhmannei Uziel*, vol. 2, page 498; and prayers from the year 1952, Ibid., page 496; Ibid., vol. 3, page 516.

Praying for the Defenders of Our Faith

Independence Day printed by the Ministry of Religions on behalf of the Chief Rabbinate, in the "Order of Independence Day" edited by Rabbi Moshe Zvi Neriah (1913-1995), and in the prayer orders for this day printed by members of the religious kibbutz.[39] In some synagogues, it was also said every Sabbath.[40] In Zionist prayer books, it was printed for

---

39 Regarding the booklets of the Ministry of Religious Affairs, "Tikkun" and the booklet of the Religious Kibbutz, see Aaron Ahrend (above, footnote 7), 23-27 (Hebrew). Also, in a few prayer books from the same period, these prayer orders were incorporated. See Katz (above, footnote 37), 809 (Hebrew). In the *Siddur Shirah Hadashah* (Jerusalem: Eshkol, 1949), there is a prayer for the well-being of the country at the end of the prayer book after the Song for Lag BaOmer, but this prayer book does not include Independence Day prayer orders because they were established after its publication.

40 The sages of Tripoli in Libya published a proclamation on 1 May 1949, in which they established an annual prayer order for Independence Day. This included a prayer of thanksgiving that was composed "for Israel Independence Day" to be recited in both the morning and afternoon prayers. In this prayer, they also mentioned the soldiers, saying: "And for all our brave-hearted heroes and the leaders of the Israeli army, we say: May the Lord be with you, mighty heroes of valor." After reciting this prayer, one is to recite the prayer for the well-being of the country, "which we customarily recite in all the communities of Tripolitania after the reading of the Torah and the Haftarah on Shabbat and holidays." The proclamation was published in *Tehumin*, vol. 13 (1992-1993): 123 (Hebrew). See also Yosef G'i'an, *Zohar Moshe* (Zekher ha-Rav Moshe) (Netanya: Beganei Hayyim, 1992), 203-204 (Hebrew). In the communal regulations of Tirat Tzvi from 1957 and Ein Ha-Netziv from 1966, it was determined to recite a prayer for the well-being of the State of Israel each Shabbat. In the regulations of Eliyahu HaNavi in 1968, it was determined to recite it on the Shabbat when the new month is blessed. In the regulations of Nir Etzion from 1970 or thereabouts, it was determined to recite it on the Shabbat when the new month is blessed and on holidays.

recitation every Sabbath from the 1960s onwards.[41] And in most of the prayer books of Yemenite Jews in Israel, an updated "Hanoten Teshua" prayer was printed.[42]

Alongside the new prayer formulations of the Chief Rabbis, as we have seen above, there were rabbis who objected to any change in the synagogue orders and especially to the recitation of new prayers. Instead,

41 This prayer can be found in the *Siddur Tefilat Yisrael* (Tel Aviv: Massada, 1964), and also in the same prayer book, 1969, following the Torah reading on Shabbat. In the *Siddur Siah Tefilah* (Jerusalem: Rabbi Hiyya Institute, 1967), it is located after the Mi Sheberach for the congregation. Since in most regular prayer books, this prayer has not yet been printed, in many synagogues, it is read from a separate page. In many synagogues of the Eastern Sephardic tradition, this prayer has not been said until today, and it is not included in their prayer books, such as the following prayer books: *Hazon Ovadia* (Jerusalem 1988), *Kol Yaakov* (Jerusalem 1993), *Avodat Hashem* (Holon 1995), *Kol Eliyahu* (Jerusalem 1997). See the following footnote for more information.

42 On the day of the declaration of the state, Rabbi Shalom Yitzhak Halevi (1890-1973), the leader of the Yemenite Jewish community in Israel and one of the Chief Rabbis, requested that a blessing for the well-being of the country be composed. When his request was not answered, he adapted the prayer "HaNoten Teshuah" with some modifications and distributed it in the month of Sivan, 5708 (1948) for recitation every Shabbat after the Torah reading. See Yehiel Yitzhak Halevi, *Siach Chachamim*, vol. 1 (Jerusalem 1995), 64 (Hebrew). This prayer has been included in most Yemenite prayer books to this day. Rabbi Yosef Kapach (1917-2000), in his article "Arabic Translations of the 'Shemoneh Esrei' Prayer," *Tarbiz*, vol. 26, no. 2 (December 1956): 198-199 (Hebrew), argued that "HaNoten Teshuah" was a later addition prompted by fear of the authorities and was not part of the original Yemenite text. Therefore, when the prayer for the well-being of the country was disseminated, it was established in place of "HaNoten Teshuah." See *Siddur Sha'arei Tziyon* (Jerusalem 1952); and see below (footnote 58). In the Tripoli Jewish community as well, a prayer for Israel, based on "HaNoten Teshuah," was composed. See Yosef G'i'an (above, footnote 40), 202 (Hebrew). Also, see "Additional Prayers" below, Section 4.

during and shortly after the War of Independence, they distributed ancient prayers of the great ones of Israel suitable for times of trouble and incorporated a short request for the protection of the soldiers.[43] For example, the Ashkenazi Badatz rabbis in Jerusalem published a page titled: "This request is suitable to be said when opening the Ark on the holy Sabbath and on Monday and Thursday." The main part of the page includes a "Yehi Ratzon" prayer based on a prayer composed by Rabbi Haim Yosef David Azulai, known as Chida (1724-1806) with a few changes.[44] The most significant change is the addition of a section in the middle of the prayer with a request for protecting the warriors, as follows:

> "And our brothers who repel [the enemy] in harsh warfare, shield and save [them], and fulfill in them the verse that is written 'Five of you shall chase a hundred, and a hundred of you shall chase ten thousand; and your enemies shall fall before you by the sword,' and the verse that is written 'The Lord will cause your enemies who rise against you to be defeated before you; they shall

---

43 This practice was common. For example, during World War II, the ultra-Orthodox community in Jerusalem disseminated a prayer composed by Rabbi Moses (Hatam) Sofer (1762-1839), in the year 1809, during the Napoleonic Wars, with some modifications. See the text of Rabbi Moses Sofer in his work *Sefer ha-Zikaron* (Pressburg 1839), 18 (Hebrew), and the version of the ultra-Orthodox community in Yosef Unna, "Prayer for Peace in Times of War by Maran He-Hatam Sofer z"l," *Beit ha-Knesset*, vol. 3, no. 8-9-10 (May – August 1948): 329 (Hebrew).

44 A copy of the page, without a date, is located in the National Library of Israel. In the library catalog, it is noted as "circa 1950." However, it's possible that the page was printed a couple of years earlier. The prayer of the "Chida" (Rabbi Chaim Yosef David Azulai) can be found in his booklet *Kaf Nachat*, Section 4. See *Avodat Hakodesh* (Israel 1975), 47a (Hebrew).

come out against you one way, and flee before you seven ways.'"

Through this short section, which is mostly verses and not a new formulation, an actual dimension was added to the ancient prayer of an important rabbi, who composed prayers based on the acceptance of the Ari (Rabbi Isaac Luria).[45]

Another initiative was taken by the Kabbalist Rabbi Mordechai Attia (1898-1978) during the War of Independence: he printed thousands of copies of chapter 34 in the Book of Isaiah, which deals with the destruction of Edom and the redemption of Israel, and worked to have it recited in public.[46]

MILITARY RABBINATE PRAYERS FOR THE WELFARE OF IDF SOLDIERS

---

[45] Another example of this phenomenon is a page printed by rabbis from the town of Rehovot, who are of Yemenite origin, titled "Prayer for the Salvation of the Settlement and the People of Israel." This is a prayer that contains Kabbalistic hints and was copied from a handwritten manuscript attributed to the great Yemenite poet and Kabbalist Rabbi Shalom Shabazi (1619-1710). In the middle of the prayer, the following sentence is included: "And save and rescue all those who stand on guard, the young men and young women among your people Israel, who are giving their lives to save the lives of your people Israel from the hands of their enemies and for the settling of the Land of Israel." This sentence is an addition and is not from the words of Rabbi Shalom Shabazi. A copy of this page without a date can be found in the National Library of Israel. In the library catalog, it is noted as "circa 1950." However, it appears that the page was printed before the year 1950, as the printers mentioned that they copied the prayer due to the severe situation prevailing in the land.

[46] See David Zion Laniado, *Li-Kedoshim Asher Ba'aretz* (Jerusalem 1980), 137 (Hebrew). I am thankful to Dr. Uzi Fuchs for bringing this initiative to my attention.

Praying for the Defenders of Our Faith

After the War of Independence, rabbis began to formulate special prayers for the welfare of soldiers, designed to be suitable also for peaceful times. On the eve of Rosh Hashanah 5710, the Military Rabbinate in Jerusalem printed a prayer book for the High Holy Days for IDF soldiers, which is a reproduction of a regular prayer book in the Sephardic tradition with a few additions. In "Laws of the High Holy Days for Soldiers" at the beginning of the prayer book, Rabbi Shlomo Goren (1918-1994), the Chief Military Rabbi, established: "All those called to the Torah in synagogues in military camps should say a 'Mi Sheberach' for the President of the State, the Prime Minister and Minister of Defense, and the Chief of Staff and his officer colleagues." After the Haftarah blessings, the following Mi Sheberach was added (emphasis in the original):

> "May He who blessed our fathers Abraham, Isaac, and Jacob bless the esteemed leaders of Israel, R. Chaim son of Ozer Weizmann, President of the State of Israel, and R' David son of Avigdor (Ben-Gurion), Prime Minister of Israel and Minister of Defense, along with all the ministers of the government, and General Jacob son of Abraham Zvi (Dori), Chief of the General Staff, and all the commanders under his command, and all the soldiers of the Israel Defense Forces who stand guard over our land and the cities of our God, from the border of Lebanon to the wilderness of Egypt, and from the great sea to the entrance of the desert, on land, in sea, and in air. May the Holy One, blessed be He, reward them for their service, protect them, and deliver them from all distress and trouble, remove from them all illness, and grant them success in all their endeavors. May He grant them wisdom and insight from Himself and send

a blessing in all their handiwork. May He silence those who hate us, crown them with a crown of salvation and a wreath of victory. And may it be fulfilled in them what is written: 'For the Lord your God is the one who goes with you to fight for you against your enemies, to save you.' And let us say, Amen."

This prayer was composed by Rabbi Shmuel Avidor HaCohen (1926-2005), assistant to Rabbi Goren and religious affairs officer in the first two years of the Military Rabbinate, who handled the printing of this prayer book.[47] In this Mi Sheberach, first, the President of the State and government members are mentioned, and apparently, the request "and direct them with good counsel before Him" is directed towards them, originating from the prayer for the peace of the state, but the main focus of the blessing is the IDF soldiers and their commanders. The language of presence found in this prayer, "our land... our God," expresses the closeness of the worshippers to the soldiers. In prayer books for soldiers printed in subsequent years, for example, on the eve of Rosh Hashanah

---

47 This is what his brother, Rabbi Menachem Hacohen, conveyed to me. We will add evidence to his words: Shortly before the printing of the prayer book, Rabbi Shmuel Avidor Hacohen composed, at the request of Rabbi Goren, a Scroll called "Devar HaTikumah." This Scroll was publicly recited by Rabbi Goren on the night of Independence Day in 1949, after the festive evening prayer at the Yeshurun Synagogue in Jerusalem. For the text, see *Chief Rabbinate of Israel* (above, footnote 28), 964 (Hebrew); and Katz (above, footnote 34), 847-848 (Hebrew). In this Scroll, among other things, there is a series of supplications, and the first of them is dedicated to the soldiers: "Our God and God of our ancestors, please be with the pipes of the soldiers of Israel who stand guard over our land and the cities of our God, from the border of Lebanon to the desert of Egypt and from the Great Sea to the entrance of the Arabah." This passage, starting with "those who stand," is also found at the beginning of the Mi Sheberach for the soldiers. Therefore, it can be concluded that both sections were authored by the same individual, namely Rabbi Shmuel Avidor Hacohen.

Praying for the Defenders of Our Faith

1955, this Mi Sheberach is found with a few changes, the main ones being: a. The names of the leaders of the state and army are not specified, and instead of the section "His Excellency... command colleagues," it is written: "The President of the State of Israel, the Prime Minister of Israel and his ministers, the Chief of the General Staff and his command colleagues." b. There is no mention of it being a Day of Judgment, and instead of "and inscribe them... their brethren," it is written: "In their days and in our days may Judah be saved and Israel dwell securely, and may the Redeemer come to Zion. So may it be His will." These changes allowed the Mi Sheberach to be said on any occasion.[48]

During Operation Kadesh on November 2, 1956, Rabbi Goren introduced a Mi Sheberach dedicated to IDF soldiers. He encouraged the community "to be recited it in all synagogues during Shabbat following the Torah reading."[49] Here is its version:

48 In the synagogue of the Turkish expatriates, Yismach Moshe, in the neighborhood of Yemin Moshe in Jerusalem, there is a memorial book, at the head of which is a prayer for the well-being of the heads of state and the IDF (Israel Defense Forces), which was apparently composed in the mid-1950s. It can be assumed that it was influenced by the wording in the IDF prayer book. Below is the prayer from Reuven Gafni, *Beit Tefilah: Hidden Synagogues in the Heart of Jerusalem* (Jerusalem: Yad Yitzhak Ben Zvi, 2008), 40 (Hebrew): "Blessed is He who blessed our forefathers, Abraham, Isaac, and Jacob, Moses and Aaron, David and Solomon. May He bless the head of the government [space left for writing his name] and the members of the Knesset. May He bless the Israel Defense Forces and all the soldiers who stand on guard, and at their head the Chief of Staff. May the Lord protect them and inscribe them in the book of good life. So may it be His will, and let us say, Amen."

49 See, for example in *ha-Tsofeh Literary Supplement* (2 November 1956): 8 (Hebrew). Shabtai Rosenthal, *Masuah Le-Dor* (Jerusalem, 1972), 128 (Hebrew), testifies that the prayer for the well-being of the soldiers was written with the consent of Rabbi Tzvi Pesach Frank.

"May He who blessed our fathers Abraham, Isaac, and Jacob bless the soldiers of the Israel Defense Forces who stand guard over our land and the cities of our God from the Lebanon border to the Egyptian desert and from the Great Sea to the entrance of the Arava, on land, in the air, and at sea. May the Lord make our enemies who rise up against us be struck down before them. The Holy One, blessed be He, will guard them and save them from all trouble and distress and from every plague and illness, and will send blessing and success in all the work of their hands, subdue our enemies under them and crown them with a crown of salvation and a wreath of victory, and fulfill in them the verse: 'For the Lord your God is He who goes with you to fight for you against your enemies to save you,' and let us say Amen."

In this version, there are a few changes from the previous version, primarily the President, Prime Minister, and their ministers are not mentioned, and the sentence "and direct them with good counsel before Him" that is directed towards the leaders of the state is omitted. Omitting the state leaders was probably due to the custom that existed then in many synagogues to say every Shabbat "a prayer for the peace of the state" in which "its leaders, ministers, and advisors" are mentioned. This version of the Mi Sheberach was included in the prayer books printed by the Military Rabbinate for soldiers in subsequent years. Examples include the High Holy Days prayer book published on the eve of Rosh Hashanah in 1958 and 1959, as well as the prayer books exclusively published for IDF soldiers, such as Tefillot LeChol HaShanah from

1960. And from 1963 onwards it was established in the "Unified Version" prayer book for IDF soldiers.[50]

Another blessing for soldiers was incorporated into the Grace After Meals in the Passover Haggadah "Unified Version" that the Military Rabbinate printed for soldiers starting from 1956. After the sentence "May the All-Merciful bless my father, my teacher, and my mother, my teacher," etc. in Grace After Meals, the sentence was added: "May the All-Merciful bless the State of Israel and the soldiers of the Israel Defense Forces." Rabbi Goren explained that this custom is based on the ruling of Maimonides (Laws of Blessings 4:7) that a guest adds a blessing for the host, "and we are guests at the table of the State and the Israel Defense Forces and we are obliged to bless them."[51]

We will return to the days of the Sinai Campaign. In the archive of the Chief Rabbinate of Israel, handwritten prayers by the Chief Rabbi, Rabbi Isaac Herzog, have been preserved, composed around the time when Rabbi Goren published the Mi Sheberach. One prayer was dedicated to the welfare of IDF soldiers and a second prayer included a memorial for IDF fallen soldiers. The prayer for the welfare of the soldiers is worded as follows:

> "May He who blessed our fathers Abraham, Isaac, and Jacob bless our brothers, the soldiers of the Israel Defense Forces, who stand guard over the land to

---

50 This prayer book was compiled by Yitzhak Alfasi, as Rabbi Menachem Hacohen informed me.

51 See the *Haggadah for Passover for IDF Soldiers, Uniform Text* (Tel Aviv: The IDF Chief Military Rabbinate, 1956), 8, 73 (Hebrew). Rabbi Menachem Hacohen informed me that he added the "Harachaman" prayer, and Rabbi Goren wrote the commentary. Later on, "Harachaman" was incorporated for the well-being of the soldiers in the Grace After Meals (Birkat Hamazon) in some prayer booklets and in *The Koren Siddur*, the American edition, unrelated to the location of the meal.

protect Zion, the home of our life. He will strengthen their hands and eternally crown them with a crown of victory. And in His mercy, He will enable us to soon see the complete redemption of Israel and the fulfillment of the prophecies of the prophets of Israel from ancient days for the peace of the entire world, Amen and Amen."

This version was likely not published widely, perhaps because Rabbi Goren's version had already been published. A week after Rabbi Goren published his version, the Chief Rabbinate called on the public to pray on Shabbat for the welfare of IDF soldiers, without specifying which prayer to say.[52] On 23 July 1957, the Chief Rabbinate determined: "The Mi Sheberach prayer for IDF soldiers should be said when opening the ark while the congregation is standing,"[53] and it seems that the determination referred to Rabbi Goren's Mi Sheberach. It can be assumed that the Chief Rabbinate's support for the version published by Rabbi Goren stemmed from the fact that his version was distributed to the general public in the newspaper and in mahzorim for soldiers.

It seems that Rabbi Goren's activity in formulating the Mi Sheberach for the welfare of the soldiers and its dissemination should be seen against the backdrop of his particular approach to the IDF. Many rabbis who ruled on military matters assisted the religious soldier in observing mitzvot while in the pressing conditions of a military camp or during wartime, but they did not see themselves as responsible for the entire military's activity. In contrast, Rabbi Goren believed that the establishment of the IDF created a new reality: it is not a matter of a

---

52 See *ha-Tsofeh Literary Supplement* (9 November 1956; Hebrew).

53 From the protocol of the Chief Rabbinate, see Katz (above, footnote 28), 1359 (Hebrew). It is not mentioned here that the Mi Sheberach should be recited every Shabbat, but it is clear.

religious soldier in a gentile army who needs halachic guidance, but of Jewish sovereignty and a Jewish army, the "Holy Forces." Therefore, halachic guidance for a religious soldier is not enough; halachic rules must also be established for the entire Jewish army regarding moral issues related to war and the use of weapons per se.[54] Indeed, Rabbi Goren endeavored to shape the IDF on the principles of Halacha, both in formulating the Chief of Staff's orders on religious matters for the entire IDF, and in responses to halachic questions from soldiers, as well as in writing rulings on general issues of the ethics of warfare. And if the IDF is perceived as an army that operates according to the Jewish heritage, it is natural to integrate a prayer expressing affection for the soldiers into the synagogue every Shabbat. The mention that IDF soldiers guard "our land and the cities of our God" while stating its biblical borders fits in with that perception. Against this background, the variety of prayers that Rabbi Goren composed for soldiers to recite, such as the Traveler's Prayer for a paratrooper and a pilot,[55] and his insistence that the name of God also be attached to the "Yizkor" for IDF fallen soldiers, should be understood.[56]

54 See Arye Edrei, "War, Halakhah, and Redemption: The Military and Warfare in the Halakhic Thought of Rabbi Shlomo Goren," *Cathedra*, no. 125 (September 2007): 125-130 (Hebrew).

55 These prayers are mentioned in Pinchas Peli (above, footnote 5). Rabbi Goren composed additional prayers related to the IDF, such as the Mi Sheberach prayer, presumably in 1974, for the IDF soldiers held captive in Syria to recite every Shabbat after the Torah reading "until their swift release." A copy of it is found in the Archives Department of the National Library of Israel (file V1803/א). Later on, he wrote a more general version of the Mi Sheberach for all IDF captives, which is almost in the same text. A copy of it can be found in the National Library of Israel.

56 See Ilana Shamir, *So They Shall not Be as though They Had not Been, Establishing State-run Commemorative Patterns: The Unit for the*

Incorporating the Mi Sheberach for IDF Soldiers into Synagogues

Until the late sixties, saying the Mi Sheberach for IDF soldiers every Sabbath in synagogues was not common. The prayer books printed during those years did not incorporate a prayer for soldiers, except, as mentioned, the "Unified Version" of the IDF, so it was not widespread. Also, it was not established to be recited in the regulations of the Zionist synagogues of that period.[57] Even in the prayer arrangements for Independence Day, there was no prayer for soldiers. Presumably, there was no perceived need, as soldiers were already mentioned, as mentioned, in the prayer for the peace of the state, which was popular in Zionist synagogues.[58] Furthermore, the prayer for the peace of the state was a new prayer, but it served as a substitute and continuation of the practice that had been in existence for hundreds of years in the diaspora to say "He who gives salvation" every Sabbath. In contrast, saying a special prayer for soldiers every Sabbath was an absolute novelty that had not existed before; while it is almost a natural prayer due to the establishment of the organized body of the IDF that did not exist previously, it was still an innovation and therefore not inclined to be adopted.

From the late sixties onwards, the Mi Sheberach for soldiers began to

Commemoration of Fallen Soldiers (Tel Aviv: Ministry of Defense, 2004), 98-99, 220-221 (Hebrew).

57 In the *Siddur Tefilat Yisrael* (in both editions) and in the *Siddur Siah Tefilah*, there is no prayer for the well-being of the soldiers. This prayer is not mentioned in the regulations of Tirat Tzvi from 1957, Tel Giborim from 1964, Ein Hanatziv from 1966, and Eliyahu Hanavi from 1968.

58 It is possible to speculate that this may be the reason why Rabbi Yosef Kapach, included the prayer for the well-being of the State in the prayer books he edited, did not include the Mi Sheberach for the soldiers, neither in the *Siddur Shivat Tzion* nor in the *Siddur Siah Yerushalayim*.

Praying for the Defenders of Our Faith

be recited in synagogues, in addition to mentioning soldiers in the prayer for the peace of the state. Perhaps the background to its revitalization was the great concern in the country prior to the Six-Day War and the great victory in this war. Initially, it was set to be recited in the prayer arrangements for Independence Day,[59] later it was established to be recited on special Sabbaths and eventually every Sabbath.[60] Its recitation every Sabbath spread in synagogues mainly due to its printing as part of the Sabbath prayers in prayer books in the seventies.[61] It was customary to recite it in Zionist synagogues in the State of Israel and even abroad, and in some Eastern Haredi synagogues.[62] In Ashkenazi communities, it was said after reading the Torah: before lifting the Torah scroll or after

---

59 In the Siddur Am Yisrael, it is found at the end of the Siddur, after "Seder Tefilot Chag Ha'atzmaut." In *Siddur ha-Tefillot le-Yom Ha'atzmaut of the Religious Kibbutz* (Tel Aviv: The Religious Kibbutz, 1969) it is included after the Torah reading.

60 In the regulations of Kfar Maimon from 1971, it is determined that the prayer for the well-being of the state and the Mi Sheberach for the soldiers should be recited "at least once a month, on Shabbat following the blessing for the new month, and on holidays." In the regulations of the religious youth group from 1972 and in the parents' council regulations from 1979, it is determined to say the Mi Sheberach for the soldiers on holidays. In the regulations of Nir Atziyon from 1970, it is approximately determined to say it every Shabbat and holiday.

61 It was printed in the year 1970 in the *Rinat Yisrael* prayer book in the Ashkenazi tradition, and in the year 1974 in the *Rinat Yisrael* prayer books for the Eastern Jewish communities and *Imrei Fi Hashalem* prayer book for the Eastern Jewish communities. It was also printed in the year 1981 in the *Koren* prayer book, among others.

62 Regarding its recitation outside of Israel: It can be found in prayer books for Jews living outside of Israel, such as *Rinat Yisrael* for Jews living outside of Israel, *Tefillat David* with a translation into Ladino, and *Koren* in the American edition. For its recitation among ultra-Orthodox Jews of the Eastern communities, please see below.

"Yekum Purkan."[63] The congregation stands during its recitation[64] and responds "Amen" at the end of the recitation, to express identification with the prayer.[65] And in the communities of the Eastern congregations,

---

63 In some prayer books, it is found before the Torah reading (e.g., in prayer books like *Rinat Yisrael* and *Koren*). In others, it is recited after the Prayer for the Welfare of the State of Israel. In the regulations of Aderet Eliyahu and Ohel Nechama, it is specified to be recited before "Hagbaat Sefer Torah." In Ohel Nechama, it is also mentioned that the gabbai should recite it. In Ramat Modiim, it is specified to be recited after the "Yekum Purkan." This is also implied in the regulations of Givat Rimon, which state that during its recitation, the person holding the Torah should stand next to the congregation's representative.

64 Some regulations specify that it should be recited while standing, such as in Ohel Nechama and Givat Rimon. In Givat Rimon, it is even specified that even the person holding the Torah should stand for this prayer. However, in most communities, this practice is not followed, and in Ein HaNatziv and Beit Zur, it is explicitly stated that the person holding the Torah should sit.

65 Sitting during the recitation of this prayer has been seen as an act of opposition to it. Rabbi Moses Tsvi Segal, *Dor v'Dor* (Jerusalem: Ministry of Defense, 1986), 35 (Hebrew), described that in 1911, when the author was seven years old and living in Ukraine, he learned the verse "You shall not place a foreigner over you," and when the congregation stood to recite the prayer for the well-being of the Russian Tsar, "I sat as an act of protest against accepting the rule of a foreign monarch over Jews in contradiction to the written Torah of Moses. The synagogue officials could not force me to stand, which caused discomfort to my father. Since then, when it came to 'Mi Sheberach' for the Tsar, I would leave the synagogue." My uncle, David Ahrend, opposed the recitation of Hallel on Independence Day. He told me that in one of the early years after the establishment of the state, he prayed on that day at the Horev synagogue in Jerusalem and heard the rabbi instructing everyone to stand and say Hallel. His response was: "I will sit and say 'Lo Lanu.'" On the other hand, David Tamar, "Olelot," *ha-Tsofeh Literary Supplement* (2 January 1998): 6 (Hebrew), wrote that when Rabbi Shlomo Zalman Auerbach prayed in a synagogue where they recited a prayer for the well-being of the State, he would stand during its recitation. There were protests against individuals who did not stand during

it is said when opening the ark before taking out the Torah scroll.⁶⁶

In contrast, the Ashkenazi Haredi public and some of the Eastern Haredi public refrained from saying a prayer for the peace of the soldiers, and all the more so did not say a prayer for the peace of the state, and in the prayer books in their synagogues, there is no prayer for the peace of the soldiers.⁶⁷ It seems that there are several explanations for this phenomenon that do not contradict each other:

1. The Haredi public is very conservative, especially regarding the world of the synagogue, and it is not inclined to change the order of prayers or add new prayers.⁶⁸

2. One of the reasons that the majority of the Haredi public did not serve in the IDF was that this community opposed the establishment of a secular state in the Land of Israel, and did not want to participate in a body like the IDF, which was clearly perceived as a Zionist institution.⁶⁹

---

the recitation of "HaNoten Teshuah," see Gafni (above, footnote 48), 89 (Hebrew).

66 This is its location in the siddurim of the Eastern communities.

67 Even in the calendars published in Israel that provide detailed daily customs, there is no prayer for the soldiers. See, for example, *Luah Davar Be-Itto; Luah Halakhot VeHalikhot Temidim K'Sidram; Luah HaHalakhot VeHaMinhagim*. For a unique case abroad, see "Additional Prayers," Section 9.

68 The opposition to changes in prayer was one of the reasons for the resistance of ultra-Orthodox rabbis to adding a lamentation (kina) for the Holocaust. See Mordechai Meir, *Elegies in Memory of the Holocaust for the Ninth of Av* (Jerusalem: Orhot, 2003), 23-24 (Hebrew).

69 In the ultra-Orthodox world, there was a comparison made between conscription into the IDF and the severe phenomenon of the conscription of Jewish youth into the armies of Eastern European nations in the 19th century. See Mordechai Zalkin, "Children of God and Children of Men: Rabbis, Yeshiva Students, and Nineteenth-Century Conscription into the Russian Army," in Avriel Bar-Levav, ed., *Peace and War in Jewish Culture*

Consequently, this community avoided praying for the well-being of IDF soldiers, as such a prayer constitutes a declaration of identification with the soldiers' actions, and this community did not want to express public identification and convey a positive attitude towards a Zionist organization like the IDF.[70]

3. The Haredi public found it difficult to express public identification with IDF soldiers when it did not enlist in its ranks.[71]

4. Most IDF soldiers were not observant, so the Haredi public refrained from praying for their peace.[72] However, during times of war

> (Jerusalem: Shazar, 2006), 219-220 (Hebrew). For the reasons behind the exemption of the ultra-Orthodox from conscription, see Meital Gez, "The Integration of the Religious Soldier into the Military System in the Early Years of the IDF (1948-1953)," (MA thesis, Bar-Ilan University, Ramat Gan, 2004), 35-42 (Hebrew).

70 See Menachem Friedman, *Haredi Society: Sources, Trends, and Processes* (Jerusalem: Jerusalem Institute for Israel Studies, 1991), 125-126 (Hebrew). It should be emphasized that Rabbi Goren's Mi Sheberach is not recited in the ultra-Orthodox sector, even though it does not include the phrase "State of Israel" but rather "our land."

71 It is possible that this is also the reason why there is no discussion in the rabbinic literature of the ultra-Orthodox Ashkenazi world regarding the recitation of this prayer.

72 See *Eved Hashem* (Holon 1996), 178 (Hebrew), who opposes the recitation of the prayer for those who do not observe the commandments. For the status of the hiloni stance within the ultra-Orthodox community, see Amir Mashiach, "Feeding Him to the Wicked and He Dies: The Position of Rabbi Yosef Shalom Elyashiv Towards the Apostate Jew," *Moreshet Yisrael*, vol. 9 (2012): 131-148 (Hebrew). See also "Changes in the Text," section 2 below.

> There were others who proposed different reasons for not reciting this prayer. In 1979, a Haredi yeshiva student told me that soldiers in the Israel Defense Forces should be happy, as the Haredi public includes them every Sabbath in the congregational blessing in the phrase "with all the holy congregations." Another explanation I heard was that Rabbi Goren was a

Praying for the Defenders of Our Faith

in the State of Israel, the Haredi synagogues used to recite Psalms or the passage "Our brothers, the whole house of Israel," that is, utterances suitable for times of trouble that do not mention the State of Israel and IDF soldiers.[73]

Non-enlistment of the Haredim in the IDF led to a sharp controversy between them and the citizens of the state who served in the IDF, who saw it as immoral behavior.[74] Among the national-religious public, this controversy found expression every Sabbath in saying Mi Sheberach for the soldiers. This prayer was said by the emissary of the public with patience, and the congregation stood and gave it much attention and answered "Amen" at the end. All this out of a desire to express overt support for the subjects of the prayer, IDF soldiers who defend the citizens of Israel, support from which implicit protest against those who refrain from saying the prayer for the peace of the soldiers is derived. From time to time, among those who recited this prayer, there

controversial figure, and therefore his prayer was not accepted. On Rabbi Goren's position in the religious world, see Chaniel Nahari, "Development of Halakhic Literature for Soldiers from 1880 to 1975," (MA thesis, Bar-Ilan University, 2003), 72-73 (Hebrew), and Abraham Horowitz, *Orhot Rabbeinu*, vol. 5 (Bnei Brak 2005), 173-175 (Hebrew).

73 See, for example, Abraham Horowitz (above, footnote 72), 71, 75-76 (Hebrew). An exceptional text is found at the beginning of the pamphlet "Shema Elokim Rinasi" [Hear, O God, My Cry], Jerusalem [1991], issued by the Jerusalem Municipality's Department of Culture. According to the directive of the Jerusalem Rabbinical Court, due to the difficult security situation during the Gulf War, it is necessary to add on Mondays and Thursdays the Mi Sheberach prayer for the soldiers of the Israel Defense Forces, the Soldiers of the U.S. Army, and their allies.

74 See, for example, Shahar Ilan, *Haredim Ltd.* (Jerusalem: Keter, 2000), 114-118 (Hebrew); Guy I. Seidman, *The Right to Serve in the IDF* (Tel Aviv: Perlstein-Ginsburg, 1996), 195-196 (Hebrew). For the attitude of the religious Zionist public toward exemption from IDF service, see Meital Gaz (above, footnote 69), 44-47 (Hebrew).

were those who expressed sharp protest against those who refrained from reciting a prayer for the peace of the soldiers.[75]

It is possible to look at the recitation of the Mi Sheberach for IDF soldiers in a broad view. The national-religious public saw itself as a partner in the rise of the State of Israel and its formation, and it found it appropriate to express this view in the synagogue through various Zionist behaviors. These behaviors differentiate the Zionist synagogue and characterize it over the Haredi synagogue. Here are examples of such behaviors: A. Recitation of a prayer for the peace of the state and Mi Sheberach for soldiers every Sabbath and special prayers for

---

[75] See, for example, Yona Emanuel, "Review of 'Sefer Mishpatei Shaul', by Rabbi Shaul Yisraeli," ha-Ma'ayan, vol. 37, no. 4 (July 1997): 73 (Hebrew); Uri Wurzburger, "Note: A Prayer for the Peace of IDF Soldiers and the Peace of the State," ha-Ma'ayan, vol. 33, no. 3 (March 1993): 63-64 (Hebrew); Knesset Proceedings (2 June 1993), 5417-5418 (Hebrew). Rabbi Zvi Yehudah Kook used to say that anyone who does not say a prayer for the well-being of IDF soldiers has "a lack of appreciation"; see the response of Rabbi Yossef Elnekave dated 6 July 2011 on the Morashah website. Moshe Gavra, Studies in Yemenite Prayer Books, vol. 2 (Bnei Brak: The Institute for Yemenite Rabbinical Studies, 2010), 217 (Hebrew), opposed Yemenite prayer books that omit a prayer for the well-being of IDF soldiers: "In all the early Yemenite printed prayer books, the prayer for the well-being of the state and the IDF soldiers was printed, and it is not right that some of the printers of prayer books in recent years omit these prayers, since all the great Yemenite rabbis of the generation who made Aliyah, such as Rabbi Yosef Kapach, Rabbi Yeshayahu Meshorer, Rabbi Hayim Kasar, Rabbi Yosef Tsubiri...wrote these prayers in their prayer books or instructed to pray for the well-being of the state and the IDF soldiers... There is in it a forced gratitude from people who benefit from the state's foundation and the preservation of security institutions, but they do not acknowledge and appreciate it." It should be noted that a special prayer for the well-being of soldiers is not present in prayer books before the 1970s.

Independence Day and Jerusalem Day;[76] B. Hanging the Israeli flag on the roof of the synagogue from Memorial Day for the Fallen Soldiers of the Wars of Israel until after Jerusalem Day; C. Commemorating the fallen IDF soldiers, mostly by their relatives, members of the synagogue, by dedicating holy objects in their memory: synagogues, Torah scrolls, curtains, memorial plaques, etc.[77] Also, prayers are said in their memory on memorial days and on Memorial Day for the Fallen Soldiers of the Wars of Israel. It is also common to have a regular study in the synagogue or distribute the study of the tractates of the Mishnah among the members in their memory; D. Incorporating holy books of rabbis with a national-Zionist view into the synagogue's library.[78] These behaviors,

---

76 In many synagogues, prayers were sometimes recited for the well-being of the settlers in Yehuda, Shomron, Azza, and the Golan Heights, as well as prayers against the disengagement from the Gaza Strip and its consequences. See Dalia Marx, "Every Mouth's Prayer: Prayers Written for the Disengagement Process (Summer 2005) and its Aftermath," *Akdamot*, no. 18 (2007): 119-139 (Hebrew).

77 A synagogue where the memorial motif stands out is the Achdut Yisrael synagogue on Jaffa Street in Jerusalem, named after the fallen who were hanged by gallows. The synagogue houses a memorial board listing the names of all the fallen from the Etzel and Lehi, as well as an additional plaque commemorating those who were hanged by gallows during the mandate period. This synagogue served members of the Brit HaHashmonaim movement, most of whom later joined the Etzel and Lehi. It also served as a meeting place for fighters against the British. For more information about this synagogue and its memorial activities, see Gafni (above, note 48), 162-176 (Hebrew). Extensive memorialization for IDF soldiers is found in the synagogues on IDF bases.

78 In ultra-Orthodox synagogues, such practices are not common. However, occasionally, a Zionist synagogue may change its character due to population changes and become ultra-Orthodox. In such cases, they may inherit memorial plaques with the names of IDF casualties that were originally established by the early worshipers. Examples of this can be found in Reuven Gafni, *The Jerusalem Nussah: Synagogues and Ethnic Communities*

and others not mentioned, create a national-Zionist atmosphere and a sense of partnership of the worshipers with the institutions of authority and the army of the State of Israel. They also influence, consciously or subconsciously, the ideology of the worshipers.

Additional Prayers for the Welfare of IDF Soldiers:

The Mi Sheberach for soldiers, which originated from the Military Rabbinate, is the famous and widespread version of the prayer for the welfare of IDF soldiers, but it is not the only version. Over the years since the establishment of the state, several more prayers for the soldiers' welfare have been connected, some unrelated to the Mi Sheberach and some that have incorporated it into their content.[79]

1. Rabbi Prof. Ezra Zion Melamed (1903-1994) published a book of laws and customs in 1955, in which a section titled "Expression of our Rise in Prayer" was included. In this section, he proposed new prayers of his own creation, justifying his words by noting the importance of acknowledging the miracle of national liberation and the establishment of the state through additions to the prayer. His prayer versions might inspire greater men than him to compose a worthy creation. He composed two prayers dedicated to IDF soldiers. One brief prayer to be

---

in Central Jerusalem (Jerusalem: Yad Yitzhak Ben Zvi, 2011), 160, 406-407 (Hebrew), and see Ibid., 154. For more information about synagogues, see Aaron Ahrend, "Regulations of Synagogues in Recent Generations," *Kenishta: Studies of the Synagogue World*, vol. 3 (2007): 51-58 (Hebrew).

79 See above (footnote 48). An interesting testimony is provided by Yair Harlap, *Shirat HaYam* (Beit El: Yair Harlap, 1992), 464 (Hebrew), regarding Rabbanit Yocheved Harlap, the wife of Rabbi Yosef David Harlap. She was known for her daily commitment to pray the Mincha prayer with a congregation in the synagogue, as she dedicated this particular prayer for the welfare of the IDF soldiers.

added during the Blessing of the New Moon, its main content being the success of the soldiers in the campaign:

> "May it be Your will, God of the heavens, that You stand to the right of the Israel Defense Forces, and grant wisdom and understanding to the commanders, and strength and might to the soldiers, to subdue all our enemies and repel all who rise against us. With His mighty arm, may He protect them, as it is written, 'The Lord of Hosts shall defend them,' and let us say, Amen."

The second prayer is called "Mi Sheberach for the IDF," and the main section includes a request that God blesses "all the young men of Israel standing in the campaign," protect them during war, and that they return to their homes healthy. This prayer also includes a plea for healing for the sick of Israel and "for all the injured and wounded," and at the end of the prayer, a request for blessing for the praying congregation and anticipation for redemption.[80] This Mi Sheberach was not influenced by the version that was in the IDF prayer books, which was not known at that time in synagogues outside the army. The version of Rabbi Melamed was customarily recited in his days in Jerusalem in the synagogues in which he used to pray,[81] but since it was not printed in a prayer book, it was not recited elsewhere.

---

80 Ezra Zion Melamed, *Pirkei Minhag ve-Halakhah* (Jerusalem: Kiryat Sefer, 1955), 194 (Hebrew). Further on Rabbi Melamed, see Noah Aminoah, "The Man of Torah and Science: The Scientific Work of Ezra Zion Melamed," *Jewish Studies*, no. 35 (1995): 103-117 (Hebrew).

81 Rabbi Melamed used to pray at the Ohel Yitzhak Synagogue in Kiryat Moshe, Jerusalem, and at the Kesai Rachamim Synagogue in the Nahalat Zion neighborhood, which was founded by his father, Rabbi Rahamim Melamed-Cohen (1865-1932). Rabbi Rahamim Melamed-Cohen served as the Rabbi of the Persian Jewish community in Jerusalem.

2. Yosef Hasid printed in 1963 a prayer book "The New Complete Prayer of Beit David and Shlomo" for the Eastern communities. At the beginning of the prayer book, "Mi Sheberach for IDF soldiers" was printed, with instruction "to be said in all synagogues on the holy Sabbath at the time of opening the ark."[82] It is an expanded version of the Mi Sheberach published by Rabbi Goren in 1957, which includes a series of biblical verses for protection and defense at its end. The author of the version leaned towards the world of Kabbalah, as one of the verses at the end of the version is brought thus: "For he will command his angels regarding you (using the divine name YHVH) to protect you in all your ways (using the divine name KLK)." The author of this version is unknown, and it has been accepted by some members of the Eastern communities to this day. Some have recited it with certain changes.[83]

3. The Rabbi of the city of Haifa, Rabbi Yosef Messas (1892-1974), originally from Morocco, composed another version of a prayer for the soldiers' welfare.[84] The prayer was composed in Iyar 1967, six days before the start of the Six-Day War, and was printed as a single page, not within

---

82   The *Siddur Tefilat he-Hadash ha-Shalem Beit David u-Shlomo* (Jerusalem, 1963).

83   Thus, for example, in the Kol Eliyahu prayer book, two versions are found: the "Short Version," which includes an abbreviation of the Hasid version, and it is also similar to the version of Rabbi Goren, and the "Long Version," which includes the Hasid version with slight modifications. Abbreviations of the Hasid version are provided in prayer books like *Siah Siftoteinu*, and *Tefilat ha-Hodesh Nusah Shami*.

84   See Etai Mor-Yosef, "The Leadership and Rabbinate of Rabbi Yosef Messas," *Masekhet*, no. 6 (2006): 171-195 (Hebrew). Shlomo Miarah discusses the scholars of the Abuhatzeira family in *Geonei Mishpachat Abuhatzeira*, vol. 4 (Hebron, 2014), 447-473 (Hebrew).

a prayer book.[85] It is a petitionary prayer built in the form of a liturgical poem addressing God in the second person, constructed with rhyme and meter and an acrostic of the letters Alef-Bet in its twenty-two lines. A preamble to the first line addresses God with words containing the initials of the Tetragrammaton: "Y-H the good and source of blessings." The initials in the last line of the prayer are "Yosef Messas." The author prefaced the prayer with short opening words, in which he also explained why he composed it in the format of a piyyut. And so, his language:

> "Blessings for the head of the IDF. Since every prayer arranged according to Alef-Bet has great value…[86] therefore, with God's help, I arranged it according to the order of Alef-Bet. I also saw in the name of the book Bnei Yissachar, every prayer in which all its sentences have 26 vowel movements in each sentence, corresponding to

---

85   The page in question was officially sanctioned by The Western Jewish Diaspora Council, and was distributed in local synagogues under their jurisdiction. The text was later printed in Rabbi Yosef Messas's book, *Ner Mitzvah* (Jerusalem: Hama'arav Press, 1969), 207, as well as in *Otzar ha-Mikhtavim*, vol. 3 (Jerusalem: Ma'arav Printing, 1998), 1762 (Hebrew). At the outset of the prayer, there is a notation that reads: "Before the Torah scroll is taken out on Shabbat and holidays, we have the custom in the Land of Israel to recite this blessing for all the soldiers of the Israel Defense Forces [IDF]. Composed by Rabbi Yosef Messas, may his memory be blessed, the Chief Rabbi of Haifa." The information regarding the creation of this prayer was relayed to me by Rabbi Elad Portal, representing Rabbi Eliyahu Messas, the son of Rabbi Yosef Messas. Rabbi Yosef Messas also composed the "Shir Kavod L'Tzahal" (Song of Honor for the IDF) following the Six-Day War, as documented in *Ner Mitzvah* (Jerusalem: Hama'arav Press, 1969), 169-175 (in Hebrew).

86   Berakhot 4b: "Rabbi Elazar said in the name of Rabbi Avina: Anyone who recites the Song of David (Psalm 145) every day three times is assured a share in the World to Come. What is the reason? Shall I say it is because it contains the whole alphabet…."

the Tetragrammaton, will not return empty, therefore I toiled and built every house with movements as the Tetragrammaton, may He do for His name's sake. And my name and my family in the last house, I am, היו״ם [=HaKatan Yosef Messas]"

In this poetic prayer, Rabbi Goren's Mi Sheberach is embedded, and additional requests are added in eloquent language and verse fragments that the Almighty will bless the IDF, grant them victory over their enemies, bring redemption closer, and sanctify His name in the world. Here are individual lines from the prayer:

"May You bless the Israel Defense Forces, O exalted and uplifted God, the living God,

Who constantly stands guard over our land and the cities of our God, they stand without idleness.

The borders of our holy land extend from Lebanon to the desert of Egypt.

They are bound and connected, even from the great sea to the entrance of the desert, between the lips."

It seems that Rabbi Messas, who was known for his deep concern for the soldiers of the IDF,[87] believed that Rabbi Goren's version of the prayer was too brief and should be expanded for the well-being of

---

87 For example, as recounted by his son, Rabbi Eliyahu Messas, in his approbation to the book of Gavriel Elkubi, *Tseva Hashem* (Kokhav Yaakov: Atzmit, 2003): "When young soldiers would come to him [=Rabbi Messas] to receive his blessing, he would stand them beside the mezuzah and bless them from the depths of his heart, and recite a blessing (without mentioning God's name and sovereignty), that He has granted us the privilege to establish a glorious army in the State of Israel. Afterward, he would give each of them a small silver coin as a token of blessing in their hands to accompany them on their way."

Praying for the Defenders of Our Faith

the soldiers. Furthermore, in Rabbi Goren's version, the address to the Almighty is in the third person: "May He bless," etc., while Rabbi Messas' prayer addresses the Almighty in the second person: "You shall surely bless... Remember the merit of our forefathers... Strengthen and fortify them," etc. Addressing in the second person creates a sense of direct conversation with the Almighty. Rabbi Messas' version of the prayer was recited in several synagogues in Haifa during his time, including the "Nishmat Hayyim" synagogue where he used to pray.

4. With the approval of the UN on the establishment of the State of Israel on 29 November 1947, Rabbi Dr. Pinchas Wolf (1875-1968), rabbi of the Mekor Chaim synagogue in Petah Tikva, composed a new prayer that constitutes an adaptation of the prayer "Hanoten Teshuah." Instead of a prayer for a king or ruler, it refers to a prayer for "the Kingdom of Israel being established in the Land of Israel," though there was no mention of the army of Israel. This prayer was recited in Rabbi Wolf's synagogue, and after the establishment of the state, a change was made: instead of "the Kingdom of Israel being established in the Land of Israel," they said "the existing State of Israel in the Land of Israel." The prayer served as a substitute for the prayer for the state's welfare that was said in other synagogues. In 1969, when Rabbi Goren's Mi Sheberach for soldiers began to penetrate synagogues, they incorporated most of the Mi Sheberach for soldiers into Rabbi Wolf's "He who gives salvation," and thus to this day, the prayer "He who gives salvation" is recited there every Sabbath. However, the well-known prayer for the state's welfare is not recited there.[88]

88 The original text by Rabbi Wolf is cited in Yoel Rappel, "A Sixty-Year-Old Attributed Prayer," *Makor Rishon* (18 September 2008). The version currently recited in the Mekor Chaim synagogue is cited in Yehuda Friedlander, "Prayer for the Welfare of the State," *Yeda Am*, vol. 36-37 [no. 71-72] (April 2011): 112 (Hebrew). Both Rappel and Friedlander wrote that Rabbi Reuven Katz (1880-1963), Chief Rabbi of Petah Tikva,

5. Yechiel Shmaya printed in the year 1980 a collection of prayers, among them "Mi Sheberach for the Soldiers of Israel."[89] The author's name is not mentioned there, but it is clear that he was familiar with Rabbi Goren's version and wrote a prayer of similar length but in a completely different version. In Rabbi Goren's version, the praying congregation is alluded to in the present tense: 'our land and cities of our God,' 'our enemies,' 'our haters,' while in this prayer there is no reference to the worshipers and the formulation is in the hidden tense, which is a distant language, such as: 'standing guard to save their brothers and protect their people.' In this version, after requesting protection for the soldiers, there is a request to God to instill in the soldiers' hearts His love and fear, to heal the illnesses of Israel, particularly the wounded soldiers, and to send them "complete healing of body and soul."[90] It is unknown where this prayer was recited.

6. The Kabbalist Rabbi Yinon Chouri (1925-2004), a teacher in schools and subsequently the Rosh Metivta in the Tunisian yeshiva 'Kisei Rachamim' in Bnei Brak, composed a prayer for the well-being of IDF soldiers in the year 1982 or slightly earlier.[91] This is an

composed the prayer and sent it to the Chief Rabbis of Israel, suggesting that they instruct the public to recite it every Shabbat. However, Reuven Feuchtwanger, a member of the Mekor Chaim synagogue, informed me that Rabbi Wolf actually composed the prayer and provided its text to Rabbi Katz. Rabbi Wolf also composed a prayer for the Holocaust victims, which is still recited in this synagogue to this day.

89 See Yehiel Shemaia (above, footnote 5), 45 (Hebrew).

90 Regarding changes in the Mi Sheberach, see below.

91 The prayer was printed with Shushan Chouri, *The Zaddik in the Teachings of Rabbi Nahman of Bratslav* (Be'er Sheva, 1994), 227-228 (Hebrew). It was composed at the request of Rabbi Moshe Burta (1896-1986). Regarding Rabbi Yitzhak Chouri, see Shushan Chouri, *Shemesh Yinon* (Bnei Brak, 2005), 434 (Hebrew). It is recounted that Rabbi Moshe Burta recited this

exceptionally long prayer spanning two pages, which is not related at all to Rabbi Goren's 'Mi Sheberach.' The prayer addresses God in the second person. It incorporates verses from the Torah such as the Priestly Blessing, Jacob's 'The Angel who redeems' blessing, and Moses's prayer for Miriam. Some verses are written as they appear in the Torah and then in reverse. There are few Kabbalistic hints in the prayer. This prayer is distinguished in several aspects from other prayers for soldiers. For example, the worshiper is supposed to mention the name of a specific soldier, as follows:

> "Master of the Worlds... Bless Your people, Israel, and the soldiers of the army of Israel, and among them (Ploni son of Plonit) with the triple blessing in the Torah, etc."

The words 'Your people, Israel' are opening words that do not intend to expand the assembly of the blessed beyond the soldiers, and this entire prayer focuses on the soldiers. Rabbi Chouri used the phrase "the army of Israel" and later expressed "the soldiers of Israel," not adopting "the soldiers of the Israel Defense Forces."[92] The prayer includes a variety of requests for the soldiers: that no harm befalls them, that they are saved from terrorists, bandits, wild animals, and traffic accidents; that their enemies fear them, and that there is increased camaraderie among them and between their friends and their commanders. There is also a request for their spiritual-religious strengthening,[93] as follows:

> "Instill in their hearts Your love and Your fear, and let the spirit of the Lord rest upon them, a spirit of wisdom

---

prayer during the Lebanon War that took place in the year 1982. It was composed in that year or earlier.

92 Regarding changes, see below.

93 On this matter, see below.

and understanding, a spirit of counsel and might, a spirit of knowledge and fear of the Lord; and save them from the evil inclination and from all sin and iniquity and from every bad trait… and let them return in peace to their homes… and establish a faithful house in Israel for Torah and testimony."

This prayer was not widely distributed, and it seemingly was not recited regularly in synagogues. Its length was undoubtedly one of the reasons for this.

7. Rabbi Avigdor Nebenzahl (born 1935), who is the rabbi of the Jewish Quarter in Jerusalem, has been reciting a special version of a prayer for the well-being of the soldiers every Sabbath for decades in the 'Minyan Vatikin' in which he prays at the Western Wall. Here is the wording of his prayer:

"May He who blessed our forefathers Abraham, Isaac, and Jacob, Sarah, Rebecca, Rachel, and Leah, bless the protectors of the holy [places] and the holy land. May the Holy One, blessed be He, guard them and return them to their homes healthy and whole, and may He cast down our enemies beneath them, for the entire congregation prays for their welfare, and may He send a blessing into the work of their hands along with all their Israeli brethren, and let us say Amen."

Regarding the background to this prayer, Rabbi Nebenzahl explained to us that he was asked to pray for the well-being of the soldiers, and therefore he composed this prayer, as there is no "holiness" in the common Mi Sheberach found in prayer books.[94]

---

94 Just before reciting the prayer for the well-being of the soldiers, Rabbi Nebenzahl would lead the congregation in an additional prayer that he

Praying for the Defenders of Our Faith

8. In 1949, the Chief Rabbi of England, Rabbi Israel Brodie (1895-1979), composed a prayer for the peace of the State of Israel. This prayer is shorter than the well-known prayer for the peace of the state and does not mention the IDF soldiers. He established it in the Siddur published by the United Synagogue organization in England, edited by him in 1962.[95] His successor in office, Rabbi Immanuel Jakobovits (1921-1999), edited a new edition of the Siddur that was printed in 1990.[96] In this edition, Rabbi Brodie's prayer for the peace of the State of Israel is found with slight changes, and in the middle was added a section on the IDF soldiers:

> "Our Father in Heaven, please command the IDF soldiers, protectors of our Holy Land, guard them from all trouble and distress and send a blessing and success in all their handiwork."

The expression "protectors of our Holy Land" is taken from the prayer for the peace of the state, and the sentence "guard them... their

---

composed. Its text is as follows: "May He who blessed our fathers, Abraham, Isaac, and Jacob, Sarah, Rebecca, Rachel, and Leah, bless our brothers who are persecuted in all the lands of their enemies. May the Lord save them and return them to their homes, whole and unharmed, as it is written: 'And the redeemed of the Lord shall return and come to Zion with singing; everlasting joy shall be upon their heads; they shall obtain gladness and joy, and sorrow and sighing shall flee away.' And may they merit the speedy arrival of the righteous Redeemer in our days. And let us say, Amen." I received the texts of these two prayers from my cousin, Moshe Ahrend.

95 *The Authorised Daily Prayer Book of the United Hebrew Congregations of the British Commonwealth of Nations*, ed. Israel Brodie (London: Eyre and Spottiswoode, 1962).

96 *The Authorised Daily Prayer Book of the United Hebrew Congregations of the Commonwealth*, ed. Immanuel Jakobovits (London: Singer's Prayer Book, 1990).

handiwork" is based on Rabbi Goren's Mi Sheberach. It seems that the inclusion of this section on the IDF soldiers was influenced by the penetration of the Mi Sheberach for the IDF soldiers in the State of Israel.

9. The ultra-Orthodox yeshiva Shaar HaTorah – Grodno, in the Kew Gardens neighborhood of New York serves both as a yeshiva and a regional synagogue. In 2001 with the entry of the U.S. Army into Afghanistan, they established the practice of reciting the prayer "Hanoten Teshuah" there for the United States government. This came about when one of the neighborhood residents, Dr. Mordechai Hacohen, who is a passionate Zionist, argued that while it is indeed an ultra-Orthodox yeshiva, since they pray there for the well-being of the President of the United States, it is also appropriate to pray there for the well-being of the soldiers of the Israel Defense Forces. The head of the yeshiva, Rabbi Zelig Epstein (1914-2009), one of the great Torah scholars in the United States, accepted his words, and as a result, the synagogue's gabbai (and teacher at Yeshiva Shaar HaTorah – Grodno), Rabbi Yosef Licht, composed a prayer for the well-being of the IDF soldiers and the Jewish people in the Land of Israel. The treasurer recites this prayer every Shabbat after "Hanoten Teshuah." Here is the wording:[97]

> "May He who blessed our forefathers, Abraham, Isaac, and Jacob, bless and safeguard our brethren, the children of Israel, the residents of our Holy Land, and our brethren, the children of Israel, who stand on guard to protect them and defend them from all sorrow and harm. In merit of this, may the Holy One, blessed be He, safeguard and deliver them from every trouble and distress, from every plague and illness, and may He send

---

97 As conveyed to me by Shalom Simcha Licht.

blessings and success in all their endeavors, along with all their Jewish brethren, and we say, Amen."

The very recitation of this prayer in an ultra-Orthodox Yeshiva is a great innovation. It seems that the fact that it is a version said in an ultra-Orthodox Yeshiva has led to the following phenomena: the prayer is very short; it includes not only the soldiers but also all the Jews of the Land of Israel, and they are mentioned before the soldiers; "The IDF soldiers" are not mentioned but "our brothers, the children of Israel who stand on guard" etc.

Thus is the connection of the aforementioned versions to the version of Rabbi Goren: Versions 1, 4, were combined before Rabbi Goren's version was distributed, and once it was distributed it was incorporated, as mentioned, into version 4. In versions 2, 3, Rabbi Goren's version was incorporated, and their authors did not see additions and expansions as impairing his version. And while the authors of versions 5-9 were familiar with Rabbi Goren's version, they did not see themselves obligated to his version, since it is not a prayer originating in the Bible or with the sages, but a version of a contemporary rabbi.[98] This in addition: the author of version 6, and perhaps also the author of version 5, was a member of the Eastern communities, and they did not see themselves as subject to Rabbi Goren who was an Ashkenazi rabbi, and the authors of versions 8-9 lived outside Israel and certainly were not subject to the Chief Rabbi in Israel.

Finally, we will mention here the prayer of non-Jews for the peace of IDF soldiers. Since the establishment of the State, many members of the Druze community have served in the IDF, and the religious people of this community have tended to compose a prayer for the peace of the

---

98 Additionally, there were those who distanced themselves from the activities of Rabbi Goren and his rulings. See above (footnote 72).

soldiers and distribute it in their villages. The prayer includes a request that God guard all IDF soldiers from disasters and accidents and protect the State of Israel. This prayer does not have a fixed version and even the time of its recitation is not fixed, but it is said as needed and the situation in the private homes of religious Druze families whose sons serve in the IDF, but not in the prayer houses of the Druze in which only the ancient fixed prayers are said.[99]

---

99 This is what I heard from Dr. Jaber Abu Rokan, an expert on Druze customs. Incidentally, Rabbi Ovadia Yosef, *Hazon Ovadia: Aveylut*, vol. 3 (Jerusalem: Ma'or Yisrael, 2011), 238 (Hebrew), ruled that when a Druze soldier is killed in the service of Israel's security, it is appropriate to recite the memorial prayer in the synagogue for the elevation of his soul. In the context of reciting "El Malei Rachamim" for non-Jewish officers, see Ayzik-Meyer Dick, *Rabbi Shemayah Mevarech Ha-Mo'adot*, trans. Dov Sadan (Jerusalem: Bialik, 1967), 95-103 (Hebrew).

Changes in the Wording of Mi Sheberach for IDF soldiers

We have seen that alongside the Mi Sheberach for IDF soldiers, which Rabbi Goren disseminated during the Sinai Campaign, additional prayers were connected, some of which were not influenced by him at all, and some of which enveloped it with many prayers and verses until it was almost unrecognizable therein. We will return now to Rabbi Goren's version. Those who adopted his version generally insisted on saying it as written and in its original language.[100] However, over the years, especially from the 1980s onward, many who recited the Mi Sheberach made minor changes, resulting from their perspective on one issue or another.[101] There are changes that have entered the prayer books, and there are changes that were practiced in specific communities without being found in any prayer book. The modifiers belonged to different groups: scholars of the Eastern and Yemenite communities, nationalist Ashkenazi rabbis, and members of non-Orthodox movements that tend to change the wording of the prayer. The changes can be categorized according to five topics.

1. Naming the soldiers: There were those who changed the expression "soldiers of the Israel Defense Forces." In many prayer books of the Eastern communities, this expression was shortened, and "Israeli

---

100 In the Ramat Modi'in communal ordinances, it is stipulated not to alter the printed and accepted text without the instructions of the Chief Rabbinate of Israel.

101 Also, the Hanoten Teshuah prayer had variations in its text. See, for example, Jacob Mazeh, *Zikhronot*, vol. 4 (Tel Aviv: Yalkut, 1936), 32-39 (Hebrew); Jacob Levi, "Childhood Memories in the Khal Adas Jisroel in Berlin," *ha-Ma'ayan*, vol. 4, no. 4 (June 1964): 12 (Hebrew). For changes made by congregants in the Prayer for the State, see Aaron Ahrend (above, footnote 7), 192-200 (Hebrew).

soldiers" was established instead, both in the title of the prayer and in the body of the prayer.[102] The abbreviation may have stemmed from a desire not to highlight the secular institution or the militarism.[103] And the one who adopted this abbreviation did so to emphasize that at times the IDF needs to be a proactive army and not just a defensive one.[104]

2. Spiritual strengthening for the soldiers: There were those who added a sentence of prayer for the spiritual-religious strengthening of the soldiers. For example, after the words "on land, in the air, and at sea," "and inspire upon them a spirit from above and return them in complete

---

102   For example, in the following prayer books: *Hazon Ovadia, Kol Yehuda, Kol Mitzion, Avodat Hashem, Ish Matzliach, Ohr HaHayyim, Darkei Avot, Revid HaZahav.*

103   Rav Zvi Yehudah Kook raised this issue, expressing it as follows in his *Conversations of Rabbi Zvi Yehudah on the Book Orot*, vol. 2, ed. Shlomo Aviner (Jerusalem: Hava Library, 2006), 371 (Hebrew): "Some people say, 'The army – it's not beautiful, it's materialistic, it's physical, it's materialistic.'" He expressed his disagreement with this approach. Rabbi Oury Amos Cherki, *Siddur Beit Melukhah* (Jerusalem, 1991), 156 (Hebrew), objected to changing "Chayalei Tzahal" to "Chayalei Yisrael" (Soldiers of the IDF to Soldiers of Israel) and stated: "There is a mitzvah obligation in mentioning the name צבא (army) which is a sacred use that enables the fulfillment of the mitzvah of conquering the land (Nahmanides in *Sefer HaMitzvot*, Positive Commandment 4)." This concept can be traced back to the ideas of Rav Kook, see, for example, *Conversations of Rabbi Zvi Yehuda: Genesis*, ed. Shlomo Aviner (Jerusalem: Hava Library, 1983), 382 (Hebrew). However, it should be noted that in the prayer formulated by Rabbi Shmuel Avidor Hacohen (see above, footnote 47), the phrase "Chayalei Yisrael" (Soldiers of Israel) is used, and Rabbi Shlomo Goren also used this expression, for example, in the opening of his Mahzor for the High Holidays for the Soldiers of the IDF, printed on the eve of Rosh Hashanah in 1960.

104   So holds Rabbi Eliezer Melamed, the head of the Beit El Yeshiva. See his response from the year 2002 on the Beit El Yeshiva website (Yeshiva.org.il).

repentance" was added;[105] and elsewhere was added: "Because the entire congregation blesses them and prays for them, the Holy One, blessed be He, will illuminate His face to them, strengthen their spirit for His love and fear, and fortify their arm to do His will."[106] And there are those who, after the request that God keep the soldiers "from all plague and illness," added "and strengthen them in their spirit and body."[107] These additions stemmed from the fact that many IDF soldiers were not religious, as well as from the pervasive secular atmosphere that prevailed in the IDF. Contrary to all these, there were those who opposed such changes, as they imply criticism of IDF soldiers.[108]

105 *Siddur Geulat Yisrael.*

106 The recitation of this prayer in the Ramban Synagogue in Jerusalem has followed this custom since its founding in 1962. The addition to the prayer was instituted by Meir Medan (1915-1989), a prominent figure who had been involved with the Lehi (Lohamei Herut Yisrael), the Jewish paramilitary organization in Mandatory Palestine during the 1940s, and served as secretary of the Committee of the Hebrew Language, and was an expert on prayer texts.

107 In the following prayer books: *Imrei Fi HaShalem, Avodat HaShem, Ish Matzliach, Revid HaZahav, Tefilah LeMoshe,* and see also our discussion above regarding Rabbi Yinon Churi's version. By the way, Rabbi Shlomo Aviner composed "Tefilat HaChayal" against the background of integrating female soldiers into combat units in the IDF, in which the soldier says the "Yehi Ratzon" prayer, emphasizing the sanctity of the camp and maintaining distance from women during military service. This text of this prayer was printed in the weekly Torah booklet *BeAhavah U'BeEmunah,* no. 667 (17 May 2008): 15 (Hebrew).

108 Cherki (above, footnote 108), 157 (Hebrew), wrote: "God forbid to add things that imply a disparagement of the soldiers of the IDF, such as 'and may they return in complete repentance,' as if the soldiers are more sinful than other segments of the public. Aren't there many very righteous and innocent among the soldiers? And should every Mi Sheberach made for a person or any community mention that they should return in repentance?" See also the response of Rabbi Yossef Elnekave (above, footnote 75).

3. The activity of the soldiers: It has already been mentioned above that in reciting the prayer for the peace of the soldiers, its reciters expressed their worldview. This can be seen in the changes in the wording of the prayer that were made following the evacuation of the Gush Katif settlements in the Summer of 2005 by IDF soldiers. This evacuation was conducted by the military system and created a certain confusion in the relationship of some opponents of the evacuation to IDF soldiers. On the one hand, the IDF was perceived as a "deportation army" and therefore not worthy of blessing, and on the other hand, it is the army that protects the people of Israel, and most of its soldiers are not part of the evacuation mechanism. The solution was to insert changes into the prayer so that it would be possible to pray for the peace of IDF soldiers without identifying with the evacuation of the settlements. Some proposed omitting the sentence "and send... their hands," since in his opinion not all the deeds of their hands deserve success and blessing, only their wars against an external enemy.[109] Another correction was to add to the sentence "and send a blessing in all the work of their hands" the word "the good" or the word "for good."[110] This addition is meant to indicate that the prayer is that IDF soldiers will succeed only if they act for good and not if their action is for evil.

From another direction: The Progressive Movement in Israel (Reform) omitted the sentence dedicated to victory over the enemy: "The Lord will place our enemies who rise against us stricken before them," and instead of the conclusion "He will subdue our enemies... to save you," a quote from the prophecy of Micah (4:3-4) was brought:

---

109 See the responsum of Rabbi Yaakov Ariel, the Chief Rabbi of Ramat Gan, in the year 5765 (2005) on the Yeshiva Beit El website (Yeshiva.org.il).

110 For example, the prayer text used in the Jewish community in Hebron. In the *Siddur Ateret Tiferet*, an additional phrase is inserted: 'ke-daat ve-ke-halakhah' (according to Jewish law and custom).

Praying for the Defenders of Our Faith

> "And it will be fulfilled in them the scripture 'and they will beat their swords into plowshares and their spears into pruning hooks, a nation shall not lift up a sword against a nation, nor shall they learn war anymore, and each man shall sit under his vine and under his fig tree, and there will be no one to make them afraid.'"

This change is one of a whole series of changes that the Reform Movement has made in the wording of the prayer, intended to emphasize the universal foundation in prayer and to omit sections that seem to offend the nations or express joy at the fall of Israel's enemies.[111]

4. State borders: In the Mi Sheberach prayer, the borders of the country that the IDF soldiers safeguard are specified. However, the location of the soldiers' activities has also changed from time to time in the wake of wars. Therefore, after the entry of the IDF into Lebanon during the First Lebanon War, some changed the phrase "from the border of Lebanon to the border of Egypt" to "from Lebanon and Syria to" and

---

111   The quotation is from the *Siddur HaAvodah SheBaLev*. On the universalist tendency in Reform prayers, see Eric L. Friedland, *'Were Our Mouths Filled With Song': Studies in Liberal Jewish Liturgy* (Cincinnati: Hebrew Union College Press, 1997), 317-325; and Dalia Marx, "Ideological, Theology and Literature in Reform Liturgy in Israel," *Kenishta: Studies of the Synagogue World*, vol. 4 (2010): 231-235 (Hebrew). And see below (footnote 119), and the text near footnote 130. Regarding the expression 'Veyadber soneinu techteihem' (Our enemies will speak in their stead), I heard from Prof. Yossef Shilhav that around 1988 there was a debate among students at The Harvard Hillel Orthodox Minyan at Harvard University about whether to include this expression. Those who opposed it argued that it was too militant and violent.

so on.[112] Others used "from Lebanon to the border of Egypt"[113] or "from Lebanon to the border of Egypt."[114] Some replaced "from the border... to the Arabah" with a shorter phrase: "wherever they are."[115] Some added before or after "on land, in the air, and at sea": "and also wherever they are," or "and wherever they are."[116] There were those who omitted 'from the border... the Arabah' because of the belief that the borders of the Promised Land would extend to the Euphrates River.[117] And some opposed changing the expression "from the border of Lebanon."[118]

112 *Siddur Shaarei Komemiyut*, based on the rulings of Rabbi Mordechai Eliyahu. Regarding this change, see the words of Rabbi Mordechai Eliyahu in Responsa, *Shu"t ha-Rav ha-Rashi (1990-1993)* (Jerusalem: Darkhei HaHora'ah L'Rabanim, 2009), 50-51 (Hebrew). Also, see also the determination of Rabbi Mordechai Eliyahu that the text of Mi SheBerach for soldiers is not obligatory and can be changed (Ibid., page 162).

113 In the *Siddurim Kol Eliyahu* (in both versions) and *Pe'er ha-Tefillah*.

114 The decision of the Chief Rabbinate of Israel on the eve of Rosh Hashanah in 2005 and a similar decision in the *Siddur Tefilat HaChodesh*.

115 The Siddur Ateret Avot. This abbreviation was suggested by Rabbi Eliyahu Bakshi-Doron, then Chief Rabbi of Safed. See the announcement *ha-Tsofeh* (9 December 1997): 1 (Hebrew).

116 Former, the opinion of the Chief Rabbis of Israel in a letter dated 25 November 1992; Siddurim Avi Chai for Shabbat, Siah Yisrael (in small print and square brackets). Latter: Hasid (above, Additional Prayers, section 2); *Siddurim Kol Eliyahu* (in the long version), *Siah Siftoteinu, Shaarei Komemiyut*, and *Tefillat He-Hadash*.

117 So does Rabbi Zalman Melamed. Also, in *Siddur HaAvodah SheBaLev*, the boundaries were also omitted, possibly to shorten it following the Reform tradition.

118 In the response of Rabbi Avraham Shapira dated 28 February 1988, which is found in the archives of the Chief Rabbinate of Israel, he answered: "There is no place to 'amend' prayers that were established by eminent rabbis in the past. The phrase 'from the border of Lebanon' does not refer to the political border between Israel and the state of Lebanon. Geographically,

5. Expansion of the Blessed: The 'Mi Sheberach' prayer, in its essence, was dedicated to the IDF soldiers, but there were those who changed its wording to expand the circle of those blessed. Some added after 'the soldiers of the Israel Defense Forces': 'and the other security forces,' in order to include those working for the country's security outside the framework of the IDF, such as the police, personnel of the General Security Service, and the Mossad.[119] Some added after 'He shall safeguard and save our soldiers' the word 'us,'[120] or the words 'and all our fellow members of the House of Israel.'[121] Others replaced 'and crown

---

the Upper Galilee and the mountains of southern Lebanon constitute one geographical region. From the history of Jewish settlement in the northern part of the Land, Jewish communities that were located in the Upper Galilee, which today are, from a political perspective, within the territory of Lebanon. Therefore, the words 'from the border of Lebanon' have a broader significance beyond geography and do not only refer to the political border." See also Hillel Unsdorfer, "On the Text of 'Mi Sheberach' for IDF Soldiers," *ha-Tsofeh Literary Supplement* (12 February 1993): 7 (Hebrew).

119 In this manner, additional phrases were added to *Siddur Avi Hai for Shabbat*. The Chief Rabbinate of Israel established on the eve of Rosh Hashanah in 2005: "And the Security Forces." These words were added to the Siah Yisrael Siddur in a small font and in square brackets. In the *Siddur HaAvodah SheBaLev*, "and the rest of our defenders" was added. Perhaps "defenders" was chosen over "land" to give the prayer a more universal character (see above, footnote 111). A similar expansion occurred with the name "Memorial Day for IDF Soldiers," which was changed in 1981 to "Memorial Day for the Fallen Soldiers of Israel's Wars." During the Gulf War, on 5 February 1991, Rabbi Moshe Zvi Neria sent a letter to the Chief Rabbinate of Israel suggesting adding after "on land, in the air, and at sea": "and all the forces of the nations standing in battle formations against our adversaries," and later, instead of "our soldiers," using "all the soldiers."

120 *Siddur Avodat HaShem; Siddur Revid HaZahav.*

121 *Siddur Geulat Yisrael.*

them… establish them' with 'and crown us… establish us.'¹²² Some added a request for the sick at the end of the prayer after the words 'to save you': 'and all those in need of healing, He shall send His word and heal them and deliver them from their ailments.'¹²³ Some added after the words 'He shall bless': 'the settlers,' and also later, it reads 'He shall safeguard and save the settlers and the soldiers,' because, in their view, the settlers have sacrificed more in recent years than anyone else for the sake of the nation and the land, whether as citizens or soldiers.¹²⁴ These changes did not fundamentally alter the prayer, as it remains dedicated to the request that the Lord protect the IDF soldiers.

One version in which significant meaningful changes were made is found in the siddur "Od Yosef Chai" for the Eastern Jewish communities.¹²⁵ In this siddur, there is a heading "'Mi Sheberach' for the IDF soldiers and the Torah scholars," and underneath it is written:

> "It is well-known that the text of the prayer [for soldiers] commonly found in prayer books was written in cooperation with the 'poets of the nation' … We therefore present an amended version, with the guidance of the 'luminaries of the nation.'"

Here, for the first time, the editor of the prayer book reveals the reason for changing the text: the original text was written as "together with 'The

---

122 *Siddur Avodat Hashem; Siddur Revid HaZahav.*

123 In the version of the prayer as established by Medan (see above, footnote 106).

124 Rabbi Eliezer Melamed, the Rabbi of the Har Bracha settlement. See his response from the year 2006 on the website of Yeshivat Beit El (Yeshiva. org.il).

125 *Siddur Od Yosef Hai*, ed. Yosef Haim Mizrahi (Jerusalem: Kollel Ner Refael Tzedakka, 2007).

Praying for the Defenders of Our Faith

Poets of the Nation.'" The reference is to the writer Shai Agnon (1887-1970), known here as "the Accuser," who believed that he composed the Mi Sheberach prayer for the soldiers. However, as mentioned, his coauthors were Rabbi Shmuel Avidor Hacohen and Rabbi Shlomo Goren. Agnon did not participate in composing this prayer but rather in composing the prayer for the well-being of the state.[126] "The Luminaries of the Nation" refers to Rabbi Mordechai Eliyahu and Rabbi Ovadiah Yosef, who edited the prayer book and were shown the new text by the editor, and they gave their approval.[127] Below is the new text of the "Mi Sheberach."

> "May He who blessed our holy and pure ancestors, may He bless, guard, protect, and assist the soldiers of Israel, and to the avreichim, the yeshiva students, and to the young pupils of the house of study, who stand guard over our land and the cities of our God, wherever they may be. The King of Kings, in His mercy, shall guard them and grant them life, and from all trouble, distress, plague, and illness, He shall save them. May the Lord make our enemies rise against us, and those who hate us come to smite us, and may He establish a decree against them, and may it be fulfilled that the Lord, your God, walks with you to deliver you. In their days and ours, may Judah be saved, and Israel dwell securely, and the Redeemer shall come to Zion. And so, may it be His will, and let us say, Amen."

In this version, there are several minor changes compared to Rabbi Goren's text, but the main difference is the expansion of the blessings, as

---

126 Yoel Rappel (see above, footnote 5), 617 (Hebrew).

127 So I heard from the editor of the prayer book.

indicated in the title: "For the Israeli Soldiers and the Torah Scholars." The prayer according to this version is not dedicated solely to the IDF soldiers but also "to the avreichim, the yeshiva students, and to the young pupils of the house of study." The expansion is based on the perspective that in defending the land of Israel, both soldiers and Torah scholars share a role. This text serves as a middle ground between those who recite the prayer for the well-being of the soldiers and those who refrain from doing so, as mentioned earlier. Mi Sheberach, which includes a prayer for the "Sons of the Torah," serves as a compromise between the two approaches: the identification with the soldiers is somewhat weakened because alongside it exists an identification with the youth of the yeshivas and the graduates who are Torah scholars.

A different interpretation can be found in the Siddur Mishkan Aharon for the Edot HaMizrach Communities.[128] In this prayer book, there is no Mi Sheberach for the soldiers, but before the Torah scroll is taken out, two prayers are included. One is titled "Prayer for the Salvation of the People of Israel, the Land of Israel, and the Holy Places," composed by Rabbi Yehuda Fatiyah (1859-1942). In this prayer, there is no request for the Land of Israel and the Holy Places but a plea for God to protect the Jewish people in exile. The second prayer is called "Prayer for the Land of Israel" by Rabbi David Suleiman Sassoon (1880-1942). In this prayer, the request is made for God to bless "our brethren in the Land of Israel... and place them securely, and instill in their hearts the governance of the country according to the laws of the Torah," etc.[129] These two prayers do not mention the soldiers of the IDF, as their

---

128 *Siddur Mishkan Aharon*, ed. Rabbi Ezra Batzri (Jerusalem: Machon ha-Ketav, 2007).

129 The sentence "And He gave... the Torah" seems to be an addition because Rabbi David Suleiman Sassoon passed away before the establishment of the State.

authors passed away before the establishment of the IDF. Reciting these prayers before the Torah scroll is taken out is intended to serve as a kind of substitute for the Mi Sheberach prayer for the soldiers, which is found in some prayer books of the Eastern Communities.

Another prayer book in which there is no Mi Sheberach for soldiers is the Sim Shalom siddur of the Conservative movement in the United States. As an alternative to the Mi Sheberach for soldiers, the following is included after a short prayer, "For the Welfare of the State of Israel," and a prayer for peace among nations by Rabbi Nathan Sternharz (1844-1780). This change stems from the intention to formulate prayers in a universal direction and to reduce distinctions in prayers between Jews and non-Jews.[130] In contrast, in the "V'ani Tefilati" siddur of the Conservative movement in Israel, two prayers are included: The first, "Blessing for the State and the IDF," is a lengthy blessing that includes a prayer for the State of Israel, for the IDF soldiers, and for the captives of Israel and those missing. It also includes a prayer for peace in the land and in the world. In this prayer, there is a request that the soldiers return to peace, be saved from all harm, and succeed in their endeavors. However, the request for victory over the enemies is omitted.[131] The second prayer included afterward is the familiar Mi Sheberach for IDF soldiers, under the title "Alternative Text [Chief Rabbinate]." In both of these prayers, an additional opening phrase follows "Mi Sheberach...

---

130 *Siddur Sim Shalom*, ed. Jules Harlow (New York: The Rabbinical Assembly, 1985). For the universalistic approach, see above (footnote 111).

131 *Siddur Va'ani Tefillati: An Israeli Siddur* (Tel Aviv: The Masorti Movement and The Rabbinical Assembly of Israel, 2010). Regarding the expression "Veyadber soneinu techteihem," see above (for the text near footnote 111).

v'Yaakov": "Our mothers, Sarah, Rebecca, Rachel, and Leah," with the intention of involving the female voice in the prayer text.[132]

MI SHEBERACH FOR IDF RECRUITS

In the early 1980s, decades after the recitation of Mi Sheberach for IDF soldiers every Sabbath became accepted practice in Zionist synagogues throughout Israel, prayers of Mi Sheberach began to be associated with those conscripting into the IDF. These prayers were not intended for weekly recitation but rather for use when a member of the synagogue was conscripting into the IDF. In their recitation, there is a declaration of support for the IDF in general and for the young person conscripting in particular.[133] Typically, the synagogue's gabbai would recite the Mi Sheberach after the young conscript went up to the Torah. This prayer has received various formulations by non-famous authors and is found in a few prayer books.[134] Starting in the 1990s, it also

132 On the adoption of the female form alongside the male form and the inclusion of "mothers of the nation" alongside "fathers of the nation" in Reform prayers, see Dalia Marx, "Gender in Israeli Liberal Liturgy," in Elyse Goldstein, ed., *New Jewish Feminism: Probing the Past, Forging the Future* (Woodstock: Jewish Lights, 2008), 206-217; and see below (footnote 134).

133 See the observations of Eliezer Schweid (above, footnote 1). Widespread public support for recruits was established in the bylaws of the parents' council: on one of the Shabbats of the month of Tammuz, a gathering is held for the sons and daughters going into service, on Friday night a special conversation is held in honor of the occasion, the sons will be called up to the Torah, Mi Sheberach will be recited for the IDF soldiers, and tidings shall be given to all those departing.

134 At the end of the *Siddur HaAvodah SheBaLev* of the Progressive Judaism Movement in Israel, there is a series of Mi Sheberach prayers, including one for male and female recruits: "He who blessed our warriors Joshua, David, and Judah, Deborah, Yael, and Judith, He shall bless... the male/female

appears in some religious regulations.[135] For example, the version found in the Siddur Shaarei Tefilah is as follows:[136]

> "Mi Sheberach, our fathers, Abraham, Isaac, and Jacob, may He bless... who ascended to the Torah today and is enlisting in the Israel Defense Forces. May the Lord strengthen his spirit, fortify his arm, grant him success in his path, and return him safely to his home. Amen."

Alongside these communal prayers, there is also a personal prayer for a father to say before his son's enlistment in the IDF. This prayer was

---

recruit to the ranks of the Israel Defense Forces. May it be Your will, Lord of hosts, to guide him/her safely and deliver him/her from every foe and ambush, grant success to his/her way, and preserve his/her comings and goings for life and peace from now and forevermore. And let us say, Amen." A nearly identical text is found in the Conservative *Siddur V'ani Tefillati*. Regarding the use of the feminine form and the inclusion of "mothers of the nation" in Reform prayers, see Dalia Marx above (footnote 132). The innovation of "female recruit" not only pertains to gender-specific language but also includes a public declaration of recruiting women into the IDF, which was vehemently opposed by the majority of Israeli rabbis. See the text provided below for reference.

135 In the regulations of Givat Rimmon, a text composed by Eliyahu Shultz, the synagogue gabbai, is provided: "He who blessed... He shall bless the young man... who goes forth to serve in the Israel Defense Forces. May the Holy One, blessed be He, guard and grant success in all his endeavors, and may he find favor and good understanding in the eyes of God and man. May the Holy One, blessed be He, grant him the merit to complete his service whole and healthy, and may the words 'each man shall return to his family' be fulfilled in him. Amen." The custom of reciting the Mi Sheberach for new recruits is found in other synagogue regulations as well, such as those of Bnei Brith, Ohel Nechama, and Ohel Yitzchak.

136 *Siddur Shaarei Tefilah*, ed. Yonah Zilberman (Tel Aviv: Modan, 1989), presents the text near Mi Sheberach for the soldiers before "Hagbaat Sefer Torah."

printed in the year 1980 without the author's attribution.[137] It begins with Mi Sheberach and is followed by Psalm 121 from the Book of Psalms:

> Mi Sheberach, our fathers, Abraham, Isaac, and Jacob... may He bless [mention the name of the recruit], son of [mention the mother's name], and establish in him the triple priestly blessing stated in the Torah: 'The Lord bless you and keep you; the Lord make His face shine upon you and be gracious to you; the Lord lift up His countenance upon you and give you peace.' May he be established with all the blessings that Jacob and Moses bestowed upon the children of Israel."

Parents' Prayers for Their Soldier Children

As mentioned above, we have seen a variety of prayer texts for the well-being of soldiers, intended for communal recitation. Additional prayers for soldiers, albeit less well-known, are those composed specifically for the parents of soldiers. The idea behind creating such prayers is evident: a person praying for the well-being of a soldier who is not a close family member is different from a parent praying for their own child or close relative. Typically, parents would recite regular prayers for the well-being of their children.[138] However, unique prayers were composed for parents

---

137   See Yehiel Shemaia (above, footnote 5),24 (Hebrew); and Eliyahu Zakai, *Shmira LeChayal* (Jerusalem: Yeshivat Or Yom Tov, 1992), 17 (Hebrew).

138   See, for example, Rabbi Yehuda Amital, *Resisei Tal* (Alon Shvut: Yeshivat Har Etzion, 2005), 347 (Hebrew), recounted that his grandmother, Dina Kanner, observed the custom during World War I when her son was drafted into the army. She undertook to fast every year on Mondays and Thursdays from the beginning of the month of Elul until the start of the month of Nissan, praying for his well-being.

of soldiers, which contain personal and individualized language and are not intended for public recitation or declaration of solidarity with the army. Two such prayers, one for mothers and one for fathers, are mentioned here.[139]

Fanny Neuda (1819-1894), the wife of Rabbi Abraham Neuda (1812-1854), the Rabbi of Nikolsburg, composed a prayer book for women. It was first printed in Prague in 1855 and subsequently reprinted multiple times. One of these prayers is intended for mothers whose sons serve in foreign armies.[140] This relatively lengthy prayer covers various themes and is written with devotion and solidarity with the foreign rule and land.[141] The prayer begins with the mother expressing gratitude for having a son "who is strong and capable of bearing arms in a time of war, on our land" (note that "our land" here refers to a foreign land). Following this, the prayer includes requests for her son not to stray from the path of Torah and ethics while in the military and to fulfill his military duties with dedication and loyalty. The prayer later dedicates a section to the request for protection during battle:

> "And on the day he is called to go to the battlefield, where death harvests its yield, there, God in Heaven, spread

---

139 The related topic is the inclusion of poems containing requests for the protection of sons in the military, which are not intended for parental recitation. On this matter, see Yael Levine, "Prayers of Mothers for Their Sons Serving in the Army," *ha-Tsofeh Literary Supplement* (17 November 2006): 11 (Hebrew).

140 See Fanny Neude, *Stunden der Andacht: Ein Gebet und Erbauungs-Buch fur Israels Frauen und Jungfrauen zur offentlichen und hauslichen Andacht sowie fur alle Verhaltnisse des weiblichen Lebens* (Prague: J. B. Brandeis, 1914), 103-104; and for a Hebrew translation of this prayer, see Aliza Lavie, *Women's Prayer: A Mosaic of Prayers and Stories* (Tel Aviv: Miskal, 2006), 126 (Hebrew)

141 See above, footnote 9 and on.

Your mercy upon him. May it be Your will to grant him the strength to protect and shield himself; may You fortify his arm and inspire his heart with courage. May he go forth to battle with joy, enthusiasm, and unwavering determination, with a pure heart, guarding the honor of his God and the faithfulness to his ruler, his people, and his land."

In this passage, the mother asks that God grant her son courage and that he may fight with respect for God's honor and with loyalty to the government. The prayer concludes with the mother's request that her son return at the end of his military service healthy in body and spirit, "adorned with a badge of honor for fulfilling his duties, to the joy of my heart, and for the praise and glorification of Your great name."

A prayer for a father for his son, a soldier serving in the IDF, was printed in the year 1980, without indicating the author's name.[142] The prayer is intended to be recited by the father occasionally during his son's military service. The instruction was to recite this prayer whenever possible, "at the opening of the synagogue or at any suitable time." It is also mentioned what the father should do before reciting the prayer:

> First of all, he should set aside money for charity according to his ability in honor of the soul of Rabbi Meir Baal HaNes. He should say: "This I give for the salvation of my son from his enemies and from all harm, that he may return in peace to his home." He should repeat this twice: "Eloka d'Meir Aneni."[143] Then he should give the money to humble Torah scholars or to the synagogue's

---

142 See Yehiel Shemaia (above, footnote 5), 24 (Hebrew); and Eliyahu Zakai (footnote 137), 18-19 (Hebrew).

143 See Avodah Zarah 18a.

charity boxes. If it is the Sabbath, he should intend in his thoughts the amount of the difference, which he will give to the poor the next day.

The prayer includes a request for physical protection for the son, followed by a request for his spiritual strengthening. Here is the essence of the prayer:

"Please, Lord, have mercy and compassion on me, my wife, and my beloved son, whom I have raised and nurtured until now, and who now stands on guard to protect Your holy people Israel and Your holy land. Please, Lord, watch over him when he goes out and when he comes in, along with all the soldiers of Israel, and protect him with Your kindness from enemies and all kinds of danger... And may it be Your will... to put in his heart to return in complete repentance before You, to plant Your Torah and fear of You in his heart, and to save him from all sin and transgression... And may we, I and his mother, always merit to see his wedding and all his joy, Amen, so may it be Your will."

Prayers for parents on behalf of their children, similar to those mentioned earlier, do not appear in contemporary prayer books and, as a result, remain unfamiliar to the general public.

Appendix: Supplications Against Enlistment in a Foreign Army

At the margins of our discussion dedicated to the examination of prayers for the well-being of soldiers in modern times, we briefly describe prayers that were designed as a plea so that Jews would not have to become soldiers. The conscription laws established in Europe at the end of the 18th century led to the recruitment of many Jews into foreign armies. This conscription was considered a severe threat to young Jews due to the separation from their families and communities and the difficulty in observing religious commandments within this framework. Consequently, many sought ways to exempt themselves from conscription.[144] Among the actions taken was a prayerful appeal to the Almighty to annul the conscription decree.[145] Typically, these prayers were well-known, but some individuals composed special prayers on this subject. These were private prayers preserved in handwritten form and were not printed in prayer books. Only a few such prayers have survived. Here, we describe three prayers of this kind that were composed in Italy in the 19th century.

The first prayer includes a prayer composed by a father, or it was composed for a father, concerning his sons, who are mentioned by name, that they should not be conscripted when the time comes for military service: "war, guard duty, and any military service related to warfare."

144 Michael Braver and Avraham Yaakov Braver, *Zikhronot Av u-Vno* (Jerusalem: Mosad ha-Rav Kook, 1966), 68-70 (Hebrew); Isaac Levitats, *The Jewish Community in Russia, 1844-1917* (Jerusalem: Posner and Sons, 1981), 41-43; Yeshayahu A. Jelinek, *The Carpathian Diaspora: The Jews of Sub-Carpathian Rus' and Mukachevo 1848-1948* (Tel Aviv: Goldstein Goren Diaspora Research Center, 2003), 100-103 (Hebrew). On the involvement of rabbis in Eastern Europe, see Mordechai Zalkin (above, footnote 69), 165-222 (Hebrew).

145 For example, Rabbi David, the rabbi of Novhardok, testified in 1827: "We heard that several women prayed on the graves of fathers at the cemetery, with fasting and in tears, and they asked for death upon themselves and upon their sons before they were taken to the military men." This quote is from Yisroel Meir Mendelowits, "'It Is A Decree From On High': Sermons concerning the Cantonists in the Writings of the Gaon Rabbi David of Novardok," *Yeshurun*, vol. 12 (2003): 719 (Hebrew), as well as Ibid., pp. 701, 721, 723 (Hebrew); and see further Yair Harlap (above, footnote 79), 15 (Hebrew).

He also listed the commandments that he believed would be difficult to observe in a military framework, including biblical and rabbinical commandments such as observing the Sabbath, fasting on Yom Kippur, abstaining from leaven during Passover, reciting the Shema, prayers, wearing tefillin and a tallit, "and all other commandments as practiced by our Jewish customs." Below is the text of this prayer (original punctuation retained):[146]

> Please, Lord of the world, Creator of souls, Ruler over all creatures, King of kings, the Holy One, blessed be He, kindly look and see my desire and the wish of my soul for my sons, those mentioned by name: Isaac, Elijah, Menachem, and Jacob Daniel Nissim may they live, that when they reach the age at which it is their turn and time to be called by the decree of the king and the ministers to join the army to fight against their enemies, or to be guardians of their cities and their possessions, or any other task related to the matter of war. You, merciful and gracious God, faithful King, answer me at this time and in other times when I pray about this, that they should not be sought out or called upon to go with them, because those who go and are attached to them cannot avoid doing everything to fulfill their duty in the obligatory commandments of the Torah and the Rabbis, and to spend all the days of their life in their Judaism observing the Sabbath, the afflictions of Yom Kippur, abstaining from leavened bread on Passover, reciting the Shema, in prayers, in wearing tefillin and tallit every day, and so all other commandments according to our

---

146   Collegio Rabbinico Italiano, Rome, MS 84 (#42971), folio unnumbered.

Jewish customs, and all the aspirations of my soul and my endeavors to raise and guide them in Your service, in fear of You, and in love for You through Torah and commandment, at every moment and season, and let nothing evil in the world delay them, nor an internal enemy nor an external enemy, but let them be forever calm and confident without fear and terror. Please, answer me, the most humble of all the humble, and may the words of my mouth and the meditation of my heart be favorable before You, Lord my Rock and my Redeemer. Amen, may it be Your will."

The second prayer is a brief prayer that a person composed for themselves to be said close to the drawing of lots, which determined who would be conscripted into the army.[147] This casting of lots was one of the methods for selecting conscripts for the army. The prayer includes a request that the lot that falls to the person contains a high number, granting them exemption from military service. Attached to the prayer is the rationale that through this exemption, they will be saved from transgressions, and will cleave to the Lord and His Torah. The prayer is formulated as follows:[148]

"Please, Lord, have mercy upon me. Tomorrow, as I go to draw a lot from the box of young men who are called to serve in the army, please stand on my right and plead

---

[147] See, for example, Rabbi Moses Sofer, *Responsa Hatam Sofer*, vol. 6 (Pressburg, 1865), no. 29 (Hebrew); and Yisroel Meir Mendelowits (above, footnote 145), 720 (Hebrew).

[148] LA Manuscript, University of California, Los Angeles (UCLA), BX UCLA 7/13.10, folio unnumbered. A similar work, apparently by the same author, is found in the collection of sermons of Isaac Rafael Tedeschi, UCLA BX 779.9.16, folio unnumbered.

Praying for the Defenders of Our Faith

In this prayer, with its purpose and goods, the background for the prayer is presented along with religious rationale for the request that a long subscription is provided: "For the sake of Your great Name, be You my aide all the days of my life, difficulties and transgressions, and I will cleave to You and Your Torah at all times. I will bless Your name forever and ever. Amen. *Elokai Meir Aneni*, enlighten me." (Repeat three times.)

The third prayer is found within a handwritten prayer compilation written between 1870 and 1879 by the residents of Cortemaggiore, in Northern Italy.[149] This prayer, dating from 1870, was intended to be recited before a medical examination that determined a person's fitness for military service. It was written by the brothers Nathanael, Joseph, Shimon, and Michael Muggia, who resided near Piacenza in northern Italy. The title of the prayer is "A Prayer to Avoid Enlistment in the Army," and it was designated to be recited during the Shema Koleinu blessing within the Amidah prayer. Here is the text of the prayer with punctuation added for clarity:

CONCLUSION

In the nineteenth and twentieth centuries, public prayers for the well-being of soldiers were composed, and these were generally recited during times of war involving foreign nations, in which Jewish soldiers also participated. These prayers were specifically composed for recitation in synagogues located in areas affected by the ongoing conflict, and they were discontinued once the war ended. During the War of Independence, rabbis composed various prayers, some of which included sections for the well-being of the Israel Defense Forces soldiers. In 1948, the Chief Rabbinate of Israel published a prayer for the welfare of the country, which included a section for the IDF soldiers. This prayer was incorporated into Zionist synagogues as an extension and update of the HaNoten Teshuah prayer traditionally recited every Shabbat in the Diaspora. In 1950, in response to Rosh Hashanah, the Chief Military Rabbinate offered a prayer Mi Sheberach for the President of the State, the Government of Israel, and serving among the soldiers of the IDF. In 1956, during Operation Kadesh, Rabbi Shlomo Goren published an updated version of this prayer dedicated exclusively to the soldiers of the IDF, instead of the general Mi Sheberach after the Torah reading. Mi Sheberach became popular in Zionist synagogues in Israel in the late 1960s, likely as a result of the Six-Day War. There were others who composed alternative prayers for the well-being of the soldiers, with or without a connection to the Mi Sheberach itself, for the IDF, but these did not attain a prominent status. Some proposed changes, additions, and

[149] "Cortemaggiore," *la Rassegna Mensile di Israel*, vol. 39, no. 5 (May 1973): 297-305. A facsimile of the prayer for preventing conscription is on p. 301; and see also Ibid. 299.

Aaron Ahrend

omissions in Mi Sheberach, each according to their understanding and perspective.

The world of prayer is a traditional world, but over the generations, various additions have been made to the prayer book. The changes mentioned in the article, the substitution of "Hanoten Teshuah" with a prayer for the well-being of the country, and especially the recitation of Mi Sheberach for the soldiers, illustrate the transformations that the Jewish public underwent since the establishment of the State of Israel. Through the recitation of these prayers, the Zionist public sought to express its connection to the State of Israel and its institutions. The ultra-Orthodox public, which had a selective connection to the state's institutions, refrained from reciting these prayers. However, it's important to distinguish between these two prayers. The prayer for the well-being of the country explicitly acknowledges the authority of the state and its leaders, which is why it is not recited in ultra-Orthodox synagogues. In contrast, Mi Sheberach for the soldiers does not explicitly mention the state's institutions and is entirely dedicated to the IDF soldiers. Therefore, it is recited in one form or another by many ultra-Orthodox Eastern Jewish communities, which generally have a stronger Zionist orientation compared to the Ashkenazi ultra-Orthodox community. The customs of a community regarding the recitation of the prayer for the well-being of the country and Mi Sheberach for the soldiers are among the factors that indicate the degree of its connection to the State of Israel.

Listing of Siddurim:

1. *Kol Hai: Yom Shabbat BeVeit HaKnesset*, ed. Avigdor Shinan (Jerusalem: Mishkal, 2000; Hebrew)
2. *Ohr HaHayyim* (Jerusalem: Machon Ohr HaHayyim, 2002; Hebrew)
3. *Ish Matzliah*, ed. Adir Amrutzi (based on the rulings of Meir Mazuz) (Bnei Brak: Machon Ish Matzliah, 1997; Hebrew)
4. *Imrei Fi Hashalem for the Eastern Jewish communities*, ed. Hayyim Halevi (Jerusalem, 1974; Hebrew)
5. *Beit Melukhah*, ed. Uri Amos Sharki (Jerusalem: Erez, 1991; Hebrew)
6. *Geulat Yisrael*, ed. Menachem Yadid (Jerusalem: Yeshivat Simhat Yom Tov, 1997; Hebrew)
7. *Darkhei Avot*, ed. David Shneur (Jerusalem: Minhagei Avot, 2004; Hebrew)
8. *HaAvodah SheBaLev*, ed. Yehoram Mazor (Jerusalem: Israel Movement Progressive Judaism, 1982; Hebrew)
9. *Va'ani Tefillati: An Israeli Siddur*, ed. Simcha Roth (Tel Aviv: The Masorti Movement and The Rabbinical Assembly of Israel, 2010; Hebrew)
10. *Hazon Ovadia*, ed. Yitzhak Yosef (Jerusalem: Yeshivat Hazon Ovadia, 1988; Hebrew)
11. *Mishkan Aharon*, ed. Ezra Batzri (Jerusalem: Machon ha-Ketav, 2007; Hebrew)
12. *Nusah Ahid: Le-Hayalei Tsava Haganah Le-Yisrael*, ed. Shlomo Goren (Jerusalem: IDF Military Rabbinate, 1963; Hebrew)
13. *Avodat Hashem*, ed. Adir Amrutzi (based on the rulings of Meir Mazuz) (Holon, 1995; Hebrew)
14. *Od Yosef Hai*, ed. Yosef Haim Mizrahi (Jerusalem: Kollel Ner Refael Tzedakah, 2007; Hebrew)
15. *[illegible] Avot*, ed. Sagiv Machpud (Bnei Brak: Nosach Teiman, 2004; Hebrew)

Aaron Ahrend

16. *Ateret Tiferet*, ed. Avraham Yitzhak Kilav (Jerusalem, 2013; Hebrew)
17. *Am Yisrael* (Tel-Aviv: Sinai, 1968; Hebrew)
18. *Pe'er ha-Tefillah*, ed. Mordechai Magar (2004; Hebrew)
19. *Kol Eliyahu*, ed. Shmuel Eliyahu (based on the rulings of Mordechai Eliyahu) (Jerusalem: Darkei Horaah le-Rabbanim, 1997; Hebrew)
20. *Kol Yehuda* (Jerusalem: 1990; Hebrew)
21. *Kol Yaakov*, ed. Mordechai Atiyah (based on the rulings of Mordechai Eliyahu) (Jerusalem: Yeshivat ha-Hayim ve-ha-Shalom, 1993; Hebrew)
22. *Kol Mitzion* (Jerusalem: Bezalel, 1995; Hebrew)
23. *Koren* (Jerusalem: Koren, 1981; Hebrew)
24. *Koren* (New York: OU Press, 2009; Hebrew and English)
25. *Revid HaZahav*, ed. Or Neriyah Ozeri (Bnei Brak: 2004; Hebrew)
26. *Rinat Yisrael, Nusaf Sefarad*, ed. Shlomo Tal (Tel-Aviv: Moreshet, 1970; Hebrew)
27. *Rinat Yisrael: Diaspora Version*, ed. Shlomo Tal (Jerusalem: World Zionist Organization, 1974; Hebrew)
28. *Rinat Yisrael: Eastern Communities Version*, ed. Shlomo Tal (Jerusalem: Moreshet, 1974; Hebrew)
29. *Shivat Tzion*, ed. Yosef Kapach (Jerusalem: Eshkol, 1952; Hebrew)
30. *Siah Yerushalayim*, ed. Yosef Kapach (Kiryat Ono: Machon Mishnat ha-Rambam, 1994; Hebrew)
31. *Siah Yisrael* (Kfar Adumim: Kornfeld, 2010; Hebrew)

32. *Siah Siftoteinu*, ed. Shlomo Amihud (Bat Yam: Agudat Ahim, 1992; Hebrew)

33. *Siah Tefillah*, ed. Yeshayahu Aryeh Devorkes (Jerusalem: Rabbi Hiyya Institute, 1967; Hebrew)

34. *Sim Shalom*, ed. Jules Harlow (New York: The Rabbinical Assembly, 1985)

35. *Shirah Hadashah*, ed. Hayyim David Rosenstein (Jerusalem: Eshkol, 1949; Hebrew)

36. Shaarei Komemiyut, ed. Yossef Elnekave (based on the rulings of Mordechai Eliyahu) (Jerusalem: 1995; Hebrew)

37. *Shaarei Tefillah*, ed. Yona Zilberman (Tel-Aviv: Modan, 1989; Hebrew)

38. *Tefillah le-Moshe*, ed. Refael Francis (Jerusalem: 2006; Hebrew)

39. *Tefillat David*, ed. Pinchas Brener (Caracas: Bekker, 1998; Hebrew and Spanish)

40. *Tefilat ha-Hodesh* ha-Shalem Beit David u-Shlomo, ed. Yosef Hasid (Jerusalem: 1963; Hebrew)

41. *Tefillat ha-Hodesh*: Nusah Shami (Beit El: R. Margoliyot, 2007; Hebrew)

42. *Tefillat Yisrael*, ed. Daniel Goldschmidt (Tel Aviv: Masada, 1964; Hebrew).

43. *Tefillat Yisrael*, second edition, ed. Daniel Goldschmidt (Jerusalem: Masada, 1969; Hebrew)

44. *Tefillot LeChol HaShanah: Nusah Sefarad Le-Hayalei Tzahal* (Jerusalem: Moriah, 1960; Hebrew)

45. *The Authorised Daily Prayer Book of the United Hebrew Congregations of the British Commonwealth of Nations*, ed. Israel Brodie (London: Eyre and Spottiswoode, 1962)

46. *The Authorised Daily Prayer Book of the United Hebrew Congregations of the Commonwealth*, ed. Immanuel Jakobovits (London: Singer's Prayer Book, 1990)

Listing of Synagogue Bylaws:

1. Aderet Eliyahu, in Gilo, Jerusalem (1994)
2. Ohel Yitzhak, on Lehi Street, in Rehovot (1997)
3. Ohel Nehama, Chopin Street, in Jerusalem (1996)
4. Eliyahu ha-Navi, in Ahuzat, Haifa (1968)
5. Beit Zur, on Rogozin Street, in Ashdod (c.1990)
6. Bnei Brith, on Hapisgah Street, in Jerusalem (1994)
7. Givat Rimon, in Efrat (1991)
8. Religious Youth Group, on Smolenskin Street, in Tel-Aviv (1972)
9. Tirat Zvi, Kibbutz (1957)
10. Kfar Maimon, Yishuv (1971)
11. Minyan Horim, in Kiryat Moshe, Jerusalem (1979)
12. Nir Etzion, Moshav (c. 1970)
13. Ein ha-Natziv, Kibbutz (1966)
14. Ramat Modi'im, Hashmonaim (1999)
15. Tel Ganim, in Ramat-Gan (1964)

Dr. Aaron Ahrend, a senior lecturer in the Department of Talmud and Oral Law at Bar-Ilan University, has published many studies on Talmudic commentary and Jewish liturgy.

Soldiers of Israel

Meir Bar-Ilan

SOLDIERS OF ISRAEL STAND GUARD over our land and the cities of our God, around the clock, throughout the year, and when necessary, they sacrifice their lives for the sake of the people and the land.

To be an Israeli soldier is not merely an obligation; it is a merit. It is the right to connect to the chain of generations, not only through Torah and commandments, as part of the covenant that the Almighty made with our forefathers, but also through defending the people of Israel and the land that was promised to our forefathers.

One who joins the Israel Defense Forces does not unite solely with the State of Israel but also with all the heroes of Israel throughout the generations. They faithfully continue the legacy of King David's warriors, who fought the battles of Israel. They unite with the fighters of Judah the Maccabee, who battled to liberate the land from foreign rule and for the sake of our Holy Temple.

Praying for the Defenders of Our Faith

They join the army of the rebels against Rome, which attempted to impose foreign rule and idol worship upon us. The warriors of Israel throughout the generations bequeathed the land to us in 1948, and they liberated Jerusalem from foreign rule in 1967.

Israel rebels against the values of the nations of the world ever since we became a nation, starting from the time when Abraham the Hebrew was on one side of the river, while all the others were on the other side. We have been rebelling against the forces of evil and falsehood not yesterday and not the day before. The nations of the world know this well, and they simultaneously admire us and despise us for our achievements and for being different from all other nations. The State of Israel was founded on the warriors of Israel throughout the generations, on heroes who sacrificed themselves on the altar of our God. Yes, the binding of Isaac was not a one-time event but an ongoing event, generation after generation, as the youth of the nation, as well as reservists, were bound on the altar. This courage is evident in every war anew. Concerning them, it is said, "Heroes of might, who do His bidding."

Even the daughters of Israel joined in the battles of the Lord. Like the daughters of Zelophehad, they sought to receive their inheritance in the land of Israel, knowing that the land of Israel is acquired through suffering. Many daughters did not settle for supporting roles in combat but asked to fight side by side with male soldiers for the sake of the people of Israel. With supreme courage, they proved themselves to be faithful successors of the Prophetess Deborah and of Judith. In the recent battles, our enemies were struck before them. The men fought like lions, and the women fought like lionesses. The young lion of Judah!

When the sons of Gad and the sons of Reuben intended to exempt themselves from military service, Moses rebuked them, saying (Numbers 32:6): "Shall your brothers go to war while you sit here?" It turns out that anyone who enlists in the army of Israel against its enemies fulfills the commandment of Moses, especially the commandment of inheriting the land, and acquires his portion in this world and in the world to come. Israeli soldiers, when they go into battle, know well that they may die in battle, yet they do not falter and courageously engage with the enemy to vanquish them under the name of the Lord. Over the years and after many battles, heroes of Israel fill row after row in military cemeteries. The fallen knew what they were heading towards, and even so, they did not seek respite, weakness, or excuses. Every soldier who dies in his duty, the Archangel Michael comes and offers his soul before the Throne of Glory.

To Rabbi Yosef Caro, there appeared a Maggid (heavenly teacher) who came to him from the higher worlds and revealed to him the secrets of Torah. The Maggid informed him: "You will merit to ascend to the Land of Israel this year, and afterwards, you will merit to be consumed in sanctification of His name. You will then merit to be consumed in the Land of Israel publicly to sanctify My name openly, and you will ascend as a burnt offering on My altars." As is well known, Rabbi Yosef Caro surrendered his life for the sake of his God only in a metaphorical sense. In contrast, many soldiers of Israel have had the opportunity to fulfill this commandment and be bound on the altar of His blessed name, as it is written (2 Samuel 1:19): "The gazelle of Israel lies slain on your heights! How the mighty have fallen!" The sons of Abraham, our forefather, who bound his son Isaac, when they serve in the army, they serve as priests in their service, Levites in their guard duty, and proclaim His blessed name at every moment. Israeli soldiers, armed with courage, go out to battle to aid the Lord, thus reinforcing the covenant and the oath that the God of Israel swore to Abraham, Isaac, and Jacob.

Meir Bar-Ilan is Professor Emeritus of Jewish Studies at Bar-Ilan University. His area of scholarly research is primarily in the history of the Jewish people during antiquity, particularly the Biblical and Talmudic periods.

Prayer for The IDF Soldiers and Liturgical Refuge

Elisheva Baumgarten

As a Jew and as a historian, it has always been incredibly meaningful to me that I can open a siddur from the twelfth century, follow most of the davening (liturgy), and feel at home with many of the prayers. Jews throughout the ages said many of the same prayers that we recite in the twenty-first century. As a historian, I delight in the changes and additions to the prayers, understanding them in the context of the events for which they were composed or added. As a mother, when my children complain about the words of *tefillah* that they find removed and sometimes incomprehensible, I often explain that these words connect us to the previous generations and provide us with ways to express ourselves in the different situations we encounter in our lives, at times when words can be hard to find.

Elisheva Baumgarten

The prayer for the IDF soldiers is one I have long appreciated. It begins with "mi sheberakh" ("He who blesses"), a liturgical formula originating in the Middle Ages when prayers of this type flourished. Currently recited every week on the Sabbath, the prayer for IDF soldiers reflects their centrality and importance in Israel, and the constant worry for them, even in times of relative calm. It thus reflects both tradition and current concerns.

Since Oct. 7th, repeating the words of this prayer has felt inadequate, to say the least. Religion and God's will play a terrifying role in this war. Hamas, a religious movement, perpetrated atrocious attacks on Israelis that anyone who believes in the sentiment: "Beloved are humans for s/he was created in the image [of God]" Avot 3:14) finds impossible to comprehend. And within Israel, unprecedented divisiveness, much of it centered around religion, has made an unbearable situation even worse. So many belligerent words have been uttered in the name of God. So many people are telling us what God wants. How do all of these words correspond with the prayers we say? How can words provide any kind of solution?

In Israel, a standard response since October 7th has been "ein milim" (there are no words) to describe the abyss we currently inhabit. And in the absence of words, there have, instead, been incredible and awe-inspiring deeds: those of the hundreds of thousands of men and women who immediately took up arms and put themselves in harm's way to defend our borders and engage in combat with the terrorists; those who organized help centers and are taking care of the evacuees from the south and the north and providing for the soldiers wherever they are.

Returning to the siddur since October 7 has been difficult, but the prayer for the IDF soldiers provides a beacon of light. In the prayer for the soldiers, the division between God and human beings is straightforward. The prayer does not tell God what to do or specify what God wants

Praying for the Defenders of Our Faith

us to do. We simply ask God to protect the soldiers and help them succeed wherever they are, fighting for them. We pray and bless them wherever they are and ask God to lead them. The prayer does not call for vengeance, but for security and success. Those are words in which I, and perhaps others, can find hope and solace. *Lu yehi.*

Professor Elisheva Baumgarten teaches in the Departments of Jewish History and History at the Hebrew University of Jerusalem, where she holds the Prof Yitzhak Becker Chair for Jewish Studies, and is the Academic Head of the Jack Joseph and Morton Mandel School for Advanced Studies in the Humanities.

On Grassroots Jewish Activism

Yosef Begun

JEWS ARE A PEACEFUL PEOPLE. In addition to the direct instructions in Jewish tradition to "love peace and seek peace…," centuries of living in dispersion without their own land, country, and a capable army to protect the people contributed to this disposition. The history of ancient Jewish kings also provides examples that martial prowess was not their chief virtue. For instance, to the legendary King David, known as a warrior, God reproached him for shedding much blood in wars and did not permit him to build the Temple in Jerusalem. The priests and teachers educated the people: they should endure, pray, and wait; the non-Jews had power and strength, but the time would come when God would send the Messiah to the Jews, who would save them and lead the people to the Promised Land.

But the Messiah did not come, and no miracle of salvation occurred. World War II came, the Holocaust, the death of 6 million Jews. The realization of the groundlessness of religious reliance on salvation led to national activities for the recreation of a Jewish state. Along with the state, a Jewish army was established, which defeated the armies of Arab states that attacked the newly born Jewish state. The Jewish people, despite suffering immense losses, managed to rejuvenate and create a modern Jewish state on the Promised Land. 2000 years (!) after the Romans destroyed Jerusalem and expelled the Jews from their land, the victory of the Jewish army in the War of Independence made the miracle of establishing a Jewish state possible.

We live in a unique time in Jewish history, simultaneously tragic and heroic. In the 20th century, two totalitarian regimes made it their goal to find the "final solution to the Jewish question." Hitler organized the Holocaust - the physical murder of millions of Jews, while Stalin pursued the same goal through cultural genocide, depriving Jews in the USSR of their spiritual foundations of existence.

In modern times, new challenges have arisen. On October 7, 2023, Hamas terrorists committed a heinous act by launching an attack in the southern part of the country on the border with Gaza while a large number of young people, Israeli citizens, and visitors from other countries had gathered for a dance and music festival. 1,200 participants of the festival and residents of kibbutzim were killed, and more than 5,000 were injured. The terrorists took more than 200 hostages with them. It's a case of the new being well-forgotten old: our enemies today, Arab terrorists, have powerful patrons, just as it was during the time of the Soviet Union, which did not recognize the "Zionist Israel" as a legitimate state. In our time, the UN continues to pass anti-Israel resolutions, and Israel once again finds itself fighting for survival, this time against the vast Arab and Muslim world that refuses to accept the existence of the Jewish state.

In the context of all these events, Jews from the former USSR, especially those who had the experience of being activists in the struggle against the all-powerful KGB, cannot forget the fight for the right to repatriate to the homeland of their people, for the opportunity to learn their language and preserve their culture. The exodus of Russian Jews is compared in its drama and scale to the biblical Exodus from Egypt. The solidarity of Jews worldwide in supporting the struggle of Soviet Jews had a momentous significance and became the guarantee of another miracle in Jewish history - the mass exodus from the empire of the red pharaoh. I had the privilege of being among those who spent many years in that struggle. Here, I would like to recount some illustrative episodes from those years of collective struggle for the freedom of Soviet Jews.

In early May 1988, shortly after making Aliyah, I was invited to a meeting with President Ronald Reagan. During a special ceremony, the President of the United States handed me a metal bracelet and said to me, "This bracelet was given to me by one of the leaders of American Jewry. It says, 'Prisoner of Zion Joseph Begun,' and it indicates the date of your arrest. For almost a year, this bracelet sat on my desk as a reminder of the difficult fate of Soviet Jews. Now you are free, and I am glad to pass this to you." I was profoundly touched by the gesture, and upon expressing my gratitude to the President, I felt compelled to mention (this was well before the significant Aliyah of the 1990s): "Mr. President, it's too early to remove this item from your desk. Many Soviet Jews still need your help." Such bracelets with the names of Prisoners of Zion in the USSR, one of which ended up on the President's desk, were distributed among American Jews in large numbers at that time.

Another meeting on the same topic occurred in a different place and under different circumstances. In the ward of a Jerusalem hospital where I was staying, an elderly nurse regularly cleaned and distributed medicines to the patients. Upon learning my surname, she approached me excitedly and said that she had sent me letters in prison.... Yehudit, as she was called, mentioned that she had also been sending letters to other

Jewish prisoners in the USSR. She did this for many years without any "directive from above." The characters in these episodes - the American president and the Israeli nurse - symbolically represent thousands and thousands of people in different countries, from various walks of life, who helped us in the USSR, the refuseniks and activists. Through their efforts, a broad public movement was created, a "second front" in the struggle for the freedom of Soviet Jews. This movement was led and directed by Jewish organizations: secular and religious, official and public, women's, student's, local and national. These structures of public Jewish life often conduct so-called "Jewish wars" among themselves, but when it came to the struggle for their brothers and sisters in the USSR, they forgot their disagreements. The selfless, united struggle of world Jewry for Soviet Jews, which stands as an outstanding historical example that Jews around the world are indeed one people.

Who were the organizers of this movement? Then quite young, Yaakov Birnbaum and Glenn Richter became the founders in the early '60s of the organization "Students for Soviet Jewry" (Student Struggle for Soviet Jewry). Glenn Richter dedicated his best young years to this work, sacrificing an academic career. I met Glenn in the late '80s, almost a quarter of a century later, and he told me about the lengthy process of American Jews realizing the necessity to fight - indeed, to fight, even in a democratic society - for the rights of their fellow Jews on the other side of the Iron Curtain. For the overwhelming majority of American Jews, demonstrations and mass actions were psychologically unfamiliar at that time. Discrimination and repression against Jews were seen as part of the Soviet regime, from which all citizens of the country suffered. Gradually, however, understanding of the tragic situation in which Soviet Jewry found itself began to penetrate the consciousness of Americans. Elie Wiesel's book "Jews of Silence", written following the author's trip to the USSR, where he described the state policy of destroying the national self-consciousness of Soviet Jews, contributed to this awareness. The intensified guilt for the passivity of American Jewry in the fate of the Jews of Europe during World War II played an important role in realizing the need to stand up for Soviet Jewry. In 1962, a small group of people came to the Soviet consulate in New York to deliver Passover matzah to the Jews of the USSR through its staff. Such actions became the "harbingers of change" in support of Soviet Jews.

The organization "Student Struggle for Soviet Jewry" was seen by many as a fringe group of idealists and even radicals. Its initial leader was Yaakov Birnbaum, a native of Germany, who was brought out of Nazi Germany as a child by his parents. He was a man of messianic faith and a prophetic disposition. His grandiose plans to mobilize international public opinion and political groups for the liberation of Soviet Jewry appeared visionary at the time - many of them were later realized.

But the most active figure in implementing these ideas was Glenn Richter. Below is an excerpt from the book by Israeli journalist Yossi Klein Halevi, who was a teenager in New York at the time and began participating in the struggle for his distant Soviet compatriots.

I met Glenn Richter one afternoon in 1965. He stood on a Borough Park street corner, offering leaflets to passersby. A green trench coat hung shapeless on his long, thin body... On his lapel was a button that read: "Student Struggle for Soviet Jewry."

"Take a leaflet, read it, and give it to a friend," he repeated over and over in a staccato chant. When a woman passed him with a baby carriage, he dropped a leaflet under its canopy. "Babies can help too," he said.

He began making a speech to the impervious crowd, enunciating each syllable. "We are fighting to save a quarter of the Jewish people. You can make a difference. This time, we won't be silent." I was his only audience.

Glenn became both the director and manager, and secretary of a small student group at the beginning, which dedicated itself to activities far from the interests of the wider public. But his almost religious faith in the righteousness of his goals and the cohesive activism of his fellow campaigners led to the movement gaining strength. In 1964, around 1,100 students gathered for a demonstration in support of the rights of Soviet Jews in front of the Soviet Mission to the United Nations.

In this situation, even official Jewish organizations deemed it necessary to establish an umbrella organization called the "National Conference on Soviet Jewry." Its leadership consisted of representatives from the Jewish leadership who had close ties to the American administration. Initially, the "National Conference" preferred to operate through lobbying using "quiet diplomacy." However, at the same time, more and more new associations emerged, dissatisfied with the cautious tactics of the Jewish establishment. They believed it was necessary to bring more activity and propagandistic "noise" to the struggle for the rights of Soviet Jews.

The Jewish Defense League, founded by Rabbi Meir Kahane, behaved provocatively, disrupting the activities of official Soviet representations in the USA. Its activists disrupted the appearances of Soviet cultural figures. Kahane and his followers' scandalous activities angered the American authorities and several Jewish organizations concerned about their respectability. In historical perspective, the actions of the Jewish Defense League contributed to shifting the issue of Soviet Jews from the last pages of the American press to the front pages.

Local organizations, uniting "ordinary people" (grass-roots organizations), created a movement that became an alliance of unofficial public organizations in support of Soviet Jews. Branches of the "Union Council for Soviet Jewry" appeared in Washington, New York, Chicago, Philadelphia, and Los Angeles. The grassroots organizations of the

National Council worked on a voluntary basis, involving housewives and students. Their leaders included Pamela Cohen (Chicago), Lynn Singer (New York), and Jane Intrator (Toronto), who organized demonstrations, rallies, and pickets locally. After the harsh verdict against the "aircraft hijackers," activists on Long Island held a car demonstration near the "Soviet dacha," in which five thousand people participated. In Glenn Richter's organization, "Students for Soviet Jews," which reached a membership in the thousands, they came up with bracelets bearing the names of Zion prisoners and long-term refuseniks. Many Americans wore them, and one of them was kept on the desk of the President of the United States.

Golda Meir's response to the question about Israel's secrets to victory, "We have nowhere to retreat," remains relevant today, just as it was in her time. We have no other choice but to win in this war against Hamas. Since the destruction of the Jerusalem Temple in the 1st century CE, Jews have lived in dispersion as a disenfranchised minority in different countries at the mercy of other nations. We were despised as "Christ-killers," and for many centuries, we were victims of mass killings and expulsions long before the establishment of the Jewish state. 200 years ago, first in France and then in other European countries, Jews gained equal rights, left the ghettos, and actively participated in the economic and cultural life of their host countries. But anti-Semitism did not disappear; Jews continued to be blamed for the woes of other nations, now for capitalism and later for socialism. Two totalitarian ideologies of the 20th century declared the "final solution to the Jewish question" as their goal. Hitler implemented the physical extermination of millions of Jews, while Stalin attempted to achieve this "solution" through forced assimilation by denying Jews in the USSR access to Jewish culture. 75 years ago (May 1948), the establishment of the State of Israel was proclaimed, and the Jewish people revived their national state in their historical homeland. This historic event transformed Jews into subjects of history, capable of determining the destiny of their existence.

Saving Jews from Physical Annihilation. "Never again!" - After the war, the ashes of the Holocaust burned in every Jewish heart. It became clear to everyone who survived that there was no other protection against the repetition of such a monstrous tragedy except for a Jewish state and a strong Jewish army. The wise Ben-Gurion understood this and insisted on accepting the proposal to divide Palestine under any conditions. The State of Israel is today the sole guarantor of the continued existence of the Jewish people, both in our time and in future generations.

Protecting Jews from Assimilation. Throughout a 2000-year-long diaspora, Jews lived in various countries as a national minority. During the Middle Ages, when Jews lived in a religious Christian environment, they relatively easily managed to preserve their distinctive (cultural, religious) existence because there was a theological dogma that allowed Jews to live in a Christian state in a separate, humiliated state and thus serve as living witnesses to the punishment for refusing to believe in the Christian Messiah. With the advent of the modern era and the beginning of the era of open democratic regimes in European countries – which was a relief for the powerless Jews of that time – the danger of assimilation began to grow. In today's global world, preserving the national characteristics of relatively small ethnic groups becomes problematic. And again, it is the State of Israel that serves as the Jewish national home where they are protected not only from the threat of physical annihilation but also have all the opportunities to continue being Jews in the modern, open, borderless world. A Jew in Israel, secular or religious, remains a Jew in any case, spiritually connected to the past of their people, preserving and developing its heritage, and passing it on to the future.

In conclusion, Jewish activism, rising from personal initiative to global influence, showcases the adaptability and strength of the Jewish community. Facing past and present challenges, it continually advocates for autonomy, justice, and self-determination. This activism not only confronts adversity but propels the community towards a hopeful future, ensuring the Jewish identity remains vibrant and committed to the ideals of peace and justice.

"Black Saturday" 7 Oct 2023 is called Small Holocaust: less victims and small-scale territory, but the same essence. Hamas killed Jews, all of them, for they are Jews, as Hitler did. Again we are getting terrible lesson. Tragedy is sobering. Israel has experience to fast rigging. Hundreds of thousands of reservists began fighting in a matter of days, and the defeat of Hamas began immediately. On such days, the unity of Israel is manifested to the maximum. Flights to Israel have been overwhelmed by the Israelis seeking to return home and defend it. At such a time, the country's leaders forget their differences, put aside party disputes and the struggle for primacy. They unite to develop joint decisions for victory. Jews again remember that they are One People with one destiny all around world, in the Land of Israel and in the Diaspora. And this still happens today. We are joined together as after Holocaust by the idea Never Again! We have no choice to win Hamas. Our slogan again: "Together We Will Win," Am Yisrael Chai!

Yosef Begun is a former Soviet refusenik, prisoner of conscience, human rights activist, author, and translator. He spent over eight years in Soviet prisons and labor camps during a 17-year period for his political activism. Despite adversity, he advocated for the emigration of Soviet Jews to Israel, which garnered international attention and pressure for his release. In 1988, Begun and his family were permitted to immigrate to Israel.

The Shield of David: Prayers as Our Binding Force

David J. Benger

ONE OF THE MOST COMMONLY mistranslated phrases in the Jewish lexicon is "Magen David." In every language I have studied, it is translated as the "Star" of David. But Hebrew speakers know, of course, that the Hebrew word for "star" is not "Magen." "Magen David," properly translated, is the "Shield of David." While the Star is a celestial being out in the universe that sparkles in the night and guides ancient navigators, the Shield is more tangible by far. The shield is something we can feel strapped tightly to our forearms (not unlike tefillin), the last line of defense between fatally sharpened steel and our flesh.

For the first time in nearly 3,000 years, Jewish people – men and women, children, elderly, toddlers and babies – are once more slaves in the land once known as Egypt. And now, just as then, columns of fire rain from the sky to rescue them. We cannot know the mechanical details of what transpired during the Exodus millenia ago. Some choose to take the story literally, and others read a metaphor. But we know that now, today, it is the IDF, the army of the independent Jewish State of Israel, that will bring back our innocent family members.

So on the one hand, how can we not pray for them? On the other hand, pray to whom exactly? The very same God who allowed the atrocities of Black Shabbat to transpire, nevermind The Holocaust and countless catastrophes (both natural and manmade)? As one of the rabbis tasked with burying the victims of October 7th put it in a widely circulated video, "God and I aren't ready to talk yet." I agree.

But for more context on how I can feel such vexation with God and still turn to prayer to express my love for the Jewish people, here is my story.

Though neither I nor my parents are old enough to remember a time before The State of Israel, its necessity for the survival and prosperity of the Jewish people was never in doubt in my house. It was always understood that a Jew who does not live at Home is living on borrowed time. Sometimes that is necessary. My family came to the US for a reason, and never seriously considered leaving. Nevertheless, Home is Home, and Jewish history is chock full of lessons when Jewish communities overstayed their welcome in their host countries.

I grew up equally certain that there was only one way to do Judaism and that was the traditionally Orthodox way, courtesy of the remarkable shluchim of the Lubavitcher Rebbe who made my family at home in this strange land. But while I was certain that this was the only right path to Judaism, I was equally comfortable in admitting that in my daily life, though I was living a Jew's life (and a proud one), I was not living a Jewish life. This hypocrisy was comfortable. I knew what kind of Judaism was right, I knew I could not live up to it, and so I admired Orthodox

Praying for the Defenders of Our Faith

Judaism like one admires a painting at a museum – with reverence and awe, but at a respectful distance.

Though my relationship to Jewish ritual practice would evolve, there is one component that would remain constant from my earliest memories in the synagogue to this day: the magical melodies of the language of prayer. Even as a small child, when I couldn't understand what was being said or why, I took comfort in the knowledge that Jewish communities across the world were saying it too. And that's what made it important.

Prayer is, foremost, about communing with the Divine. Of course. But it is also about bonding with our fellow Jews through space and time.

We pray because it is what we Jews do. We pray because prayer binds us to one another as Jews. We pray because even in the moments where we do not know whether God is listening or even in those darkest moments when we question His very existence, we know that another Jew is praying, and it is our responsibility to bring fellowship to our fellow Jews by joining in that prayer. We pray because prayer is our shield. And just as we have no land but the land of Israel, so too do the Jewish people from across the planet have no greater common binding agent than the language of prayer. We pray for the IDF and for the hostages, because it is the only thing we know for sure feels right to pray for.

And just as the six pointed emblem of the Flag of Israel serves as our nation's shield (our "magen") so too do the prayers for the IDF and for the captive hostages serve as shields of the Jewish people in diaspora. They connect us and protect us. They guard us and keep us.

The language of the two prayers to which this volume is dedicated is naturally very pious. Both begin with the words, "May he who blessed our [patriarchs]," and end with "And let us say: Amen." I make no claim that the drafters of the prayers or any individual who recites them have anything but unwavering devout devotion to God. We do not pray TO the IDF, the way we pray to God. We pray FOR the IDF. And the distinction is crucial. Nevertheless, for me, a flawed person whose devotion to God wavers, my devotion to the mission of these prayers does not. It is the language sandwiched between the "Mi Shaberach" and the "Amen" that speaks to me. Like Churchill spoke of fighting in the beaches, landing grounds, fields, and streets, so too do we speak of "from the Lebanese border to the Egyptian desert." Like the anthem "America the Beautiful" speaks of "from sea to shining sea" so too do we speak of "from the Mediterranean sea to the Approach of the Aravah."

We use our language and speak our prayers as one, and it is the power of that binding force between all of the Jewish people that the blue and white Shield of David fluttering in the wind represents.

So even in moments when "God and I are not ready to talk yet," through the language of these prayers, I am talking to my brothers and sisters among the Jewish people. That is how I tighten my shield. And for that, I am always ready.

David Benger is a lawyer with experience in international human rights and civil rights. He is an alumnus of Harvard Law School, Schwarzman Scholars (Tsinghua University), Brandeis University, and the Pardes Institute of Jewish Studies. This piece is dedicated to the Okunevs, a family who has dedicated generations to bringing the light of Yiddishkeit to the southernmost frontier of Brooklyn. The views expressed here are his alone.

Public Prayers in Times of Communal Distress

Yaron Ben-Naeh

Until the twentieth century, there was an understood "arrangement" between the Jews of the Diaspora and those in the Land of Israel: the former would support their brethren through financial contributions – as a duty or voluntarily, while the residents of the holy land pray for them in Jerusalem, the "Gate of Heaven," in Safed, at the father's tombs in Hebron, or in Tiberias. Indeed, prayers for Jews in exile, especially for those volunteering for the Jews of the land, are mentioned throughout the Ottoman period, from the sixteenth-century onwards.[1] For example, a letter from the summer of 1607 by Rabbi Shlomo Shlomel Dresnitz, who migrated from Moravia to Safed, states: "… And every Thursday, the entirety of Israel gathers after the morning prayers in a certain grand/large synagogue. There, they offer an intensely fervent prayer for

---

1   See, for example in Jacob Barnai, "The Pattern of Economic Support for the Yishuv from the Diaspora," in *The Jews in Palestine in the Eighteenth Century: Under the Patronage of the Istanbul Committee of Officials for Palestine*, trans. Naomi Goldblum (Tuscaloosa: University of Alabama Press, 1992), 53-73.

all of Israel, wherever they may be, lamenting the exile of the Divine Presence, the plight of Israel, and the destruction of our Holy Temple. They bestow blessings upon anyone who sends their funds to aid the impoverished of the Land of Israel, praying that the Almighty prolong their days and years, grant success to their endeavors, and shield them from any distress or hardship…"[2] He continues and describes additional ceremonies in synagogues and holy sites in the city and its vicinity. Even if the details are exaggerated in their idealization, there is probably a grain of historical truth here. Prayers for male and female donors are also mentioned in the writings of the Rabbinical Emissaries, known as Sheluhei de-Rabbanan (also known by the acronym Shadarim), who were sent to the diaspora in order to collect money for the four holy cities – prayers as a spiritual exchange.[3]

Here and there, remnants of evidence have survived regarding special prayers that were offered in Jewish communities within the Ottoman Empire as a means of dealing with severe calamities. These could be natural disasters, such as prolonged droughts or epidemics, or man-made calamities, like wars or sieges.[4]

---

2 Avraham Ya'ari, *Igrot Erets Israel* (Tel Aviv: Massada 1943), 198-199 (Hebrew).

3 See Yaron Ben-Naeh, *Jews in the Realm of the Sultans: Ottoman Jewish Society in the Seventeenth Century* (Tübingen: Mohr Siebeck, 2008), and earlier in Avraham Ya'ari, *Shluhei Eretz Israel* (Jerusalem: Mosad ha-Rav Kook, 1951; Hebrew); Barnai, *The Jews in Palestine*; and Matthias B. Lehmann, *Emissaries from the Holy Land The Sephardic Diaspora and the Practice of Pan-Judaism in the Eighteenth Century* (Stanford: Stanford University Press, 2014).

4 See, for example, Yaron Ben-Naeh, "Life and the Yearly Cycle," in Yaron Ben-Naeh, ed., *Jewish Communities in the East in the Nineteenth and Twentieth Centuries: Turkey* (Jerusalem: Ben-Zvi Institue 2010), 226 (Hebrew); Yaron Ben-Naeh, "Religious Life," in Yaron Ben-Naeh and Michal Held Delaroza, eds., *Jewish Communities in the East in the Nineteenth and Twentieth*

Praying for the Defenders of Our Faith

In one of the letters of the Sabbatean thinker Abraham Miguel Cardozo from the beginning of the eighteenth-century, the author boasts of his powers and narrates a story about many mass prayers of the "Togarmim," meaning the Turkish Muslims, and after them the prayers of the "uncircumcised [=that is the Christians], in abundance of idols for three consecutive days" due to a severe drought.[5] Following this, Cardozo suggested to the community leaders that he alone will pray for rain in the synagogue, or outside the city, but one of the officials wanted to continue the routine procedure – "he said that it is appropriate that tomorrow all the Jews and also/as well as the children's teachers with the children should go outside, as it once happened in Morea[6] and the rains came down, and it was a great honor for the Jews."[7] And he instructed the sexton to announce that all Jews, young and old, should go to the cemetery to pray."[8] We know of similar stories from other communities, including Jerusalem, both from Hebrew sources, as well as from reports of European travelers.

Rabbi So Amarillo, who penned the Responsa Kerem Shlomo (Salonika, 1717) and was the father of Rabbi Moshe Amarillo, the author of Responsa Dvar Moshe (3 vols., Salonika, 1742-1750), was a notable scholar in Salonika during the late seventeenth century and early eighteenth-century. In a sermon he gave, he referenced prayers made to

---

Centuries: *The Sephardim in Erets Israel* (Jerusalem: Ben Zvi Institute 2022), 129 (Hebrew).

5 See Isaac R. Molho and Abraham Amarilio, "Autobiographical Letters of Abraham Cardozo," *Sefunot*, vol. 3-4 (1959): 183-241, esp. 188-189 (Hebrew).

6 The Morea roughly coincides with the territories of modern Greece.

7 See Isaac R. Molho and Abraham Amarillio, Op. cit.

8 Ibid.

halt an epidemic in the city, likely around 1710. He wrestled with two primary concerns: the reason God inflicted them with a severe epidemic and why their prayers did not halt its progression:

> "Behold, we must understand why the Lord has acted thus towards this land. What great wrath has so inflamed Him that He has stretched forth His hand, sparing neither young man nor maiden, neither infant nor elderly people? And all this has befallen us due to our sins. This is one reason for such calamities; because we have the power to protest and yet remain silent, especially when the sins are those of immorality and wickedness."[9]

The cause of the plague lies in immoral behaviors which the community's rabbis and leaders neither condemn nor strive to prevent. In discussing why the prayers seemed ineffective, he observes to his audience: "Behold, we [=the rabbis] have discerned and identified two grave wrongs that seal the gates against our prayers. The first is the licentiousness prevalent among us due to our transgressions. The second is baseless hatred ('sinat hinam'); no individual feels the anguish of another's plight or prays on their behalf. Instead, there's malevolence, people are delighted in the downfall of others. A third reason that our prayers are left unanswered is our lack of knowledge in arranging them according to their proper form..." This reflection is set against the backdrop of their collective prayers and endeavors to combat the plague.[10]

Efforts in prayers and actions against the plague[11] also point to a lack of knowledge about the proper way to pray, the declining moral state,

---

9   Shlomo Amarillo, *Pnei Shlomo* (Salonica 1717): 76c-d (Hebrew).
10 Ibid.
11 Ibid. 77b.

and particularly the absence of solidarity and baseless hatred. Of course, this reality was not unique to Ottoman Salonica's community in the early modern period.[12]

Jews from the diaspora are currently offering both material and spiritual support through prayers, to their counterparts in the State of Israel. This practice represents a distinctively modern trend, probably originating during the period of the national settlement ('the Yishuv') in Palestine, especially during the Great Arab Rebellion (as Arabs called it) or the Riots (as Jews referred to the events), took place between the years 1936 and 1939.[13] This trend has intensified since the founding of the State of Israel and the subsequent War of Independence.

Prof. Yaron Ben-Naeh holds the Bernard Cherrick Chair in the History of the Jewish People, in the department of Jewish History and Contemporary Jewry, at the Hebrew University of Jerusalem.

---

12 For more on this, see for example Yaron Ben-Naeh, "Violence in Ottoman-Jewish Society: Izmir as a Case Study," *International Journal of Turkish Studies* [IJTS] vol. 21, no. 1-2 (2015): 1-16; Yaron Ben-Naeh, "Unknown Regulations in Ladino from Ottoman Salonika (ca. 1740)," MEAH = *Miscelánea de Estudios Árabes y Hebraicos*, vol. 65 (2016): 137-149, 219-254; Yaron Ben-Naeh and Michal Held, "The Coplas of Yomtov Magula as a Source for Jewish Life in Eighteenth Century Izmir," *Sefunot*, vol. 25 (2017): 205-284 (Hebrew).

13 For a more in-depth exploration on this topic, please refer to the articles within this volume authored by Aaron Ahrend, Nissim Leon, and Yoel Rappel.

On the Mitzvot of Daily Recitation of The Prayer for Israel's Soldiers and The Prayer for Hostages

Saul J. Berman

WHAT ARE THE IMPLICATIONS OF the general halakhic duty of Prayer for the current situation in which a barbaric attack against our fellow Jews in Israel resulted in over 1200 people being tortured and slaughtered, additional thousands being severely wounded physically and psychologically, over 70,000 Israelis displaced from their homes, over 240 Hostages taken by Hamas, and our beloved soldiers of Israel being sucked into a defensive war in which thousands of additional lives, both of Jews and of non-Jews, will be tragically lost?

Part I

A. The Duty of Petitional Prayer

It is an essential principle of the Jewish faith that God hears prayers and is responsive to them. Thus, at the end of the concluding petition of the weekday Amidah, three times daily on six days of the week, we affirm that "...For You (God) hear the prayer of your People Israel, with Compassion;" this is the version of Machzor Vitri and is the usual Ashkenaz Nusach. With broader sweep, Maimonides, and the current common Sephardi version use the following language, "...for You hear the prayers of every mouth." Rabbi Joseph B. Soloveitchik zt"l had the practice of combining both of those formulations and regularly reciting "...for you hear the prayer of every mouth and the prayer of your People Israel with Compassion."[1]

Maimonides considers daily prayer to be a Torah-based Mitzvah, one of the 613 Divinely revealed Commandments, based on the Written Law demand of "V'avad'tem – And you shall Serve the Lord your God..." (Ex. 23:25), and what he considers to be the Revealed Oral Law teaching that the legal meaning of the word "U'le'avdo – And Serve Him with all your heart and all your being ...." (Deut.11:13), is specifically

---

[1] See Saul J. Berman, "An Overview – The 'Approach' in Prayer," in *The Rabbinical Council of America Edition of The Complete ArtScroll Siddur* (Brooklyn: Mesorah Publications, 1986), xii-xvii, and Saul J. Berman, "Even a New Siddur Can't Close 'God Gap,'" *The Forward* (29 August 2009): 1,26. See, as well, Aharon Lichtenstein, "Prayer in the Teachings of Rabbi Joseph B. Soloveitchik," in *Mesorat HaRav Siddur* (Jerusalem: Koren, 2011), xv-xvii; Aharon Lichtenstein, "Prayer in the Teachings of Rabbi Joseph B. Soloveitchik," *Alon Shvut*, no. 149 (1997): 79-91 (Hebrew), translated in Jonathan Sacks, "Rabbi Joseph Soloveitchik on Jewish Faith and Prayer," in *Mesorat HaRav Siddur* (Jerusalem: Koren, 2011), xiv-xxxiv; and Dov Schwartz, *Rabbi Joseph Dov Soloveitchik on the Experience of Prayer* (Boston: Academic Studies Press, 2019).

meant to refer to prayer." While Maimonides maintains that there is no fixed text required by the Torah Law, there is specific three-fold content which must be present in the human conversation with God in order to fulfill this daily obligation, namely, expressions of Praise, Petition and Gratitude.

Nahmanides and many others take sharp issue with Maimonides on this matter and contend that the Talmudic evidence demonstrates that the entire obligation of daily prayer is based on Rabbinic legislation, not on Revealed Law. At the end of his discussion of this matter, Nahmanides adds a narrow possible area of agreement between himself and Maimonides, saying the following:

> "And if perhaps their Midrash (teaching), that the essential obligation of prayer is of the Torah, ought to be counted in the listing of the Rav [=Maimonides], we would say that it is a Commandment for times of trouble, that we should believe that He, may He be Blessed and Exalted, hears prayer, and He is the one who rescues from troubles due to prayer and crying out."

While Nahmanides does not concede to Maimonides the existence of a Torah-based duty of daily prayer, he does affirm the existence of a foundational belief that God hears our prayers when we cry out to Him, and that He responds to those prayers. Simultaneously, he also does not explicitly indicate the existence of an actual Commandment to pray at times of trouble – only to believe that if we pray, God will hear and will respond. Nevertheless, Since Nahmanides considers the Rabbinic obligation to be fulfilled with recitation of the Amidah composed in outline form by the Great Assembly under the leadership of Ezra, the content of obligatory prayer remains as Maimonides had codified it, words of Praise, Petition and Gratitude.

B. The Efficacy of Prayer

The idea that according to both opinions, either the Divine Command or Rabbinic Legislation mandated that we issue requests to God, is itself astonishing. We can easily understand that worship is constituted by words of praise or of gratitude, but why would anyone consider the making of a request to be an act of Avodah, of worship? There are many meaningful answers to this question, but they mostly point to one fundamental theme – a petitioner making a request thereby confirms her or his recognition of a human need, whether it be personal or national, whether material or spiritual. In that recognition inheres an expression of humility in the Presence of God, the understanding that we are only human and that the achievement of our goals and aspirations in every aspect of our lives are ultimately dependent upon our partnership with God in the real world.

Furthermore, we can then appreciate the extraordinary gift which God has given to us by commanding us to Pray to him with petitions. An understanding which inheres so clearly in the whole of Torah, that the Rabbinic imagination could understand its presence even in the absence of a direct Divine command. In His opening to us the path of petitions, God is opening Himself to the responsibility to hear and respond to us within our Covenantal relationship with Him. Would then God command us to engage in a useless endeavor, asking for His help when He has neither the intent to hear nor to respond to our needs? The efficacy of prayer, in the form of God's hearing and responding, is the most fundamental underlying assumption of all Prayer, believing that human prayer can actually have an impact on the unfolding of one's personal life and even of the history of the Jewish Nation.

That does not mean that there are not other goals and achievements involved in petitional prayer. Undoubtedly the recitation of the Amidah and the engagement in prayer generally, also helps the worshipper organize a clearer understanding of what her or his own priorities of needs and desires are and ought to be. No one reciting the Amidah three times a day could for a moment think that all of their time, energy and aspirations should be bound up in their personal material needs. No one who understands the meaning of the words of the Amidah could possibly think that the only significance of the Jewish Nation resides in its spiritual achievements, and not at all in its role of protecting Jews, of developing a just society and of ingathering the exiles into our national homeland.

Beyond even this, the fact that every petition in the Amidah is composed in the plural, even those which seem very personal and individual, and that the group for whom we pray is sometimes the Jewish People and sometimes all of humanity, means that we must cultivate the awareness that our individual identity is intimately bound up with our connection to our tribe and to all humans. The effectiveness of prayer thus relates not only to the attempt to persuade God to help us shape the future of our own lives, but also to aiding us in the personal shaping of own values and virtues and in helping to form deeper connections to our community and to the world within which we live.

Part II

Understanding the variety of ways in which our Prayers can be efficacious, we need to examine the implications as to circumstances under which we might have a duty to engage in Prayer beyond the Biblically or Rabbinically mandated daily Tefillot.

A. Duty to Rescue Life

One of the truly distinctive duties which Torah imposes upon each individual Jew is the responsibility to rescue a person whose life is at risk, when such rescue can be effectuated without significant risk to the rescuer.

Praying for the Defenders of Our Faith

While there are many obvious complications in the implementation of such a legal duty, there is a simple clarity to the underlying principle -- that we are not only forbidden to murder, to unjustifiably take any human life, but that we have a duty to protect the lives of persons at risk when we have the capacity to do so.

The importance of this duty is emphasized when Maimonides codifies the Laws of Murder and spends 10 of the 16 paragraphs of the very first chapter explicating the details of this Duty of Rescue. In doing so, Maimonides points out that this duty includes the privilege of using whatever force is necessary against an aggressor, including taking the aggressor's life if that is the minimal force needed to achieve the rescue of the innocent victim. He also, however, offers examples in which it might be possible to save the life of the victim by using words, such as by appeasing the aggressor, or by forewarning the victim of the threat against his life. It is specifically in relation to such a case that Maimonides asserts that:

> "If a person knows of a pagan idolator or a violent person (both of these terms are appropriate designations of Hamas terrorists) who is attacking another person, and he could appease the aggressor, but fails to do so; in this and in all analogous instances, a person who fails to act transgresses the commandment, "Do not stand idly by while your brother's blood is at risk" (Leviticus 19:16)."

What Maimonides is telling us here is that the means of rescue is not the issue in this duty. It does not matter whether the rescuer has an Uzi or a tank, or only his words. The only question is whether he has an instrument which has a possibility of achieving the desired outcome, the rescue of an innocent victim from an aggressor.

Then, if we truly believe that words of Prayer are an effective instrument which might actually save the lives of the persons for whom we are praying, then it would appear to be the case that we have a Halachic duty to pray for that outcome. And, as Maimonides teaches us, the failure to attempt rescue – here by prayer for the particular persons whose lives are at risk – would constitute a violation of great severity.

It is for this reason that many people I know, now engage in such prayer daily by the recitation of the Mi Sheberach for all soldiers of the Israel Defense Forces. As for me, I include the names of our granddaughter and the eighteen other grandchildren of my brother and late sister, Aleha HaShalom, as well as an additional list of children and grandchildren of friends and other family members.

B. Duty to Redeem Hostages

A tragic reality in the history of the Jewish People is the frequency with which we have confronted debased military forces or nations who would take Jews captive and then sell them as slaves or hold them as hostages to extort money or demand the release of arrested murderous terrorists. In instances when it was possible to do so, Jewish communities in many parts of the world would station members of the community at slave markets to purchase and then liberate Jews being sold. They acted in accordance with what became a fundamental principle of Jewish Law of Charity, as taught in Bava Batra 8a-8b, and paraphrased by Maimonides as "There is no Mitzvah (within the priorities of Tzedakah) as great as redeeming hostages. For a captive is among those who are hungry, thirsty and unclothed, and whose life is in constant danger." (Hilkhot Matenot Aniyim 8:10.)

Maimonides then goes on to address a fundamental question related to hostages, what constitutes violation of the duty to rescue hostages? Maimonides' language is quite clear on this matter. He says:

> "If someone closes his eyes to the duty to redeem, he violates three negative commandments: 'Do not harden

your heart or close your hand' (Deuteronomy 15:7), 'Do not stand by when the blood of your neighbor is in danger' (Leviticus 19:16), and 'He shall not oppress him with exhausting work in your presence' (ibid. 25:53). And he has repudiated the observance of three positive commandments: 'You shall certainly open up your hand to him' (Deuteronomy 15:8), 'And your brother shall live with you' (ibid. 19:18), 'Love your neighbor as yourself' (Leviticus 19:18), 'Save those who are taken for death' (Proverbs 24:11), and many other decrees of this nature. There is no mitzvah as great as the redemption of captives.'"[2]

2   On this passage of Maimonides, the late Professor Isadore Twersky offered a profound insight: "Emphasis of fundamental ideas, usually spiritual-moral conceptions, which should be impressed upon the reader's mind so that they will be deeply resonant, reverberating, and refreshing, results in a measure of lengthiness. The statement about ransoming captives (pidyon shevuyim), with its repetition, stringing together halakhic commands and prohibitions, and exhortation, has a deep pathos which gives the passage a rhythm of its own and almost produces a visual representation of the suffering and possible tragedy which prompt and unstinting giving of charity will prevent. One is also tempted to conclude that only a person who had traveled the Mediterranean and experienced its hazards and anxieties could have written such moving prose." See Isadore Twersky, *Introduction to the Code of Maimonides (Mishneh Torah)* (New Haven: Yale University Press, 1980), 339-340.

See also S.D. Goitein, "The Actions of Moses Maimonides for the Ransom of Captives Held in Palestine," in S.D. Goitein, *Palestinian Jewry in Early Islamic and Crusader Times in the Light of the Geniza Documents*, ed. Joseph R. Hacker (Jerusalem: Ben-Zvi Institute, 1980), 322-320 (Hebrew); Mark R. Cohen, "Maimonides and Charity in the Light of the Geniza Documents," in Georges Tamer, ed., The Trias of Maimonides: Die Trias Des Maimonides (Berlin: de Gruyter, 2005), 65-81; and Miriam Frenkel, "Proclaim Liberty to Captives and Freedom to Prisoners: The Ransoming of

The severity of the crime is quite intense, however the violation is not constituted in failing, it is in "closing one's eyes" to the duty, that is, in not investing the effort which the circumstances would allow. In most instances the effort to redeem hostages can only be effectuated by the Governing body of the community or nation. It is that governing body which needs to evaluate the possibility of engaging in military action or negotiating a deal which rescues the hostages and does not further endanger the entire community and its members. Such is the balancing required of them by the Mishna and Gemara in Gittin 45a, and the subsequent debates in the periods of the Rishonim, the Acharonim, and Contemporary Poskim. This itself is no easy task, and its achievement certainly requires both human wisdom and Divine guidance.

However, for individual citizens, the requisite efforts to achieve the liberation of hostages is generally relegated to political persuasion of decision makers, social communications to maintain pressure on all parties, and words of Prayer. Again, since we believe in the efficacy of prayer to actually impact on the outcome of such dangerous situations, then we are obligated not only to use the active tools of communication and persuasion to shape social attitudes and political decision-making, but also to engage in both communal and private prayer for the desired outcome.

The awareness of this duty to pray for the well-being and safe return of hostages is doubly significant because such redemption is part of the laws Tzedakah and Maimonides speaks with great intensity against persons who "turn a blind eye" to the challenges of charity. (Hilkhot Matenot Aniyim 10:3) Beyond that, Maimonides places great emphasis on the need to take care of the emotional needs of people in a state of

Captives by Medieval Jewish Communities in Islamic Countries," in Heike Grieser and Nicole Priesching, eds., *Gefangenenloskauf im Mittelmeerraum* (Hildesheim: Georg Olms Verlag, 2015), 83-97.

suffering as an essential element in the proper fulfillment of the laws of tzedakah. This obviously includes not only the hostage, but the families and friends of hostages as well. This is, as Maimonides points out in Hilkhot Matenot Aniyim 10:4-5, entirely constituted in words, and tone of voice and facial expressions manifesting empathy and transmitting hope, suggesting comfort and commiseration – in truly being with the other as God Himself promises to be with us in our moments of trouble.

There are numbers of different texts of Prayers for Hostages all of which allow for inclusion of the names of current hostages, which are also available. As we had seen, the efficacy of prayer is not only measured by its impact on the outcome of that which is prayed for, but also by the impact on the emotional well-being of the persons for whom the prayer is issued, and the impact on the person issuing the prayer. In the current situation, it is essential not only to be privately or communally engaged in prayer, but to assure that the emotionally affected parties are aware that these communal and private prayers are being offered up. All three levels of impact are engaged in these prayers which we are now called upon, and have the opportunity, to recite in the fulfillment of Mitzvot of Hashem.

> *May God grant wisdom and courage to the Government and people of Israel.*
>
> *May God grant success to the Israel Defense Forces in their military efforts to eradicate the idolatrous Hamas, with minimal loss of lives to the soldiers of Israel and to innocent civilians.*
>
> *May the hundreds of hostages being held by Hamas all be extracted safely.*
>
> *May the bodies of Kedoshim be returned to their families for Jewish burial.*

Saul J. Berman

May this be God's will, and May our prayers contribute to these outcomes.

Rabbi Saul J. Berman is Professor of Jewish studies at Stern College of Yeshiva University, New York and Adjunct Professor at Columbia University Law School where he is the Rotter Fellow of Talmudic Law. As an Orthodox Rabbi in Berkeley, California, Brookline, Massachusetts, and at Lincoln Square Synagogue, New York, Berman was an early participant in the Soviet Jewry and Civil Rights movements.

Powerful Moment of Prayer and Unity: Reflections on Leading the Prayer for IDF Soldiers Before a Gathering of 300,000

Chaim Dovid Berson

IN A REMARKABLE GATHERING OF solidarity and support for Israel, I had the incredible honor of leading the Prayer for the Soldiers of the IDF at the Rally for Israel in Washington DC, on November 14, 2023. As I stood before a crowd of 300,000 people, with hundreds of thousands more joining us online, the magnitude of the moment filled me with a profound sense of pride and responsibility. Now, after having returned home several days ago, I find myself in contemplation of this powerful experience from the past week.

My journey began early that morning, as I boarded one of the myriad of buses at Congregation Kehilath Jeshurun in New York City, joining physically and emotionally with thousands of others converging on Washington DC from every corner of the country. It was as though we were experiencing a taste of what we will, once again, encounter in Aliyah LaRegel – when we return to the Holy Temple in Jerusalem.

As the various travelers merged, first at a rest stop, then at the designated parking lots, then in the DC Metro, then at the National Mall, the progressive sense of shared purpose paralleled the growth of the numbers. From spontaneous HaTikvahs on the Metro, to the chantings of Am Yisrael Chai at the bus depot, the pride and passion of our connection to each other and to Israel was palpable.

While the immense crowd had previously been filled with vocal enthusiasm following the President of Israel's address, a profound stillness descended upon us as the Prayer for the Soldiers of the IDF was announced. I was summoned to the center stage the Rally for Israel in Washington DC – the largest stage of prayer that I have ever represented – and I stood before an audience numbering 300,000. The gravity of the moment embraced us all as we collectively internalized this powerful moment of prayer, transcending our individual differences.

As I began the melody, the silent swaying transformed into joined voices that amplified with each verse. The emotional weight of the occasion was heightened by the knowledge that we were standing in prayer for both Israel and the soldiers of the IDF, recognizing that as we prayed, these brave men and women were risking their lives for the sake of their nation. This outpouring of communal prayer in unity was a great Kiddush Hashem – sanctification of God's Name - demonstrating our dependence on Him, and on each other.

Praying for the Defenders of Our Faith

Upon deep reflection of this profound experience, I am filled with gratitude for the privilege of guiding the prayer during this historic gathering. It was a distinct honor to contribute to a moment that transcended the boundaries of individuality, evolving into a collective embodiment of faith, unity, and unwavering support, not only for the State of Israel but also for the broader cause of humanity.

Am Yisrael Chai!

Cantor Chaim Dovid Berson, a native of Jerusalem, holds the distinguished position of Chief Cantor at the renowned Congregation Kehilath Jeshurun on Manhattan's Upper East Side.

Reflections on the Moral Imperative of Praying for the Soldiers of the IDF

Rookie Billet

THE PRAYER FOR THE WELL-BEING of the IDF soldiers grips our hearts and souls in many ways. On a personal level, it often brings me to tears, whether I hear it in the synagogue, or watch the chief chazzan of the IDF sing it with musical accompaniment on a youtube video, or whether we view it in homemade videos of talented children with incredibly beautiful voices singing its haunting notes over the backdrop of a photo collage of our soldiers in uniform, on land, in the air, in the sea, protecting our tiny piece of land in the worst neighborhood in the world with courage, dedication, team spirit, and an unbelievable willingness to lay down their precious lives for the sake of protecting the only country we have, and its citizenry, comprised of people whose families have lived

Praying for the Defenders of Our Faith

here for centuries, and of immigrants of all colors and cultures who have been gathered here in contemporary times from all four corners of the world.

The current war has made us even more aware than we always are of the boys and girls who comprise the IDF and its holy spirit. I well know that they are men and women, but when we have visited their bases during the war to deliver vital equipment that may help them protect themselves, or be more comfortable in their tanks or their tents without any amenities of home, or give them a meal that is freshly cooked or a makeshift barbecue in the field, we look at their fresh faces, at their brilliant smiles, at their simple gratitude, at their youth and their promise, and think of them as just girls and boys, as we hope and pray that they will be kept safe and whole and healthy in mind and body by the Ribono shel Olam, the master of the universe.

In response to updates we have been sending to our friends in the diaspora about what we as civilians are trying to do to build merits for our soldiers in the divine ledger, a friend wrote to the effect that while we who have moved to Israel and cast our lot with Am Yisrael b'Eretz Yisrael have the privilege of making our small contributions in person, on the ground, what is left for her to do is to pull out her checkbook and to pray. My reply to her was that she should keep praying for the safe return of all the sons, husbands, fathers, brothers, uncles, finances, (and all the females equivalents) to the fold of their loving families, because as human beings, we ourselves can only do what we are capable of doing in our limited way, with our limited strength, influence, funds and time. But the Almighty to whom we direct our prayers is all-knowing and all powerful, and He can do anything and everything.

I find myself dedicating extra time each day to the recitation of Psalms (Tehillim) for the soldiers and of course for the captives, the wounded and the bereaved families. So many of the passages speak to our need for divine intervention when we are besieged and beleaguered by our enemies and lack the clarity to know what to do, what the next steps should be. Mentioning the names of the soldiers whose names I have collected from various sources is particularly meaningful, and on these lists, there are often multiple boys (and girls) with the same mother's name. I recognize so many of the mom's names, since they are friends of my daughter who has two sons and one son-in-law who are currently serving. I went to a Torah class last week, and the teacher opened the class with a chapter of Tehillim. One of the students told me that the teacher has three sons and a son-in-law in active duty.

One of the more inspiring aspects of unity, solidarity and comfort we are experiencing is the recitation of the prayer for the IDF by many Haredim (ultra-orthodox) whose prayer services always include Psalms, and the singing of Acheinu kol Beit Yisrael (Our brothers (and sisters), the entire house of Israel, who are in bitter straits, etc., God should have mercy on them and release them from darkness to light etc.), but whose Tefilot do not usually include the official prayer for the soldiers. To see clips of bearded Chassidim or Yeshiva men singing the prayer for the IDF is deeply meaningful, even as more and more of the ultra-orthodox find a way to serve the state in addition to being part of "Tzivos Hashem" (the 'army' of God that studies the Torah).

In sum, this war is for the very survival of Israel, and as many have said, for the survival of the western, democratic way of life, and should convince every one of us of the moral imperative to pray for the soldiers of the IDF. They are our personal messengers, our Shelichim! They have answered the call that so many of us cannot—we are too old or too young, we live in the diaspora, we are not trained, we lack the courage or the passion, or any other reason that makes us impotent. Our strength is in the unity and purposefulness of our prayers for the safe return of our soldiers so they can leave the necessity of war and destruction behind

Praying for the Defenders of Our Faith

them, and build wonderful Jewish families and assure the continuity, dignity and self-respect of the Jewish people forever.

Rabbanit Rookie Billet, who enjoyed a long and accomplished career as a Jewish Studies Educator, Yeshiva Principal, Shul Rebbetzin, and Yoetzet Halacha in the United States, has embarked on a new chapter in her life alongside her husband, Rabbi Hershel Billet, with their Aliyah to Israel.

Participation through Prayer in the Battle for Israel's Safety

Jonathan Blass

PRAYER FOR THE SUCCESS OF Israel and its armed forces is a powerful weapon that can overcome enemy forces, turn the tide of battle, and bring victory.

Yaakov Avinu tells Yosef that he wrested land from the Amorites "with my sword and with my bow" (Bereishit 48 22). Playing on the Hebrew word for "with my bow," which is a homonym of "my request," Onkelos translates Yaakov's message: "with my prayers and supplications."

Rav Kook, in his writings (Mussar Hakodesh, Orot Hakodesh vol. 3, pp. 49-54; Ein Aya Berakhot, vol. 1, ch. 1, p. 57), explains that those who raise questions about the necessity or efficacy of prayer in influencing the decisions of an all-knowing God do not adequately appreciate the power and nature of Man's will to do good. The will of a human being, created in God's image, to do good is an expression, within creation, of the

Praying for the Defenders of Our Faith

Divine will that created the world. It is a branch of that Divine will. On a day-to-day level, human will is generally used for mundane purposes that obscure, and in practice diminish, the influence of its connection to the Divine will which is its source.

But by turning to the Ribono Shel Olam, the Jew who is expressing his will in prayer activates the existing connection between his own will and Hashem's will. Acting as an extension of the Divine will, his own will carries with it the Divine power to change reality. Each of us who *davens* has already changed reality through the power of his will expressed in prayer.

Does anyone doubt that the Ingathering of the Exiles and the Rebuilding of Jerusalem that we witness today are in part the fruit of the prayers of our ancestors over the millennia, prayers that have combined with the power of our own prayers and the actions of our generation's builders and olim?

The Avnei Nezer, as referenced by his son in Shem Mishmuel (Bereishit Chayyei Sarah 5672), understands Onkelos's translation that reads "prayers" into the power of Yaakov Avinu's "bow", to imply that the ability of prayer to effect wide-reaching change is influenced by the urgency of the Will that the prayer is expressing. The distance an arrow will travel from the bow increases as the archer draws it to the point where the string is tensed to its limit.

A similar idea was expressed by his son, the Shem Mishmuel (in Purim 5677), regarding our ability to achieve a full victory over Amalek. He writes that this is guaranteed only if our determination to eradicate the evil is no less intense than that which Haman felt when he sought to exterminate us.

The people, the State, and the Army of Israel are fighting a war against the barbarians that attacked us on Shemini Atzeret and the society that spawned them: 'Peleshet ve-Yoshvei Tzur' them (Psalms

83:8) Gaza and Tyre, backed by Amalek and others. Everyone who has an effective weapon at his disposal cannot remain indifferent.

The prayer for the victory of the IDF and for the safety of our soldiers and others defending the Land and the People of Israel is an effective weapon that should be used together with the daily prayers, reciting relevant chapters of Psalms, and the prayer for the State of Israel)whose leaders should be blessed with wisdom from Above).

Our words should be said with a power of Will that speeds them across oceans to accompany and strengthen our soldiers—may God watch over and protect them—and strike at the enemies of God and Israel.

Rabbi Jonathan Blass, an alumnus of Yeshivat Mercaz HaRav, serves as the rabbi of the Neve Tzuf community in the Shomron. He also leads Ratzon Yehuda, a Zionist kollel in Petach Tikva, named in honor of HaRav Tzvi Yehuda Kook, catering to graduates of hesder yeshivot. Rabbi Blass is renowned for his extensive multi-volume work on Maimonidean philosophical thought titled "Menofet Tzuf."

Praying for Israel's Defenders

David R. Blumenthal

A PRAYER IS REALLY SERIOUS WHEN it becomes part of the accepted communal liturgy. The prayers for the State of Israel and for the Soldiers of Israel have become that. They have been placed into the liturgy in almost all Orthodox communities by the authority of the Chief Rabbinate of Israel and with the consent of the community. But, shouldn't the prayer for those who defend the State of Israel at the risk of their lives be part of our *daily* prayer?

Where is the most logical place in the daily liturgy to put the prayer for the soldiers who defend the homeland? After Torah reading (which is where it is) only occurs on days when one reads Torah. Where should it be to really be a part of our *daily* prayer?

It seems to me that the most appropriate place to pray for those who risk their lives to defend the Jewish people is in the most important daily petitionary prayer – in the Shemoneh Esreh. That is the place where we, observant Jews, make our most important petitions to Hashem, three times a day. It is where we pray for knowledge, repentance ... destruction of our enemies, blessing upon the righteous ... the messiah ... and peace. Where, then, should one insert the prayer for the security forces of the State of Israel in the daily Shemoneh Esreh?

I propose that several phrases be inserted into "*Al HaTzaddikim*" right after "*Ve'al Geray HaTzedek*." Whatever is inserted would then be followed by "*Ve'alenu*" and the prayer could continue to its end, being sure to mention "*Lekhol HaBotchim Bishmekh Be'Emet*" which would include, by kavvana (intention), all non-Jews who also support the State of Israel. I am not qualified to debate the halakhic issues of how to do this, but the common-sense goal of putting a prayer for the soldiers who defend the Jewish people into the Shemoneh Esreh itself would seem quite clear

There will be much discussion on what one should insert. This is what I propose: After *Ve'al Geray HaTzedek* one should insert the following:

... ועל גרי הצדק, ועל חיילי צבא הגנה לישראל, ועל משמר הגבול, ועל משטרת ישראל, ועל השב"כ, ועל המוסד, ועל האמ"ן, ועל היחידות המיוחדות, ועל כל כוחות הבטחון ... ועלינו

upon the soldiers of the Israel Defence Forces, upon the Israel Border Police, upon the Israel Police Force, upon the Internal Security Agency, upon the Mossad, upon the Military Intelligence Directorate, upon the special units, and upon all the security forces, and upon us."

There are ways to make this shorter but the point is clear: Mention the specific forces for which we petition Hashem's protection, and do it as part of our *daily* petitionary prayer, at the most appropriate place. I do it every day though, out of deference to the community, I do not say it in the repetition if I lead the prayers. It would be best, however, to do so.

Praying for the Defenders of Our Faith

David R. Blumenthal is the retired Jay and Leslie Cohen Professor of Judaic Studies at Emory University. He has contributed greatly to the growth of Jewish Studies, the place of Judaism in Religious Studies, interreligious dialogue, and the reframing of Judaism in light of the Holocaust, postmodernism, and poststructuralism.

Beyond Borders: A Note on Rabbi Hillel Unsdorfer's Posthumous Article on the Mi Sheberach for IDF Soldiers

Menachem Butler

IN 1973, DURING THE YOM Kippur War, the world was introduced to Hillel Unsdorfer, a remarkable soldier whose story transcends the clichés of heroism. Born in 1952, he was named after his paternal grandfather, Rabbi Hillel Unsdorfer. His grandfather had been educated at the Pressburg Yeshiva under the guidance of Rabbi Akiva Sofer and Rabbi Yosef Tzvi Duschinsky. From 1920, he served as the rabbi of Lucenec in Slovakia, renowned for his deep understanding of Jewish law and active community engagement. Tragically, he perished in the Gunskirchen concentration camp in 1945.¹

A young religious Israeli soldier, Unsdorfer served in a Nahal brigade and was stationed in a bunker along the Suez Canal. Armed only with rifles, he and his IDF unit confronted advancing Egyptian tanks. Their unit, consisting of just 42 men, held off hundreds of Egyptians for a full week. By the third day of battle, they realized that all other Israeli fortifications had fallen, leaving them as the sole remaining force in combat against the Egyptians. Reflecting a decade later, Unsdorfer remarked, "There's no way I can explain in military terms how we stood up to the attack." One remarkable example of their heroism during that week was when a fellow soldier sacrificed his life by jumping on top of a grenade that had been thrown into their fortification. Unsdorfer remembered, "If he hadn't done that, everyone would have been killed."² Despite their miniscule odds of victory, the 42 soldiers refused to surrender, even when their division commander informed them via radio that the rest of the Israeli army couldn't reach them. They persisted for

---

1   About Rabbi Hillel Unsdorfer (1892-1945), see Aharon Unsdorfer, *Beit Hillel: A History of the Lucenec Congregation and Rabbi Hillel Unsdorfer* (Jerusalem, 2008; Hebrew); and see Joachim Neander, "Auschwitz—Grosswerther—Gunskirchen: A Nine Month's Odyssey through Eight Nazi Concentration Camps," *Yad Vashem Studies*, vol. 28 (2000): 287-310; and Evelyn Zegenhagen and Stephen Pallavicini. "Gunskirchen-Wels I [aka Wald-Werke, Wels, Notbehelfsheimbau, SS-Arbeitslager Gunskirchen]," in Geoffrey P. Megargee, ed., *The Encyclopedia of Camps and Ghettos, vol. 1: 1933-1945* (Washington DC: United States Holocaust Memorial Museum, 2009), 917-919.

2   See Fern Allen, "Israeli POWs' Torah Remains a Mystery," *The Jewish Week* (16 September 1983): 3, reprinted in Fern Allen, "Hillel Unsdorfer's Unit," *The Jerusalem Post* (24 September 1993): 5. For a biography of Hillel Unsdorfer (1952-1993), see Menachem Michelson, *Hillel from the Post on the Pier* (Tel-Aviv: Yediot Ahronoth Books, 1997; Hebrew).

a few more days until Moshe Dayan, then the defense minister, ordered them to surrender, cautioning that not doing so would be suicidal. But later, shortly before they surrendered, Moshe Dayan changed his order, as he didn't want posterity to remember him as the man who gave the "Surrender" order.

Throughout their roughly month-long captivity in the custody of the Egyptian army, the Israeli prisoners of war had contact with a Red Cross representative. However, once that Red Cross representative left, they faced physical assault at the hands of the Egyptians. Unsdorfer had his personal belongings, including his watch, glasses, and kippah, confiscated, and his tzizit were forcibly ripped from beneath his shirt. Foreign journalists, reporting on the war from Egypt, captured a powerful image of Hillel Unsdorfer and his unit on their way to their captivity. In the photograph, Unsdorfer is seen embracing a Torah Scroll in his arms. This iconic image rapidly gained worldwide recognition and emerged as a lasting symbol of strength for the Jewish community in the wake of the traumatic Yom Kippur War. Rabbi Hillel Unsdorfer later served as the Rabbi at Kibbutz Beit Rimon in the Lower Galilee, where he was deeply committed to strengthening Jewish agricultural communities guided by Jewish law.

A decade after the Yom Kippur War, Rabbi Hillel Unsdorfer explained to a reporter why he chose to carry the Torah scroll across the Suez Canal and into captivity, saying, "Most of us felt we should take the Torah with us to Egypt because it watched over us while we were fighting. We felt it should stay with us and continue to guard us." Reflecting further, he added, "I have no idea how the Egyptians knew I was wearing tzizit. They took all religious symbols off us for the same reason they started the war on Yom Kippur – the war was really against Judaism and Jews, not only against Zionism and Israel." Eventually, an agreement between the Israeli and Egyptian governments led to the exchange of provisions for the Israeli prisoners of war, resulting in their release.[3]

Tragically, in 1993, two decades after his release from captivity, Rabbi Hillel Unsdorfer's life was cut short in a car accident in the Galilee at the age of 41. He left behind his wife and five children. In the week before his untimely death, Rabbi Hillel Unsdorfer submitted a thought-provoking article to the ha-Tsofeh religious Zionist newspaper.[4] His analysis of the Mi Sheberach prayer for IDF Soldiers centered on the phrase 'from the border of Lebanon,' arguing that it held broader implications than mere geography, extending beyond the political border. He emphasized the prayer's apt reflection of the daily realities faced by IDF soldiers, asserting its continued relevance without the need for changes due to shifting geographical circumstances. This insightful article, a response to Rabbi Alexander Malkiel's earlier article published the previous month in the *ha-Tsofeh Literary Supplement*,[5] was enriched by Rabbi Unsdorfer's own harrowing experiences during his captivity in Egypt, which provided him with a unique perspective on the nuances of the Mi Sheberach prayer. In the introduction to Rabbi Unsdorfer's final article in *ha-Tsofeh*, the editor poignantly reminded readers of Unsdorfer's legendary act of carrying the Torah into Egyptian captivity.

---

[3] On the nineteenth anniversary of the Yom Kippur War, several months earlier, he recounted the story of his captivity in Hillel Unsdorfer, "With All Your Strength," *Amudim*, vol. 41, no. 1 [558] (September 1992): 11-14 (Hebrew). See also Hillel Unsdorfer, "A Great Commandment to Always Be in Joy, A Great Joy to Always Be in a Commandment," *Amudim*, vol. 41, no. 5 [562] (February 1993): 160 (Hebrew).

[4] Hillel Unsdorfer, "On the Text of 'Mi Sheberach' for IDF Soldiers," *ha-Tsofeh Literary Supplement* (12 February 1993): 7 (Hebrew).

[5] See Alexander Malkiel, "Open Letter," *ha-Tsofeh Literary Supplement* (8 January 1993): 8 (Hebrew).

Rabbi Avraham Shapira, then-Ashkenazi Chief Rabbi of Israel and Rosh Yeshiva of Yeshivat Merkaz HaRav, had, several years prior, provided a historical and spiritual interpretation of the same phrase in the Mi Sheberach prayer, presenting a striking contrast to Rabbi Unsdorfer's view on the subject. Discovered later in the archives of the Israeli Chief Rabbinate, Rabbi Avraham Shapira's insights on the Mi Sheberach prayer were articulated in an unpublished responsum dated 28 February 1988. There is no indication that Rabbi Unsdorfer was aware of or had access to this document when he wrote his article in *ha-Tsofeh*. Shapira wrote: "There is no place to 'amend' prayers that were established by eminent rabbis in the past. The phrase 'from the border of Lebanon' does not refer to the political border between Israel and the state of Lebanon. Geographically, the Upper Galilee and the mountains of southern Lebanon constitute one geographical region. From the history of Jewish settlement in the northern part of the Land, Jewish communities that were located in the Upper Galilee, which today are, from a political perspective, within the territory of Lebanon. Therefore, the words 'from the border of Lebanon' have a broader significance beyond geography and do not only refer to the political border."[6]

As the fiftieth anniversary of the Yom Kippur War approached in early October 2023, renewed interest on social media highlighted the story of Hillel Unsdorfer and his unit's Torah scroll, symbolizing not only historical remembrance but also contemporary resilience. In

---

6   This responsum is fully reprinted in Aaron Ahrend, "Prayers for the Welfare of Soldiers," *Alei Sefer*, vol. 24-25 (2015): 321n118 (Hebrew). It was the source that prompted me to seek out Rabbi Hillel Unsdorfer's brief article (see previous footnote). My thanks go to Dr. Charles Berlin and the staff of the Harvard Library Judaica Division for their assistance in providing access to this periodical on microfilm, a vital resource for studying Religious Zionist history. The entire article by Dr. Ahrend is available in English translation in this volume.

2023, coinciding with this milestone, "The Stronghold," a television series dramatizing the experiences of Unsdorfer's unit, was released to commemorate the anniversary.[7]

The Torah scroll, referred to as "The Prisoner," which saw its return to Israel in 2000 through the efforts of then-President Ezer Weizmann and Egyptian President Hosni Mubarak, now resides in the IDF Military Rabbinate Corps at Shura Camp. The saga of this Torah scroll, marked by its captivity and eventual return to Israel, symbolizes renewal amid despair and serves as a beacon of hope during Israel's current conflict with Hamas. Rabbi Unsdorfer's insightful writings on the Mi Sheberach prayer reminds us "that the prayer encompasses all the IDF soldiers wherever they may be." We hope and pray for the safe return of all the hostages from Gaza, and may they be speedily reunited with their families and with all of Israel.

Hillel Unsdorfer
"On the Text of 'Mi Sheberach' for IDF Soldiers"
ha-Tsofeh Literary Supplement
(12 February 1993): 7 (Hebrew)

[Hillel Unsdorfer, the rabbi of Kibbutz Beit Rimon who died in a road accident at the age of 41, was known during the Yom Kippur War when he fell into Egyptian captivity with other fighters from The Pier Outpost and

---

[7] "The Stronghold" (2023), directed by Lior Chefetz and co-written with Nahum Werbin, is a 1h 53m film featuring stars Michael Aloni, Daniel Gad, and Amir Tessler. Set during the Yom Kippur War, it portrays a desolate Israeli outpost that endures a surprise Egyptian attack and subsequent siege. See Hannah Brown, "A Gripping Story of the Yom Kippur War," *The Jerusalem Post* (4 August 2023): 2.

left the outpost with the Torah scroll in his hands. A few days ago, Rabbi Hillel Unsdorfer sent us the article about the prayer Mi Sheberach for the IDF soldiers, and these words will be a candle in his memory. – ha-Tsofeh Editor]

On Friday, the 15th of Tevet, an article by Rabbi Alexander Malkiel was published regarding the Mi Sheberach prayer for the Israel Defense Forces soldiers. In his article, the author quotes the Mi Sheberach prayer, but in the prayer's quotation, we find a difference from what is written in the prayer books.

I would like to address the change proposed by the author. It is stated there: '… the soldiers of the Israel Defense Forces who stand guard over our land and the cities of our God, from Lebanon to the desert of Egypt.' And in a note there he writes, 'In prayer books, it is written as 'from the border of Lebanon.' But since this wording does not reflect the current reality, as our soldiers also operate beyond the border within Lebanon, it is appropriate to say 'from Lebanon' so that these soldiers are also included in this prayer. That's all."

This change, not to say 'on the border of Lebanon,' began, to the best of my memory, during the Lebanon War [in 1982]. At that time, many prayerful individuals who considered and emphasized their prayers felt the desire to pray and bless the soldiers who were fighting and dedicating themselves to our defense. Therefore, they omitted the word 'on the border,' and thus they included in their prayers the soldiers operating within Lebanon beyond the border, as indicated in the note.

Regarding such matters, our sages have said, "Anyone who adds, in fact, subtracts." While we have indeed added the soldiers located within Lebanon to our prayers, what about the soldiers sent each day from beyond the great sea or beyond the desert, to stand guard over our Land? What about the soldiers who were sent in their time to Operation

Praying for the Defenders of Our Faith

Entebbe, whose self-sacrifice added security to those of us residing in the cities of our God? Thus, one can count hundreds and thousands of actions to which our soldiers are dispatched beyond the borders and are not located in Lebanon.

And the question arises regarding these soldiers who are in a high-risk position: do we not pray for them that the Almighty will watch over them, save them, send blessings and success upon them, crown them with the crown of salvation and the wreath of victory? Do we truly only pray for those soldiers within these borders?

If so, the inquirer may ask, should we change the entire Mi Sheberach prayer to include all the soldiers, including those outside our borders? Perhaps it would be wise to omit specifying the borders altogether?

In my humble opinion, there is no need to change the prayer at all. Instead, we should return to the prayer written in the prayer books and cancel the change made by "the meticulous ones." Then we will realize that the prayer encompasses all the IDF soldiers wherever they may be. We only need to understand what we are saying.

In the Mi Sheberach prayer, we pray for the IDF soldiers who "stand guard over our land and the cities of our God," and what is our land? What are its borders? – "From the border of Lebanon to the desert of Egypt and from the Great Sea to the Aravah."

Our soldiers, who stand guard over our land, are located "on land, in the air, and at sea." This means that the passage beginning with the words "from the border of Lebanon" and ending with "to the Aravah" is essentially enclosed in quotation marks, and its intention is to encompass "our land and the cities of our God."

Even our soldiers who cross these borders in their service to the IDF do so to defend our Land within the mentioned borders. Therefore, the prayer written in the prayer books accurately reflects the daily reality.

And every military action, as it is, does not require changing the order of the prayer.

Here, I would like to express my gratitude to Rabbi Alexander Malkiel, who, time and time again, enlightens our eyes with the precision of prayer and awakens our hearts to genuine intent in prayer. May the Almighty to confirm His redemption to our prayer and with a crown of victory.

Menachem Butler, the Program Fellow for Jewish Legal Studies in the Julis-Rabinowitz Program on Jewish and Israeli Law at Harvard Law School, serves as the President of the Institute for Jewish Research and Publications and is the co-editor of this volume.

Introduction to Rav Shlomo Aviner's Commentary on the Mi Sheberach for IDF Soldiers

Menachem Butler

R ᴀᴠ Sʜʟᴏᴍᴏ Aᴠɪɴᴇʀ ɪꜱ ᴀ leading figure in Israel's Religious Zionist community. Born in Nazi-occupied France, he immigrated to Israel and quickly established himself as a profound thinker and educator. He played an instrumental role in founding the Ateret Cohanim Yeshiva in Jerusalem's Old City. In addition to his role at the yeshiva, Rav Aviner serves as the rabbi of Beit El, a West Bank community. He is renowned for his extensive writings on topics such as halakhah, Jewish philosophy, and contemporary issues, making him a sought-after authority on matters pertaining to the modern State of Israel. His reputation is further enhanced by his nuanced approach to complex subjects, demonstrating a sincere commitment to the welfare of the Jewish people, both spiritually and physically.

In his concise commentary on the prayer for the Israel Defense Forces soldiers, which is presented below in both Hebrew and English translation, Rav Aviner leads us on a journey that explores the intricate relationship between faith and action. This exploration draws inspiration from the simultaneous preparations made by the patriarch Jacob for both prayer and combat. The IDF is lauded not as an army of conquest, but as a force of defense. This defense-centric philosophy is deeply rooted in Israel's historical experience, moral compass, and scriptural teachings. Rav Aviner underscores the symbolic representation of IDF soldiers as the epitome of national unity, bridging divides of religious observance, ethnicity, and political ideology. They emerge as a singular entity, embodying the collective essence of Israel.

Rav Aviner's commentary emphasizes the omnipresence of the Divine – the Master of the Universe who has chosen and accompanied Israel throughout its history. In their dedication and sacrifice, the soldiers enact a divine commandment, furthering the values and teachings passed down by the patriarchs: Abraham, Isaac, and Jacob. The text acknowledges the challenges that have historically beset the Jewish people, highlighting adversaries who have sought their harm. However, in the contemporary era, with the establishment of the State of Israel and the formation of the IDF, a narrative of empowerment and divine favor prevails. Israel stands resilient, not solely by its own strength, but also by the unwavering divine guidance that has been its compass throughout history.

Concluding his commentary, Rav Aviner evokes a sense of collective unity, urging all segments of the nation, irrespective of their individual beliefs or backgrounds, to resonate with a unified Amen.

Praying for the Defenders of Our Faith

Amen ve-Amen.

פירוש תפילה לשלום חיילי צה"ל

תפילה: יש צורך גם בתפילה וגם במלחמה. אי אפשר זה בלי זה. יעקב אבינו התכונן גם לתפילה וגם למלחמה. זו תפילה שברכת ד' תחול על מסירות הנפש של החייל.

לשלום: האידיאל שלנו הוא שלום. אנו מצפים וכתתו חרבותם לאיטים. לפעמים גם בצבא יש שלום, ולפעמים גם באזרחות יש שנאה. אשרינו שבצבאנו יש שלום בין אדם לחברו ושלום בינינו לבין רבונו של עולם.

חיילי: יש אנשים שונים באומה. אבל בצבא כל ההבדלים נעלמים. אין דתי וחילוני, אין חרדי וציוני, אין אשכנזי וספרדי, אין תימני ואתיופי, אין ימני ושמאלני. יש חייל! הוא מתרומם לכלל ישראל.

צה"ל: צבא הגנה לישראל, זו תפארתנו, שאיננו תוקפניים, איננו כובשים, אלא אנו מגנים על עצמנו. אמר פילוסוף אחד: אני חושב, לכן אני קיים. ועתה אנו אומרים: אנו מגנים על עצמנו, לכן אנו קיימים.

מי: הוא רבונו של עולם, אדון עולם אשר מלך בטרם כל יציר נברא. הוא רבונו של עולם שבחר בעמו ישראל והוא אלהי צבאות ישראל.

שברך: רבונו של עולם מביא ברכה לעולמו, מביא ברכה לכל מי שמכין את עצמו לקבל את זאת הברכה.

אבותינו: אנחנו מה שאנחנו מכח אבותינו. תכונות אבותינו הינן שוכנות בתוכנו לנצח. אשרינו מה טוב חלקנו.

אברהם יצחק ויעקב: כל אחד עם נתיבו, כל אחד עם דרכו לעבודת ד', ואנחנו בלולים מכולם. אשרינו.

הוא יברך: ברוך אתה ד' אשר קדשנו ממצוותיו. מי שמקיים מצוות ד', מקבל ברכת ד'. קל וחומר, את המצוה הענקית של שרות בצבא, להצלת העם, להצלת הארץ, להצלת קידוש השם.

את חיילי: איזו מילה נפלאה. חייל! בכלל, היה בן חיל! כתוב בתחילת מסילת ישרים. ויש אשת חיל! תורת חסד על לשונה!

צבא הגנה לישראל: אשרינו שיש לנו מדינה. ובימינו אין מדינה בלי צבא. הרמב"ם כתב: הלכות מלכים ומלחמות. וכל המלחמות שלנו הן מלחמות בלית ברירה. מלחמות הגנה.

ואנשי כוחות הביטחון: חיילים עם מדים, חיילים עם מדים אחרים, משטרה, משמר הגבול, וגם לוחמי אש וגם שב"ס. גם חיילים בלי מדים – שב"כ ומוסד.

העומדים: הם לא עייפים, הם לא נרדמים, הם עומדים. הם תלמידי רבונו של עולם שומר ישראל, אשר לא ינום ולא יישן.

על משמר ארצנו: לו פינו מלא שירה כים, אינינו מספיקים להודות לחיילנו היקרים מכל הסוגים. אנו אוכלים ואנו שותים, אנו ישנים ואנו נחים, אנו בטוחים ואנו רגועים, וכל זאת בזכותם, כי הם עומדים על המשמר, בכל יום, ובכל עת ובכל שעה.

וערי אלהינו: כי ארצנו אינה סתם מקום מגורים, סתם מקלט זמני או קבוע, אלא היא ארץ אלהינו, ועריו הן ערי אלהינו, וכל רגב אדמה הוא לאלהינו.

מגבול הלבנון ועד מדבר מצרים: כל זה ארצנו, באמת ובצדק, על פי המוסר ועל פי ההיסטוריה, על פי התורה ועל פי התנ"ך. ועוד הרבה חסר לנו, ולא מתייאשים אנחנו, אך עתה עבודת צבאנו, היא לשמור על גבולות אלה, גבולות לא פשוטים, אך צבאנו מסור וחזק, ד' יברכהו.

ומן הים הגדול עד לבוא הערבה: גם זה כולו ארצנו, או ליתר דיוק חלק מארצנו, וגם שם צבאנו מוסר נפשו, יומם וליל, ד' יברכהו.

ביבשה באוויר ובים: איש על מחנהו ואיש על דגלו, כולם נצרכים, כולם הכרחיים, כולם אהובים, כולם גיבורים, כולם עושים באימה וביראה רצון קונם.

יתן ד' את אויבנו: ד' הוא שמנהיג את העולם, שמנהיג את ההיסטוריה, והוא עושה זאת על ידנו ומתוכנו. אנו שלוחיו הנאמנים.

הקמים עלינו: אנו מעולם לא תקפנו אדם. אנו תלמידי אהרן הכהן אוהב שלום וכולם שלום. אלא הם קמים עלינו, ואז אנו משיבים מלחמה שערה.

נגפים לפניהם: במשך אלפיים שנות גלותנו אויבינו רדפו אותנו, גנבו ורצחו, אנסו וחמסו, גרשו וביזו. ועתה המצב השתנה, בחסדי ד' עלינו. עתה אנו המנצחים והם הניגפים.

159

Praying for the Defenders of Our Faith

הקדוש ברוך הוא: רבונו של עולם הוא קדוש, מעל העולם, מעל ההויה, והוא ברוך, ממלא את העולם, ממלא את ההויה.

ישמור ויציל: הוא שומר שלא יקרה מאומה, ואם קורה דבר מה, אז הוא מציל. אנו לא לבד. אל גדול וגיבור בתוכנו, ההולך לפנינו.

את חיילינו: הם חיילינו, לא חיילי עם אחר. הם מקושטים במדים שלנו, מדברים בשפה שלנו, שייכים לעמנו ולארצנו. הם חיילינו.

מכל צרה וצוקה: באופן טבעי, במלחמה יש צרות ויש צוקות, אבל מעל כולן מתנשא גואל חי וחזק.

ומכל נגע ומחלה: יש יהודים יקרים המחפשים סגולות נגד תחלואים, והם אינם יודעים שסגולת הסגולות היא קיום תורה ומצוות, ושצבא הוא מצות המצוות, עד כדי מסירות נפש, והנו הוא המציל מכל נגע ומחלה.

וישלח ברכה והצלחה: ד' אוהב את חיילינו, משגיח על חיילינו, מתפאר בחיילינו, מספר למלאכי השרת על חיילינו. וכיוון שעבודתם קודש לד', אז רבון העולם שולח להם ברכה ושולח להם הצלחה.

בכל מעשה ידיהם: כל מעשה של חייל הינו נצרך, הינו חיוני, אינו לשוא, אינו מיותר, אלא מדוייק ומחושב.

ידבר שונאינו תחתיהם: בינתיים יש לנו שונאים. תמיד היו לנו שונאים. ועוד זמן יהיו לנו שונאים. והרבה סבלנו מאותם שונאים. אבל עתה השתנתה תמונת העולם. אנו גוברים על שונאינו, והם נשלטים על ידינו.

ויעטרם בכתר ישועה: הרבה כתרים יש, כתר תורה, כתר כהונה, כתר מלכות וכתר שם טוב. ויש כתב ישועה, בו מכתיר אותנו מלך עוזר ומושיע. מאז קום מדינתנו, מאז קום צבאנו, ישועת ד' סובבת אותנו.

ובעטרת נצחון: זה כתר עוד יותר גדול: נצחון. לאורך גלותנו שכחנו מכתר זה הגדול. עתה, בחסדי ד', מתגלה נצח ישראל, נצחון ישראל.

ויקויים בהם הכתוב: הכתוב הזה נאמר עליכם. הכתוב הזה מגן עליכם וסוכך אתכם. הכתוב הזה הוא נשמת חייהם.

כי ד' אלהיכם: הוא בורא עולם וכל העולמים, בורא תבל וכל היושבים בו, אבל מעל הכל ובתוך הכל, הוא אלהינו, שלנו, של עמנו אנו. יש לו קשר מיוחד, פנימי, עמוק, אינטימי, דווקא איתנו.

ההולך עמכם: אנו לא נעזבים, אנו לא יתומים, ד' איתנו. לאורך כל ההיסטוריה שלנו, ד' מתהלך עמנו.

להילחם לכם: ד' הוא גם איש מלחמה. במלחמה כמו במלחמה. הוא בעל מלחמות ואנו דבקים במידותיו ועוסקים במלחמה.

עם אויביכם: כי אויבינו הם אויבי ד'. קומה ד' ויפוצו אויביך וינוסו משנאך מפניך. אלו שונאי ישראל שכל השונא את ישראל שונא את מי שאמר והיה העולם (במדבר י לה רש"י).

להושיע אתכם: כי לד' הישועה. הישועה היא לד' ואנו לד', ולכן הישועה הנצחית מעטרת אותנו. ועתה השליח האלהי של ישועתנו הוא צבאנו.

ונאמר אמן: כולנו נאמר אמן. דתיים וחילוניים נאמר אמן. חרדים וציונים נאמר אמן. ימניים ושמאלניים נאמר אמן. כל האומה נאמר אמן. אמן ואמן.

Prayer: There's a need for both prayer and war. One cannot exist without the other. Jacob our father prepared for both prayer and war. This is a prayer where God's blessing will rest upon the self-sacrifice of the soldier.

For Peace: Our ideal is peace. We hope "and they shall beat their swords into plowshares." Sometimes there's peace even in the army, and sometimes there's hatred even among civilians. We are fortunate that in our army there is peace between one man and his fellow and peace between us and the Master of the Universe.

Soldiers: There are different people in the nation. But in the army, all differences disappear. There's no religious or secular, no ultra-Orthodox or Zionist, no Ashkenazi or Sephardi, no Yemenite or Ethiopian, no rightist or leftist. There is a soldier! He is devoted to the entire nation of Israel.

Praying for the Defenders of Our Faith

IDF: The Israel Defense Forces, this is our pride, that we are not aggressive, we are not conquerors, but we defend ourselves. One philosopher said: "I think, therefore I am." And now we say: "We defend ourselves, therefore we exist."

Who is the Master of the Universe: The Lord of the World who reigned before any creature was created. He is the Master of the Universe who chose His people Israel and He is the God of Israel's armies.

Who blessed: The Master of the Universe brings blessing to His world, brings blessing to all who prepare themselves to receive that blessing.

Our Fathers: We are what we are because of our fathers. The attributes of our fathers reside forever within us. How fortunate we are, how good is our portion.

Abraham, Isaac, and Jacob: Each one with his path, each with his way of serving God, and we are a blend of all. How fortunate we are.

He will bless: Blessed are You, Lord, who sanctified us with His commandments. One who fulfills God's commandments receives God's blessing. All the more so for the monumental commandment of military service, to save the people, to save the land, to sanctify the Divine Name.

Our Soldiers: What a wonderful word. Soldier! In general, be a "Ben Chayil" (man of valor)! It's written at the beginning of the "Path of the Just." And there is a "Woman of Valor"! Her tongue is a Torah of kindness!

Israel Defense Forces: How fortunate we are to have a state. In our time, there is no state without an army. Maimonides wrote: Laws of Kings and Wars. And all our wars are wars of necessity. Wars of defense.

And the security forces: Soldiers in uniforms, soldiers in different uniforms, police, border patrol, also firefighters, and also the Shin Bet

(Security Agency). Also soldiers without uniforms – the Israeli Secret Intelligence Service and Mossad.

Those who stand: They are not tired, they do not sleep, they stand. They are students of the Lord, the Guardian of Israel, who neither slumbers nor sleeps.

Guarding our land: If our mouth was full of song like the sea, we would not suffice to thank our precious soldiers of all types. We eat and drink, sleep and rest, we are secure and calm, all thanks to them, for they stand guard every day, at every moment and every hour.

And our cities: Because our land is not just a place of residence, not just a temporary or permanent refuge, but it is the land of our God, and our cities are the cities of our God, and every grain of soil belongs to our God.

From the Lebanese border to the Egyptian desert: All this is our land, truly and justly, according to morals and history, according to the Torah and the Bible. And we still lack a lot, but we do not despair. But now the task of our army is to guard these borders, not simple borders, but our army is dedicated and strong, God bless it.

And from the great sea to the edge of the desert: This too is all our land, or more precisely part of our land, and there too our army dedicates its soul, day and night, God bless it.

On land, in the air, and at sea: Each in his camp and each by his flag, all are needed, all are essential, all are loved, all are heroes, all perform the will of their Creator in awe and reverence.

God will repel our enemies: God guides the world, guides history, and He does so through us and from within us. We are His faithful agents.

Who rise against us: We have never attacked anyone. We are disciples of Aaron the priest, lovers of peace, and pursuers of peace. But they rise against us, and then we respond with a blazing war.

Who strike before them: Throughout the two thousand years of our exile, our enemies pursued us, stole and murdered, raped and oppressed, expelled and humiliated. But now the situation has changed, by the grace of God. Now we are the victors and they are the ones being struck.

The Holy One, blessed be He: The Master of the Universe is holy, above the world, above existence, and He is blessed, filling the world, filling existence.

He will guard and save: He guards so that nothing happens, and if something happens, then He saves. We are not alone. A great and mighty God is within us, leading us.

Against your enemies: For our enemies are God's enemies. "Rise, O Lord, and let Your enemies be scattered, and let those who hate You flee before You." Those who hate Israel hate the One who said and brought the world into being.

To save you: For salvation is from God. Salvation belongs to God, and we belong to God, and therefore eternal salvation adorns us. And now the divine agent of our salvation is our army.

And let us say Amen: We all say Amen. Religious and secular say Amen. Ultra-Orthodox and Zionists say Amen. Rightists and leftists say Amen. The entire nation says Amen. Amen and Amen.

Menachem Butler, the Program Fellow for Jewish Legal Studies in the Julis-Rabinowitz Program on Jewish and Israeli Law at Harvard Law School, serves as the President of the Institute for Jewish Research and Publications and is the co-editor of this volume.

Reflection on Praying for IDF Soldiers

Ruth Calderon

I GREW UP IN A SECULAR environment in Israel, where school days passed without prayers and religious rituals were foreign to my household. There lingered a sentiment, perhaps grounded, that the religious teachings from the diaspora held little relevance in our modern nation-building endeavors.

However, as I grew more introspective, I began to see the untapped wisdom and depth the older generation carried, which we might have been sidelining. This insight led me to deeply engage with the treasures of rabbinic Judaism. By reconnecting with the eloquence of our ancient scholars, I have a richer connection with prayer, deeply rooted in the richness of the Hebrew language.

When a Jewish community prays for the soldiers defending our national home, a profound bond is forged across all generations of the people of Israel. Hearts unite. And achievements that surpass mere battlefield victories become possible.

Praying for the Defenders of Our Faith

I am deeply grateful to all who hold us in their thoughts and evoke our presence during their moments of prayer.

Dr. Ruth Calderon is a distinguished Israeli academic, Talmudic scholar, and educator with a deep-rooted passion for teaching. A former Knesset member for Yesh Atid (2013-2015), she is the founder of Alma: Home for Hebrew Culture; and in 2019-2020, served as the Caroline Zelaznik Gruss and Joseph S. Gruss Visiting Professor in Talmudic Civil Law at Harvard Law School.

This Could Be You

Amichai Chasson

THE MOMENT OF TERROR IN my childhood synagogue did not appear on the High Holy Days but recurred every Sabbath. At the end of the Torah reading, when Mi Sheberach for the Soldiers of the Israel Defense Forces was said, an unusual, thin silence prevailed in the sanctuary. Although it is the most modern prayer included in the prayer book – and accordingly, also the "least holy" in the halachic hierarchy – it was held by the praying community as a prayer that must not be desecrated by a severe prohibition. One minute of concentrated, shared, holy terror.

Is this happening precisely because of its modernity, because of its absolute tangibility? For it does not deal with angels or seraphim, not with ancient kings nor with Amoraim and Tannaim, not with redemption nor with the building of the Temple, not even with rain for the farmers – but with hands that are making war at this very moment. Or more precisely: hands that enable this moment, in which Jews pray freely in their land.

Is it the concreteness that gives it such strong validity? For even the "Mi Sheberach for the sick" is recited publicly as a general prayer, not specific, without details and particulars. But here, in the Mi Sheberach for the IDF soldiers, we bless them wherever they are: "on land, in the air, and at sea," and we draw a geographical map: "from the border of Lebanon to the desert of Egypt, and from the great sea to the Arabah."

One can pray these words and imagine the lines of soldiers walking in darkness beyond enemy lines. One can imagine your brother, your sister, your father, your son, your home. You can imagine yourself. I think that is the secret of the terror of the prayer – the understanding that it could be you. Not as an image, without any "word of Torah" to connect, to explain and to interpret. It simply could be you – and by the law of life in the State of Israel, you know that it's not just "could be," but that it will be you, tomorrow morning or in the near future. There is not a single father in the State of Israel who does not ponder this accrued terror when looking at his son, as he enters into the covenant of Abraham our father.

I was a child during the first Intifada, a teenager in the second, and I enlisted in the IDF a year after the Second Lebanon War. I spent my military service, both regular and reserve, between rounds in the Gaza Strip and the tough, sad routine of the checkpoints in Judea and Samaria. Regrettably, it remained a relevant prayer, then and now.

As a child, I imagined that my prayer could save heroes in battle. As a soldier, I understood that I needed this prayer because I was not a hero, because I was standing alone in the middle of the night at the guard post on the Lebanese border, a magazine inside the weapon and a suspicious figure before me – and at that moment, I needed a prayer not to stand entirely alone.

And yet, every time anew, something is missing for me in this prayer. In fact, it lacks what could nullify it. The vision of the end of days by the prophet Isaiah: "They will beat their swords into plowshares and their spears into pruning hooks; nation shall not lift up sword against nation, neither shall they learn war anymore." This verse I inscribed on my weapon strap at the end of my basic training, and it accompanied me until the end of my service in the army. Amid the terrible war imposed upon us, it is hard to imagine that wondrous, dreamy prophetic vision, but one can pray for it, with exactly the same terror.

I conclude with a poem titled "A Trial in a Delicate Motorcade," written during my military service in the Jordan Valley, in the winter of 2008.

הַנֶּשֶׁק תָּמִיד צָמוּד לַגּוּף

מִתְפַּתֵּל בָּאוֹטוֹבּוּס לֹא נוֹגֵעַ בְּאַף אֶחָד

מְפַלֵּס דֶּרֶךְ בֵּין הַמּוֹשָׁבִים לְמָקוֹם מְרֻפָּד

לְכַתֵּת חַרְבוֹתַי לְאִתִּים חֲנִיתוֹתַי לְהַצְלֵב רֹאשִׁי לְשִׁפּוּעַ

לִמְרֹחַ לְחָיַי עַל זְכוּכִית כְּפוּלָה

מְמֻגֶּנֶת, מְלֻכְלֶכֶת מְאֹד,

מַכְבִּידָה לִרְאוֹת סִימָנֵי גְּאֻלָּה.

The weapon is always attached to the body

Twisting in the bus not touching anyone

Carving a path between the settlements to a paved place

To beat my swords into plowshares, my spears into a cruciform head

To smear my cheeks on doubled glass

Protected, very dirty,

Heavy to see signs of redemption.

Amichai Chasson is an Israeli poet, curator, and filmmaker. He currently serves as the Artistic Director and Chief Curator at Beit Avi Chai in Jerusalem.

Owning the New Implications of Familiar Words

Noah Cheses

Every Shabbat, week in and week out, our community stands up together, before the *Chazan* returns the Torah to the Ark, and recites aloud, in unison, the prayer for the Israel Defense Forces printed in the RCA Siddur. As the Rabbi, I lead the *Mi Sheberach* and invite everyone to join in with me to say the words together. On a typical week, a few dozen people do so but I still generate most of the volume. In the weeks following the Simchat Torah Massacre of 5784, I could barely hear my own voice, as the community said these words with unparalleled passion and desperation. I could hear some high pitched, cracking voices mixed with tears coming from the women's section. The intensity reminded me of the conclusion of *Ne'ilah*, which was still fresh in my memory from a few weeks earlier.

What changed was that 63 members of our community had an immediate relative–son, brother or nephew that was deployed to the front lines. Everyone knew somebody who was fighting in the IDF at that very moment and prayer became one of the strongest avenues for mitigating the gnawing feelings of helplessness in the face of horror. The words of this prayer for Israeli soldiers became somewhat of an anthem in our community, being recited and sung, as frequently if not more so than *Hatikvah*. I found myself in a situation on Shabbat afternoon in a crowd where someone suggested that we recite the *Mi Sheberach* but there were no siddurim available. Several of us looked at each other and I suggested that we could likely do it by heart at this point and indeed we did.

On a typical Shabbat, we recite the *Avinu Shebashamayim* prayer for the state of Israel before the *Mi Sheberach*. I often introduce these additional prayers with a quick update or anecdote related to Israel from the prior week. On the third Shabbat following the onset of the war, I intended to give a brief introduction but found myself sharing a lengthy reflection on the tension between these two prayers. The prayer for the state of Israel, on the one hand, is a prayer for peace, requesting that God "spread over it a canopy of peace…and grant peace to the entire land." The prayer for the soldiers on the other hand is a prayer "for the success of the soldiers in all of the tasks of their hands," which at a time of war, means the opposite of peace. If the soldiers complete their missions and accomplish their jobs, it means that there will be tremendous loss of life and a chain of intergenerational traumas will be unleashed.

I attempted to reconcile this noted tension by suggesting that our petitions for peace are for a long term peace, but that in the short term we need to reclaim the language of a just war, by praying that all the operations go as planned. It is easy to pray for the well-being of our soldiers; it is less comfortable to pray that our soldiers be successful in killing our enemies. But those are the words of the *Mi Sheberach* and we need to stand by the implication of those words at a time of war. We need to be confident in choosing "us" over "them" even if it means that there will unfortunately be inevitable civilian casualties on the other side. This is what the words of the *Mi Sheberach* compel us to grapple with and come to terms with at the time of war. We don't want peace now; we want other things now that will get us to peace later.

May we arrive at that peace within our lifetimes.

Rabbi Noah Cheses is the rav of the Young Israel of Sharon in Sharon, Massachusetts.

Hasidim Praying for Soldiers

Levi Cooper

Prayer Objectives

Prayer can be a request for divine intercession, assistance, and salvation; an appeal to the Almighty to change the planned course. "The one who blessed our ancestors … may He bless …" – we call on God who has blessed our predecessors to bestow further blessings on the object of our prayers. The objective of such prayers is change orchestrated by God.

Prayer can also be a meditative practice that provides a framework for inculcating and honing ideals, values, and objectives. While we may not fully understand those goals or even have complete faith in their virtue, prayer texts sketch the gamut of belief. "Blessed are You, O Lord, who revives the dead" – resuscitation of the deceased may well be a difficult concept for the modern mind to grasp, and the definitive

---

* Dedicated to my beloved children, and to all who selflessly and bravely protect Israel. May this research be read as a prayer for their spiritual, emotional and physical wellbeing, for their safety and success, for their speedy return home, and for peace in the Land.

statement may raise doubts about the future, yet given its prominent place in the daily prayers it clearly part of Jewish thought. Indeed, the collection of prayers can be seen as a compendium of Jewish beliefs, values, and hopes.[1] This aspect of prayer is one of the reasons why for some people it so important to insert the four Mothers into the text so that our prayers express egalitarian aspirations. Others find the change anathema to the goal of preserving the sacred past. Both opinions see prayer as a vehicle for values.

Prayer can also be an expression of sensitivity, care, and appreciation for others. Keeping someone in your prayers or reciting prayers on behalf of those in dire straits is a demonstration of commonality, camaraderie, and shared destiny.

These elements of prayer are not discrete. When reciting a prayer for hostages and explaining "since the community prays for them," we are beseeching the Almighty for their release in the merit of communal prayer, we are voicing the communal value of freedom, and we are publicly stating that the community has not forgotten those who are held in captivity.

Moreover, these are not the only elements of prayer. There are other facets to prayer such as praise and gratitude, confrontation and questions, and more. These facets may or may not be subsumed under the three elements I have sketched.

With these prayer elements in mind, this article tracks and analyses prayers for soldiers offered by contemporary hasidic masters during the war that began in Israel on Simhat Torah 5784, October 7, 2023 with the devastating massacre by Hamas that claimed some 1,200 lives, injured

---

1 See Yehuda Brandes, "Ha-tefilla ke-hagut," *Luah ha-shana shel kehillat ihud shivat tsiyon* (2006/07); Levi Cooper, "Ha-mehadesh be-tuvo be-khol yom: ma'amad birkat ha-hama be-hatseirot hasidiyot," *Daat*, no. 77 (2014): 183-207, especially p. 184 (Hebrew).

over 5,000 people, and captured 224 hostages. The finding presented herein reflect the first three weeks of the war and this paper is written as events unfold in real time.

Hasidic Prayer

In the annals of Hasidism, there have been hasidic masters who have offered prayers for soldiers, generals, and armies. The 1812 French invasion of Russia provides a well-known example, where hasidic masters took different sides and waged spiritual battle on behalf of empires. Their weaponry included prayers, theurgic practices, and worldly tactics in order to determine the outcome of the war.[2] This fascinating historical angle is beyond the present scope, and is qualitatively different to the present discussion. Unlike the IDF, those armies were not made up almost entirely of Jews, nor were they defending Jews, nor were they fighting for the Jewish State.

In general, hasidic communities do not publicly recite any version of the most accepted prayer for IDF soldiers.[3] They roundly reject the prayer because it is perceived as an assimilation of Zionist values or an acceptance of the Israeli army as the military representative of the Jewish People.[4] Reciting the prayer could even be construed as encouragement

---

2   See, for example, David Assaf, "When the Rabbis 'Met' Napoleon," trans. Daniel Tabak, *Tradition: A Journal of Orthodox Jewish Thought*, vol. 54, no. 2 (Spring 2022): 55-63.

3   Regarding the prayer see, inter alia, Yoel Rappel, "Be-khol makom she-hem," *Makor Rishon* (September 12, 2014), available here (https://tinyurl.com/yrhpmxz3); see also the other chapters in this collection.

4   For a summary of hasidic approaches to the State of Israel, see *Hasidism: A New History*, eds. David Biale, et al (Princeton: Princeton University Press, 2018), 707-739.

to fulfil the legal, civil, and social obligation to serve in the IDF, which is staunchly opposed by hasidic leadership.

For the sake of accuracy, it should be noted that there are hasidic synagogues where the prayer for IDF soldiers is recited, but these are exceptions rather than the rule. Moreover, the prayer is recited together with the *Mi she-beirakh* prayer for the sick in the middle in the Torah reading.[5] This placement should be contrasted with the practice to give the prayer its own moment during the service where it captures attention – in Sephardic synagogues when opening the ark to take the Torah out, or in Ashkenazic synagogues after Torah reading before returning the Torah to the ark.

Considering the enormity of the present situation, perhaps the common practice might be set aside? This article focuses on changes born out of the crisis of war. Have hasidic leaders issued calls to pray for soldiers at this time?

There are related wartime issues that go beyond the fieldwork conducted for this project – changes in relationship to the State of Israel, actual army service, and volunteer work for the benefit of soldiers. For example, there have been reports of Haredim – a sector that includes the hasidic community – enlisting in the armed forces. This has been a grass roots development rather than a move orchestrated by the leadership. While this is interesting from the perspective of Israel society, the numbers are yet be of significance. Reports range from 1,500 to 3,000 Haredim willing to enlist, out of a sector that has 150,000 military deferments, and at a time when there at 400,000 people enlisted

---

5   This is the practice in the Kehal Hasidim synagogue in Jerusalem's Sha'arei Hesed neighbourhood.

or mobilised.⁶ Whether or not these efforts will result in long-lasting changes remains to be seen.

Calls for Prayer

The war has affected everyone living in the State of Israel. Rocket fire from Gaza has also been directed at hasidic communities, with blaring sirens sending hasidic families into reinforced protected rooms or bomb shelters. Given this reality, it stands to reason that hasidic masters would mobilise themselves and their communities for the war effort.

Hasidism places great emphasis on prayer as a religious, spiritual, mystical, and communal practice.⁷ Considering this focus, it is possible that hasidic masters and their communities would offer intense prayer support for the armed forces. Moreover, it is possible that they would use theurgic prayer rituals to protect soldiers and ensure military victory.

Certainly, there are hasidic precedents for such action during times of trouble. Perhaps the most famous example in hasidic memory dates back to the inspiration for the movement, Rabbi Yisrael Ba'al Shem Tov

---

6   See, for example, Baruch Green, "Charedi Journalist Yanki Farber – Expect changes in the Charedi community," *VINnews* (20 October 2023), available here (https://vinnews.com/2023/10/20/watch-charedi-journalist-yanki-farber-expect-changes-in-the-charedi-community). At this time, there is no available data regarding the communal affiliation of those willing to enlist since the war began.

7   See, for example, Louis Jacobs, *Hasidic Prayer* (London: Routledge & Kegan Paul, 1972). For the latest overviews, see Biale, *Hasidism*, 183-188; Zvi Mark and Roee Horen, "Tefilah," in *Or hozer: 'olama shel ha-hasidut*, ed. Avishar Har-Shefi (Jerusalem: Maggid Books, 2022), 747-778; Levi Cooper, *Hasidic Relics: Cultural Encounters* (Jerusalem: Maggid Books, 2023), 261-295.

(Besht, ca.1700-1760).[8] In 1749, when faced with a catastrophe that was about to befall the Jewish People, the Besht interceded in heavenly spheres. First, he asked that whatever was to be visited upon the Jews be at the hands of God rather than by brutal marauders. This request was granted and a pandemic struck rather than a pogrom. Then the Besht tried to mitigate the tragedy with further supplications, but was denied on account of his prior involvement. Finally, at great personal risk – and it is unclear from the record whether the danger was physical or spiritual – the Besht tried again by offering a particular, mystically efficacious prayer to prevent the plague from entering the region. According to the Besht, this effort was successful, his request was granted, and the disease did not ravage the local community.

Those risking their lives on the battlefront might well be hoping that today's spiritual titans of Hasidism are following the legacy of the Besht and earnestly offering intercessory and mystical prayers for the IDF's success and the safety of all soldiers.[9] Moreover, the soldiers might gain strength from the knowledge that in this time of crisis, people from all walks of life are identifying with the travails of the Jewish People, even if they do not endorse the State of Israel.

---

8   For an overview, see Cooper, *Hasidic Relics*, 290-298. For in-depth analysis of the letter, see Moshe Rosman, *Founder of Hasidism: A Quest for the Historical Ba'al Shem Tov* (Berkeley: University of California, 1996; repr., with new introduction, Oxford: Littman Library of Jewish Civilization, 2013), 99-113; Chaim Elly Moseson, "From Spoken Word to the Discourse of the Academy: Reading the Sources for the Teachings of the Besht," (doctoral diss., Boston University, 2017), 35-117.

9   For such a claim regarding Rabbi Aharon Rokach of Belz (1880-1957) during the 1956 Sinai Campaign – that was recalled during the 2023 war – see Moshe Weisberg, "The Hasidic Influencer: There's Nothing to Fear from Ground Entry to Gaza," *Be-hadrei hareidim* (23 October 2023; Hebrew), available here (https://www.bhol.co.il/news/1608498).

Indeed, many hasidic masters have been quick to respond to the current situation by issuing calls for prayer in these times of trouble. Some calls have specifically mentioned the kidnapped hostages who are – as of this writing – still cruelly held in captivity.[10] Some calls have included oblique references to the war. Barring a few exceptions, soldiers have not been singled out by contemporary hasidic leadership for public prayers. The most accepted prayer for the soldiers has not been introduced into the service.

Extremes

Satmar

One of the Satmar communities that has branches in Jerusalem, Bnei Brak, and Beit Shemesh issued a call for prayer "because of the difficult situation that prevails in the Holy Land" – a nondescript acknowledgement of the grim reality.[11] The broadside in Hebrew drew

---

10 Regarding such prayers from outside the hasidic community see, for example, Ofer Sabath Beit Halachmi, "Prayer for the Redemption of Israelis Taken Captive [during the war begun on Shemini Atseret 5784]," trans. Rachel Sabath Beit Halachmi, *the Open Siddur Project* (7 October 2023), available here (https://opensiddur.org/prayers/collective-welfare/trouble/conflicts-over-sovereignty-and-dispossession/prayer-for-the-redemption-of-captive-israelis-shemini-atseret-war-ofer-sabath-beit-halachmi-2023); Sivan Rahav-Meir, "A prayer for the captives," trans. Yehoshua Siskin, *Sivan Rahav-Meir* (17 October 2023), available here (https://www.sivanrahavmeir.com/the-daily-thought/a-prayer-for-the-captives).

11 The notice was posted on *Twitter* on October 16, 2023, see here (https://twitter.com/moshe_nayes/status/1713906670445715939). The use of Hebrew may be surprising given that Satmar eschews any link to Zionism, but this should be read as Loshon ha-kodesh (the holy tongue) rather than Modern Hebrew.

Praying for the Defenders of Our Faith

on the words of the sages and announced that "our strength is only through the mouth," referring to prayer.[12] Citing the instruction of the

The broadside includes orthographic errors in Hebrew. One mistake is particularly jarring, perhaps event heretical: מלכינו instead of מלכנו, turning the word into plural and suggesting multiple Rulers.

12 *Bemidbar Rabbah* 20:4.

hasidic leader of the community, Rabbi Aaron Teitelbaum (b. 1947), the broadside declared that the *Avinu malkeinu* prayer should be added in the morning and afternoon.[13] Before signing off, the broadside calls on the Guardian of Israel – that is, God – to protect the remnant of Israel. The Satmar broadside includes no acknowledgement of the soldiers on the front lines who could serve as instruments of the Guardian of Israel.

Given Rabbi Aaron Teitelbaum's staunch opposition to the Israeli army and considering the anti-Zionist legacy of Satmar Hasidism, the broadside is unsurprising.[14] It seems that there is no way that Satmar Hasidism could put aside its fierce anti-Zionist ideology and anti-IDF stance, and pray for the safety of Israel's soldiers.

Yet Satmar's response is not an outlier on the contemporary hasidic scene. Other examples from hasidic groups that are not as vehemently anti-Zionist as Satmar are widely available via news outlets that cater to those interested in what is going in hasidic courts. One such Hebrew forum, *Parenches*, has a page dedicated to hasidic news pertaining to the

---

13 Regarding this prayer and its adventures, see David Assaf, "From Synagogue to Rock Concert: A Journey from the Prayer Service in the Wake of 'Avinu Malkeinu,'" *Oneg Shabbat* (26 September 2011; Hebrew), available here (https://onegshabbat.blogspot.com/2011/09/blog-post_26.html); Tamar Zigman, "The Incarnations of the 'Avinu Malkeinu' Piyut from the Talmud to Barbara Streisand," *The Librarians* (24 April 2018), available here (https://blog.nli.org.il/en/avinu_malkeinu_barbra_streisand).

14 For Rabbi Aaron Teitelbaum's harsh position against the IDF see, for example, Kobi Nachshoni, "Satmar: IDF draft worse than annihilation," *Ynet* (4 December 2013), available here (https://www.ynetnews.com/articles/0,7340,L-4365946,00.html). For a similar position taken by the other hasidic master of Satmar, Aaron's younger brother – and adversary – Rabbi Zalman Leib Teitelbaum (b. 1951), see Kobi Nahshoni, "Satmar: No greater offence than voting," *Ynet* (22 January 2013), available here (https://www.ynetnews.com/articles/0,7340,L-4335420,00.html).

war.[15] Prayers for Israel's fighting forces are absent from the *Parenches* forum.

As of October 23, 2023 – just over two weeks after the onset of the war – the *Parenches* forum included 157 posts, posted by 25 different writers (with some 7,900 views). Only one post mentioned soldiers of the IDF – a post about the efforts of Lubavitch hasidim to contribute to the war effort. It should be noted, however, that Lubavitch hasidim see themselves as serving in another army – *Tzivos Hashem* (the Army of God), established in 1980. While the supreme commander of Tzivos Hashem is the Almighty, "soldiers" receive[d] their marching orders from

---

15 See "Operation Swords of Iron in the Hasidic Court – [5]784," *Parenches*, available here (https://tinyurl.com/bdfzaxpc). *Parenches* – bleachers, the tiered stairs that surround the table (Yiddish: *tish*) and are filled by hasidim at well-attended communal gatherings. A few years ago, the bleachers at a hasidic gathering collapsed with tragic consequences; see Jeremy Sharon, Idan Zonshine, and Tobias Siegal, "Two killed, 184 injured in bleachers collapse at Hassidic synagogue," *The Jerusalem Post* (18 May 2021), available here (https://www.jpost.com/breaking-news/synagogue-balcony-collapses-in-givat-zeev-dozens-injured-report-668322).

the current Lubavitcher Rebbe of blessed memory, Rabbi Menachem Mendel Schneerson (1902-1994).[16]

Pashkan

One fascinating exception to the widespread hasidic pattern is the Pashkaner Rebbe: Brigadier General Hoshea Avraham Friedman Ben-Shalom (b. 1959).[17] A high-ranking officer who was born in a secular kibbutz and grew up in a religious kibbutz. Ben-Shalom (as he was known at the time) served in the famed Golani Brigade, moving up the ranks until he served as the commander of the IDF's reserve forces. He was discharged from active service in July 2017, a few months after his father passed away and the mantle of hasidic leadership passed on to him.

Short videos of the Pashakner Rebbe decked in army uniform have been released since the beginning of the war. The Pashkaner Rebbe is seen offering encouragement and calling for unity and prayers for the success of the war effort.

Admittedly, the Pashkaner Rebbe is far from representative of the mainstream hasidic community. The modern, Zionist hasidic

---

16 Note the title of Sue Fishkoff, *The Rebbe's Army: Inside the World of Chabad-Lubavitch* (New York: Schocken Books, 2003).

17 Rabbi Hoshea Avraham Friedman Ben-Shalom reportedly prefers to be called the Rebbe from Gilo, rather than Pashkan, in order to avoid conflict with his relative Rabbi Yaakov David Mendel Leib Friedman (b. 1957), who is known as the Rebbe of Bohush (succeeding his maternal grandfather, the previous Rebbe of Bohush) or the Rebbe of Bohush-Pashkan (succeeding his paternal father, who was the Pashkaner Rebbe in Jaffa from 1947 until he passed away in 1955). See Yisrael Cohen, "Sensitivity in Hasidism: The Admor from Gilo Will Organize a Yahrzeit Tish," *Kikar Hashabbat* (30 August 2017), available here (https://www.kikar.co.il/hasidism/244261). Despite this stated preference, many still refer to him as the Pashkaner Rebbe.

community that he leads is a relic from bygone days when Hasidism and Zionism often went hand in hand. In the contemporary hasidic scene, Pashkan Hasidism is a unicorn.

Acceptance without Embrace

With Satmar as a marker on one end of the spectrum of hasidic responses and Pashkan as a marker on the other end, it is the hasidic communities that are in between these extremes that are of particular interest. These communities often perform a complicated – and at times convoluted – dance of respect without identification, acceptance without embrace, gratitude without commitment, appreciation without assimilation, sympathy without empathy.

In the present climate, such hasidic communities have recognized the self-sacrifice of IDF soldiers in this difficult time. Yet true empathy is not possible, because as a community they do not serve in the IDF. They therefore cannot replicate the feeling of having first-degree relatives or close friends who have placed their lives on the line for the sake of those held captive, the Jewish People, or the State of Israel. Despite the emotional distance, they have offered prayers on behalf of the soldiers, while stopping short of a full embrace.

Boyan

On Rosh Hodesh Heshvan (October 15-16, 2023) – just over a week after the Simhat Torah massacre – the Boyaner Rebbe, Rabbi Nachum Dov Brayer (b. 1959) dispatched a book of prayers to his hasidim who have children or spouses who are serving or were mobilised.

As a rule, Boyan hasidim – like other mainstream hasidic communities in Israel – do not serve in the IDF. Notwithstanding this communal norm, Boyan's relative openness and its history of relative openness has resulted in a number of adherents who are Zionist hasidim and serve in the IDF as a matter of course. Sending a prayer book (together with a box of pralines!) was a heart-warming gesture and an expression of communal concern and understanding that parents or spouses of soldiers may be particularly anxious at this time.

The book is titled *Teḥinot 'et ratson*, translatable as "supplications [for divinely] favourable time."[18] *Teḥinot 'et ratson* is an eclectic collection of supplications for all manner of occasions: prayers for pregnant women and prayers for women who want to become pregnant, prayers for parents about their children and prayers for children about their parents, prayers to be said at particular locations and prayers to be said at particular times, and so on. The prayers were gathered from a variety of sources, including medieval texts, hasidic material, kabbalistic prayers from Sephardic and Ashkenazic traditions, and more.

The collection includes a prayer of possible relevance to the present discussion: "a supplication and request regarding the people of Israel that they should be saved from wars."[19] This prayer was excerpted from a longer supplication included in a work prepared by Rabbi Eliezer Papo (1785-1827) and printed in Belgrade in 1860.[20] The original prayer was not presented as a specific supplication for salvation from war. Moreover, the prayer does not capture the essence of a Jewish State fighting against those who would throw Jews into the sea. The reference to "Israel" is not to the modern state, but to the people. The spirit of the prayer is more in line with the Jewish experience over the last two millennia prior to Zionism: Praying that Jews would not be collateral damage in

18 Salient imprint information, such as who put the collection together, are not given. The National Library of Israel catalogue does not list the book in its holdings, but the book is widely available for purchase on the internet.

19 *Teḥinot 'et ratson*, 396.

20 Eliezer Papo, *Beit tefilla* (Belgrade, 1860), 55a-b. For the entire prayer, see ibid, 53a-59b.

Praying for the Defenders of Our Faith

wars between peoples, countries, or empires. Thus, it appears that any relevance of this particular prayer to the present war is incidental rather than intentional.

בית אדמו״ר שליט״א
מבאיאן
עיה״ק ירושלים תובב״א

ב״ה,

ר״ה חשון תשפ״ד

לאחינו בשרנו היקרים העומדים במערכי המלחמה
מחרפים את נפשם במלחמה הקשה נגד שונאי ישראל המבקשים לכלותינו
ואל בני משפחותם העומדים מאחור במסירות עילאית למען הצלת הכלל

חזקו ואמצו!
זכרו כי ה' עמנו
והוא הנותן לנו כח לעשות חיל
״יפל מצדך אלף ורבבה מימינך אליך לא יגש״

חרוטים אתם על לוח לבנו, ועל לוח לבם של כלל ישראל
וכולנו תפילה לאבינו אב הרחמן שזוכו לשמירה עליונה מכל פגע רע
כי מלאכיו יצוה לך לשמרך בכל דרכיך
להשיבכם בשלום, שלמים בגוף ובנפש
ולהצליח דרככם ללא נגע ומכאוב
ובזו הטעה עזדיר בלבנו אמונת איתן ביוצר הכל הסנהיג עולמו בחסד וברחמים
השומר עמו ישראל לעד לא יטוש ולא יעזוב שארית נחלתו
אל ירך לבבכם אל תיראו ואל תחפזו ואל תערצו
כי עיני עמנו ותלויות להצלחתכם!

ויהי רצון שנזכה בקרוב לראייתם בבית קדשנו ותפארתנו
בשוב ה' שבות עמו וישראל נטע בה תשועת עולמים

It is notable that the collection does not include a prayer for soldiers, suggesting that those involved in the book's production were targeting an audience that would have no need for such a prayer. At first blush, it is incongruous to present an assemblage of prayers to parents and spouses of soldiers with the most pressing, relevant, and meaningful prayer absent from the collection. A letter stuck to the inside cover of the book serves as a significant counterweight:

While the book was delivered to parents or spouses of soldiers, the letter is actually addressed to the soldiers and their families. The wording draws on biblical verses and the text exudes pathos, respect, encouragement, and resilience. Given the uniqueness of the letter, it is worth rendering into English:

> To our dear brothers, our flesh, who stand in battle formations
>
> Who endanger their lives in the difficult battle against those who hate Israel, who seek to destroy us
>
> And to their families who stand behind [them] with supreme dedication for the sake of saving the entirety
>
> **Be strong and be brave!**[21]
>
> **Remember that God is with us**
>
> **And He gives us strength to wage war**[22]
>
> **"A thousand will fall by your side and ten thousand at your right hand, none will come near you"**[23]

---

21 Deuteronomy 31:6.

22 Ibid, 8:18.

23 Psalms 91:7.

Praying for the Defenders of Our Faith

> You are etched on the slate of our heart, and on the slate of the heart of the entirety of Israel
>
> And we are all praying to our Father, merciful Father, that you will merit supreme safeguarding from all harm
>
> For He will charge his angels regarding you, to safeguard you in all your ways[24]
>
> To return you in peace, complete in body and in soul
>
> And to cause you to have success in your journey without injury and pain
>
> And in this hour we will inculcate in our heart the faith of the mighty one [Abraham] in the Creator of all, who rules His world with kindness and with mercy
>
> The one who forever safeguards His nation Israel[25] He will not abandon and He will not forsake the remnant of His heritage[26]
>
> Let not your heart be faint, fear not, and do not tremble and do not be terrified[27]
>
> For the eyes of our people are looking attentively at your success!
>
> And may it be the will [of God] that we will soon merit to see you in our holy and our beautiful house[28]

---

24 Ibid, v. 11.

25 From the *Hashkiveinu* blessing recited in the *Ma'ariv* evening prayer.

26 Paraphrasing Psalms 94:14; Micah 7:18.

27 Deuteronomy 20:3.

28 Isaiah 64:10.

> When the Lord turns the captivity of His people[29] and
> Israel is saved by the Lord, an everlasting salvation[30]

It worth considering what this letter is and what it is not. The letter is not a public prayer offered by the leader of a hasidic community. In fact, it is unclear whether the letter was public knowledge or not. The weekly email that includes information about what happened in the Boyan communities around the world, *Mei-hana'aseh ve-hanishma*, made no mention of the books dispatched even though it was posted on October 20, 2023, four or five days after the letter was written. The letter is also not a mystical prayer for divine intercession, styled after the Besht's theurgy. There is not explicit mention of the State of Israel or the IDF, and even the word soldier is absent. Nonetheless, the context and vibe of the letter is unmistakable. This is a strongly worded voice of support and caring; it is an acknowledgement of the dangers faced by the soldiers and an appreciation of the significance of their service for all of Israel. From this perspective, the letter fills some of the functions of prayer – a recognition that IDF service at this time is a laudable enterprise and an expression of gratitude for those risking their lives to defend Israel – the people and the country.

Vizhnitz

One of the Vizhnitzer Rebbes, Rabbi Yisrael Hager (b. 1945), is another interesting exception. Like other mainstream hasidim, Vizhnitz hasidim do not actively support the Israeli army. Yet for a fuller background image, it is worth mentioning two army-related quirks in the history of this hasidic community.

---

29 Psalms 14:7.

30 Isaiah 45:17.

First, Rabbi Eliezer Hager (1924-2015), hasidic master of Seret-Vizhnitz in Haifa from 1964, served in the pre-State Haganah, saw action in Haifa, and was wounded in battle.[31] Second, in 1965 Rabbi Yisrael Hager's younger sister, Surah'le (b. 1946) married Rabbi Yisakhar Dov Rokach (b. 1948) – the Belzer Rebbe in-waiting (and current Belzer Rebbe). An invitation to the wedding was sent to the then-IDF commander-in-chief, Yitzhak Rabin (1922-1995). The invitation was written in Hebrew rhyme, with an acrostic of his surname, and published in the general Hebrew press:

> *The head of the general staff of our glorious and mighty army!*
>
> *In the Israel Defence Force on the land, at sea, and in the air*
>
> *He subdues peoples under you and nations under your feet*
>
> *They will be smitten before you, God will deliver our enemies into your hands*[32]

Despite these historic peculiarities, Vizhnitz hasidim do not serve in the IDF, nor do they regularly say a prayer for the well-being of Israelis soldiers.

With this in mind, it was certainly a newsworthy event when Rabbi Yisrael Hager chose to say a prayer for the soldiers on the first Shabbat following the massacre. After he was called to the Torah in his Bnei Brak synagogue and completed the reading, he added the following prayer:

---

31   Tsadok Eshel, *The Battles of the Hagana in Haifa* (Tel Aviv: Misrad Habitahon, 1978), 398 (Hebrew); Yael Ron, "Testimonies of the Fighters of 1948: How We Liberated the City of Acre," *Srugim* (9 May 2011; Hebrew), available here (https://tinyurl.com/3a385z4k). Eliezer was Yisrael's first cousin once removed.

32   *Maariv* (17 February 1965): 18 (Hebrew).

מי שברך אבותינו אברהם יצחק ויעקב, הוא יברך וישמור ויעזור ויגן ויושיע לכל אחינו בית ישראל, העומדים במערכה מול שונאי ישראל, בעבור שכל הקהל מברכים אותם ומתפללים בעדם. בשכר זה הקב"ה ישמרם ויצילם מכל רע, וידבר עמים תחתם, ורדפו מהם חמשה מאה ומאה מהם רבבה ירדופו, ובכל אשר יפנו יצליחו, ונפלו אויבינו לפניהם לחרב, וישובו לשלום לאהליהם. להחלימם, לרפאותם, להחזיקם ולהחיותם, וישלח להם רפואה שלמה מן השמים לכל איבריהם וגידיהם בתוך שאר חולי ישראל, רפואת הנפש ורפואת הגוף, השתא בעגלא ובזמן קריב ונאמר אמן.

ומי מהם שנפל בשבי, הקב"ה ימלא רחמים עליהם ויתנם לרחמים לפני שוביהם, ויוציא ממסגר אסיר, ויקרא לשבויים דרור ולאסורים יפקח קוח, וישיבם לבתיהם בשלום במהרה, אמן.

He who blessed our ancestors, Abraham, Isaac, and Jacob, may He bless and safeguard and assist and protect and save all our brethren, the house of Israel, who stand in the battle against those who hate Israel. As the entire congregation blesses them and prays for them. In merit of this, may the Holy One, blessed be He, watch over them and save them from all harm, anghd cause peoples to be subject to them,[33] and let five of them pursue one hundred, and a hundred of them will pursue ten thousand,[34] and wherever they turn they will succeed, and our enemies will fall before them by the sword,[35]

---

33 Paraphrasing Psalms 18:48; 47:4.

34 Paraphrasing Leviticus 26:8.

35 Paraphrasing Leviticus 26:7 and 8.

and they will return in peace to their tents. [God will] cause them to recuperate, heal them, strengthen them, and revive them. And may He send them from heaven complete recovery for all their limbs and their sinews, together with all Jews who are ill, healing of the soul and healing of the body, now, soon and in the near future, and let us say Amen.

And whoever has fallen into captivity, may the Holy one, blessed be He, be filled with mercy for them, and grant them mercy before their captors, and rescue the prisoner from confinement,[36] and proclaim release for the captives and liberation for the imprisoned,[37] and speedily return them to their homes in peace, amen.

The event was widely reported in the Haredi press and in the Religious-Zionist press, both in Hebrew and in English, and rightly so – there was no historical precedent for the Vizhnitzer Rebbe's conduct.[38]

---

36 Paraphrasing Isaiah 42:7.

37 Paraphrasing Isaiah 61:1.

38 Reported by Yisrael Cohen, October 14, 2023, https://twitter.com/Israelcohen911/status/1713228163977781343. See also Itzik Brandwein, "Ha-'admur 'arakh tefilla le-shlom ha-lohamim ve-ha-hatufim," *Arutz Sheva*, October 14, 2023, https://www.inn.co.il/news/616686; "The Mi Shebeirach for Soldiers Recited by the Vizhnitzer Rebbe," *Matzav.com*, October 15, 2023, https://matzav.com/the-mi-shebeirach-for-soldiers-recited-by-the-vizhnitzer-rebbe; *Parenches*, October 15, 2023, https://tinyurl.com/yyu2kcfn; "Ahdur be-'am IL – hasidei Vizhnitz yatsu la-darom," *Rotter*, October 15, 2023, https://rotter.net/forum/scoops1/817010.shtml; "Kir'u le-shlom ha-hayalim ve-he-hatufim et nusah mi she-beirakh she-hiber rabbi Menahem Mendl Gefner ztl," *Moked Tehillim Artzi*, October 17, 2023, https://www.tehillim-center.co.il/article/8010.

To be sure, this is not the standard prayer for Israeli soldiers, and it is immediately apparent that there is no explicit mention of the soldiers of the Israel Defence Forces. Notwithstanding, news outlets that reported the event were clear that the prayer was for IDF soldiers.

The Vizhnitzer Rebbe did not make up the text (though making up such a text is not necessarily problematic). The text was composed by Rabbi Menahem Mendl Reuven Gefner (1905-1988).[39] Rabbi Gefner moved to the Land of Israel in 1924, and is famous for instituting the annual *Birkat kohanim* gathering at the Western Wall. The event was first held on Tuesday, 3 Kislev 5731 (December 1, 1970) at seven o'clock in the morning. In the following years, the event was held five times a year. Nowadays, it is conducted biennially on the intermediate days of Sukkot and Pesah, and attracts tens of thousands of people.[40]

The prayer appears in the hagiographic account of Rabbi Gefner's life written by his grandson, Rabbi Baruch Gefner, who is affiliated with Vizhnitz Hasidism and is a follower of Rabbi Yisrael Hager. This two-volume biography, published in 2001, is coloured by contemporary Haredi ideology, including much vitriol against serving in the army. Thus, when recounting the events of 1948 that culminating in the establishment of the State of Israel, armed fighting against the Arabs is depicted as futile. Prayer was the only avenue for Jewish survival, and

---

39   For recollections about Gefner by his grandchildren, see Baruch Gefner, "Inseparable from the Kosel: Remembering Rabbi Menachem Mendel Reuven Gefner, zt"l, Upon His 30th Yahrtzeit, 18 Teves," *Hamodia*, January 22, 2018, https://hamodia.com/frominyan/inseparable-kosel-remembering-rabbi-menachem-mendel-reuven-gefner-ztl-upon-30th-yahrtzeit-18-teves; idem, *Olamo shel hasid* (Bnei Brak: B. Gefner, 2001); Brindi Stern, "'Olamo shel hasid – r. Menahem Mendl Gefner," *Ma'agar sippurei moreshet*, August 6, 2023, https://tinyurl.com/mr4yvfje.

40   See Baruch Gefner, *Kuntras birkat kohanim he-hamonit 'al yad ha-kotel ha-ma'aravi* (Jerusalem: B. Gefner, 1992).

Praying for the Defenders of Our Faith

"on this front, Rabbi Mendl Gefner positioned himself as the military leader."[41] Using army terms, the grandson explained how Rabbi Gefner martialed the troops for a continuous attack against the enemy: "While people were walked around the streets looking for sandbags to block the windows of their house out of fear of the bombings, [Rabbi Gefner] would stand in the middle of the city ... and call with gusto [*hayil*]: "Psalms, gentlemen, Psalms alone will help us!"[42]

The message is clear: battles are won with prayers. The narrative continues in this vein with the sound of artillery fire competing with the sounds of prayer of "Rabbi Mendl Gefner and his troops" who repeatedly completed the entire book of Psalms, prayed, blew the *shofar*, and recited *selihot* and other supplications for a full one hundred days.[43] At the end of each prayer shift [*mishmeret*], Rabbi Mendl Gefner would add the aforementioned prayer.[44] The chapter concludes with victory over the Arab armies credited without hesitation to the Psalms and prayers.[45]

Rabbi Mendl Gefner's text was recalled some years later in the context of the 1973 Yom Kippur war. The war formally ended with a

---

41 Ibid, 620.

42 Ibid, 622. The Hebrew term *hayil* (translated here as gusto) is also a military term. Wrinkles appear in the narrative when some of those committed to reciting Psalms are injured or killed by bombs (ibid, 627-629)

43 Rabbi Baruch Gefner repeatedly referring to these hundred days, suggesting that this was not just a turn phrase. Alas, he does not spell out when these hundred days were and why specifically one hundred days.

44 Ibid, 622-627. The Hebrew term *mishmeret* (translated here as shift) is also used in the military. These prayers were printed in a pamphlet on 7 Adar I 5708, February 17, 1948: *Kuntras teshuva u-tefilla u-tsedaka* (Jerusalem: Chevrath Tehilim Kehal Hakodesh Shebyerushalaim, 1948). According to Rabbi Baruch Gefner, it was his grandfather who decided the order of prayers and printed the pamphlet.

45 Gefner, *Olamo shel hasid*, 2:630.

ceasefire agreement between Israel, Egypt, and Syria that came into effect on October 24, 1973. Alas, fighting continued and over 300 Israeli soldiers were held captive, most by Egypt, some by Syria, and a few by Lebanon.[46] It was in this context that Rabbi Gefner's text was re-printed on November 1, 1973, a week after the official end of the war.[47]

46 In the second half of November 1973 over 200 captive Israeli soldiers (including nine airmen who had been taken during the 1967-70 War of Attrition) were exchanged for some 8,300 Egyptian soldiers. Further exchanges with Syria and Lebanon occurred in the first week of June 1974.

47 One page notice dated "Thursday, of the portion 'and God blessed him' [Genesis 26:12; from the Torah reading of Parshat Lekh Lekha], [5]734"; that is, 6 Heshvan 5734 or November 1, 1973. The notice was printed on the letterhead of Chevrath Tehilim Kehal Hakodesh Shebyerushalaim [sic.]

The 1973 text was slightly different from the 1948 version, which was the version that the Vizhnitzer Rebbe reportedly recited. The most significant difference was invoking the names of more ancestors, including the Four Mothers:

> "May He who blessed our ancestors, Abraham, Isaac, and Jacob, Moses Aaron David and Solomon, Sarah Rebecca Rachel and Leah …"

Furthermore, the page included an important postscript:

> "The above version was approved by the *gaon* of Tchebin, may the memory of the righteous be a blessing, and the rabbi the *gaon* Rabbi Isser Zalman Meltzer [1870-1953], may the memory of the righteous be a blessing."

The "*gaon* of Tchebin" is a reference to Rabbi Dov Berish Weidenfeld (1881-1965), who served as the rabbi of Trzebinia, Poland from 1923 until the outbreak of the Second World War. Rabbis Meltzer and Weidenfeld were two of the most respected Talmudists in Jerusalem at the time, and their imprimatur was a strong endorsement. The circumstances of their approval, presumably in 1948, are not detailed.[48]

While the Vizhnitzer Rebbe's addition on that first Shabbat after the slaughter – October 14, 2023 – was widely reported, no such reports were forthcoming a week later on Shabbat, October 21, 2023. It seems that the addition was a one-time response to the gravity of the military situation and the enormity of the tragedy that had unfolded in the preceding days.

– the same organisation that printed the 1948 pamphlet of prayers (above, note 42). The page was reproduced in Gefner, *Olamo shel hasid*, 2:629.

48 Rabbi Baruch Gefner (*Olamo shel hasid*, 2:626) notes that the approval was given in 1948. It is not clear whether there is an independent source for that information, or whether it is inferred from the 1973 notice.

Immediately after the item became public, one talkback was sober in his assessment that this was not a watershed moment, even though the Vizhnitzer Rebbe deserved credit for his response:

> "I suspect that this was pulled out of the back of the drawer for use in the undeniably difficult matzav [situation] we are in. Using it in a regular basis could be misunderstood as an approval to join our brothers, i.e chayalim [soldiers] or army, in defending the house of Yisroel [Israel]. No mention of the Land of Israel, or the illegitimate State of Israel. Still, all respect is due the Rebbe for acknowledging that this is an unprecedented point in our history."[49]

Looking forward

Could it be that these initial responses and glimmers of respect and appreciation might herald a wider shift in the contemporary hasidic approach to service in the IDF? As the war continues, will hasidic masters instruct their follows to pray for soldiers defending the country? Will we see hasidim who rise and sleep under the blanket of the very freedom that the Israeli army provides for them, offer regular, public prayers for their safety? Or perhaps, they might even pick up a weapon and stand a post? Initial indicators are, alas, not promising, as the support and prayers seem to be idiosyncratic, fleeting, or private.

Time will tell.

---

49 The comment was posted on *Matzav.com* by someone identified only as Aaron.

Praying for the Defenders of Our Faith

Levi Cooper is an Orthodox Jewish teacher, author, and community leader who lives in Tzur Hadassah, Israel. He is a faculty member of the Pardes Institute for Jewish Studies in Jerusalem, where he teaches Talmud, Rambam, and Hasidism. Originally from Australia, Cooper lectures extensively on the topics of law and Halakha, Jewish spirituality and Hasidic thought. Since 1996, he has also served as a historian with Heritage Seminars.

A Parent's Greatest Pride

Pini Dunner

From a simple phone call requesting socks to a grand gesture of community support, an extraordinary humanitarian mission began in the wake of the tragic events of October 7th, sparked by our son Meir – a 21-year-old reserve sergeant in the Israeli military.

Soon after the war began, Meir reached out from his military base with a modest request for thick socks to withstand the cold nights. This appeal quickly transformed into a wave of generosity within our Beverly Hills community, evolving into a significant effort to support those serving on the front lines of the Israel-Hamas conflict.

It started with a couple of boxes of socks and thermal underwear, but it soon grew to hundreds of boxes, filled with a variety of supplies including protein bars, phone chargers, flashlights, toiletries, and a variety of tactical gear. The community's effort also extended to providing much needed supplies for families displaced by the war, providing them with essentials like baby food and diapers.

This collective act of kindness culminated in an extraordinary gesture – the donation of a cargo plane to swiftly deliver these care packages. This initiative, all of which originated from Meir's simple call to his parents to help him stay warm, became a significant humanitarian project, showcasing the power of empathy and action. It highlights the Jewish community's deep-rooted love for Israel and for its people.

As parents, the pride we feel for our soldier son Meir is beyond words. Every day, he demonstrates remarkable bravery and commitment, standing on the front lines to protect and serve Israel. Meir's dedication is not just a testament to his own strength and character, but it also resonates with our deepest convictions as a family. Israel is the essence of who we are, and our son serving in the Israeli military, defending the Jewish homeland from the evils of terrorism, truly reflects the values we instilled in him.

For us, Meir's IDF service is much more than just a job he needs to do; it is a courageous act of devotion to his country and to the Jewish people. Meir's willingness to face challenging conditions, and his unwavering spirit in the face of adversity, fill us with overwhelming admiration. In these trying times, his actions reinforce our faith in the next generation – showing us that there is great hope for the future.

Am Yisrael Chai!

Rabbi Pini Dunner is the Senior Rabbi at Beverly Hills Synagogue.

From Yoav's Legacy to Today's Frontlines: Israel's Resolve and the Prayer that Binds Us

Atara Eis

IN COMPOSING THE PRAYER FOR the welfare of IDF soldiers, Rav Shlomo Goren referenced Yoav's battle cry in Bnei Yisrael's war against Ammon: "Let us be strong and resolute for our people and the land of our God; the Lord will act as He sees fit" (II Samuel 10:12). As Israel responds to the unfathomable Simchat Torah massacre with its just war to eradicate Hamas and to free the hostages taken to Gaza, these words orient our posture toward the current crisis, making this prayer a critical part of our spiritual preparation.

David sends a delegation to do *hesed*, to comfort King Hanun of Ammon after his father's death. David's kind deed presumed a positive relationship with Hanun, despite the prohibition to develop

Praying for the Defenders of Our Faith

any relationship with Ammonites (see Deuteronomy 23:7, Bamidbar Rabba 14:3, 21:5). David's gesture of comforting the Ammonite King Hanun was misinterpreted as a spying mission. This resulted in a two-pronged conflict: Hanun not only humiliated David's delegation but also instigated a two-front war against Bnei Yisrael, drawing other adversaries into the battle. What was meant as a goodwill gesture became a glaring misinterpretation, echoing modern-day distortions and "fake news." A familiar tale, isn't it?

During his battle preparations, Yoav exhibits steadfast courage. He assumes the most challenging position and instructs his soldiers to stand firm, not just for their people, but also for the cities of their God. This valor, now witnessed firsthand by modern Jews, is something that remained distant to us during millennia in the diaspora. However, in spite of Yoav's meticulous strategy, he recognizes that ultimately, "God will do what He deems best in His eyes."

The Homefront significantly bolsters the morale of soldiers on the Front. Rav Goren's prayer is a poignant reminder that God's guidance and will underpin both our triumphs and setbacks. Invoking the words "Arei Elokeinu" imparts a profound lesson of faith, especially relevant and critical in our current times. After enduring a year of intense disagreements spanning left to right across the Israeli political spectrum, there is now a unified stance on the legitimacy of the justness of this war in the face of such pure evil. Nobody questions whether we should take Hamas at their word regarding their willingness to achieve their evil charter, given the tiniest breach in our defense system. My sense from the powerful videos of our soldiers on the Front is that they have zero questions on their purpose right now; they understand that this is the greatest existential threat to Israel and the Jewish people in more than fifty years.

For those in the Diaspora, particularly those navigating the challenges of the media's war and on college campuses, this prayer offers crucial solace and strength. Confronted with an overwhelming wave of Hamas propaganda, it's deeply concerning to witness individuals from "Western, Educated, Industrialized, Rich, Democratic" backgrounds seemingly endorsing or justifying Hamas' egregious actions. The tale of Yoav reminds us not to yield to calls for a premature ceasefire, emphasizing the need to see this milhemet mitzvah through: the total dismantling of Hamas. Our path is clear, guided by the moral imperative to act for the sake of the Cities of our God. History has shown us the repercussions of our goodwill being misconstrued, often with perilous consequences. In these dire times, we fervently pray, with unwavering faith, for God's intervention against our adversaries.

Rabbanit Atara Eis serves as the Associate Dean of International Affairs at Nishmat – The Jeanie Schottenstein Center for Advanced Torah Study for Women in Jerusalem, Israel, and Director of Nishmat's Miriam Glaubach Center for U.S. Yoatzot Halacha.

The Great Story

Emuna Elon

As I lie down and rise during these horrific days, when it is so difficult to sleep and so difficult to wake, I remind myself that my personal story is merely a modest fragment within the great story of the Jewish people. Not that I've ever forgotten this: the great story of the Jewish people sits with me at home, and walks with me on my way, and has surrounded me since I first recognized my own existence. I've always understood that I'm an integral part of it, but during these trying days, I hold onto this awareness like a lifeline.

Every human being understands that they don't begin and end with their physical body, and that their life is not just the hyphen that will be engraved on their tombstone between the dates of their birth and their death. It seems that this understanding, whether consciously or unconsciously, is what motivates most people to honor their parents, have children, acquire friends, and contribute to society. Humans are defined by the ability to "speak," that is, to communicate with others and connect with the collective. And manifestations of patriotic loyalty are common, of course, in every nation and language.

But it seems that only among the Jewish people, participation in the great story is the default choice for every individual. Throughout history, many Jews have tried to escape this default choice – and time and time again a Magen David (or a Swastika) was painted on the wall of their home and the great story informed them: I am here. Many Israelis have tried to relate to the State of Israel as a "regular" country, like any other country, and time and time again, the great story proves to them that it's not possible: the State of the Jews – the one with a flag inspired by a tallit (prayer shawl) – is a state whose very existence is a miracle, and this miracle does not operate according to the conventional norms applied anywhere else.

When I pray, during these dreadful days, for the wellbeing of the Israel Defense Forces, my heart goes out to my own combat soldiers: my son, and five of my adorable grandchildren. I am so proud of the IDF and so proud of my beloved and courageous family members – delicate young souls, lovers of beauty and music, lovers of God and humanity – who embarked on their mission and went to fight for our people with their heads held high and sparkling eyes. But there is a weight that these days often bear on me, a feeling of distress that overpowers me and gnaws at my pride and my faith. And it's as if this current distress has been fused and melted, within me, into all the distress I had experienced here in previous wars and terror attacks, all the distress experienced right now by Jews in Israel and around the world and all the distress that had been the inheritance of our nation throughout history.

I think about the twelve-year-old Jerusalem girl I was in June 1967, when I ran home from school in the morning that the Six-Day War broke out. I ran fast, because in the previous weeks the Arab countries had threatened to destroy Israel and throw all its citizens into the sea. As I passed through King George Street, the Jordanian shelling from

Praying for the Defenders of Our Faith

the direction of the Old City began, and shells whizzed and exploded around me until I reached my parents' house and took shelter.

Israel survived that war and the wars that followed, the process of The Return to Zion continues and before our very eyes the exiles are being gathered and the dry bones are reviving. But what would I say to that girl right now? What could I tell her in October-November 2023 and what can I tell my grandchildren, if not the great story that even now – like in June 1967, like always – all our individual events are nothing but short chapters in its endless narrative?

We didn't choose to be the chosen people. It's much more comfortable – certainly much more "progressive" and "up to date" – to be like everyone else. Wearing a T-shirt with a "liberal" slogan printed on it is much more pleasant than donning the striped robe and having everyone else wanting to throw you into the pit. But the one who blessed our fathers and our mothers chose us from all the nations and chose all of us, and each one of us, to be the main characters in the great story. These days, filled with fear and bravery, force us, through pain we never imagined we could endure, to acknowledge that. The one who blessed our fathers and our mothers goes with us to fight for us against our enemies to save us, and we say, Amen.

Emuna Elon is a renowned novelist, journalist, and women's rights advocate. Raised in a family of prominent rabbis and scholars, she has a background spanning Jerusalem and New York.

Prayer, Strength, and Confronting Evil

Rachelle Sprecher Fraenkel

IT SEEMS THAT THE PRAYER for the peace of the IDF soldiers is an expansion of the relevant paragraph in the prayer for the peace of the state: "Strengthen the hands of the defenders of our Holy Land, and bestow upon them the deliverance of our God. Crown them with the crown of victory, grant peace in the land, and everlasting joy to its inhabitants." This is the fundamental ethos of the IDF, and it's a source of pride to us: Ours is a Defense Force, and more than any other military culture, its legacy is a profound aspiration for peace.

But it seems that the war of Shemini Atzeret/Simchat Torah, was a watershed moment. amidst the immense pain, loss, and mourning, a unique form of heartbreak is felt: the revelation (or re-revelation) that people are capable of losing their human image. That man could so horrifically betray the image of God in which he was created. This is not about horrors described in history books; it's happening here and now; these are our neighbors.

Praying for the Defenders of Our Faith

Following the abduction and murder of our son Naftali and his two friends Eyal and Gilad in 2014, I had a profound conversation with Rabbi Adin Steinsaltz. He offered an insightful interpretation of a familiar prayer, shedding light on its deeper theological implications. We often recite "oseh shalom u'voreh et hakol" in our prayers, translated as "He who makes peace and creates everything." However, Rabbi Steinsaltz pointed out that this is a more palatable version of a more challenging verse from Isaiah: "Oseh Shalom u'Voreh Ra, Ani Hashem Oseh Kol Elleh," which means "He who makes peace and creates evil." This original verse confronts us with a stark and complex view of the divine role in the balance of peace and evil in the world, a perspective especially poignant in the aftermath of personal tragedy.

In the world created by the Almighty, there exists both peace and evil. During that time, Rabbi Adin elaborated on this concept in a lesson centered around the verse from Psalms 97:10: "O lovers of the Lord, hate evil." He explained that those who love the Lord must acknowledge the full reality of the Almighty, including the presence of evil. While we often try to shield children from evil, he noted, we cannot remain in a childlike state of ignorance forever.

Decades ago, in *Kol Dodi Dofek*, Rav Joseph B. Soloveitchik expressed: "Judaism, with its realistic approach to man…understood that evil cannot be blurred or camouflaged and that any attempt to downplay the extent of the contradiction and fragmentation to be found in reality will neither endow man with tranquility nor enable him to grasp the existential mystery. Evil is an undeniable fact. There is evil, there is suffering, there are hellish torments in this world." But lovers of the Lord, their duty and mission are to despise wickedness. Those who love the Lord abhor evil.

In the Talmud Berakhot 7a, Rabbi Yochanan and Rabbi Meir have a disagreement about how Moshe's third request, "Please show me your ways," was answered. The request was to understand the divine conduct in the world, why do righteous people suffer and how to fathom the problem of evil? Rabbi Yochanan says that Moshe's request was granted, suggesting that Moshe lacked a broad perspective, but when the information in his possession was completed, he was able to comprehend. On the other hand, Rabbi Meir disagrees and implies God tells Moshe such knowledge is beyond his capacity. Essentially saying "You are flesh and blood, it's beyond your league."

In a profound reflection on the enduring question of theodicy, Rabbi Lord Jonathan Sacks offered a compelling perspective in one of his final interviews, a month before his passing in November 2020. Addressing the troubling and often asked question, "Why do bad things happen to good people?" Rabbi Sacks shared a thought-provoking meditation that delves into the nature of divine intent and human understanding: "God does not want us to understand why bad things happen to good people. Because if we ever understood, we would be forced to accept that bad things happen to good people. And God does not want us to accept those bad things. He wants us to not to understand so that we will fight against the bad and the injustices of this world. And that is why there is no answer to that question because God has arranged that we shall never have an answer to it."

That response from Rabbi Sacks has given me much strength, and continues to do so.

In human history, there are many cases of nations who were strong and wicked. There are some examples of nations who were weak and righteous. The State of Israel is one of the rare experiments in creating a people who strive to be strong and righteous. It's usually expressed in the effort to maintain a society that embodies justice, compassion, and mercy. In this historic point in time, the ability to be strong and righteous is expressed in the need to use strength to fight evil, to use the power of light to overcome darkness. This is not the natural state of mind for the righteous. The righteous usually prefer kindness and compassion. But there are times when tenderness is the refuge of the wicked.

Nowadays defense is not enough. The failure of defense exposed the face of evil and cast a mission on the army that prides itself on being a defense force that is Herculean – or better yet – biblical (Eicha 3:66) in its dimensions: "You shall pursue them with fury, and you shall obliterate them from under the heavens of the Lord."

Rabbanit Rachelle Sprecher Fraenkel, a renowned Yoetzet Halacha and educator, directs Matan's Advanced Halakha Program and teaches Talmud and Halakha at Nishmat.

Prayer and Redemption: The Commandment to Pray in Turbulent Times

David Fuchs

I N *Berakhot* 42a, the Talmud says:

> "Rabbi Ḥiyya bar Ashi said, Rav said: There are three that immediately follow each other: Immediately following placing hands [on the head of a sacrifice], is slaughter; immediately following redemption, is prayer; immediately following washing of the hands [*Mayim Aḥaronim*, before *Birkat haMazon*], is the blessing."

The *Talmud Yerushalmi, Berakhot* 1:1, quotes Rabbi Abba bar Yirmiya, who cited the sources for all three pairs:

> "Immediately following placing hands, is slaughter – "He shall lay a hand upon the head of the burnt offering… The bull shall be slaughtered" (Lev. 1:4-5). Immediately following washing of the hands, is the blessing – "Lift your hands toward the sanctuary, and bless the Lord" (Ps. 134:2). Immediately following redemption, is prayer – "May the words of my mouth [and the meditations of my heart be acceptable before You, Lord, my Rock and Saviour" (Psalms 19:15). What is this followed by? " May the Lord answer you in time of trouble, the name of Jacob's God keep you safe" (ibid. 20:2)."

A noticeable difference between the three pairs is that while in the first two, the order of the verses is the same as that of the *halakha* which is derived from the juxtaposition, in the third the order is reversed: we learn that the Silent Prayer (the *Amida*) follows the blessing of Redemption after the Shema, from the fact that a verse about prayer is followed by a Psalm which pleads for being saved from an attack.

This reversal indicates that prayer has a two-fold meaning: it is both a reaction to the past, and a petition for the future. However, prayer is also an obligation laid upon us – the Sages have instituted a framework of three daily prayers, and according to some opinions, this follows a positive commandment by the Torah to pray. Prayer does look towards both the past and the future – but it is grounded in the present.

In the following, I will attempt to delineate the contours of this obligation, following the opinions of several of the *Rishonim* (early authorities). None of the ideas presented here will be original or novel – but some readers may not know them all, and at least, it might serve as a reminder to those who know them already.

Prayer as a Duty

In the preface to *Mishne Torah*, the Rambam enumerated the 613 Torah commandments, in what amounts to a summary of his *Sefer HaMitzvot* (Book of Commandments). The first four commandments present the fundaments of Jewish faith: belief in the existence of God and his unity, and love and awe of Him. The fifth commandment is:

> "To pray to Him, as it is said (Ex. 23:25): "You shall serve the Lord your God" – "service" means prayer."[1]

The Rambam enlarged upon this in the opening halakha of *Hilkhot Tefilla* (the Laws of Prayer):

> "It is a positive commandment to pray every day, as it is said (Ex. 23:25): 'You shall serve the Lord your God'; the Sages learned by oral tradition that this "service" is prayer.[2] And it is said (Deut. 11:13): 'and to serve Him with all your heart' – the Sages said (*Taanit* 2a): "Which is the service that is in the heart? It is prayer'… but the Torah specified no designated time for prayer."

According to the Rambam, the manner of service required from us is daily prayer. However, his opinion was not accepted across the board, and in fact, it contradicts the Talmud in *Berakhot* 21a:

> "The recitation of Shema and Birkat HaMazon (Grace after Meals) are by Torah law, while prayer is a rabbinic decree."

---

1   *Sifrei, Ekev* 42.

2   The method of inferring this meaning was explained by the Ramban, which will be quoted below.

One might reconcile Rambam's ruling with the statement made by the Talmud if we contextualize it as referring to the immediacy of the mitzvot: the Torah designates specific times for the recitation of *Shema*, while *Birkat HaMazon* follows immediately upon the conclusion of a meal; while the time, and indeed manner, of prayer was only determined by the Sages, and the Torah's enjoinment may be fulfilled by postponing prayer to a later time, as long as it is once a day.

However, the *Tosafot* accepted the simple reading of the Talmud, explaining by it the dispute in *Berakhot* 20b whether "הרהור כדיבור דמי" (contemplation is tantamount to speech), and consequently whether one who is impure may fulfill the commandment of reading *Shema* voicelessly, or must he utter the words with his lips (21a q.v. והרי):

> "It should be said that according to Ravina, this works out well: since contemplation is tantamount to speech, he [the impure person] may be required to recite *Shema* and *Birkat HaMazon*, which are *deOraita*, more than prayer that is [only] *deRabanan* [and therefore, the obligation might be voided in case of impurity]; but according to Rav Ḥisda, according to whom contemplation is considered as nothing – In what way is *Shema* different from prayer?"

Rav Joseph B. Soloveitchik apparently agreed that this is the most straightforward reading of the Talmud; but rather than this leading him to rejecting the Rambam's approach, he called attention to its novelty, lauding it as no less than revolutionary:

> "When our Master [Rambam] said that prayer is mandated by the Torah, and identified it with the service

of the heart – he had redeemed both love and awe,³ indeed our entire religious experience, from muteness. A voice was granted them.

The lover may now express his longing; the awe-stricken – his fear and trembling; the humble and lowly – his helplessness; the misguided – his bewilderment; and the joyful – his spirit's hymn. All this within the framework of prayer.

The service within the heart found its grounding in the actual, matter-of-fact world. Life's experience and the prayer are the two poles, within which the great service of God takes place."⁴

Prayer as a Grace

It is unclear though, why defining prayer as a *Mitzva mideOraita* is what redeems "our entire religious experience, from muteness"? Why would a *Mitzva mideRabanan* not suffice? It might be that the Rav is pointing to a different point – a direct commandment may be needed to enable praying. In *Berakhot* 61a, the Talmud warns:

> "Rav Huna said that Rav said in the name of Rabbi Meir: One's words should always be few before the Holy One, Blessed be He, as it is stated: 'Be not rash with your mouth, and let not your heart be hasty to utter a word

---

3   As we pointed out above, the enjoinments to love God and to be in awe of Him are the two which immediately precede the duty to pray, according to the Rambam's ordering of the 613 Commandments. To the best of our knowledge, the Rav hasn't made that point.

4   'Reflections on prayer', 6; in *Halakhic Man* (p. 241 in the Hebrew edition).

before God; for God is in heaven, and you upon earth; therefore, let your words be few' (Ecclesiastes 5:1)."

Indeed, any time we approach God in prayer, we preface it by a supplicatory verse – even before *Shaharit* [the morning prayer], despite the requirement of juxtaposing redemption and prayer![5] The Talmud was aware of this difficulty, and resolved it (*Berakhot* 4b):

> "How can one juxtapose [redemption to prayer] in the morning? Didn't Rabbi Yohanan say: Before, one recites: "Lord, open my lips [that my mouth may declare Your glory]" (Psalms 51:17)? Afterward, one recites: "May the words of my mouth [and the meditations of my heart be acceptable before You, Lord, my Rock and Saviour" (Psalms 19:15)! Rather, there, since the Sages instituted that one must recite: " Lord, open my lips…" it is considered as an extended prayer."

This was explained in the siddur attributed to Rabbi Shlomo ben Shimshon of Germaisa:[6]

> "This is the beginning of the prayer, and therefore not an interruption between redemption and prayer."

Before beginning the first of the nineteen blessings, we say this verse, imploring God to enable, and perhaps to allow, us to approach Him in prayer.[7] This might be perceived as a preparation, composing ourselves

---

5 i.e. the Morning Prayer should be preceded without interruption by the invoking of God's redemption of Israel from the bondage of Egypt.

6 Worms. Rabbi Shlomo was a colleague of Rashi, and was among the martyrs murdered in the 1096 Worms massacre during the First Crusade.

7 See Rav Ezra Bick, *Shemoneh Esrei: Exploring the Fundamentals of Faith through the Amida Prayer*, who devoted a whole chapter to the role and significance of this verse (p. 11-20 in the Hebrew edition).

and directing our thoughts towards Him,[8] but it is also a reaction to the recalling of God's might and majesty,[9] immediately before it. In this context, how dare a mere human open his lips and try to declare His glory?

Rav Soloveitchik probably understood that such prayer is only possible after being granted a special Grace by God. Prayer is not just an obligation laid upon us, to present ourselves once a day, parading with the "thousands upon thousands served Him, Myriads upon myriads attended Him" (Daniel 7:10) – but also a special permission to speak: one loves, is awe-stricken, feels humble, misguided or joyful; all these he would pour forth if he only could. The Rambam asserts that he not only may, but verily he must, approach the Lord in prayer.

No matter what feelings of fear, anxiety, pity, rage, loathing, distrust or even fundamental doubt we might have – we are permitted, and even enjoined, to express them in prayer before God, asking for soothing, relief and guidance.

---

8   See *Shulhan Arukh, Orah Hayim* 98:1.

9   See *Mekhilta deRabbi Yishmael, BeShalah (massekhta deShira)*, 3:
    "This is my God" (Ex. 15:2) – Rabbi Eliezer says: from where do you learn, that a designated maidservant (שפחה חרופה) saw on the Sea what neither Isaiah or Ezekiel ever saw? As it is said (Hosea 12:11): "[For I granted many visions], and spoke parables through the prophets", and it is written (Ez. 1:1): "the heavens opened, and I saw visions of God".
    Unlike the "visions and parables" which other prophets received, or even the "visions of God" which Ezekiel saw, which are open to interpretation and even misunderstanding – the Midrash asserts:
    When the Holy One, Blessed be He, revealed Himself on the Sea – none needed to ask: who is the King? As soon as the saw Him, they recognized Him, and said all: "This is my God, and I will enshrine Him" (Ex. 15:2).

Praying for the Defenders of Our Faith

Prayer as Service

As a matter of fact, the idea that prayer was a positive commandment by the Torah, was not original to the Rambam. Rav Saadia Gaon opened his אזהרות (admonitions), a *piyyut* in which he enumerated the 613 commandments,[10] with the line:

את ד' א-להיך תירא, ואותו תעבוד בתפילה; ערב ובקר יחדוהו, באות וטוטפת לתהילה.

Fear the Lord your God, and serve him with prayer; evening and morning proclaim His unity, glorifying Him with a sign and an emblem (the *Tefillin*)

According to Rav Saadia, prayer is intertwined with the recitation of the *Shema*, and the wearing of *Tefillin*: Fear of God prompts us to serve Him, by wearing a servant's insignia and declaring absolute fealty to Him, as well as by worship, and waiting upon Him for our daily bread. If so, it seems obvious that the requirement is for a daily service, as per the Rambam's ruling. Rav Soloveitchik's view of prayer as an opportunity

---

10   It might be debated whether Rav Saadia considered all of the commandments he mentioned as binding *mideOraita*. After all, other Geonic lists (most famously, the *Halakhot Gedolot*) included Rabbinic decrees as well. In their understanding, the Talmud's calculation (*Makkot* 23b-24a):

Rabbi Simlai taught: 613 mitzvot were given to Moses: 365 prohibitions corresponding to the number of days in the solar year, and 248 positive mitzvot corresponding to a person's limbs. Rav Hamnuna said: What verse is the source? "Moses commanded to us the Torah, an inheritance [of the congregation of Jacob]" (Deuteronomy 33:4). Torah, in its numerical value [*gimatriyya*], is 611; "I am [the Lord your God]" and: "You shall have no [other gods]" (Ex. 20:2, 3), we heard from the mouth of the Almighty.

- is not necessarily an exact and authoritative count (as the Rambam considered it), but rather a mnemonic. In any case, the Rambam did not attack Rav Saadia on this front like he did the *Halakhot Gedolot*; and as he must have known the אזהרות, he probably accepted this to be Rav Saadia's opinion.

to express before God our innermost emotions, hopes and fears, adds a second dimension to the simple devotion required.

However, the basis of prayer is in standing in attention before the Lord, to serve Him and to hear His message (this connects prayer to study of the Torah, a point which will be further developed below). And even in periods of confusion, grief or even despair – we must still come before Him, even if it seems mechanical, and a pure formality; we may hopefully be granted an "opening of the lips", to speak and no longer be dumb.[11]

Prayer as a Plea

The Ramban offered a completely different interpretation of the commandment:

> "The essential meaning of the verse 'and to serve Him with all your heart' is a command that all our service to the Blessed God will be done with all our heart, i.e. with clear intention and complete devotion to His Name… And when the Sages taught in the *Sifrei*: 'You shall serve the Lord your God' – 'service' means study; alternatively, it means prayer[12] – is merely a support (אסמכתא); alternatively, it might mean that an essential part of service is studying the Torah, and praying to Him in times of trouble, and turn our eyes and hearts to Him alone, 'as the eyes of slaves follow their master's hand' (Ps. 123:2)."

---

11 See Ezekiel 24:15-27.

12 *Sifrei, Ekev* 42.

Ramban suggests two different viewpoints, which are at odds with those of Rav Saadia and the Rambam. At first, he simply rejects their reading of the Midrash, suggesting it is no more than an allusion, adjuring us to pray and study with all our heart as part of our service to God. The second suggestion accepts that study and prayer are the centerpiece of this very service.

The study of Torah is clearly a *Mitzva deOraita*; is the same true of prayer? The *Kesef Mishne*[13] tends to think it is not; however, the consensus among later authorities is that Ramban ultimately followed his second suggestion, and considered prayer to be a *Mitzva deOraita* in certain times: when a person, a community, or the whole of Israel[14] are in dire need, we must turn our eyes and hearts to God and to Him alone.[15] It is a great privilege to be able to plead before the King; but beyond the opportunity, it is an obligation laid upon us, to place our hopes and trust in Him.

This by no means negates or even belittles the need for our own human exertions, to strive for deliverance by the best of the means we have; but this must be accompanied by a passionate *cri de cœur*, to Him with whom our true salvation lies.

---

13 On *Hilkot Tefilla* 1:1.

14 See the prayer of Solomon at the consecration of the Temple, I Kings ch. 8.

15 This is clearly the opinion of the Meiri, in his *Essay on Repentance* (חיבור התשובה): "This is in order to awaken us in the times of our trouble, so that we will observe and understand that all has comes to pass by the hand of the Lord, and this is the meaning of "you shall sound [short blasts on the trumpets, that you may be remembered before the Lord your God]" i.e. prayer (*Shever Gaon*, 1:1)."

David Fuchs

Prayer as Awareness

Another understanding of the essence of prayer might be gleaned from the list of commandments in the introduction to the *Halakhot Gedolot*. As a rule, *Behag* (בעל הלכות גדולות, as the author is commonly known) does not refrain from including *Mitzvot deRabanan* in his count; however, he does not mention the *mitzva* of prayer at all in this section. However, *mitzva* 25 by his count is "one hundred blessings every day," following *Menaḥot* 43b:

> "It is taught, Rabbi Meir would say: A person is obligated to recite one hundred blessings every day, as it is said: 'And now, Israel, what [*ma*; Rabbi Meir interprets the verse as though it said *me'a* – one hundred] does the Lord your God require of you' (Deuteronomy 10:12)."

Behag considered this to be one of the commandments, and it was put in high relief by the pupils of Rashi, in their compilations of his halakhic rulings – *Sefer haPardes*, *Sefer haOre*, and the Vitry *Maḥzor* all open with Rabbi Meir's declaration. To achieve this count, we recite three times a day the nineteen blessings of the Silent Prayer.

Even if one accepts Rabbi Meir's opinion as binding, this is clearly a Rabbinic enactment, based on the implication of a misreading of the verse. However, despite its far-fetched sourcing, this opinion states a broader vision, which encompasses all our daily experience: we must live in a state of constant awareness of the benevolent presence of the Lord, and react to everything that happens by addressing Him, thanking and blessing Him for His creation. Rabbi Yehuda Amital has often quoted the very last Midrash in *Midrash Tanḥuma* (*veZot haBrakha*, 7):

> "…these are the righteous, who even after death are called 'living'… but the wicked, even during life are called 'dead'… for he sees the sun rise, and yet does not say the

blessing 'who forms light'; [sees the sun] set, and does not say the blessing 'who brings on evenings', eats and drinks but does not say the blessing on them. But the righteous say a blessing on every thing the eat, drink, see or hear."

This might even explain why the Talmud did not consider prayer to be a positive commandment: we need to attain a consciousness, which perceives in the whole world surrounding us the marks and traces of its Creator. This combines the daily routine which Rav Saadia described, with Ramban's urging to be attentive and direct all our pleas and questions towards God. This is not a positive commandment in and of itself, but rather an all-encompassing way of life.[16]

It is not a formal obligation laid upon us, but the natural expectation from us to truly live – to which the Sages only added the formal framework, by defining and phrasing the actual prayers to be said. But prayer is essentially our spontaneous reaction to the world, one of joy and wonder, as Rav Kook stated in siddur *Olat Re'iyah*:[17]

התפילה היא לנו, ולעולם כולו, הכרח גמור, וגם התענוג היותר כשר שבתענוגים.

[Prayer is for us, and for the whole world, both an absolute necessity and the most appropriate of all joys][18]

16 Compare to Principle four, in Rambam's *Book of Commandments*: The fourth Principle is that one should not count *mitzvot* that include the whole Torah.

17 In his preface, התפילה המתמדת של הנשמה [the constant prayer of the soul], 6.

18 Rav Amital discussed Rav Kook's words at length here: ואני תפילה | תורת הר עציון (etzion.org.il) (in Hebrew).
    The Rav connected Rav Kook's idea with the interpretation of prayer as a special grace granted by God to Man, and enlarged upon the importance of

Conclusion

The debate among the *Rishonim* as to whether by praying we follow a positive commandment revolves upon the different way of understanding the essence of prayer: addressing the Lord is a multi-faceted experience, and intuitively it should come from a person's own volition and not be simply a discharge of an externally-imposed duty. While the Sages prompted us by instituting a framework for the times and content of prayers, did they do so in response to a Torah mandate?

The Rambam defined a daily prayer as a positive commandment, indeed the very first in his enumeration of mitzvot which involves concrete action, rather than faith or emotional response. This despite the Talmud stating explicitly that prayer is a Rabbinic enactment. It is probable that the Rambam understood the Talmud as referring to the specifics of prayer, which were indeed instituted by the Sages.

Rav Soloveitchik saw the Rambam's understanding as no less than revolutionary, a redemption of Man's state in this world, by enabling him to approach God. in his reading, prayer is a special grace granted to us.

However, the source the Rambam cited points at a different view, which was already hinted at by Rav Saadia Gaon – that of prayer as a service, offered to God. We were created His glory, and we owe Him service, which is rendered by a daily act of worship.

The Rambam's approach is usually contrasted to an approach suggested by the Ramban: that daily prayer is indeed only a Rabbinic enactment, but the Torah directs us to call upon God in times of need. The essence of prayer is in accepting Him as our Rock and Savior, which is shown in times of need. Normal, tranquil times do not call for such a response.

> a natural, honest prayer – something which would be the natural result of the awareness mentioned above.

Praying for the Defenders of Our Faith

A fourth viewpoint might be deduced from *Behag*, who did not mention prayer in itself as a positive *mitzva* at all – but included it in a *mitzva* to say one hundred blessings a day. This *mitzva*, which was greatly emphasized by the pupils of Rashi, implies that prayer is the primary expression of a larger obligation: the requirement to be constantly aware of God's presence in the world, and to react to all we experience by addressing Him. This may not be a formal commandment, one of the 613, but is rather a call for a heightened consciousness.

It is astonishing that the pupils of Rashi, living in the harrowing, turbulent time of the Crusades, where able to persevere in their ability to live this way; by doing so, they preserved the *Mesora* of Torah and *Mitzvot*, and handed it down to us.

May we be able, if not to emulate their faith, at least to be inspired by it, and find a glimmer of hope in these turbulent times.

Rabbi David Fuchs, a renowned scholar and editor, studied at Yeshivat Har Etzion from 1994 to 2007 and received his rabbinic ordination from the Chief Rabbinate of Israel. Between 2007 and 2020, he led the Hebrew liturgical projects department at Koren Publishers in Jerusalem, where he was instrumental in editing the New Koren siddurim and machzorim in both Hebrew and English. He resides in Alon Shvut, Israel, with his family. Presently, Rabbi Fuchs contributes to scholarly projects with Dicta, the Steinsaltz Center, Mada Toratecha Institute at the Sulamot organization, and at the Jerusalem College of Technology.

Prayers in Jerusalem Amidst the War of Independence: A Protective Booklet for IDF Soldiers

Uziel Fuchs

During the 1948 War of Independence, Jerusalem faced a siege and various parts of the city were bombarded by Arab forces. The atmosphere was thick with fear. My grandfather, Rabbi Mordechai Attia (1895-1978), navigated this crisis by drawing inspiration from the Talmud in Ta'anit 15a. They carried the Torah scrolls into the city square and there, they offered their prayers. He, along with Rabbi David Laniado (1899-1969), who was the rabbi of one of the synagogues in his neighborhood, led the reading from the Book of Isaiah, Chapters 34-

Prayers in Jerusalem Amidst the War of Independence

35. These chapters vividly depict God's war with the nations and Israel's triumphant return to its Land, transforming the barren desert into a flourishing oasis, and they concluded with the verse: "And the redeemed of the Lord shall return, and come with singing unto Zion…." In Isaiah 35:3, the evocative verse, "Strengthen the weak hands, and make firm the feeble knees," resonates deeply, highlighting the profound intent of these assemblies: to embolden and fortify the spirits of Jerusalem's residents.[1]

In that year, 1948, amidst the war, Rabbi Attia published a small booklet titled "Beit Yosef." The booklet comprises verses, teachings from the sages, as well as words of encouragement from the author. This compact edition was designed to fit into the pockets of soldiers, and its cover proclaimed it to be a "charm and protection for IDF soldiers."

Among other things, he calls on the soldiers to unite around faith, and he wrote:

חוברת זו היא קול קורא אל חיילינו, אחינו הגבורים העומדים במערכה וממשיבים מלחמה שערה ומפליאים את מכותם באוייב ומשלחים בהם מהומה, אימה ופחד. אל גיבורים אלה מופנים דברינו אנא אחרים יקרים! דעו נא את גודל אחריות השעה המוטלת על כולנו, שעת הרת עולם זו תובעת ודורשת מאתנו להתלכד סביב דגלנו הנאמן מדור דור שסמלו הוא האחדות, האמונה בצורה ישראל, ובשיבה אל המקור בכל המובנים... ולא הועילו המים הזדונים של מלכויות הרשע להעבירנו מעל דתינו ולהכחידנו מעל פני האדמה; כן עכשיו שומה עלינו, ביתר עז ומרץ, להתאזר יותר ויותר בדברים אלה שבזכותם גם אנו נכניע את כל הקמים עלינו, ואף אם יהיו רבים נצח ננצחם בעזרת צור ישראל.

---

1   For several memoir stories about the reading of these chapters in Jerusalem and their impact on the residents, see *Ateret Mordechai: The Life and Times of the Kabbalist Rabbi Mordechai Attia*, ed. Eliyahu Attia (Jerusalem: Yeshivat ha-Hayyim ve-ha-Shalom, 2015), 66-69 (Hebrew).

This booklet serves as a clarion call to our soldiers, our heroic brethren who stand unwaveringly on the frontlines. They emerge from harrowing battles, striking fear into the hearts of their adversaries, causing chaos, terror, and dread. To these champions, our words are directed: Beloved brothers, recognize the gravity of the responsibility that this pivotal hour places upon us all. This epoch-making moment beckons and mandates us to rally around our steadfast flag, an emblem of unity, faith in the essence of Israel, and a return to our roots in every sense… The malevolent waters of wicked kingdoms failed to divert us from our faith or to annihilate us from the face of the earth; so now, it rests upon us, with increased strength and fervor, to arm ourselves more and more with these principles. By their merit, we too will subdue all who rise against us, and even if they are numerous, we will eternally triumph over them with the help of the Rock of Israel.

His gatherings, his booklet, and his prayers were meant to encourage the fighters, to instill faith in them, to unite the fighters around eternal values, and to prevent fear.

Dr. Uziel Fuchs is the Head of the Department of Oral Law at Herzog College, and on the Faculty in the Department of Talmud, Bar-Ilan University. He is the author of *The Geonic Talmud: The Attitude of Babylonian Geonim to the Text of the Babylonian Talmud* (2017).

Prayers in Jerusalem Amidst the War of Independence

The Siren-Interrupted Meditation on the IDF Soldiers' Prayer

Tova Ganzel

THE CENTRALITY OF THE PRAYER for the well-being of the IDF soldiers lies primarily in its ability to prompt each of us in prayerful reflection to pause and dedicate our thoughts to our very own soldiers, those guardians standing vigil over our homeland. Yet, it's crucial to understand that this is merely the initial layer of its profound significance.

The profound strength of this prayer is rooted in its ability to act as a unifying force, bridging Jewish communities both within Israel and across the diaspora, week after week. This prayer seamlessly integrates elements from a liturgy that has been recited for countless generations, with scarcely a shift in its essence, into our present narrative, particularly since the establishment of the State of Israel. There's a raw honesty in its simplicity, where each of us finds a reflection of our soul in every word. It's not just a prayer of a singular community, but one that resonates in

Praying for the Defenders of Our Faith

Jewish hearts worldwide, momentarily aligning Jewish contemplations globally with the heartbeat of Israel. Whether voiced in harmony by the congregation and cantor, whispered or pronounced, cried out or sung, there's a moment where, with the contributions of both men and women, all voices converge in a collective call to the Divine. Its significance is underscored by its inclusion in the prayer books of Orthodox communities, a testament to its resilience. It has gracefully navigated the challenges of modernity, overcoming reservations tied to Reform tendencies, ensuring that the time-honored Prayer liturgy retains its integrity, as it has for generations upon generations.

In the midst of the present conflict's darkness, we've had the opportunity to introspect, to re-encounter the essence that shapes our identity. This war, with its tumult and trials, has rejuvenated the spirit of our people. It's a conflict where the bonds and resilience of every segment of our society are palpably manifested at the forefront. I envision a day, not too distant, where our prayer for the welfare of the IDF soldiers will undergo a subtle refinement, a nuance of inclusivity. We'll not only speak of our male soldiers but also honor our valiant female warriors. We'll remember not just our male captives but also recognize our captive women. Beyond merely acknowledging our security forces, we'll salute the vigilant emergency response teams that stand ready.

The piercing siren on Shmini Atzeret/Simchat Torah in Jerusalem abruptly interrupted our prayers. We returned home from our synagogue service, having missed out on praying for our soldiers' welfare and without reciting the rain prayer for the year 5784. This omission weighs on my heart, yet it also serves as a catalyst for reflection and growth. As a collective, we seek to restore the spirit, tapping into the depths of our capacities, united in our concerns for all who stand as our nation's protective shield. They are the ones who ensure the continuity of our existence in a Jewish state in the Land of Israel. From this backdrop, we embarked this year on the study of the Book of Genesis, recognizing that even creation has room for improvement. The echoes of those unsung prayers reverberate, spanning the vast expanse from one end of the world to the other.

Dr. Tova Ganzel is a Senior Lecturer at the Multidisciplinary Department of Jewish Studies and is the Head of Cramim, the Jewish Studies Honors Program at Bar-Ilan University.

Bringing Hadar to Eretz Tzvi

Simha Goldin

THE BEAUTIFUL MELODY OF 'ERETZ Tzvi' was Hadar's constant companion from the day he enlisted until his tragic death. He carried the spirit of the song into battle. Operation Jonathan became a defining chapter of his journey. Yoni's remains were eventually brought home. Today, we must continue to uphold this legacy and return Hadar and other Israeli hostages home.

I am often asked why Hadar held such a deep affection for the song 'Eretz Tzvi'.

On the day Hadar embarked on his military journey, he made 'Eretz Tzvi' his personal anthem. 'Eretz Tzvi' was there with him throughout his journey—during his days as a new recruit, a soldier, a commander, a rookie officer, and finally, as a commander of fellow soldiers.

Why did he connect so profoundly with this particular song, you might ask? Sadly, I find myself speaking on behalf of my son, who was taken from us at the tender age of 23, shortly before his scheduled wedding. His body was tragically seized and remains in the hands of the very adversaries he courageously faced, akin to the hero in the song.

While I cannot engage in a conversation with him, I feel compelled to answer on his behalf. Through smiles, through gestures, through reenactments, he demonstrated a deep affection for the lyrics of Talma Alyagon, the melody crafted by Dubi Zeltzer, and the profound message that it carried. Every verse held a special meaning for him, and he found new inspiration in each line. His enthusiasm was evident as he would often exclaim, "Did you hear that? 'Eretz Tzvi'—did you hear that? 'Bound in good and bad'—did you hear that?"

Hadar firmly believed in the responsibility of the Jewish army to safeguard every Jew in distress worldwide. This conviction was a guiding principle that influenced every aspect of his life. At its core, it embodied an aspiration for rebirth and the embrace of a new spirit, one that symbolized the resilience of the Jewish people as they stood on their ancestral soil, confronting the global challenges before them.

Operation Jonathan served as the defining marker along this path. The IDF forces operating in Uganda became the trailblazers, and the commander who made the ultimate sacrifice embodied unwavering determination. Hadar viewed their heroic actions as a model for his own generation, and this sentiment found its expression in the powerful and evocative 'Eretz Tzvi' song. The song encapsulated the ideals deeply rooted in Israeli culture and fortified by biblical connections and the challenges faced by the nation.

Praying for the Defenders of Our Faith

בַּחֲצִי הַלַּיְלָה הֵם קָמוּ	"At midnight, they arose,
וְהִכּוּ בִּקְצֵה הָעוֹלָם	And struck at the end of the world,
כִּבְנֵי רֶשֶׁף חָשׁוּ	Like the sons of Reshef, they felt the silence,
הִרְחִיקוּ עוֹף	They drove away the bird,
לְהָשִׁיב אֶת כְּבוֹד הָאָדָם	To restore the honor of humanity."

The biblical hero Samson, who, in the dead of night, seized the city gates of Gaza, which had been firmly closed against him. With unparalleled strength, he hoisted the heavy gate, its two sturdy doorposts, and even the crossbar onto his shoulders, carrying this colossal burden all the way from Gaza to Hebron.

"At the stroke of midnight, they ventured forth to the ends of the Earth, the edge of the world itself." According to our sources, the "end of the world" is the most remote and formidable place, a realm even beyond the enigmatic Sambatyon River, deemed impassable and forever isolating the ten lost tribes. Just like the sons of Reshef, they encountered profound silence, akin to a rearranged verse from Genesis. As Job's Book reminds us, "When does a person born of a woman" shall the "sons of Reshef raise birds." The sons of Reshef symbolize a stark departure from the ordinary human condition.

However, as Talma Alyagon aptly notes, the messengers of the Jewish people, the IDF, alter this equation. When the Israel Defense Forces step in to protect and rescue fellow Jews, they transform into formidable forces much like the sons of Reshef.

"Shall we persist in labor? Most certainly, as we are not serpents, and we shall never forsake our own. Our mission is to restore the dignity of humanity, to bring back the honor of mankind to their rightful home, the 'Eretz Tzvi.'"

אֶל אֶרֶץ צְבִי	"To the 'Eretz Tzvi,'
אֶל דְּבַשׁ שְׂדוֹתֶיהָ	To its honeyed fields,
אֶל הַכַּרְמֶל וְהַמִּדְבָּר	To the Carmel and the desert,
אֶל עַם אֲשֶׁר לֹא יֶחֱשֶׁה	To a people that will not be heedless,
שְׁאֵת בָּנָיו לֹא יַפְקִיר לְזָר,	That will not abandon its sons to strangers,
אֶל אֶרֶץ צְבִי שֶׁבְּהָרֶיהָ	To the 'Eretz Tzvi,' with its mountains,
פּוֹעֶמֶת עִיר מָדוֹר לְדוֹר	Once a city, from generation to generation,
אֶל אֶרֶץ אֵם לְטַבּוּרָהּ	To the motherland to whose navel,
קְשׁוּרִים בָּנֶיהָ בְּטוֹב וּבְרַע.	Bound to her sons in good and bad."

Towards the 'Eretz Tzvi,' we find that the profound poem and our nation's leadership erred in participating in a ceremony marking the 40th anniversary of the Raid of Entebbe. Entebbe no longer holds significance for us; we've moved far beyond the confines of Uganda. The ceremony should have transpired at Tzvi's airport, right at the very spot where the sons of Reshef once brought captives and the wounded, overlooking the bountiful fields, the majestic Carmel, the vast desert,

Praying for the Defenders of Our Faith

the city nestled amidst the hills, and the venerable Tavor, to which its devoted sons remain bound through both adversity and prosperity. This verse, cherished deeply by Hadar, remains etched in our hearts: "To the Land, if it's Tavor, bound are its sons in good or bad."

Lately, my thoughts have been consumed by this verse. It speaks of the Land of the Mother, where her sons stand united with Tavor, steadfast through thick and thin. I think of the courageous among us, ready to embark on any journey, to lend their unwavering support in every conceivable way. These are individuals who grasp the essence of the Land of the Mother, who comprehend the enduring bonds that unite her sons through all circumstances.

Nearly fifty years ago, this promise was made – a vow that even in the face of danger, in times of strength, in the unwavering resolve of a nation, we shall not be indifferent, nor shall we abandon our sons to the care of strangers. Today, the good people who choose to stand beside us ask themselves the same question – to affirm that they are truly the offspring of the Land of the Mother, bound to us through Tavor, and unwaveringly present in both good and bad times. For we are a nation that does not forsake its sons to the care of strangers.

בַּחֲצִי הַלַּיְלָה עוֹבֶרֶת	"At midnight, a hot wind passes
בִּשְׂדוֹתֵינוּ רוּחַ שָׁרָב	In our fields, the parched land
עֲרָבָה אִלֶּמֶת תַּרְכִּין אָז רֹאשׁ	Silent, mute, then the head bends
עַל אֲשֶׁר עִם שַׁחַר לֹא שָׁב	For the one who did not return with dawn"

And indeed, the price exacted was profound, intertwined with solace. Much like the words of the prophet Isaiah, Talma Alyagon etched her lament upon the pathways of her memory, for with the dawn, he did not return. In the return to Zion, to the 'Eretz Tzvi', the prophet proclaims a path and a way. The desert blossoms, waters and streams gush forth in this arid land, and glory is restored to Carmel. Feeble hands find strength, and faltering knees regain their fortitude. Indeed, on that very night, the mute barren land bowed its head, for he did not return with the dawn. Our tears mingled with the chamomiles in the field, and joy and sorrow wove themselves together in the tapestry of our day.

The sons of Reshef, who, despite being human, did not forsake their brethren to the care of strangers. They brought back the sons of Reshef who did not return with the dawn. The night transformed into day, the sons of Reshef descended, and the honor of humanity was restored, bringing Yoni back to his homeland – to the 'Eretz Tzvi'.

Hadar, my son, readied himself in the desert to defend the 'Eretz Tzvi' and protect the dignity of humanity. He stood ready to traverse to the ends of the Earth for this noble cause. As the IDF assembled on the border of Gaza, he sketched an invitation to his own wedding on his military equipment lists. A frame adorned with tree branches, birds, and pomegranates, beginning to ripen at the end of Tamuz. Inside the frame, he inscribed the profound words of the great poet Harav Kook, harmonizing them with the verses of the composer Talma Alyagon. It was the whispered essence of existence in the 'Eretz Tzvi'.

He went to battle, and for nine years now, his body has been held by the enemy. From their vantage point, Yoni and Hadar observe us, waiting for our choices and actions. They watch over their families, their fellow soldiers, their people. The question looms: will we choose to act as the sons of Reshef, or as mere mortals bound by toil? They bear witness to a nation that does not remain indifferent, a nation that does not abandon its sons to strangers. Shall we continue to leave our sons in the hands of others?

Yoni's family gathered his letters, creating a written testimony that illuminates a life of giving and excellence. But within the Goldin family, this is not sufficient. In Hadar's case, the sacred duty of the sons of Reshef remains unfulfilled, and before our very eyes, this sacred duty crumbles and disintegrates, taking with it the Carmel, the desert, the city, the field of chamomiles, the fabric of his day, and, above all, the honor of humanity, both in life and in death. The honor of mankind, embodied by Yoni and Hadar, is our collective honor—a reflection of who we were and, more importantly, who we aspire to be.

Dr. Simha Goldin is the Director of the Goldstein-Goren Diaspora Research Center at Tel Aviv University. He is the father of Lt. Hadar Goldin, a fallen IDF soldier who has been held captive by Hamas in Gaza since 2014. Along with his wife, Dr Leah Goldin, Simha has led the efforts to return his son along with the other fallen soldier and civilians that have been held hostage in Gaza for the last nine years.

[An earlier version of this article appeared in Yediot Aharonot, Sabbath Supplement (7 June 2016)]

God's Presence and Israel's Wars

Alon Goshen-Gottstein

As we think of soldiers and Israel – both Biblical and contemporary – going to war, we are invited to reflect on the very nature of war making. Who is it that is fighting? The question might seem trivial. After all, it is the army, human soldiers, who are going to war. This is, indeed the framework within which the prayer for the soldiers of the IDF is recited. Yet, the biblical prooftext that is offered at the conclusion of the prayer invites us to reconsider what might seem obvious at first sight. "For the Lord your God goes with you, to fight on your behalf with your enemies, in order to save you (perhaps: in order to make you victorious)" (Deut. 20:4). The prayer itself speaks of God protecting and saving our soldiers and ניגפים לפניהם (please use here whatever translation you are using for the prayer). The prayer, then, seems to suggest that it is the soldiers who are doing the fighting and that God, in turn, helps them by bringing about the requested outcome. But something more is said in the prooftext. It is not simply that God helps or supports the soldiers. In fact, it is God who goes with them and it is *he* who fights.

The question of agency is a broader issue of religious thought and finds expression in a range of fields, extending in Hassidic thought even to the question of true agency in performance of mitzvot and good deeds. It is particularly pronounced when it comes to Israel's warmaking. Consider Psalms 44, which says: "It was not by their sword that they took the land, their arm did not give them victory, but Your right hand, Your arm, and Your goodwill, for You favored them" (Psalms 44:4). Of course, one might still consider this as an expression of God's *support* at time of war. The continuation of the Psalm could justify such an understanding. "Through You we gore our foes; by Your name we trample our adversaries. I do not trust in my bow; it is not my sword that gives me victory; You give us victory over our foes; You thwart those who hate us" (Psalms 44:6-8).

Weapons of war are used, suggesting soldiers are conducting the war. Yet true salvation comes from God. In other words, God is the true warrior. More than God accompanying us in times of war, the image is one of God as the actual warrior, an ancient image first articulated in *shirat hayam* in Ex. 15.

There is a still more radical expression of dependence on God in times of war. If one reviews the formula "fear not", one realizes that there are two different uses of this formula in the Bible. The first is found, for example, in the just cited context of the battle at the reed sea, that turns out to be God's own battle. "But Moses said to the people, "Have no fear! Stand by, and witness the deliverance which the Lord will work for you today; for the Egyptians whom you see today you will never see again" (Exodus 14:13).

Here is the extreme case. God engages in battle alone. Israel is actually to remain silent, or inactive. Contrast this with where "the Lord said to Moses, 'Do not fear him, for I give him and all his troops and his land into your hand. You shall do to him as you did to Sihon king of the Amorites who dwelt in Heshbon'" (Numbers 21:34). Moses is going to war and the same formula is used, suggesting reliance on God, while engaging in battle. Thus, God's presence in the battlefield is not simply a promise. It is a means of shaping a religious attitude. Moses goes to battle with a sense of trust and fearlessness, because of God's promise. (Actually, the verse does not speak of God's actual presence in the battlefield, in which case this verse might present yet another model).

What does all this say to us with reference to the prayer for the IDF soldiers? I believe the tension between the text of the prayer and the cited prooftext is an important tension. It raises the question of agency, in other words who is doing the fighting, and what types of synergy are possible between human and divine action. This is, as the verses suggest, not a theoretical question. Its consequences are trust – "do not fear" – and the attitude with which one goes to war.

The framers of the prayer, and whoever is attentive to it (for me, this is the first time I have payed any serious attention to it), sought protection and success for soldiers at battle. Yet, the vision of success and the religious vision of battle-making may be much more far reaching as both the prooftext and other biblical sources suggest. Going to war, like any other activity, especially religious activity, is an activity to discover who is the true actor. We are invited to offer the prayer not only as a means of protecting and supporting our soldiers. The vulnerability and precarity that war places us in is an invitation to deeper trust. This trust is based on the recognition that the ultimate actor at war is God himself. This is not an easy vision to realize, neither for those whose hands engage in war, nor for those who support them in prayer. But this is precisely the point of potential spiritual growth that war invites us to. It is also the point of transformation and surrender to divine will at war.

May we, then, offer this prayer as an opportunity for the wider community and for the soldiers at war to deepen in faith and to enter the journey of discovery in which human and divine actors blend and come together to achieve God's purposes.

Rabbi Dr. Alon Goshen-Gottstein is the founder and director of the Elijah Interfaith Institute since 1997. His work bridges the theological and academic dimension with a variety of practical initiatives, especially involving world religious leadership.

Let Dead Words Become Prayers Again

Ithamar Gruenwald

IN BIBLICAL TERMS, THE LIFE of the People of Israel swings between blessings and curses, between life and death (Deuteronomy 19, 19). Initially, these entities indicated moral principles or guidelines, but history has transformed them into existential realities. The choices of life and blessing is the obligatory setting, for both individuals and communities, thus contextualizing the opposites, death and curses, in a wider context than their physical manifestations.

Indeed, death means the annihilation of everything that matters, of order, meaning, hope, and, in our case, the use of words in a humane context. We are approaching November 9 and 10, which in 1938 signaled the events of the Kristallnacht. Deplorably, the distance from the smashing of Jewish property in Germany to rendering words as shredded pieces of glass is alarmingly short. As long as prayers evolve as blessings and life enhancing factors, curses should not get a hearing. But what kind of prayers can currently be said to break through the walls of the dark dungeons of speechlessness? As the Psalmist says, "I keep a muzzle on my mouth, as long as the wicked are in my presence" (39, 2).

The Prophet Jeremiah (chapter 9) addresses this issue, advocating the parlance of wailing and its dire sonic overtones:

> *The sound of wailing is heard from Zion:*
>
> *'How ruined we are!*
>
> *How great is our shame!*
>
> *We had to leave our land*
>
> *because our houses were in ruins.*
>
> *Now, you women, hear the word of the LORD;*
>
> *open your ears to the words of his mouth.*
>
> *Teach your daughters how to wail;*
>
> *teach one another a lament.*
>
> *Death has climbed in through our windows*
>
> *and has entered our fortresses;*
>
> *it has removed the children from the streets*
>
> *and the young men from the public squares.*

Indeed, there can be no better way of addressing the current situation than do the words of the Prophet Jeremiah. The eruption of inhuman cruelty which marks the events of October 7 has incurred loss and bereavement on a scale that escapes comprehension. It has left many and worthy speechless.

Amidst the current state of horror, marked by physical disaster, agony, and pain, what can empower words to regain their praying potentials? Furthermore, how can supplicatory words, when somehow pulled together, overcome the dirty manifestations of an utterly moral eclipse, of blatant forms of speech, unleashed in so-called enlightened argumentations followed by organized demonstrations? The collapse of a sober scale of human values, of basic forms of moral judgement and justice, as shown by and in certain academically affiliated circles and their morally blind followers, should clearly signal the horrific dangers of antisemite eruptions embedded in these brutal attempts to divest words of their innocent meaning and human values. In face of this all, who will now come and teach our daughters "how to wail"?

We should be very explicit and clear over this: The sword of deathly events that cut through the south of the Land of Israel defies every notion of moral, humanely inspired, dignity. These were moments of a total eclipse of human light, and there is nothing that can hold words back from gravitating into the destructive powers of a black hole. Words have indeed become redundant in the face of the horrific reality.

And this, too, has to be clear: In face of the dire events, ruthlessly crushing evil is the only gateway to hope, to faith, and to the ultimate regaining for words their true meaning, The normally shocking notion of the inevitable form of justice implied by "evil for evil", has under the circumstances become the unfortunate equation that aims at sustaining peace and clear reasoning. The utter destruction of the powers of evil should help words regain their power to convey justice, to communicate trust, and to enact their potential of redressing pain and agony.

After they have mentally ceased to be the gateways to prayers of supplication, to any kind of human dignity, words may find rescue in the prophecy of Ezekiel, whose words so shockingly address the scenes we have seen: "Can these bones live?" And this is what God is expected to say to these bones: "I will make breath enter you, and you will come to life." May God help us see this prophecy become true.

My words come from Yerushalayim, the city whose name signifies, in Hebrew, wholeness and peace. They call for meetings in moments of prayer for the physical and mental wholeness of those who in the words of Isaiah 5, 20 expose those who "call evil good and good evil, put darkness for light and light for darkness." The well-being of those who enlisted in this war is in the interest of everyone who puts his trust in a humanity that is given its uninhibited chance to show its true face. Hopefully, this war will regain for life its natural prospects that are worth living and for words their true meaning.

Currently, the shattering words of the poet who wrote The Lamentations of Jeremiah prevail, "For death has come up into our windows" (9:20). However, the yearning of many around the world – Jews, Christians, and Muslims, alike – to pray is still there. This is a prayer I wrote several years ago:

> *Bless us, our Father,*
>
> *All of us as one,*
>
> *With grace and love,*
>
> *With courage and righteousness,*
>
> *With fraternal compassion and purity of heart;*
>
> *So that we who pray --*
>
> *Shall no longer pray one against the other;*
>
> *And that all the sons of Abraham,*
>
> *Shall see the virtues of the light*
>
> *That makes peace shine --*
>
> *Bright, truthful, and full withits life-giving fruits.*

Ithamar Gruenwald is Professor Emeritus at Tel-Aviv University, where he dedicated his academic career to Jewish and religious studies. He lives in Jerusalem, Israel.

Not Heeding the Slippery Watershed Between Hostile Words and Their Catastrophic Consequences

Ithamar Gruenwald

THE WATERSHED THAT DIVIDES BETWEEN hostile words and the ruthless manifestation of evil is thin and alarmingly fragile. When control and restraint are carelessly dismissed, which currently is the case among critics of Israel at war, this is what, in the words of William Shakespeare, happens. They "Cry havoc and let slip the dogs of war" (*Julius Caesar* Act 3. Scene 1, line 91). In other words, today's critics of war should be alerted to the fact that wars of survival have a wider range of implications than to those who are fighting them. In their distorted

Praying for the Defenders of Our Faith

vision, these critics of the war expose themselves to the risks of becoming the victims of the war of tomorrow.

No moment should be lost in sounding an alarm call warning against the misjudgment of the concerns aroused by the current torrential flooding of vocal outcries. Clearly, one should carefully abide by the rules of civilized free speech. However, the right for free speech should not be misused to undermine its risky potentials of streaming unwarranted and shattering consequences.

In the wake of the dark days of World War One, the Irish-born poet William Butler Yeats wrote these lines:

> …Things fall apart; the centre cannot hold;
>
> Mere anarchy is loosed upon the world;
>
> The blood-dimmed tide is loosed, and everywhere
>
> The ceremony of innocence is drowned.
>
> The best lack all conviction, while the worst
>
> Are full of passionate intensity.
>
> (*The Second Coming*, 1919)

There can be no better words than these to describe the present situation in what has become the Holy Land first to Jews, and then to Christians and Moslems. In the words of the Spanish Mystic, St. John of the Cross, we have reached the "dark night of the soul." It characterizes events in several Academic institutions in the United States, but not only there. Deplorably, it has become obscenely fashionable among "enlightened circles" to engage in misinformed and prejudiced forms of discourse. They cannot but stream blind hate and even unrestrained violence against Jewish students and faculty, their mental and physical wellbeing.

Much of this is contextualized in the terms of traditional outbreaks of antisemitism. However, there are good reasons to see in this kind of contextualization a rather simplified characterization of the events. When asked to do so, many of those who surf on the tides of misinformation will fail to give a coherent and sustainable account of what really is at stake. In fact, there is very little that can specifically motivate their arguments and actions, beyond their fascination with states of chaos.

Their protestations resonate with a blindfolded illusion that anarchy carries with it liberating potentials. No reasonable and sustainable forms of argumentation are taken into consideration. In their view, the State of Israel, and its war against Hamas, can provide only vulnerable forms of justification. However, misjudging apparent injustice can lead nowhere but to what in the words of the poet amounts to "Mere anarchy is loosed upon the world."

This message is written on November 9, which in 1938 marked the events of the Kristallnacht. In that night, Jews in Germany and Austria realized how dark the night can be when blind hate followed by unrestrained and uncontrolled riots is allowed to spread. The smashing of windows and the burning of synagogues was a preamble to much graver events culminating in the physical extermination of millions of Jews.

No mistake can be made about this: There is very little that can effectively stop words from being turned into acts of violence. The current hate discourse can easily spill over and become a pogrom-cult in which the physical wellbeing and the cultural assets of Jew are seriously endangered.

It is with horror that one observes the shrinking distance between the ruining of Jewish property in Germany and Austria to the current events in the south of the country. Words, like glass, can easily be smashed and become broken pieces with dangerously sharp cutting edges. Indeed, hate creates all kinds of shortcuts, notably those between verbal discourse and violent action. In other words, addressing the issue in terms of "this cannot and should not happen on our premises" may retrieve some sympathy but does not look evil straight in the eye.

In short, the learned distinction maintained between words and deeds fails in face of the energies in which violence is hatching. Thus, the denunciation of antisemitism falls short of what really is at stake, namely, an educational failure which for a long time has tolerated misbehavior as expressions of juvenile zeal. This failure highlights the condemning words of the poet, "Things fall apart, the centre cannot hold". The bond created in several American campuses between Students for Justice in Palestine and the Jewish Voice for Peace may be viewed by many as an unholy marriage between, what tin reality is, a misdirected form of reasoning and expression.

Notwithstanding these comments, this must be said loud and clearly: In face of all this, there are laudable humanitarian voices that deserve a decent hearing and proper attention. They should not be allowed to be submerged in hate-oriented statements and demonstrations. They are the treasure houses in which the aims of this war are crafted: the release of the captives, the annihilation of terror, and the restoration of peaceful existence.

With is in mind, let us all that we can to give life to the consoling words of the Prophet Amos (chapter 9):

> The time is surely coming, says the Lord,
>
> when the one who plows shall catch up with the one who reaps
>
> and the treader of the grapes with the one who sows the seed;
>
> the mountains shall drip sweet wine;
>
> and all the hills shall flow with it.

Ithamar Gruenwald

I will restore the fortunes of my people Israel,

And they shall rebuild the ruined cities and inhabit them;

And they shall plant vineyards and drink their wine,

And they shall make gardens and eat their fruit.

I will plant them upon their land,

And they shall never again be plucked up

out of the land that I have given them,

Says the Lord your God.

Ithamar Gruenwald is Professor Emeritus at Tel-Aviv University, where he dedicated his academic career to Jewish and religious studies. He lives in Jerusalem, Israel.

Mi Sheberach for Shluchei Mitzvah?

Neriah Guttel

THE INQUIRER POSES A QUESTION: Is there a necessity or a proper occasion for a Mi Sheberach—on behalf of those who are prepared to lay down their lives for their loyalty to God, to the Jewish People, and to the Land of Israel? These individuals demonstrate a commitment to self-sacrifice that is unparalleled. Does such profound dedication necessitate or warrant the recital of a Mi Sheberach prayer for them?

My answer, in unequivocal terms, is: Yes, indeed.

The Sages indeed taught us that 'agents of a mitzvah are not harmed' (Pesahim 8b), yet in parallel, they also taught us that this is not said in a situation where 'harm is frequent,' and they added and said that generally 'we do not rely on miracles' (Pesahim 64b), and certainly in a place where harm is common – we do not rely on miracles (Kiddushin 39b).

This principle is frequently adopted by us: "I will lift up my eyes to the mountains – to the parents" (Bereishit Rabbah 68:2), and "From the elders I gain understanding" (Tehillim 119:100). And so, go forth and learn from our forefathers and foremothers, who did not rely on miracles, and often took the spindle of strategy into their hands. Abraham and Isaac said of their wives that they were "sisters", due to danger; our father Jacob prepared to meet Esau with a gift, with prayer, and did not rule out the alternative of war; the prophet Samuel wondered how to fulfill God's command to anoint David – "How can I go? If Saul hears it, he will kill me" (I Samuel 16:2), and it is written about this in the book "Duties of the Heart" (*Shaar ha-Bitahon*, Part 4, Chapter 1):

> "And it is not considered a deficiency in his trust in God, but that zeal in this matter is praiseworthy... And if this were a shortcoming in his trust, the answer to him would be 'I cause death and I bring to life'... as He said to Moses... 'Who has made man's mouth etc.'. And if Samuel, despite his complete righteousness, did not take lightly to enter into even a minor cause among the causes of danger, even though he would have entered it by the command of the Creator... all the more so it was disgraceful for others... And as we said in matters of life and death, so we say in the obligation to seek causes of health, food, clothing, and shelter – with the clarification of his faith that the causes are not helpful in this at all, except by the decree of the Creator."

And so it is also in the conduct of wars, as explained by Nahmanides in his commentary on the sending of the spies by Moses at the request of the people of Israel (Bamidbar 13:2):

> "Israel said, as is the way of all who come to fight in a foreign land, that they send scouts ahead to know the ways and the approaches to the cities, and upon their return, the strategists go at the head of the army

to direct them on the paths, as the matter that is said (Shoftim 1:24) "Show us now the entrance of the city," and they will give them counsel on which city to fight first and from which side it will be convenient to conquer the land, and so they said explicitly (Devarim 1:22) "And bring us word again by what way we should ascend, and into which cities we shall come," meaning the cities that we shall enter first and from there we shall go throughout all the land. And this is a fitting strategy for all conquerors of lands, and so did Moses himself as it is said (Bamidbar 21:32) "And Moses sent to spy out Jazer," and so with Joshua the son of Nun (Joshua 2:1) "Two men to spy secretly," and therefore it was good in the eyes of Moses. For the Torah does not rely on miracles, but rather commands those who are fighting to arm themselves, to be vigilant, and to prepare ambushes, as the scripture came in the war of Ai (Joshua 8:2) which was according to the word of God, among many other sources.

This is what the Maimonides wrote in his famous letter to the sages of Montpellier (*Iggerot HaRambam*, vol. 2, ed. Rabbi Yitzchak Shilat, page 280) that the kingdom of Israel was lost and our sanctuary was destroyed and we have reached until today because they did not engage in the study of warfare and ways of conquest.

And if there exists a fixed human obligation to exert effort, then all the more so is this effort required in times of danger, when the Satan prosecutes (Jerusalem Talmud, Shabbat 2:6), and especially in times of danger – people are taken without justice (Babylonian Talmud, Hagigah 4b-5a). On these matters, Rabbi Abraham Isaac Kook wrote:

"The individuals who are killed unjustly in the revolution of the flood of the war participate in the concept, 'the death of the righteous atones,' they rise above in the root of life and the essence of their lives brings a general quality of good and blessing to the overall structure of the world in all its values and senses. Afterward, at the cessation of the war, the world is renewed in a new spirit and the feet of Messiah are revealed even more. According to the extent of the war in quantity and quality – so increases the expectation of the feet of Messiah through it."[1]

It is therefore obligatory to make every human effort, and it is the same law for all spiritual effort, and to bless and hope that:

מי שברך אבותינו – הוא יברך את חיילי צבא ההגנה לישראל, ונאמר אמן.

"He who blessed our fathers – may He bless the soldiers of the Israel Defense Forces, and let us say Amen."

Rabbi Prof. Neriah Guttel, a distinguished Israeli rabbi and scholar, serves as the head of the research department at Mercaz Torah v'Medina in Nitzan and is a community rabbi at the Redlich Synagogue in the Givat Shaul neighborhood of Jerusalem. His research has significantly influenced both religious and academic circles. He has taught at various academic institutions and contributed to publications on Halakhic and Zionist thought. Rabbi Guttel is a senior member of a dedicated team in the IDF Military Rabbinate, tirelessly involved in the sensitive and critical task of identifying victims from the October 7, 2023, massacre.

---

1 *Orot ha-Milhamah*, 1 (Hebrew), translation from *Rav Kook's Orot*, trans. Bezalel Naor (Jerusalem: Maggid, 2022), 131.

A Voice of a Proud and Concerned Father: A Letter from Rav Aharon Lichtenstein to Soldiers in War

Aviad Hacohen

THE SECOND LEBANON WAR BEGAN on the 16th of Tammuz 5766 (July 12, 2006). Amidst the conflict, many students and graduates of Yeshivat Har Etzion, including Rav Shai Lichtenstein, son of Dr. Tovah and Rav Aharon Lichtenstein, and his friends Aviad Friedman, Meir Ben-Shahar, Eli Sizel, Yair Cohen, Shamir Landau, Moshe Shpeter, Yochai Stern, and Gabi Porten, were mobilized by Emergency Order ("Order 8") to join the IDF's operations deep within Lebanon. The intensity of the war made it nearly impossible for these soldiers to maintain regular contact with their families, limited mostly to infrequent and brief phone calls.

As the war neared its end, Aviad Friedman (hereafter: Aviad), was called back to Israel and attended the funeral of his cousin, Lt. Col. Gilad Sussman, a Shin Bet member and reserve Paratroopers Brigade soldier who was killed in action on the 15th of Av, 5766 (August 9, 2006). The funeral, held in Kfar Saba, stretched late into the night. Afterwards, Aviad traveled to Neve Daniel in Gush Etzion, and considered a late visit to Shai Lichtenstein's parents to relay Shai's wellbeing. Despite the late hour, he decided to proceed, reaching their home in Alon Shvut after midnight. Dr. Tovah, opening the door to Aviad's unexpected visit, was comforted by the news of her son and quickly called for Rav Aharon. The ensuing conversation, both heartfelt and brief, led to Rav Aharon entrusting Aviad with two letters – one for Shai and another for his unit.

Aviad, scheduled to return to Lebanon early the next morning, suggested taking the letters immediately to avoid delays. Rav Aharon quickly wrote the two letters and handed them to Aviad. He then expressed a concern: "How can one letter reach so many soldiers from our group? Maybe I should make copies at the yeshiva office." Seeing an opportunity to help, Aviad proposed taking the letters himself and making the copies en-route to Lebanon. Appreciating the gesture, Rav Aharon offered Aviad a blessing for a safe return. He shared that since the war's onset, particularly during the 'bein hazmanim' intercession break, he had committed "to intensify his studies."

On Friday morning of Shabbat Parashat Eikev, Aviad journeyed northward to rejoin his unit in Lebanon for the concluding phase of the war. The letters from Rav Aharon, photocopied and distributed by Aviad, reached his fellow soldiers, and provided a morale boost while sparking considerable excitement.

Three days later, on Monday morning, the IDF forces began their withdrawal back to Israel. They left Lebanon and went to Meron to pray the morning prayer at the tomb of Rabbi Shimon bar Yochai. In a poignant moment, each soldier recited the Gomel blessing of gratitude and the atmosphere was further uplifted as they joined in singing Tov LeHodot Lashem, from (Psalms 92:1-2), singing: "It is good to praise the Lord and sing praises to your name, Most High: Proclaiming your kindness in the morning and your faithfulness at night."

The next day, one of their friends at Yeshivat Har Etzion had his wedding. Rav Aharon Lichtenstein officiated the ceremony, and at its conclusion, he approached each of the soldiers who returned from Lebanon, embraced them warmly, and blessed them with emotion.

This letter is being published in full for the first time, including an English translation, with the exception of a few indecipherable words, thanks to the generosity of Aviad Friedman. We also extend our gratitude to Rabbi Mosheh Lichtenstein, Rosh Yeshiva of Yeshivat Har Etzion, and Rabbi Dov Karoll for their invaluable assistance.

– Aviad Hacohen (trans. and ed. Menachem Butler)

[2006 photo: Rav Aharon Lichtenstein visits his students from Yeshivat Har Etzion, including his son Rav Shai Lichtenstein, serving in the IDF in Northern Israel. This image is shared with the permission of the Lichtenstein family.]

ב"ה, עש"ק לסדר למען ירבו ימיכם וימי בניכם[1]

לכבוד
חברי ש.י. לנשק, לשלֵם

איינני יודע בדיוק כיצד ולמי למעֵן שורות אלו. חלק מהקבוצה - בעיקר אלו שלמ-
דו בישיבת הר עציון- אני מכיר, וחלק, לא. עם כמה, אתם שהייתי בבית מדרשנו,
נשמרו קשרים לאורך שנים, ועם חלק, לא. לכמה, שמי מוכר, ולכמה, לא. ובכן,
אכתוב כמה שורות לכלל היחידה, ולסיום, איחד כמה שורות לקבוצה מסוימת.
בעוד כמה שבועות נקרא: "כי תצא מחנה על אויביך ונשמרת מכל דבר רע"[2].
העיר רש"י: "שהשטן מקטרג בשעת הסכנה" (כלומר, ולפיכך, דווקא אז יש צורך
בזהירות יתירה). אך לא רק השטן מתעורר בשעת הסכנה ולא רק קיטרוגו מת-
להם. מתעוררת, לא פחות, אהבה מתוך דאגה, ודאגה מתוך אהבה.

התקשרות והתחברות, זיקה קיומית ולכידות אישית וחברתית. בראש ובראשונה,
כמובן, בין השותפים לברית הגורל והיעוד כאחד, החשופים לסיכונים יחד והחו-
תרים למשימה יחד.

אך גם, ברמה שניה, בין חברת העורף – בעיקר, משפחות וחברים, אך לא רק הם –
אשר בשליחותם אתם פועלים ולמענם אתם מקריבים. אולי הדבר מובן מאליו אך
משנתגלגלה לפתחי אפשרות להביע את המובן, לא הרפיתי ממנה. ובכן, לא רק
גיבוי ועידוד אלא אהבה ורעות שלוחים אליכם מלב עוקב ודואג, מחובר ומקושר.

ומלב גאה. התרגשתי עד כדי דמעות ממש בשמעי מה ביקשתם שיובא לכם מן
העורף, כשנמסר שנפתחה צוהר להעברת חבילה: דפים מאמצע מסכת יומא שח-
סרים לכם זה כמה ימים, על מנת שתוכלו, ככל שיתאפשר, להדביק את הפיגור
ולהתקדם הלאה[3].

איזו גבורה ואיזו עדות להגשמת "עשה תורתך קבע" – לא בהכרח במובן הכמותי,
אלא האיכותי: תורה שאיננה נלמדת בהזדמנות אלא שהחיבור אליה והמחויבות
כלפיה מוטבעת לעומק בלומד ובאישיותו.

---

1 דברים יא, כא. המכתב נכתב ביום ששי, עש"ק עקב, י"ז במנחם אב תשס"ו, 11.8.2006.

2 דברים כג, י.

3 באותם ימים נלמדה מסכת יומא במסגרת הדף היומי. בני החבורה שיצאה לקרב, לקחו אתם צילום של מספר דפים מן המסכת, אך לא שיעורו מתחילה שיצטרכו לשהות זמן כה ממושך בלבנון.

Praying for the Defenders of Our Faith

ממש "תורה שלמדתי באף" המתוארת ברמב"ם על פי חז"ל⁴ כמקדמת אדם לקראת רכישת כתר תורה. הלוואי שלא הייתם מוצבים במבחן זה, ואשריכם שאתם עומדים בו. ואשרי העם שאלו בניו.

ומי יתן ותזכו לחזור, כל אחד למקומו, בשלום ובשלווה, להמשך בנייה אישית ומשפחתית, ולעשייה ויצירה ביישובו של עולם ובביצור והעמקת חיי הרוח ועבודת ה', על כל תכניה, לאי"ט [=לאורך ימים טובים], ומי ייתן ויתקיים בנו בקרוב ה' עז לעמו יתן ה' יברך את עמו בשלום.

בחיבה ובהוקרה,

אהרן ליכטנשטיין

• • • • •

With divine assistance, on the Sabbath eve [of Parashat Eikev, which includes the verse] "for the sake of prolonging your days and the days of your children,"⁵

To Shai's dear friends,

I'm unsure how and to whom to address these lines. Some members of the group –primarily those who studied at Yeshivat Har Etzion – I know, and some, I do not. With a few, those with whom I learned in our beit midrash [study hall], connections have been maintained over the

---

4 רמב"ם, הלכות תלמוד תורה ג, יב: "אין דברי תורה מתקיימין במי שמרפה עצמו עליהן. ולא באלו שלומדין מתוך עידון ומתוך אכילה ושתיה. אלא במי שממית עצמו עליהן ומצער גופו תמיד. ולא יתן שינה לעיניו ולעפעפיו תנומה. אמרו חכמים דרך רמז: 'זאת התורה אדם כי ימות באהל' - אין התורה מתקיימת אלא במי שממית עצמו באהלי החכמים. וכן אמר שלמה בחכמתו 'התרפית ביום צרה צר כחכה.' ועוד אמר 'אף חכמתי עמדה לי' - חכמה שלמדתי באף, היא עמדה לי". ומקורו במדרש, ילקוט שמעוני קהלת ב, ט.

5 Deuteronomy 11:21. This letter was written on Friday, Parashat Eikev, the 17th of Menachem Av, 5766 (August 11, 2006).

years, and with some, not. To some, my name is familiar, and to others, it is not. Therefore, I will write a few lines to the entire group, and in conclusion, I will dedicate a few lines to a specific subgroup.

In a few weeks, we will read: "When you go out to battle against your enemies and take precautions against anything evil."[6] Rashi explains: "The Satan accuses at the time of danger" (meaning, therefore, extra caution is needed at that time). However, not only the Satan awakens in moments of danger, and not only is it his accusation that is strengthened. Love also awakens, to no less a degree, love out of concern, and concern out of love.

Connection and bonding, existential affinity and personal and social cohesion. First and foremost, of course, between the partners in the conjoined covenant of fate and destiny, who are exposed to dangers with one another and pursue their common mission together.

Yet also, on a second level, among the homefront community – primarily, families and friends, but not only them – the ones who have sent you to serve and for whom you sacrifice.

Perhaps this is self-evident, but as I have been given the opportunity, I did not refrain from expressing the obvious. Indeed, not just support and encouragement, but also love and brotherhood, are sent to you from a heart that is following and is concerned, strongly and deeply connected.

And from a proud heart. I was actually moved to tears upon hearing what you requested to be brought to you to the frontlines when there was a small window of an opportunity to deliver a package: pages from the middle of Tractate Yoma that you've been missing for several days, so that you can, as much as possible, close the gap [=of the daf yomi

---

6   Deuteronomy 23:10.

learning] and progress onward.⁷ What courage and what testimony to the fulfillment of עשה תורתך קבע ['establish Torah as a fixed practice'] – not necessarily in a quantitative sense, but in a qualitative one: Torah that is not learned casually but rather the connection to it and the commitment towards it are deeply embedded in the learner and in his character.

Indeed, this is precisely תורה שלמדתי באף, the "Torah I have learned through suffering" that is described by Maimonides according to the Sages,⁸ as it advances a person towards the acquisition of the crown of Torah.

Would that it were that you were not tested in this way, and how fortunate you are that you have withstood the test. And fortunate is the nation that these are its children.

May the Almighty grant that you will merit to return, each one to his place, in peace and tranquility, to continue personal and familial development, and to engage in creation and creativity in settling the world, and in the refinement and deepening of spiritual life and the

---

7   In those days, Tractate Yoma was taught as part of the Daf Yomi [the daily page learning of the Talmud]. The members of the group that went into battle took with them a photocopy of few pages from the tractate but did not initially imagine that they would have to spend such a long time in Lebanon.

8   See Maimonides, Laws of Torah Study 3:12: "The words of Torah are not upheld by one who indulges himself in them, nor by those who study them for pleasure or enjoyment. Rather, they are upheld by one who toils in them, distresses his body continually, does not allow sleep to his eyes, or slumber to his eyelids. The Sages said this in a hint: 'This Torah, when a person dies in the tent, the Torah is upheld only by one who kills himself in the tents of the scholars.' And Solomon said in his wisdom: 'In the day of adversity, consider: God has made one as well as the other.' And he further said: 'Even my wisdom stood by me, the wisdom I studied with effort stood by me.'" And its source is in the Midrash, Yalkut Shimoni, Kohelet 2:9.

service of God, in all its aspects, for many good days to come. And may it soon come to pass for us that God will grant strength to His people and God will bless His people with peace.

With affection and honor,

Aharon Lichtenstein

Rabbi Dr. Aharon Lichtenstein (1933-2015), a disciple of Rabbi Joseph B. Soloveitchik, received his rabbinic ordination from Yeshiva University and earned a PhD in English Literature from Harvard University. He initially served as a Rosh Yeshiva at Yeshiva University. In 1971, he relocated to Israel and assumed the role of Rosh Yeshiva at Yeshivat Har Etzion, a hesder yeshiva founded by Rabbi Yehuda Amital in Alon Shvut, where he served alongside Rabbi Amital.

Professor Aviad Hacohen serves as the President of Sha'arei Mishpat Academic College and previously held the position of Dean at its Law School. His extensive academic research encompasses Mishpat Ivri, human rights, criminal law, civil law, and their intersections with Jewish law.

Praying for the Defenders of Our Faith

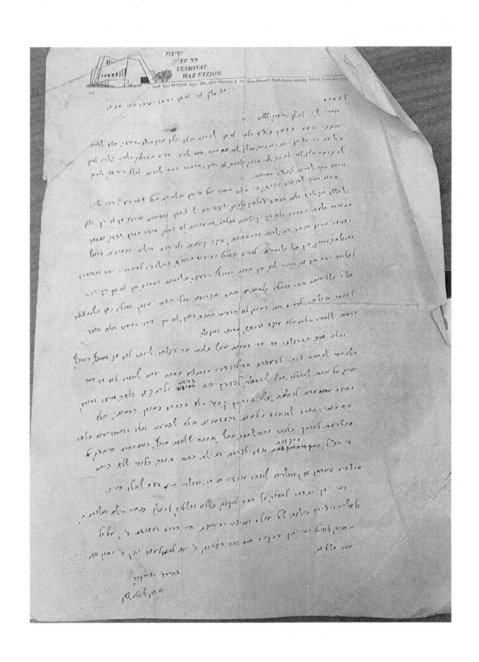

Neither Seen nor Found: Why is the 'Mi Sheberach' Prayer for IDF Soldiers Absent in the Lithuanian Haredi Community?

Aviad Hacohen

A. Introduction

On Friday, 12th of Marcheshvan 5784 (27 October 2023), like the three weeks preceding it, the front pages of Israeli newspapers (such as *Haaretz*, *Israel HaYom* and *Yedioth Ahronoth*) were dedicated to descriptions of the horrors of the terrible war. It began on the morning of Simchat Torah, when Hamas launched a horrifying campaign of destruction in which approximately 1,200 people were

Praying for the Defenders of Our Faith

abused, tortured, and murdered, including the elderly, women, and children, as well as several hundred soldiers, police officers, and security forces personnel. In addition to them, about 240 people, ranging in age from infancy to the elderly, were abducted to the Gaza Strip area, with no information regarding their fate.

In the first twelve pages of *Yated Ne'eman*, the 'official' newspaper of the Degel Ha-Torah, the party of the Lithuanian Haredi community,[1] there was almost no mention of this. The day before, on the evening of Thursday, Rabbi Baruch Mordechai Ezrachi, a senior and the eldest member of the Council of Torah Sages of the Lithuanian Haredi community, head of the "Ateret Israel" yeshiva, one of the greatest disseminators of Torah in the world of Torah and yeshivas, and a unique figure, passed away. He was 94.

The following day, the front page of *Yated Ne'eman*, featured a large headline announcing his passing. Not only this: All 14(!) of the first newspaper's pages were dedicated to the deceased and his extensive life and legacy. Mourning notices covered every corner, and at the their top part appeared, in prominent black letters, the 'customary' headlines in such cases: "Woe to the ship that lost its captain," "A world of darkness covered us," "Torah, Torah, gird yourself with sackcloth and wallow in ashes," "All the splendor has departed from the daughter of Zion," "A voice of wailing is heard from Zion," "How are we plundered," "The sun has set," "A pillar of fire ascended to the heights," "Mourn alone for yourself," "Oh, who will give us in his stead," "Jerusalem has lost its precious vessel," "Alas, the crown of Israel has fallen," "The angels have overcome the strongholds, and the Holy Ark has been captured."[2]

Among the thousands of words in these first twelve pages, the newspaper did not dedicate even a single word to the war[3] or to the IDF soldiers fighting on the front, to the hundreds of bereaved

families, to the thousands of wounded, or to the families of the captives, abductees, and missing persons.

The only reminder that a bloody war between the IDF and the murderous terrorist organization Hamas was indeed taking place at that very moment was a tiny notice that appeared in the top corner of the first page. It contained the words of Rabbi Dov Landau, Rosh Yeshiva of the Slabodka Yeshiva and leader of the Council of Torah Sages, the spiritual leader of the Lithuanian Haredim, which read as follows:

> "Due to the **difficult situation** that many yeshiva students are unable to attend the funeral, efforts should be made to arrange eulogies in the higher yeshivas and Kollel's during the seven days of mourning in memory of this great sage of blessed memory. There is splendor in his study of Torah and spreading it to the thousands who have heard his lessons and the many who have drawn from his waters over the years, and those in the Talmud Torahs and educational institutions should recite Psalms and speak words of remembrance at the time of the funeral."

A stranger who happened upon the first pages of *Yated Ne'eman* and those of the other, general-'secular,' newspapers published on that very day,[4] or a historian scrutinizing them fifty or a hundred years from now, would think they were written in different countries, perhaps on different planets.

The disregard for the difficult military campaign was further manifested in the eulogy spoken at the funeral of Rabbi Ezrachi, which took place two days later, on Sunday morning. Due to the war and security concerns, the Home Front Command prohibited[5] gatherings of more than 300 people anywhere in the State of Israel, whether indoors or outdoors.[6] This includes shopping centers and other venues. This did

Praying for the Defenders of Our Faith

not prevent **tens of thousands**(!) of people, mostly from the Lithuanian Haredi community, from crowding into the Bayit VeGan neighborhood of Jerusalem, where the funeral procession began.[7]

A naive reader, unfamiliar with the various nuances of the Haredi newspapers, who would glance at the first pages of *Yated Ne'eman* on that day, might think that "the difficult situation" referred to the death of Rabbi Ezrachi. Only from page 14 onwards did news related to the war appear. Yet, in many of the reports, there is talk of "the difficult situation in the Land of Israel."

Note this: in the main headlines of the newspaper,[8] reference is made to "the difficult situation in the Land of Israel," but the terms "Israel,"[9] "war,"[10] and certainly the full name "Israel Defense Forces"[11] do appear rarely, if at all, in the main headlines. The careful use in the newspaper's headlines of the term "the difficult situation" is not coincidental. It appears in the 'official' announcements signed by the great Torah scholars throughout the entire period following the outbreak of the war, up to the time this article was written. Indeed, as in other contexts, here too the term often used in Hebrew, בעזרת השם having a dual meaning: "With the help of God" and "with the help of the right name," in the right terminology. In the Lithuanian Haredi community, words and every nuance or connotation still have significance. On the surface, someone might think that this phenomenon illustrates the existence of a disconnect between two worlds, the Israeli society on one hand and the Lithuanian Haredi community on the other, to the extent that sometimes it seems they operate in two parallel, utterly unconnected universes.

Despite the picture painted by the pages of *Yated Ne'eman*, one must be very careful before drawing conclusions solely from it. As in other issues, in this matter too, the gap between the written word and reality is often very large. The printed newspaper reflects the 'desired' reality, at least in the eyes of some of the ideologues of the Lithuanian Haredi community,[12] while the actual reality may be completely different. Many – if not most – members of the Lithuanian Haredi community are aware of what is happening "outside,"[13] are knowledgeable about the course of the war and are concerned – along with all of Israel – for the safety of IDF soldiers, and some of them, although very few, even enlisted in the IDF after the war began with other Haredim.[14]

Moreover, alongside the *Yated Ne'eman* newspaper which serves as the 'official' channel of the Degel Ha-Torah party, there are parallel communication channels in this community, which do not adhere to the use of the aforementioned terminology. In the Lithuanian Haredi community, there are thus two parallel channels: the 'official' one, which often gives less expression to the IDF's part in the campaign, and the 'reality' channel, where IDF soldiers receive expressions of appreciation, if not admiration, as in the public. Be that as it may: is seems that the Mi Sheberach prayer, the prayer for the peace of IDF soldiers, is not said in any of the synagogues and yeshivas of the Lithuanian Haredi community. And not without reason.

Like leavened bread on Passover, the explicit and full name – not its abbreviation – of the "Israel Defense Forces" is in the category of "shall not be seen" and "shall not be found" in the 'official' newspaper of the Lithuanian Haredi faction throughout the year.[15] When describing the fierce battles occurring in the war, they are at times described in a passive voice: "The territory was conquered and cleansed," "The buildings were destroyed," "The Hamas command center was attacked, the security quarter was conquered," "The tunnels of Jenin were destroyed." Sometimes the newspaper uses a third-person hidden voice: "The forces conquered, the forces advanced," without specifying who these anonymous, nameless forces are. When it wishes to mention the names of the war's navigators and army spokespersons in its headlines, *Yated Ne'eman* will use acronyms. Thus, for example acronyms are used for IDF, the army Chief of Staff or the IDF spokesperson, but again, the explicit name "**Israel Defense Forces**") will never appear. Even the acronym IDF will not appear in the main headline but only, if at all, in the **sub**-headlines[16] or in the body of the news article.[17]

This phenomenon may easily explain why the Mi Sheberach prayer for IDF soldiers – which mention the full name of "**Israel Defense Forces**" – is not recited in the synagogues and study halls of the Lithuanian Haredi community of yeshiva and Kollel students, and it seems unlikely that it will be recited there in the near future. Indeed, despite the natural tendency to attribute this omission as a disdainful attitude on the part of the Lithuanian Haredi community towards the soldiers' self-sacrifice or to a lack of gratitude towards them, this is not necessarily the case. As will be detailed below, the strong objection to reciting a special prayer – even in a different version – stems from a series of ideological and social factors, some of which also influence actions in other areas and are not specifically directed towards the IDF. Moreover, it should be emphasized, as also becomes clear from other articles in this book,[18] that the Haredi community is not monolithic in this matter, and the positions of the 'Hasidic' Ashkenazi Haredim and the 'Sephardi' Haredim on this issue are not the same as those of the 'Lithuanian' Haredim. Furthermore, even within the community of rabbis and students of yeshivas and Kollel's in the Lithuanian Haredi community itself, there are nuances, both in worldview in general and in their stance on this particular issue.

We will seek to shed light on the ideological background of the Lithuanian Haredi community's attitude towards the IDF in general, and the "Mi Sheberach" prayer for IDF soldiers in particular. In doing so, we will also examine whether, alongside the demonstrated disregard for the IDF, "alternative paths" have also been created through which this large community, can express its participation and partnership in the sorrows of Israel during times of war and peace.

B. Historical Background

The attitude of the Haredi community in general, and of the Lithuanian Haredi community within it, towards the State of Israel[19] and the IDF has undergone significant changes since the establishment of the State of Israel. In the early days of the state, this community struggled for its survival. After the Holocaust that decimated Jewish communities throughout Europe, including the major centers of Jewish learning, Haredi leaders sought to revive and reestablish the world of yeshivas, mainly in Israel and the United States. They received tangible support from the State of Israel in pursuance of this goal, while maintaining a separation from the state's institutions and not identifying with it on an ideological level.

This relationship was also reflected in the Haredim's attitude towards the security forces and the IDF, both before and after the establishment of the state.

Prior to the establishment of the state, some yeshiva students, from among the small number who were in Israel at the time, joined underground organizations (mainly the Irgun and Lehi), some of them doing so secretly and others openly. During the siege of Jerusalem,[20] and after the establishment of the state, throughout the War of Independence and even afterwards,[21] many haredim, particularly those from Lithuanian yeshivas,[22] enlisted in the IDF.[23] So much so that in the years 1948-1949, Agudat Israel published "Agudat Israel's Bulletin for Enlistees," which contained many expressions of the haredim's partnership in the security efforts.[24]

The Lithuanian Haredim's part was also noticeable in the senior command of the Military Rabbinate: Rabbi Shlomo Goren, the Chief Rabbi of the IDF, was a graduate of the Hebron Yeshiva, as were many of his senior staff, including Rabbis Shmuel Eliezri,[25] Yitzhak ha-Levi Epstein,[26] Avraham ha-Levi Horowitz,[27] Dov Cohen,[28] Shimon

Rafiko,[29] Yehuda Shulman;[30] rabbis of the younger, second generation such as Rabbis Avraham Avidan (Zemel),[31] Ephraim Tzemel,[32] Chaim Menachem Baksht;[33] Shlomo Zalman Kook,[34] and military rabbis of the third and fourth generation like Rabbis Mordechai Abramovsky,[35] Ram Moshe Ravad,[36] and others.[37] Indeed, there were also many graduates of Lithuanian Haredi yeshivas who served in other IDF units as regular soldiers. This was the case already during the War of Independence, in an organized manner through "Gedud Tuvia" (Tuvia's battalion)[38] and other specific frameworks for Haredim such as Haredi Nahal,[39] or as individuals in regular units.[40] This continued in later periods until the early 1980s.

The enlistment of haredim in the military service both prior to the establishment of the state and in the subsequent period had the approval – explicit or 'silent' - of most of the major hareidi leaders. To such an extent that before the establishment of the state, in January 1948, an internal circular was issued by the Command Committee for People's Service, of the central office of Agudat Israel in Israel, stating the party's decision regarding the obligation to report for 'people's service' for those aged 17 to 25, and volunteering for those aged 26 to 45, in order to "protect Jewish life and property from murder and destruction." The circular called on everyone to rebuke anyone who did not obey this directive, stating:

> To all those who have not yet responded to this call, we now turn to them personally to awaken them to their duty to their people and their land in this difficult hour.
>
> The murderers' hand is extended to anyone who is called by the name of Israel, **and therefore, no person of Israel shall be exempt from defending life and property.** 'Shall your brethren go to war while you sit here'?

Praying for the Defenders of Our Faith

Agudat Israel will therefore operate with the full weight of responsibility **to denounce any evasion from service of any kind whatsoever."**[41]

Given this, it is not surprising that in the 1950s, groups of uniformed soldiers routinely visited the Ponovezh Yeshiva in Bnei Brak, participated in the Yarchei Kallah gathering, and were warmly received by the head of the yeshiva, Rabbi Yosef Shlomo Kahaneman, who even hosted them in his home. Not only was this not done in secret, but a photo of the soldiers that were invited by Rabbi Kahaneman to the Ponovezh Yeshivah appeared in a promotional booklet of the yeshiva. Rabbi Goren maintained connections with the Hazon Ish and consulted with him, among other things, on different halakhic questions and issues related to military service.

Soldiers who participated in the Yarchei Kallah gathering of the Ponovezh Yeshiva in 1956 gather at the home of the yeshiva's dean. Standing: Rabbi Yosef Shlomo Kahaneman, the head of the yeshiva. To his left is Rabbi Shlomo Goren, the Chief Rabbi of the IDF, and to his right is Rabbi Shimon Rafiko.

The decline in the connection between IDF soldiers and the Lithuanian Haredi community was a gradual process. As the "society of learners" of the Lithuanian Haredi community grew, the number of Lithuanian Haredim serving in the IDF decreased. In the early years of the state, most Lithuanian Haredim lived in mixed cities like Tel Aviv, Haifa, and Petah Tikva. Even if many did not serve in the IDF, their family members or neighbors often did, thus maintaining a tangible, daily connection to the army and those serving in it. Over time, this connection weakened, partly due to the 'ghettoization' of the Haredim in general and the Lithuanian Haredim in particular. They began to concentrate in cities which became predominantly if not exclusively haredi (e.g. Modi'in Illit, Beitar, Bnei Brak) and separate neighborhoods (such as the northern neighborhoods of Jerusalem, alongside others like Beit VeGan, Ramot Eshkol and Har Nof, which over the years became predominantly Haredi neighborhoods).

Instead of integration, from the 1980s onward, there are more Haredi leaders who encourage a trend of "ghettoization" – separation and consolidation of the Haredi society within itself, with an increasing – even if not absolute – disassociation from the rest of Israeli society. Parallel processes of 'Israelization' that began emerging here and there (such as entering the workforce in non-Haredi workplaces,[42] using advanced technology like cell phones and computers, and to a lesser extent, pursuing academic studies and joining the workforce) created a backlash, leading the "eyes of the community," the leaders of the Lithuanian Haredim, to intensify their statements against any attempt of closeness, certainly not integration, with the general Israeli society. From the 1980s, the issue of "equal burden," and the enlistment of yeshiva students in the IDF, which has always loomed in the background, moved more and more to the forefront and became one of the main points of tension and dispute between the general Israeli society and the Haredi community. It also became a key issue in Haredi politics. Alongside the process of 'Israelization,' there was also an increasing process of separation and 'ghettoization'. Military service – a foundational and defining component of Israeli identity – became a negative symbol, if not one of outright "impurity," in certain segments of the Lithuanian Haredi community. Any 'son of Torah' worthy of the name, belonging to the Lithuanian Haredim, was commanded to abstain, separate, and distance himself from it, in the sense of "turn away from evil."[43]

C. The Ideological and Educational Dimensions

The avoidance of reciting the Mi Sheberach prayer for IDF soldiers **also** has an ideological background. Even if not all – or even the majority – of those within the Lithuanian Haredi community who refrain from reciting it are aware of, agree with, or are familiar with its specific content, it looms over them like a constant black shadow.

Alongside the sociological erosion in the day-to-day connection between the "society of learners" of the Lithuanian Haredim and the rest of Israeli society, a complete ideological framework was created to separate the Lithuanian Haredim from Israeli identity in general, and the IDF in particular. Within this framework, some leading Torah scholars[44] and leaders of the Lithuanian Haredim sought to establish a pure ideological doctrine to justify the Lithuanian Haredim's separation from sharing the national burden, giving it an ethical justification, and glorifying their abstention from the IDF and everything related to it. Increasingly within the Lithuanian Haredi community, voices argued that the real "Defense Army" for Israel consists of Torah scholars who "kill themselves in the tents of Torah," and not the soldiers of the IDF, who die defending the people and the land.

The primary argument, which is also powerful in many other contexts, is related to the strict adherence to the principle of conservatism that is embedded in significant parts of the Haredi community's ways, especially in prayer rituals. This principle is often formulated in the words of Rabbi Moshe Sofer – known as the Hatam Sofer, who said, "The new is forbidden by the Torah."[45] This means that anything 'new' is inherently invalid, regardless of whether it pertains to dress codes, Torah study, or prayer.[46] For this reason, there is resistance – at least on the surface – to any introduction of secular studies into the religious education system, and there is widespread opposition to any changes in the traditional liturgy and synagogue ritual. This last issue is particularly sensitive given that one of the prominent differentiators between the "innovators" – the non-Orthodox movements, the Reform and Conservative – and the Orthodox, focused on synagogue rituals (location of the bimah, use of an organ, removal of partitions and mixed seating, prayers in vernacular, and changes in the liturgy).

Therefore, even in cases where there is no halakhic concern in adding a prayer like Mi Sheberach to the service, not as a fixed prayer but in between, such as after the Torah reading, between Shacharit and Musaf, the Lithuanian Haredi community refrains from adopting it. While the Yekum Purkan prayer in Aramaic, added nearly two thousand years ago during the time of the Babylonian exile,[47] and directed to the well-being of its leaders, has gained a status of quasi-sanctity, any new addition to the prayer – even if relevant and meaningful to our current reality – is rejected outright.[48]

This is even more so when the prayer's integration into the service was promoted by distinctly Zionist figures, in this case, the then Chief Rabbi of the IDF, Rabbi Shlomo Goren. In his specific case, the opposition to him was even more intense, especially after his involvement in the "Mamzerim Affair" from the early 1970s, leading to an unofficial 'ban' on him in the Haredi community, with its rabbis and spiritual leaders distancing themselves from him as much as possible.

In this specific case, even the wording of the prayer itself arouses opposition among certain segments of the ideological leadership of the Haredi public. Firstly, the use of the combination "IDF – Israel Defense Forces" carries a subtle, albeit implicit, challenge against the Haredi perception (which, even if not accepted by all, has deep roots within parts of this community and its leaders) that according to Torah, it is the Torah itself and not any other entity that "guards and saves," who protects and rescues, only the Torah and not the entity called the Israel Defense Forces. It should be noted that even though the origin of this expression is in the words of the Sages in the Talmud,[49] its common usage today, including during the COVID-19 pandemic, where it served as a pretext to avoid vaccination among some segments of the Haredi public, does not necessarily reflect its original meaning and context.[50]

Behind this argument lies another message, not always publicly expressed for 'diplomatic' reasons, but deeply embedded in this ideology: It is inconceivable that an army of a 'secular' state, with non-Jewish soldiers and many Jewish soldiers who do not observe Torah and mitzvot, are the ones "protecting" the Jewish people. In this context, even the inclusion of verses or mentioning God's name within the prayer cannot, according to them, atone for this sin of replacing trust in God with reliance on a flesh-and-blood defense system. The expression of this reservation is found in various verses frequently cited – mainly in writing but also orally – in articles and speeches disseminated among the Lithuanian Haredi community throughout the year, and especially during times of war and danger. Verses relevant to times of distress, war, and danger were polished and began to be used frequently.

For example, verses such as "The Lord will fight for you, and you shall hold your peace" (Exodus 14:14); "Some trust in chariots, and some in horses: but we will remember the name of the Lord our God" (Psalms 20:7); "Through God we shall do valiantly: for He it is that shall tread down our enemies" (Psalms 60:12); "A horse is a vain hope for deliverance; despite all its great strength it cannot save" (Psalms 33:17); "Asshur shall not save us; we will not ride upon horses: neither will we say any more to the work of our hands, Ye are our gods" (Hosea 14:3); "Alas! for that day is great, so that none is like it: it is even the time of Jacob's trouble; but he shall be saved out of it" (Jeremiah 30:7), and similar verses are often heard in this context.

Alongside them, various other expressions are frequently used, from the sayings of the sages such as the previously mentioned "Torah protects and saves," or expressions from the language of prayer such as "Only on You do our eyes depend." The verse "The voice is the voice of Jacob, but the hands are the hands of Esau" (Genesis 27:22) is also widely used to highlight the heritage whereby Esau – the ultimate enemy – fights with his hairy hands, while Jacob fights through his mouth and prayer. This interpretation is based on the rabbinic interpretation[51] of the verse in Isaiah (41:14): "Fear not, thou worm Jacob," meaning: just as a worm's strength is only in its mouth, so Jacob's strength is only in his mouth, and this is linked to the verse in Psalms (149:6): "The high praises of God in their throat, and a two-edged sword in their hand."

These words of the Sages sometimes support newer statements, such as "We have no one to rely on but our Father in Heaven,"[52] the promise attributed to the Hazon Ish (widely used during the Gulf War) – as conveyed by his nephew, Rabbi Hayyim Kanievsky – in the name of Rabbi Turchin: "It is assured that in the Torah city of Bnei Brak, no bombs will fall."[53]

In an address delivered in 2013, Rabbi Kanievsky added the words of the Zohar: "The only advice to subdue and escape from the nations is solely through the power of engaging in the Torah, as it is written in the Holy Zohar (Parashat Beshalach, 58a), "There is nothing in the world that can break the strength of the nations except for the time when

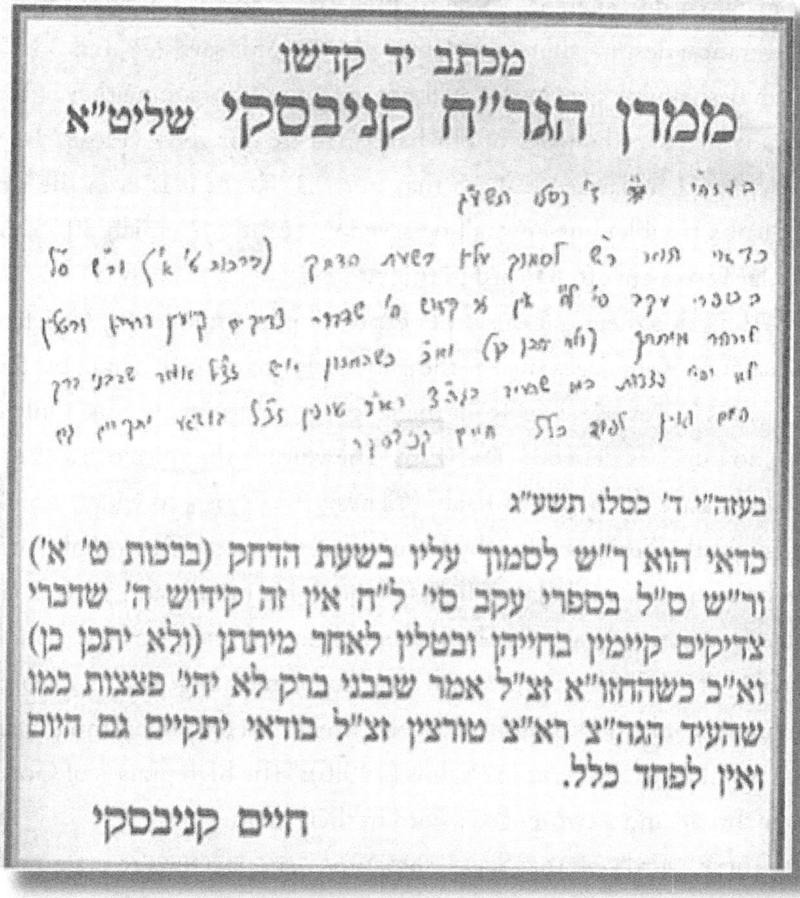

Praying for the Defenders of Our Faith

> מכתב יד קדשו
> ממרן הגר"ח קניבסקי שליט"א
>
> בע"ה י' כסלו תשע"ג
>
> [handwritten text]
>
> בעזה"י ד' כסלו תשע"ג
>
> כדאי הוא ר"ש לסמוך עליו בשעת הדחק (ברכות ט' א')
> ור"ש ס"ל בספרי עקב סי' ל"ה אין זה קידוש ה' שדברי
> צדיקים קיימין בחייהן ובטלין לאחר מיתתן (ולא יתכן כן)
> וא"כ כשהחזו"א זצ"ל אמר שבבני ברק לא יהי' פצצות כמו
> שהעיד הגה"צ רא"צ טורצין זצ"ל בודאי יתקיים גם היום
> ואין לפחד כלל.
>
> חיים קניבסקי

"You should not fear at all." The letter of Rabbi Hayyim Kanievsky from the year 5773-2013 during the period of missile fire from Gaza, during Operation 'Pillar of Cloud.'

Israel engages in the Torah, as long as Israel is engaged in the Torah, the right hand is strengthened and breaks the strength and might of the nations." Also, in advertising, use is made of the sayings of the Sages to encourage the engagement in Torah study as a shield against the calamity of war. For example, an advertisement calling for "Avreichim [=married students] and yeshiva students" to come to "a special assembly of strengthening in light of the challenges of the time" appeared under the headline "Through the merit of the Torah and its learners, the world will be saved." Alongside it, a saying of the Sages in "Tana Devei Eliyahu" (Chapter 6) was brought: "If you see that troubles are looming and coming, run to the chambers of Torah, and immediately the troubles will flee."

Parallel to emphasizing the value of peace and expressing reservations about war[54] due to the concern of *"pikuach nefesh"* [=the concern for the endangerment of human life] inherent in it,[55] the voices of these speakers often also express significant reservations about any admiration for power in general, and for the Israel Defense Forces in particular. This attitude, according to some Haredi rabbis, could lead to the feeling of "my power and the might of my hand," i.e., the feeling that human power and might – and not God – are responsible for military achievements. Indeed, a complete doctrine has developed to combat this phenomenon on an ideological basis. The textual foundation for this doctrine is based on the admonishment in Deuteronomy 8:14-18, cautioning against the tendency, when things are going well, to believe that it is a person's own powers alone are what gave rise to his accomplishments:

> "Take care lest you forget the Lord your God, by not keeping His commandments and His ordinances and His statutes, which I command you this day... And your heart be lifted, and you forget the Lord your God... And you say in your heart, 'My power and the might of my hand have gotten me this wealth.' But you shall remember the Lord your God, for it is He that gives you power to get wealth."

Rabbi Elazar M. Shach (1899-2001), who was the head of the Ponevezh Yeshiva in Bnei Brak, and a leader in the Lithuanian Haredi community at the end of the twentieth-century, expressed strong words on this matter. Regarding the Yom Kippur War, he referred to "false faith of 'My power and the might of my hand have gotten me this wealth.'" And he added: "... this war came and shattered this approach from its foundation. The arrogant idea that the IDF is an invincible army shattered to pieces... Only prayers stood by us, and only the Almighty saved us... This war undoubtedly came to shatter the foreign influence of 'my strength and the might of my hands.'"[56]

IDF officers in Rabbi Shach's home. From left to right: Rabbi Shach, Rabbi Shlomo Lorenz (the political leader of the Lithuanian Haredim); General Shlomo Lahat, Head of IDF Personnel (first right)

A sharp expression of opposition to this approach was voiced lately by Rabbi David Cohen, head of the 'Hebron' Yeshiva, one of the flagship institutions of the Haredi yeshiva world. In an interview conducted by the leaders of the "Lev Shomea" organization about two weeks after the outbreak of the war,[57] when the conflict seems to be at one of its peaks, he expressed the danger in the attitude of "my power and the might of my hand":

> "We do not know the calculations of heaven, but after the Six-Day War, there was in the country an intoxication of greatness and power. They said then that the IDF is the strongest and greatest army in the world, and when the Yom Kippur War broke out, our rabbis said that there was then an exaggerated feeling of 'my power and the might of my hand.' I still remember from the yeshiva days, the discussions about this by our revered leaders, head of Hebron Yeshiva Rabbi Yechezkel Sarna of blessed memory, the supervisor Rabbi Meir Chodosh of blessed memory, and Maran HaGaon Rabbi Chaim Schmulevitz of blessed memory, about how the notion of 'my power and the might of my hand' shattered before our eyes. Even now, after fifty years of more or less maintaining a stance, there was a similar feeling, and now it has shattered in the same way. Especially in recent times, irresponsible people have spoken many terrible words in the manner of 'my power and the might of my hand,' about power, and in some places, no one reflects on this situation, a situation of terrible dangers, from the south with Hamas, from the north Hezbollah, behind them Iran, and the Iranian ruler speaks like Hitler in his time, wanting to destroy all the inhabitants of the Holy Land, and it is a situation of danger, and from their perspective, nothing exists except for words of arrogance and bluster, recklessness like no other… and again they return and speak 'my power and the might of my hand' in a terrible and threatening manner, words of pride

and arrogance, people are being slaughtered before your eyes and you stand powerless, and you continue with 'my power and the might of my hand.' I observe among the young boys who are drawn after all the formulas of degradation and pride towards the authorities, that they are reckless and irresponsible people, and here again, heaven has sent us a reminder, to understand that people have gotten used to this terrible propaganda that this is redemption, we have a state, the power of the people of Israel, and forget that as long as the Messiah has not arrived, we are still in exile. And this 'my power and the might of my hand' has also penetrated us, we see with our own eyes that according to the way of nature, we have no possibility to live here, and we have no one to rely on but our Father in heaven."

The significant blow that Hamas caused to Israel's security on the first day of the "Operation Swords of Iron" served as a tool for these ideologues to prove their point: Despite Israel's clear superiority in planes, tanks, submarines, and other war machinery, and despite its advanced technological means, and even being considered (according to "foreign publications") a nuclear power, Israel was unable to prevent the terrorists from infiltrating its territory and carrying out acts of horror, murder, and massacre within its borders. According to the thinking of these Lithuanian Haredi thinkers, this is another expression of the collapse of the concept of "my power and the might of my hand," as if military force and technological means have the power to win battles, and not that it is God who "has done all this." This approach, which completely or partially ignores the contribution of the IDF to the security of the State of Israel and its residents, is prominent in the extreme faction of the Haredi community, primarily represented by the "Jerusalem Faction."

This faction effectively continues the legacy of Rabbi Yitzchak Zev (Velvel) Soloveitchik, the Brisker Rav. While many leaders in the Lithuanian Haredi world, including Rabbi Chaim Schmulevitz, Rabbi Elazar M. Shach, Rabbi Shlomo Zalman Auerbach, Rabbi Gershon Edelstein, and Rabbi Hayyim Kanievsky, believe that soldiers who fell in battle can be considered 'martyrs' who died sanctifying the name of God, one of the leaders of the Jerusalem Faction stated that since many soldiers do not observe commandments, it is forbidden to pray for their well-being, and it is preferable that they die(!!).

This stern and harsh approach of the leaders of this faction is also evident during the recent war, Operation Iron Swords, as in the example of Rabbi Yisrael Bunim Schreiber from Ashdod.[58] In response to a question from one of his students about the appropriate attitude of "Bnei Torah," Yeshivah and Kollel students toward fallen soldiers, distanced himself from the implied message in the question. He responded with a counter-question: "I want to ask a question: What is the proper attitude towards recognizing the good and the effort of those who collect the garbage every morning? What is the right attitude? The same question exactly."

He then added: "It's not our concern why it happened to those who were killed. We don't work in the records of hell, and we don't work in the records of paradise. It's not our business why they were killed, whether they deserved it or not. It's not our business, and we're not supposed to judge it. We're not supposed to accuse them or defend them. **What do they have to do with us? They have no connection to us.** God sent a situation of war here that is troubling everyone, and we need to think about that. The attitude toward the victims, who said there should be an attitude? What is your connection to them? Why are you supposed to relate to them? Not for or against, and it doesn't matter if they are righteous or wicked. What is their connection to you? They are connected only because a great disaster has occurred, and they are directing themselves to you. You need to inquire why they are directing themselves to me, as the magnitude of the disaster, so is the magnitude of those directing themselves to me. What about them? What are they? What is my business with them?"[59]

Another reason for avoiding the prayer relates to the educational and social aspects. Naturally, a glorified army like the IDF, with its airplanes, submarines, armored corps, and weaponry, can evoke admiration and awe in the heart of every observer, especially among teenagers who often crave such "excitements." Mentioning the army "inside the house," in the synagogue and in the study hall, during prayer, grants validation and endorsement to the IDF and those who serve in it, and might, God forbid (according to their view), entice some of the Haredi community to leave the halls of Torah and "the society of learners," and to carve out "broken cisterns" for themselves within that very army.

It goes without saying that in most cases, this concern is completely unfounded. The Lithuanian Haredi community, despite the 'ghettoization' characteristic of many of their lifestyle practices, do not live in outer space and are aware of the existence, power, and actions of the IDF.

Not mentioning its name in the synagogue does not significantly change this reality. Nevertheless, at least externally, the name of the IDF will remain akin to leavened bread on Passover, "neither seen nor found, neither remembered nor mentioned."

D. From the General to the Specific: Alternatives to the 'Mi Sheberach' Prayer

Considering all the above, the Lithuanian Haredi public's abstention from reciting the Mi Sheberach prayer for IDF soldiers does not necessarily stem from wickedness or hardheartedness. Alongside its ideological and educational foundation, this abstention reflects their reluctance to identify – certainly publicly and during prayer – with the Zionist enterprise, of which the IDF is a prominent symbol. Alongside all this, most of the Haredi public genuinely cares for the peace of all Israel and recognizes that despite the lofty and elevated rhetoric about trust in the Divine, the State of Israel – and they as part of it – still need a strong and robust army to protect their peace and security.

The principle of mutual responsibility, as well as partnership in times of crisis, also obliges members of this community to act in times of trouble and not to continue their regular routine with indifference, let alone insensitivity, to what is happening around them.

In light of this, there have been created what might be called "alternative pathways" to the Mi Sheberach prayer, seeking to express identification with those hoping for Israel's victory over its enemies, remembering the holy souls who sacrificed their lives for the defense of the people and the land, entreating God for the healing of the wounded, and for the return of the captives, the kidnapped, and the missing to their homes. However, this is done without being enticed to follow the customary ways of prayer and outcry found in other sectors, rather, intentionally setting up a distinction from those customs.

Primarily, these circumventing steps are taken using traditional methods that have been accepted from generation to generation in Jewish society and particularly in the Haredi community. These include reciting chapters of Psalms – by schoolchildren – and in general,[60] calling for fasting and penitence, holding prayer and outcry assemblies, 'worldwide days of prayer,' participating in acts of Kiruv Rechokim, and encouraging strengthening the observance of commandments particularly those regarded to be efficacious for purposes of protection.

Praying for the Defenders of Our Faith

בס"ד, שלהי מר חשוון תשפ"ד

אגודים בצרה לשפוך תחינה

עת צרה היא ליעקב וממנה ייוושע, תולעת יעקב אין כוחה אלא בפה

לרגל המצב הקשה בארץ ישראל, בימים אלו שמחוץ תשכל חרב ומחדרים אימה, קוראים אנו לאחינו בית ישראל בכל מקומות מושבותיהם בארץ ישראל ובגולה, להתכנס בעת רצון יום ב' **ערב ראש חודש כסליו הבעל"ט**, אנשים, נשים ותינוקות של בית רבן לזעוק, להתחנן ולהריע, ולהתעורר בתשובה, כל קהילה ומנהגה באמירת תהילים או לנוהגים להתפלל תפילת י"ג קטן בער"ח אשר יש בכחה לבטל גזירות.

בהיכלי הכוללים, בישיבות הגדולות והקטנות, ובבתי הכנסיות בכל אתר ואתר יתכנסו להתפלל ברוב עם, ובמוסדות החינוך של תשב"ר ובבתי יעקב מכיתות ז' ומעלה ובסמינרים. נשים שיש להן האפשרות תתכנסנה בעזרות נשים בבתי הכנסיות, ומי שאינו יכול להצטרף לתפילת הרבים, ישתתף במקומו ויצטרף יחד עם כלל ישראל בתפילה הכוללת.

ואין לנו על מי להישען אלא על אבינו שבשמים
והן קל כביר לא ימאס תפילת רבים
וישמע קול שוועתנו ויחון אותנו ברחמים גדולים ובתשועת עולמים

מועצות גדולי התורה

| דגל התורה | אגודת ישראל | מועצת חכמי התורה |

וגם אנו מצטרפים לקריאה הנ"ל
מועצת גדולי התורה באמריקה

A rare call from three major Torah councils to convene "due to the difficult situation in the Land of Israel."

For instance, regarding the "advancing of the zman" – the period of study in yeshivas – during "Operation Protective Edge," which erupted during Simchat Torah, the following week was still part of the traditional 'bein hazmanim' intercession break in the Lithuanian Haredi yeshivas. Despite this, community leaders called on yeshiva students to start the new semester early, even before the official date of "Rosh Chodesh Cheshvan." Among women, the mitzvah of 'hafrashat challah' holds a special place as it is traditionally believed to have a special power of protection from death and other harms.[61]

Alongside this, there were calls to enhance the observance of commandments, such as establishing additional study sessions beyond the usual, or accepting the Sabbath earlier than usual, in the hope and expectation that these actions will join the circle of merits of the people of Israel and assist them in the war effort that was imposed upon them.

Additional aspects of mutual responsibility were manifested in the aid provided to fighting soldiers. Beyond financial donations and packing food supplies for soldiers, a special call was made within the general Haredi society to assist the soldiers in fulfilling the mitzvah of tzitzit (ritual fringes), which according to Jewish tradition also has the power to protect and save. Hundreds of Lithuanian Haredi men and women mobilized to sew tzitzit (in military camouflage colors!) and tie the tzitzit strings, so that they could be distributed en-masse to soldiers at the front. In addition, *"seudat amenim"*[62] and *"hafrashat challah"* gatherings[63] were held for the benefit of IDF soldiers, even within families belonging to the Lithuanian Haredi community, actions perceived as possessing a charm for protection and success.

From the description of all the above, a clear picture emerges of a gap between the genuine, sincere, and substantial concern within the Lithuanian-Haredi community for the safety of their brethren, including the soldiers among them, and the public face put forth that seemingly 'ignores' them and is unwilling to explicitly pray for their well-being

Praying for the Defenders of Our Faith

through the explicit utterance of Mi Sheberach for the IDF soldiers or for the well-being of the captured and missing ones.

A call from the Yeshiva Council to convene "in this time of trouble."

E. Is There a Chance That This Picture Will Change in the Foreseeable Future?

Despite the significant changes occurring within the Haredi community, particularly in the Lithuanian branch, it seems that this image of reality will not change in the foreseeable future. IDF spokespersons – and subsequently, various media outlets – highlighted the initiative of approximately 2,000 Haredim (including yeshiva students from overseas) who approached the recruitment office with a request to enlist in the IDF to undergo a shortened basic training and integrate into the military support system. Indeed, compared to the entire population of yeshiva students, this remains a small minority.[64] The fact is that despite all the attention drawn by the war and its horrors, the majority, if not all, of yeshiva students and kollel members in the Haredi world have remained within their institutions and have not turned to the recruitment office.

This phenomenon has also led several prominent yeshiva leaders[65] to publicly denounce this "dangerous and harmful" trend (in their view). It can be assumed that the publicity surrounding these statements will lead to a "boomerang effect" of increased resistance to any move towards leaving the yeshiva or kollel for the purpose of military service.

It can also be assumed that the reluctance stemming from the perception of "my strength and the might of my hand" will increase and resonate in the halls of Torah and the yeshivot, growing stronger as we approach the upcoming Hanukkah holiday. During this holiday, it is customary to celebrate the heroism of the Maccabees and their military victories, with a clear allusion to our present-day reality.

Endnotes

1. I am grateful to my colleagues Professor Benjamin Brown, Dr. Shlomo Tikochinsky, Adv. Amy Yourman and Mr. Menachem Butler, who assisted me in clarifying several issues. All emphases in the quotes are mine unless otherwise stated.

   This party, with its spiritual leaders, heads of yeshivas, and political representatives, represents the core of the Ashkenazi-Lithuanian Haredim (as opposed to Sephardi Haredim and Ashkenazi-Hassidic Haredim). According to various estimates, this group of Lithuanian Haredi numbers several hundred thousand people today. *See the research mentioned by Kimmy Caplan and Yael Becher, Studying Israeli Haredi Society: A Scholarly Inventory* (Jerusalem: The Israel Democracy Institute, 2022), 73 (Hebrew), regarding the positions of other groups, particularly more extreme ones, both to the right, such as the HaEidah HaHareidi and "Neturei Karta." In many ways, the positions of these groups were influenced by the positions of Haredi leaders in the early years of the state, such as Rabbi Yosef Zvi Duschinsky and Rabbi Yitzchak Zev (Velvel) Soloveitchik, the Brisker Rav. Their "followers" are the adherents of the "Jerusalem Faction" (headed, until his passing, by Rabbi Shmuel Auerbach), and its newspaper *Ha-Peles*. From the "left" side of the Haredi map, we should consider more "modern" groups, such as the "New Haredim," the "Israeli Haredim," and the "Workers Haredim." For more information of the Lithuanian Haredi faction, see Immanuel Etkes, "On Shaping the Image of 'the Gedolim' in Haredi Lithuanian Hagiographic Literature," in Benjamin Brown and Nissim Leon, eds., *The Gedolim: Leaders Who Shaped the Israeli Haredi Jewry* (Jerusalem: Magnes, 2017), 21-69 (Hebrew), and Benjamin Brown, "The Fundamental Components of Haredi Ideology (Hashkafah)," in Kimmy Caplan and Nissim Leon, eds., *Contemporary Israeli Haredi Society: Profiles, Trends and Challenges* (London: Routledge, 2024), 32-66.

2   This type of strong wording in announcements of mourning is routinely used in thousands of ads and eulogies in the Haredi world. They have become commonplace and trivialized, sometimes to the point of absurdity, losing their power and uniqueness. For instance, Similar expressions were widely heard at the time of mourning for Rabbi Shach, Rav Kanyevsky, Rav Steinman, Rav Edelstein and many others. On this bleak phenomenon of the "prepared eulogy," as if written in a "template" in which only the names of the deceased are replaced, see Aviad Hacohen, "How Do We Eulogize?" *Shabbaton*, vol. 23 [no. 1145] (7 November 2023) (Hebrew), available here (https://shabaton1.co.il/?p=35153).

3   A prominent expression of this can be found on the second page of the newspaper. An editorial article was titled "Lost Weapons **of War**," but its content was not dedicated to the difficult and ongoing war that rages on the southern front, in the Gaza Strip. Instead, the loss referred to is the passing of the Great Rabbi Baruch Mordechai Ezrachi. The article emphasized his status as a "hero of Torah" and a "man of valor" in the "war of Torah" and concluded with remarks about the need for "the defense of Torah especially in this difficult time."

4   For the sake of completeness, it should be added that one reading the other "secular" newspapers, would probably not be apprised of the death of Rabbi Baruch Mordechai Ezrachi, one of the Torah giants of the generation. The reader encountered only horrifying images of war, both at the front and in the civilian sphere, with soldiers on tanks, planes bombing various sites in Gaza, heartbreaking photos of families mourning their loved ones at their graves, and detailed descriptions of the bloodshed in the Gaza Strip because of the Israeli attacks at that very time. From the examination I conducted, it appears that the news of Rabbi Baruch Mordechai Ezrachi's passing appeared in all major "secular" media outlets, primarily on their websites rather than in printed editions. For example, in the newspaper "Haaretz": "Rabbi Baruch Mordechai Ezrachi, an elder of the Torah sages, passes away at the age of 94," Haaretz.co.il; and "From the Greats of

the Generation": Rabbi Baruch Mordechai Ezrachi passed away at the age of 94," Kan.org.il, and more.

5   Home Front Command Releases Updated Guidelines (israelnationalnews.com).

6   Despite the perceived aversion to the military, at least publicly, in recent years, the Home Front Command has developed a special relationship with the Haredi community, primarily due to the Home Front's handing of the COVID-19 pandemic. During this period, several Haredi settlements, notably the city of Bnei Brak, were significantly affected by the spread of the pandemic, and infection rates and morbidity among them increased significantly. To cope with this challenging reality, the Home Front Command enforced population concentration guidelines in these areas. Former Major General Roni Numa, who served as the commander of the Home Front Command, was appointed as a "special project manager" for dealing with COVID-19 in the Haredi community. As a result of this involvement, the infection rate in these areas indeed decreased significantly, and Major General Numa and the Home Front Command received widespread praise for their efforts.

7   During the careful procession, the police warned that they would stop the funeral procession due to the presence of individuals who had gathered dangerously on the barriers set up in the area. In the midst of the eulogies, which lasted for about two and a half hours, the funeral procession departed towards the Mount of Olives cemetery, this time – according to the security forces' instructions – with the limited participation of only a few dozen people.

8   This is in contrast to the content of the news reports, in which the term "war" is mentioned more than once.

9   The avoidance of using the name "Israel" for the secular state instead of the sacred Halachic term "Eretz Yisrael" is well-known and does not require proof. Even Rabbi Joseph B. Soloveitchik, the leader of the "Mizrachi" movement in the United States, consistently refrained from using the 'secular' term Israel even in addressing letters, and

always insisted on using the halakhic term "Eretz Yisrael" (or "Eretz Hakodesh"). See Aviad Hacohen, "'For You Shall See the Land, But You Shall Not Enter It': On Rabbi Joseph B. Soloveitchik's Candidacy for the Tel Aviv Chief Rabbinate and the Riddle of his Subsequent Refraining from Visiting Israel," in Dov Schwartz, ed., *Religious Zionism: History, Thought, Society*, vol. 9 (Ramat-Gan: Bar-Ilan University Press, 2023), text near footnote 63, and footnotes 134, 152, especially footnote 165.

10 The term "war" is used at times in contemporary Torah literature, including those produced by members of the Haredi community. Nevertheless, there is still a reluctance to use it frequently in the main headlines of *Yated Ne'eman* or in statements issued by contemporary Haredi leaders. For example, in statements published during times of war, a more common and vernacular expression such as "in light of the difficult situation" is preferred. In some of the ideological literature within the Haredi community, the term 'war' is reserved for the "true" wars in the world of Torah, known as "Wars of God," "the war of Torah," or "the war against the evil inclination," rather than wars involving flesh and blood. It is possible that the use of the term "war" and the definition of the "difficult situation" as 'war' in general and as a mandatory war (mitzvah war) in particular (as it is a war explicitly meant for the "assistance of Israel from the hand of their oppressors" – see Maimonides, Mishneh Torah, Laws of Kings and Wars 5:1), which would then necessitate a thorough halakhic inquiry regarding whether the Haredi public, including its Torah scholars, is allowed to exempt itself from active participation in such a war, in view of the words of Moses: "Shall your brothers go to war, while you sit here?" (Numbers 32:6) and in accordance with the guidance of our Sages: "In a mandatory war, everyone goes out to war, even a groom from his room and a bride from her canopy" (Mishnah Sotah 8:7).

11 It is entirely possible that the limited use of the explicit name 'IDF' (Israel Defense Forces) and the reluctance to praise it and its soldiers stems partly from concerns about groups 'to the right' of the Degel Hatorah circles. Foremost among these groups are the 'Peleg' or the

'Jerusalem Faction' (or as they are referred to in the Haredi-Lithuanian sector, the 'Etznikim,' named after the letters 'עץ' [Etz] that were used to represent them in the past in elections. The members of the 'Peleg' have declared an uncompromising war against any association with the army, to the extent that their spiritual leaders instruct their followers to refrain from even going to the enlistment office to obtain an 'exemption from service.' Concurrently, they organize massive protests (often turning violent) against attempts to draft haredim into the IDF and against the arrests of deserters who did not report to the enlistment office to obtain an exemption from service. See Nissim Leon, "The Haredi Scholar – Society and the Military Draft in Israel: Counter-Nationalism and the Imagined Military Symbiosis," in Eyal Lewin, et al., eds., *Comparative Perspectives on Civil Religion, Nationalism, and Political Influence* (Hershey, PA: IGI Global, 2016), 210-225; and Elisheva Rosman, "Haredim and Conscription to the IDF Perspectives, Perceptions, Prospects," in Kimmy Caplan and Nissim Leon, eds., *Contemporary Israeli Haredi Society: Profiles, Trends and Challenges* (London: Routledge, 2024), 90-109.

12 In this matter as well, there have been past allegations that the newspaper reflects only the position of the more moderate leaders of Bnei Brak, such as Rav Steinman as opposed to the more hardline positions of Rav Shach or the Jerusalem leadership. Over the years, opposite claims have been heard, suggesting that the newspaper reflects the position of the more moderate leaders of Bnei Brak but not the more 'extreme' leaders of Jerusalem. This allegation led, among other things, to the establishment of the newspaper *Ha-Peles*, which reflects the more strict and extremist positions of the "Jerusalem Faction."

13 The knowledge is acquired through alternative means, such as non-kosher mobile phones, various telephone lines providing news to the haredi sector, the internet, Facebook groups, WhatsApp, and alongside them, the 'traditional' sources for transmitting rumors and information by word of mouth.

14 Generally, in the internal division of the Haredi community, among yeshiva graduates who enlist in the IDF, a significant portion comprises those from Sephardic Yeshivot, followed by the Hasidim. Meanwhile, the typical Lithuanian Haredi take the last place in this hierarchy.

15 The disregard for the "explicit name" is also evident in other sectors of the ultra-Orthodox Jewish community, even in its more moderate sections. For example, Rav Shaul Alter, a prominent Gur Hasidic Rabbi who had previously served as a Rosh Yeshiva in the main Gur Hasidic court but more recently established his own, visited the Sheba hospital that treated injured IDF soldiers from the Nahal Brigade—a gesture that set him apart from many of his Hasidic counterparts. His "court" even published a notice mourning the death of Eitan Dov Rosenzweig, may his memory be blessed, a Religious Zionist soldier from Alon Shvut who regularly visited the Tish of Rav Shaul's Hasidic court. However, the notice did not mention, even indirectly, the name of the army or the fact that he fell in combat and during the war. It stated, "We participate in the heavy mourning for the sacrifice of the sanctification of God of one of our unique study hall members… and he merited to nurture Torah, fear of God, and piety from our Rabbi, the head of our yeshiva, may he live long and well."

16 Another typical and consistent phenomenon in the *Yated Ne'eman* newspaper is the pattern involves adding different 'verses' from the bible and other Jewish sources at the end of any significant news headlines. For example, after a headline describing the intention to release captives, the words "He [namely, God] will bring them out of darkness" or "He will bring them out of distress to spaciousness." Similarly, after a headline describing the tough fighting in Gaza, the words of the verse (Psalms 127:1) "Unless the Lord watches over the city, the guards stand watch in vain" (*Yated Ne'eman*, 22 November 2023, p. 1). This practice extends to various headlines, where verses from prayers or biblical texts are incorporated to emphasize or relate to the news content. In response to Prime Minister Benjamin

Netanyahu's statements regarding the "Hamas intrigue," the words "Not by might, nor by power" are added. Following a statement by the Hezbollah leader, the verse "Annul the counsel of our enemies" from the prayer "Avinu Malkeinu" is included. In the context of the arrest of the general manager of the Shifaa Hospital in Gaza, the phrase "They will heap up secrets against Your people" is included. In the weekly additional headlines, the words "Days of war" are emphasized, followed by the verse "and we will go in the name of our God" (*Yated Ne'eman*, 24 November 2023). It appears to be a consistent feature in the newspaper's reporting style.

17 Due to the need to occasionally use the term "war" in the main headlines, the newspaper employs creative methods such as converting the term "war" into "Operation Iron Swords" or "ground maneuvers." Generally, significant segments of the Haredi public tend to ignore and consign to oblivion terms originating in halakhic discourse or carrying religious significance that have been 'secularized' in modern Hebrew and are commonly used in this other sense, e.g., "the sports temple", [היכל] "the sanctuary of the Knesset,[משכן הכנסת] " . An exception to this rule is the use of the title "defense minister," [in Hebrew: שר הביטחון, a term equal of "security minister"] even though this term also carries a significant ideological and religious load, differing entirely from the ideological realm: the level of security in God, which is one of the foundations of Jewish faith. See, for example, the well-known book by the Hazon Ish, Rabbi Abraham Isaiah Karelitz (1878-1953), "Emunah u-Bitachon" (1954); or in recent articles by R.J.Zwi Werblowsky, "Faith, Hope and Trust: A Study in the Concept of Bittahon," in Joseph G. Weiss, ed., *Papers of the Institute of Jewish Studies London*, vol. 1 (Jerusalem: Magnes Press, 1964), 94-149; Aharon Lichtenstein, "Bittachon: Trust in God," De'ot, no. 45 (1976): 352-355 (Hebrew); Aharon Lichtenstein, "Bittachon: Trust in God," in *By His Light: Character and Values in the Service of God*, ed. Reuven Ziegler (Jersey City: Ktav Publishing House, 2003), 134-161, a translation of Aharon Lichtenstein, "Bittachon: Trust in God," in Moshe Halbertal, et al., eds., *On Faith:*

Studies in the Concept of Faith and Its History in The Jewish Tradition (Jerusalem: Keter, 2005), 131-144 (Hebrew); and see also Benjamin Brown, "The Hazon Ish: Faith, Trust and Obedience to God," in Naftali Rothenberg, ed., *Meditations on the Parasha* (Tel Aviv: Yedioth Ahronoth, 2005), 385-394, and Daniel Stein, "The Limits of Religious Optimism: The Hazon Ish and the Altar of Novardok on Bittahon," *Tradition: A Journal of Orthodox Jewish Thought*, vol. 43, no. 2 (Summer 2010): 31-48.

18   See the articles by Aaron Ahrend, Levi Cooper, and Nissim Leon in this book.

19   It goes without saying that there exists a strong correlation between the relation of this public towards the State of Israel, on the ideological as well as the practical level, and their attitude towards the Israel Defense Forces (IDF). Extensive literature has been dedicated to the Haredi community's stance towards the state. Notable works on this topic include Aviezer Ravitzky, *Messianism, Zionism, and Jewish Religious Radicalism* (London & Chicago: The University of Chicago Press, 1996); Benjamin Brown, *The Hazon Ish: Halakhist, Believer and Leader of the Haredi Revolution* (Jerusalem: Magnes, 2011), 243 (Hebrew). Additionally, see Benjamin Brown, *The Haredim: A Guide to their Beliefs and Sectors* (Tel-Aviv: Am Oved, 2017; Hebrew); Benjamin Brown, "Haredi Judaism and the State," in Yedidia Z. Stern, et al., eds., *When Judaism Meets State* (Jerusalem: Israel Democracy Institute 2015), 77-268 (Hebrew); Zvi Weinman, *From Katowice to the Fifth of Iyar: Episodes in the History of Haredi Judaism and Agudat Israel, and Their Doctrines* (Jerusalem: Vatikin, 1995; Hebrew) Yohai Hakak, "Haredim, Zionism, and the State of Israel," in *Men in Black: A Journey to the Wellsprings of Israeli Politics – Haredi Men in the Likud* (Jerusalem: The Israel Democracy Institute, 2006): 11-18 (Hebrew); Yosef Fund, *Separation or Participation: Agudat Israel confronting Zionism and the State of Israel* (Jerusalem: Magnes, 1999; Hebrew). For an up-to-date bibliography, see Kimmy Caplan and Yael Becher, *Studying Israeli Haredi Society: A Scholarly Inventory* (Jerusalem: The Israel Democracy Institute, 2022).

20 See Yuval Frankel, "Haredi and Religious Judaism in Jerusalem during the Siege," *Zionism*, vol. 18 (1994): 247-289 (Hebrew)

21 A few months before the establishment of the state, in the month of Adar 5708 (February 1948), a festive gathering took place to mark the founding of the "Religious Service." The meeting was attended by David Ben-Gurion, the leader of the Jewish Agency, Yaakov Dori, the head of the National Defense Forces (and later the first Chief of Staff of the IDF), and members of the Jewish Agency's leadership, Rabbi Judah Leib Maimon and Moshe Shapira, along with representatives of Agudat Yisrael and the Chief Rabbinate, including Rabbi Benjamin Mintz and Rabbi Kalman Kahana. For a detailed description, see Yitzhak Meir, *Not by Might, nor by Power: The Military Rabbinate and Religious Services – Laying the Foundations for Religious Life in the IDF* (Bnei Brak: The Association for the Study of the History of Bnei Brak and Ginzach Kiddush Hashem, 1999), 12 (Hebrew). For a more detailed account, see Moshe Ehrenwald, *The Haredim During the War of Independence* (Ben-Shemen: Modan, 2017; Hebrew).

22 It should be noted that the clear distinction that exists today between "Haredim" and "non-Haredim" was much more blurred during those years. All observant individuals stood on a single continuum, and the "pious" among them in the observance of commandments were referred to as "Haredim," even if their worldview was completely aligned with the Zionist-religious perspective. For example, Rabbi Joseph B. Soloveitchik consistently referred to the members of the "Mizrachi" movement as part of "Haredi Judaism" in all his writings. See Aviad Hacohen, "'For You Shall See the Land, But You Shall Not Enter It': On Rabbi Joseph B. Soloveitchik's Candidacy for the Tel Aviv Chief Rabbinate and the Riddle of his Subsequent Refraining from Visiting Israel," in Dov Schwartz, ed., *Religious Zionism: History, Thought, Society*, vol. 9 (Ramat-Gan: Bar-Ilan University Press, 2023), 207n152 (Hebrew); and Benjamin Brown, *The Haredim: A Guide to their Beliefs and Sectors* (Tel-Aviv: Am Oved, 2017), 12-13 (Hebrew). During the second half of the 20th century, the term "haredi" gradually became more firmly established, partly due to

interested parties who appropriated it to imply that only they, and no others, were truly "Haredim for the sake of God." This term was also used to stigmatize people identified with non-Zionist movements and parties such as Agudath Yisrael and the factions to their right.

See also Moshe Bar-Asher, *Leshonenu Rinna: Liturgical Studies: Language, Style, Content, Versions, and Customs* (Jerusalem: Reuven Mass, 2015), 198-199n77 (Hebrew), who writes: "Up until the 1940s, those of Religious Zionist persuasion still embraced the label 'Haredi Jews'. However, in the latter half of the twentieth-century, 'Haredim' came to denote those who observe commandments to an extreme extent, distinguished by their unique appearance and their pronounced dissociation from Zionism and the state (a topic I hope, God willing, to delve into in a dedicated study of the evolution of the term "Haredi"). Notably, it stands as the sole Hebrew word that underwent a transformation in meaning during the twentieth century, a period marking the rebirth of Hebrew as a spoken vernacular, amidst the societal shifts in the Land of Israel."

23 See Moshe Ehrenwald, *The Haredim During the War of Independence* (Ben-Shemen: Modan, 2017); Kimmy Caplan and Yael Becher, *Studying Israeli Haredi Society: A Scholarly Inventory* (Jerusalem: The Israel Democracy Institute, 2022), 27 (Hebrew) and references there; and Benjamin Brown, *The Hazon Ish: Halakhist, Believer and Leader of the Haredi Revolution* (Jerusalem: Magnes, 2011), 247.

24 See Eldad Naor, "The War of Independence in Jerusalem: Criticism in the Area of Security, as Reflected in "Hayoman" of Agudat Israel (March–April 1948)," in Amiram Gonen, ed., *The Journal for the Haredi Society Research*, vol. 5 (April 2018), 94-131 (Hebrew), available here (https://jerusaleminstitute.org.il/wp-content/uploads/2019/07/מלחמת-העצמאות_pub.pdf).

25 Rabbi Shmuel Eliezeri (1907-1991) was one of the disciples of the Chofetz Chaim after World War I in Shumyachi, and later wandered with the yeshiva and the Chofetz Chaim to various cities around Lithuania. During this time, he had the privilege of studying Torah from prominent Lithuanian rabbis, including Rabbi Elchonon Wasserman, Rabbi Eliyahu Dushnitzer, Rav Boruch Ber Leibowitz, and Rabbi Chaim Ozer Grodzinski, who was the co-founder of the

Vaad ha-Yeshivot in Vilna and served as the first chairman of the Moetzes Gedolei Torah, the rabbinical advisory board to the Agudath Israel. Eventually, after Rabbi Shmuel Eliezeri's immigration to Israel, he studied at Yeshivat Merkaz HaRav and served as a rabbi in the Beit VeGan neighborhood and later in Tel Aviv.

26 Rabbi Yitzhak ha-Levi Epstein (1912-1965) studied at the Kletsk Yeshiva in Lithuania and was a close disciple of Rabbi Isser Zalman Meltzer and Rabbi Elazar Menachem Man Shach. After immigrating to Israel, he continued his studies at the Hebron Yeshiva. Rabbi Epstein was one of the founders of the military rabbinate and completed his service with the rank of Lieutenant Colonel. He served as a rabbinical judge (Av Beit Din) in Tel Aviv and was an editor of the Talmudic Encyclopedia.

27 Rabbi Avraham ha-Levi Horowitz (1920-2004) was the son-in-law of Rabbi Chaim Yehuda Leib Auerbach and the brother-in-law of Rabbi Shlomo Zalman Auerbach.

28 Rabbi Dov Cohen served as the first chaplain of the Israeli Air Force. He was born in Lithuania, raised in the United States, and later immigrated to Israel. He became a student of Rabbi Nosson Tzvi Finkel, the Alter of Slabodka in the Yeshivat Knesset Yisrael (later known as Yeshivat Hebron), when it was still located in Hebron. Many descriptions of Rabbi Dov Cohen's service in the IDF can be found in his memoirs, published in *Zikhronotav Shel HaRav Dov Cohen* (Jerusalem: Feldheim, 2010; Hebrew), and adapted to English in *To Rise Above – The Amazing Life of HaRav Dov Cohen zt"l A Journey to Greatness Against All Odds* (Jerusalem: Feldheim, 2016). On Rabbi Nosson Tzvi Finkel, the Alter of Slabodka in the Yeshivat Knesset Yisrael, see Shlomo Tikochinsky, *Torah Scholarship, Mussar, and Elitism: The Slabodka Yeshiva from Lithuania to Mandate Palestine* (Jerusalem: Shazar, 2016; Hebrew).

29 Rabbi Shimon Rafiko (1915-1980) was born in Lithuania and studied at the Slabodka Yeshiva. He considered himself a disciple of Rabbi Yehezkel Bernstein, known as the author of "Divrei Yehezkel,"

from Slabodka. During the Holocaust, he survived in the Kovno Ghetto. After the war, he received rabbinical ordination in Germany and served as a rabbi in displaced persons camps until his immigration to Israel. In Israel, he married (as a second marriage) the daughter-in-law of Rabbi Shlomo Yosef Zevin, a member of the Chief Rabbinate Council of Israel and the editor of the Talmudic Encyclopedia. Rabbi Rafiko held various positions, including serving as the Chief Rabbi of the Central Command and heading the Kashrut and Shabbat Department in the IDF Military Rabbinate.

30 Rabbi Yehuda Shulman (1911-2001) lost his father at the age of one and was raised by his mother and brother. He studied in various yeshivas, including those in Baranovich, Radin, and Hebron. He was the brother of Rabbi Mordechai Shulman, who served as the head of the Slabodka Yeshiva in Bnei Brak and was a prominent figure in the Musar movement. Rabbi Yehuda Shulman was also the son-in-law of Rabbi Asher Kerstein, who served as the rabbi of Afula.

31 Rabbi Avraham Avidan (Zemel) (1938-2022) studied at the Tiferet Zion yeshiva in Bnei Brak, which was founded by the Hazon Ish, and at the Hebron Yeshiva. He was a student of Rabbi Yosef Sholom Elyashiv. Rabbi Avidan served, among other roles, as the military rabbi of the Jerusalem district and as the deputy chief military rabbi of the Israel Defense Forces.

32 Rabbi Ephraim Tzemel (1935-2022) was born in Jerusalem to a Lithuanian family (his mother descended from the "HaSaba MiKelm" family). He served, among other roles, as the rabbi of the Paratroopers Brigade and the rabbi of the Israel Air Force. After his release from the IDF, he served as a Rosh Yeshiva at Yeshivas Ohr Sameyach in Jerusalem, was counted among the close associates of Rabbi Shach, served as a member of the spiritual leadership of the Chief Rabbinate Council, was the head of the Daf Yomi branch of "Degel Hatorah" in Jerusalem, and also served as the secretary of the Council of Torah Sages of "Degel Hatorah." His son-in-law, Rabbi Yisroel Zicherman,

Rabbi of Achuzas Brachfeld in Modi'in Illit, was a member of the "She'arit Yisrael" Beit Din of the Lithuanian-Haredim.

33 Rabbi Chaim Menachem Baksht (b. 1932) studied at the Tiferet Zion yeshiva in Bnei Brak and at the Hebron Yeshiva, and in the Shevet MeYehuda Kollel Dayanut. During his service in the IDF, he served, among other roles, as the Chief Rabbi of the Southern Command, the Navy Rabbi, and as the Deputy Chief Military Rabbi with the rank of Brigadier General.

34 Rabbi Shlomo Zalman Kook (1929-1971) was the son of Rabbi Raphael Kook, the Rabbi of Tiberias, and the nephew of Rabbi Abraham Isaac Kook. He studied at the Hebron Yeshiva and joined the Haganah at the age of 16. He married Judith, the daughter of Rabbi Dov Katz, the author of the five-volume *Tenuat ha-Mussar* book series. After their marriage, they lived in Ramsgate, England from 1954-1957, where he served as Rosh Yeshiva of Montefiore Theological College. In the year 1958, he assumed the position of the military rabbi for the Jerusalem district and served in that role for seven years. Following that, he served as a Dayan in Tel-Aviv and then as the Chief Rabbi of Rehovot until he tragically passed away in a car accident, along with his wife and two of their children. See Cyril Domb, "Rav Shlomo Zalman Kook and Montefiore College," *Le'ela*, no. 43 (April 1997): 35-38.

35 Rabbi Mordechai Abramovsky (b. 1947) studied at the Hebron Yeshiva and was ordained as a rabbi by the yeshiva's leaders, Rabbi Yehezkel Sarna and Rabbi Moshe Hevroni. He enlisted in the Israel Defense Forces (IDF) after the Yom Kippur War and served, among other roles, as the rabbi of the Gadna youth corps, the IDF rabbi of the paratroopers, and the head of the Division of Personal Status and Burial. Today, he serves as the rabbi of Zikhron Yaakov. His brother-in-law, Rabbi Mordechai Neugroschel, is one of the contemporary leaders of the Baaley Teshuva and Keiruv movement and well-known public figure in the Lithuanian Haredi community.

36   Rabbi Ram Moshe Ravad served as a rabbi in the Israeli Air Force with the rank of Major. Within the framework of the Air Force, he promoted the "Shachar" program for the integration of Haredi individuals. Even after his retirement, he continued to work on advancing the service of Haredim in the Israel Defense Forces.

37   Prominent outliers in this landscape of those coming from Lithuanian yeshivas were several rabbis who had studied at Yeshivat Merkaz HaRav. These included Rabbi Mordechai Piron (1921-2014), who was the Deputy to Chief Rabbi Goren; Rabbi Shear Yashuv Cohen (1927-2016), who was a son of Rav David Cohen the Nazir and son-in-law of Chief Rabbi Goren; Rabbi Gad Navon (1922-2006), who was born in Morocco and studied in yeshiva there, and would later serve as the third Chief Rabbi of the IDF; and Rabbi Yitzhak Meir (1918-2005), a Gur Hasid and later mayor of Bnei Brak. See Shifra Mescheloff, "Establishing the Independent Status of the IDF Rabbinate: From Rabbi Goren to Rabbi Piron," in Aviad Hacohen and Tsvi Tal, eds., *Safra ve-Saifa, The Book and the Sword: Rabbi Mordechai Piron Jubilee Volume* (Jerusalem: Mahanayim, 2013), 366-389 (Hebrew); Aharon (Roni) Kampinsky, "The IDF Military Rabbi: Between a Cohen Anointed for War and a Religious Services Provider," *Religions*, vol. 11, no. 4 (2020): 1-14; and Haggai Huberman, *Rav Aluf: Biography of Rabbi Mordechai Piron* (Jerusalem: Bet-El Publishing, 2021).

38   "Gedud Tuvia" (named after its commander, Tuvia Bir, a graduate of the Kol Torah yeshiva), also known as "The Yeshiva Students Battalion," operated in Jerusalem following the establishment of the state, from May to November 1948. Its establishment was the result of an agreement between the central command of the Jewish community, on one side, and the Yeshivot Committee with the participation of the chief rabbis of Israel and the Va'ad Edah HaChareidis, on the other side. Its goal was to incorporate the students of yeshivot who resided in Jerusalem into the city's defense forces. An examination of the battalion's roster (as reported in the blog post "Revelation: The Satmar Recruits Following the Agreement of the Gaavad"), available here

(http://kvarhaya.blogspot.com/2017/10/blog-post.html), reveals that it included young men from Jerusalem yeshivot and Hasidic backgrounds who also served in the IDF. Examples include Rabbi Aharon Nahum Miletski, who served as a gabbai in the household of Rabbi Shach and gabbai of the Itzkovitz Synagogue in Bnei Brak, and his brother Moshe Chaim Miletski, sons of Rabbi Haikel Miletski, the head of the Chayei Olam yeshiva, who was associated with the leaders of the Haredi Agudat Yisrael movement. Jacob Chaim Sarna, son of Rabbi Yehezkel Sarna, head of the Hebron Yeshiva (and later head of the Hebron Yeshiva – Geula), and Rabbi Aharon Chodosh, son of Rabbi Meir Chodosh, who served as the mashgiah ruhani of the yeshiva, who were also part of the battalion.

39   The Nahal Haredi, which later changed its name to the Netzah Yehuda Battalion, operated from its inception under the close supervision of individuals from Tzeirei Agudat Israel, led by Rabbi Moshe Haim Sheinfeld. For more on this unit, see Ze'ev Drori, *Between Faith and Military Service: The Nahal Haredi Battalion* (Jerusalem: The Floersheimer Institute for Policy Studies, 2005), David Zoldan, *The Yarmulke and the Helmet: The Story of the First Haredi Army Unit* (Tel-Aviv: Yedioth Ahronoth, 2009); and most recently in Elisheva Rosman, "Haredim and Conscription to the IDF – Perspectives, Perceptions, Prospects," in Kimmy Caplan and Nissim Leon, eds., *Contemporary Israeli Haredi Society: Profiles, Trends and Challenges* (London: Routledge, 2024), 90-109. For additional insights, see the testimony of Dr. Jacob Weinroth, a graduate of the Ponovezh Yeshiva, who was drafted into the IDF as part of this unit. It's worth noting that in the late 1970s, soldiers of the Haredi Nahal underwent shortened basic training and were also involved in diamond cutting work in the Haredi moshav of Komemiyut, which is now part of the Hazon Yehezkel educational institution. See Aviad Hacohen, "And Jacob Went On His Way," in Gershon Gontovnik, Avi Weinroth, and Haim Zicherman, eds., *Sefer Jacob Weinroth* (Jerusalem: Nevo, 2022), 61-172 (Hebrew)

40 An example of this phenomenon is the enlistment of Rabbi Yehuda Amital (1924-2010), who was the founder and co-Rosh Yeshiva of Yeshivat Har Etzion. Rabbi Yehuda Amital (Klein) studied in yeshivas in Hungary, survived labor camps during the Holocaust, and immigrated to Israel in 1944. He studied at the Hebron Yeshiva in Jerusalem and the Kletzk Yeshiva in Pardes Hanna. He married Miriam, the daughter of Rabbi Zvi Yehuda Meltzer, the head of the Etz Chaim Yeshiva, and was ordained as a rabbi by his wife's grandfather, Rabbi Isser Zalman Meltzer. The day after the declaration of the state, he enlisted in the IDF and participated in the War of Independence as a soldier in the 7th Brigade, in battles at Latrun and in the Western Galilee. He documented his experiences as a soldier in an article in Yehuda Amital, "The Path of the Religious Soldier in the War of Independence," in *HaMa'alot MiMa'amakim* (Jerusalem and Alon Shevut: Agudat Yeshivat Har Ezion, 1977), 96-107 (Hebrew), which was analyzed in Aaron Ahrend, "Serving in the IDF in the Teachings of Rabbi Yehuda Amital," *Bar Ilan's Parashat Hashavua Study Center* (7 May 2011), available here (https://etzion.org.il/en/holidays/yom-haatzmaut/serving-idf-teachings-rabbi-yehuda-amital-zl). It is important to note that this phenomenon is not limited to graduates of Zionist-oriented yeshivas but also includes individuals who initially grew up in religious Zionist environments, later turned to Haredi yeshivas, and subsequently enlisted in the IDF, such as Rabbis Yehoshua Ben-Meir (b. 1947), Mordechai Halperin (b. 1946), Benjamin Be'eri (b. 1940), Avraham Sherman (b. 1941) and others.

41 The document can be found in the archive of Religious Zionism at Bar-Ilan University, file 494, and it was published by Benjamin Brown, *The Hazon Ish: Halakhist, Believer and Leader of the Haredi Revolution* (Jerusalem: Magnes, 2011), 247 (Hebrew).

42 In this context, it is important to underscore once again the distinction between the "traditional" Haredim and the "modern," "working" Haredim, also referred to as "Israeli Haredim." As mentioned, these are shades and nuances along a spectrum, and the boundaries between

the various groups are not always precisely delineated. Regarding the new Haredim, see Benjamin Brown, *The Haredim: A Guide to their Beliefs and Sectors* (Tel-Aviv: Am Oved, 2017; Hebrew), and David Zoldan, *The New Haredim* (Modiin: Kineret, Zmora, Dvir, 2021; Hebrew).

43 At the same time, the military also made efforts to recruit Haredi individuals, both due to a surplus of manpower in certain areas and out of concern for the tasks and limitations that would be imposed on the army. These limitations included budgetary constraints (many Lithuanian-Haredi individuals were "over the Rubicon" in terms of age, married, and had families, which imposed a significant financial burden on the military budget) and practical considerations (such as the inability to integrate them into mixed-gender units, the requirement for strictly kosher food, and more).

44 It is permissible to say that even within the ideological field, there are nuances and variations among the Haredi public. For example, some tend to distinguish between the Hazon Ish followers from Bnei Brak and the students of Brisker Rav (who mainly reside in Jerusalem), and between them and the "Zilberman" followers, students of Rabbi Yitzchak Shlomo Zilberman (1929-2001). Given the differences between these groups, there is also some political representation for each of them. For example, Knesset members Moshe Gafni (b. 1952) and Yisrael Eichler (b. 1955) represent the rabbis of Bnei Brak, while Knesset member Uri Maklev (b. 1957) "represents" the Jerusalemite public, and Knesset member Yitzhak Ze'ev Pindrus (b. 1971) is associated with the students of Rabbi Zilberman.

45 This, even though it has been proven that the Hatam Sofer himself did not always refrain from adopting 'new practices,' and used the principle not only in order to reinforce stringent practices but also to avoid following new stringencies. See Maoz Kahana, *From the Noda be-Yehuda to the Hatam Sofer: Halakhah and Thought in Their Historical Moment* (Jerusalem: Shazar, 2015; Hebrew).

46 In practical terms, there have been considerable shifts in lifestyle across generations, influenced by sociological and economic changes, such as the increased participation of women in the workforce, and technological advancements, including the use of electronic devices. Yet, at the level of stated principles, the adage has maintained its perennial relevance and applicability.

47 On the origins of *Yequm Purkan*, see Charles Duschinsky, "The Yekum Purkan," *Sefer Zikkaron Likvod ha-Dr. Shmuel Avraham Poznanski* (Warsaw, 1927; repr. Jerusalem, 1969), 182-198; and Neil Danzig, "Two Insights from a Ninth-Century Liturgical Handbook: The Origins of *Yequm Purqan* and *Qaddish de-Hadata*," in Stefan C. Reif, ed., *The Cambridge Genizah Collections: Their Contents and Significance* (Cambridge: Cambridge University Press, 2002), 74-122.

48 For this reason, in most non-Haredi communities, there is also an avoidance of saying lamentations that were composed after the Holocaust. In some Israeli communities, new lamentations have been added to the traditional order of lamentations, including those composed by figures whose connection to the Haredi public is beyond doubt, such as the Bobover Rebbe, Rabbi Shlomo Halberstam or Rabbi Shimon Schwab, the rabbi of the Khal Adath Jeshurun community in Washington Heights, New York, and one of the important ideologues of Agudath Israel in the United States. In this context, it is also appropriate to mention the conservative position of Rabbi Joseph B. Soloveitchik. Despite being a leader of Modern Orthodoxy in the USA, in everything related to prayer orders, Rabbi Soloveitchik maintained a wholly conservative stance. Thus, he wrote regarding the addition of lamentations on Tisha B'Av: "On Tisha B'Av, we fast and mourn for all the tragedies and all the disasters of Jewish history throughout the generations... Not only for the disasters that occurred on it, but for every exile, every tragedy, every disaster that befell the Jewish people over the generations." He added a reservation about adding special lamentations composed after the Holocaust: "The six million Jews are certainly worthy of being mentioned on Tisha B'Av. But we do this within the framework of the lamentations

that we already say on that day... The described sights and the words of despair, mourning, and sorrow are not different." For more on this subject, see Jacob J. Schacter, "Rabbi Joseph B. Soloveitchik zt"l on the Tisha B'Av Kinos," *Jewish Action*, vol. 54, no. 4 (Summer 1994): 8-12; Jacob J. Schacter, "Introduction," in Rabbi Joseph B. Soloveitchik, *The Lord is Righteous in All His Ways: Reflections on the Tish'ah be-Av Kinot*, ed. Jacob J. Schacter (Ktav Publishing House, Inc.: Jersey City, 2006), xi-xix; See Jacob J. Schacter, "Holocaust Commemoration and Tish'a be-Av: The Debate Over 'Yom ha-Sho'a,'" *Tradition: A Journal of Orthodox Jewish Thought*, vol. 41, no. 2 (Summer 2008): 164-197; Jacob J. Schacter, "The Rav and the Tisha B'Av Kinot," in Zev Eleff, ed., *Mentor of Generations: Reflections on Rabbi Joseph B. Soloveitchik* (Jersey City: Ktav, 2008), 303-314; and Ephraim Kanarfogel, "The History of the Tosafists and their Literary Corpus According to Rav Soloveitchik's Interpretations of the Qinot for Tishah B'av," in Ephraim Kanarfogel and Dov Schwartz, eds., *Scholarly Man of Faith* (New York: Yeshiva University Press, 2018), 75-107.

Similarly, Rabbi Yekutiel Yehuda Halberstam, the Klausenberger Rebbe, himself a Holocaust survivor who lost almost his entire family – his wife and nine children – opposed the integration of new Holocaust lamentations into the prayer. See Tamir Granot, "The Revival of Hassidism in the Land of Israel after the Holocaust: The Ideological, Halachic and Social Doctrine of the Admor Rabbi Yekutiel Yehudah Halberstam of Sanz-Klausenburg," (PhD Dissertation, Bar-Ilan University, 2008; Hebrew).

49 The clarification of the expression can be found in Sotah 21a, in the context of a broader discussion of actions that may "protect" a person from various harms. It states as follows: "Rabbi Yosef says: A mitzvah [commandment]—when one engages in it, it protects and saves him. When one does not engage in it, it protects him, but it does not save him. Torah—both when one engages in it and when one does not engage in it, it protects and saves him."

50 For additional information on this subject, you can consult Rabbi Neria Guttel, "On Whom Does the Torah Protect?" *Mercaz*

Torah v'Medina (29 October 2020), available here (https://www.toramedina.org.il/-מי-על/קורונה-מדינה-מכת/המרכז-ושיעורי-מאמרי התורה-מגינה/). It goes without saying that no one in the Lithuanian-Haredi community leaves their house or car door unlocked, nor do they abstain from medical treatment when necessary, solely on the basis that the Torah "guards and shields."

51 Midrash Tanhuma, Beshalah, 9.

52 Based on the words of the Talmud in Sotah 49b.

53 For further information on this topic, see the article by Chanani Breitkopf, "Did the Assurance of Rabbi Hayyim Kanievsky That Missiles Won't Fall on Bnei Brak Hold?" *Kikar Shabbat* (19 October 2023), available here (https://www.kikar.co.il/haredim-news/s2rqbz). My colleague and friend, Professor Benjamin Brown, drew my attention to the fragility of this "assurance." According to him, the initial source of its existence is the book "Eileh Toledot Yitzchak," in which the Hazon Ish assured during the War of Independence that in this month, no missiles would fall on Bnei Brak. When asked why he suddenly permitted himself to make a prophecy, he replied that when Jews are worried, it is a mitzvah to console them. As Professor Benjamin Brown puts it, "This 'psychological exercise' turned this statement into a mystical talisman." Regarding the "development" in this matter, consider, for example, the statements made in the name of Rabbi Yitzchak Zilberstein, the rabbi of the Ramat Elchanan neighborhood in Bnei Brak, in 2019, where this assurance was based on "the merit of sanctifying the name of God and using kosher electricity on Shabbat." On another occasion, when asked if the assurance also applied to other Haredi settlements besides Bnei Brak, he replied that indeed, the Hazon Ish did not say his words only about Bnei Brak but added, "But obviously, the words are true for other settlements as well because the clarification of the Hazon Ish's assurance is due to the observance of Shabbat by the residents of Bnei Brak, and if so, anywhere Shabbat is observed – the assurance applies, and the security is that no missiles will fall." This "assurance" then took

on a life of its own (for example, the question asked of Rabbi Hayyim Kanievsky by a Torah scholar who lived in a building in Ramat Gan, bordering on Bnei Brak, inquiring if the assurance of the Hazon Ish that missiles wouldn't fall on Bnei Brak also applied to him, to which Rabbi Kanievsky replied that indeed, the assurance applied to this building as well...).

54 The worldview presented here stands in stark contrast to the worldview of some spiritual leaders of Religious Zionism who saw the war as a miracle and even attributed value to it. For example, Rabbi Kook wrote in praise of war, in works that which were eventually published under the title "Orot Ha-Milhamah" (The Lights of War). Among other things, he wrote: When there is a great war in the world, the power of Messiah is aroused. The time of song (zamir) has arrived, the scything (zemir) of tyrants, the wicked perish from the world, and the world is invigorated and the voice of the turtledove is heard in our land. The individuals who are killed unjustly in the revolution of the flood of the war participate in the concept, "the death of the righteous atones," they rise above in the root of life and the essence of their lives brings a general quality of good and blessing to the overall structure of the world in all its values and senses. Afterward, at the cessation of the war, the world is renewed in a new spirit and the feet of Messiah are revealed even more. According to the extent of the war in quantity and quality – so increases the extent of the feet of Messiah through it." See Rav Avraham Yitzhak ha-Kohen Kook, *Orot ha-Milhamah*, 1 (Hebrew), translation from *Rav Kook's Orot*, trans. Bezalel Naor (Jerusalem: Maggid, 2022), 131.

55 This important topic goes beyond the scope of this article. We will only mention that the political worldview of some of the leaders of the Lithuanian-Haredi community, such as Rabbi Elazar M. Shach, who advocated for the return of territories in exchange for a peace agreement and the prevention of war, emanated from this worldview, among other things. See Benjamin Brown, "Rabbi E.M. Shach: Admiration of Spirit, Critique of Nationalism, and Political Involvement," in Neri Horowitz, ed., *Religion and Nationalism in*

Israel and the Middle East (Tel-Aviv: Am Oved, 2003), 278-342 (Hebrew); and Moshe Hellinger, "The Criticism of Democracy in Rabbi E.M. Shach's Thought," in Erich Kofmel, ed., *Anti-Democratic Thought* (Exeter: Imprint Academic, 2008), 123-138.

56   These remarks by Rabbi Shach were first published the following year in the *Digleinu* magazine in 1974 and were later quoted in other sources, such as Rabbi A.Y. Nesher, *Sha'arei Emunah u-Bitachon* (Bnei Brak, 2012), Part II, p. 209 (Hebrew). Despite his ideological perspective, Rabbi Shach publicly expressed his appreciation for the soldiers of the Israel Defense Forces on a personal level. The son of Rabbi Shach, Dr. Ephraim Shach (1930-2011), served as a soldier in the Irgun and later in the Israeli Defense Forces as did two of his children, who are Rabbi Shach's grandchildren. According to an oral tradition, during a tour by IDF commanders in Bnei Brak and at the Ponevezh Yeshiva, the commanders visited Rabbi Shach's home. When they entered, he stood up and said to them: "You are important people, very important. You are guarding the Land of Israel excellently, and we owe you a lot of thanks for your actions. We know how to recognize and appreciate your contribution here," and he added, "Out of respect for these important people, I stand."

57   See Chizki Stern, "The Blow We Endured, the Struggle, and the Questions of the Children | Q&A on War with Rav David Cohen," *Kikar Shabbat* (19 October 2023), available here (https://www.kikar.co.il/yeshiva-world/s2s2yx).

58   Rabbi Yisrael Bunim Schreiber (b. 1958) heads the "Netiv Daat" Yeshiva in Jerusalem and serves as the rabbi of the "Bnei Pinchas" Lithuanian Haredi community in Ashdod, which was led by his father, Rabbi Pinchas Schreiber, until his passing. He studied at the Ponevezh and Brisk Yeshivas and taught in the Ramat Elchanan neighborhood in Bnei Brak, one of the strongholds of the Lithuanian Haredi community.

59   Later, after a public storm erupted following these statements, Rabbi Schreiber "clarified" that he apologizes for the misunderstanding of

his words and their misinterpretation. In an advertisement published in the *Yated Ne'eman* newspaper (dated 21 November 23), he stated: "Clarification. Quoting my words regarding the war as published in the media distorts their meaning. And certainly, there was no intention, God forbid, to harm. Yisrael Bunim Schreiber."

60 In this matter as well, there is a special place for certain chapters of Psalms that are customarily recited specifically in times of danger, such as chapters 91 ("Shir Shel Pega'im"), 130, and more.

61 See Tamar El-Or, "A Temple in Your Kitchen: *Hafrashat Hallah* – The Rebirth of a Forgotten Ritual as a Public Ceremony," in Ra'anan S. Boustan, et al., eds., *Jewish Studies at the Crossroads of Anthropology and History: Authority, Diaspora, Tradition* (Philadelphia: Penn Press, 2011), 271-293, 404-405.

62 For a brief bibliographical analysis on the *seudat amenim*, see Shnayer Z. Leiman, "A Puzzling Passage in a Book Intended for Jewish Children, with a Tentative Bibliography of Religious Books that Discuss the Mitzvah of Answering "Amen'," *The Seforim Blog* (22 November 2006), available here (https://seforimblog.com/2006/11/shnayer-leiman-on-puzzling-passage-in).

63 On Rosh Chodesh 5784, (14 November 2023), a *hafrashat challah* ceremony of this kind was also held in the main entrance of the Supreme Court building, attended by some of its judges, including Israeli Supreme Court President Esther Hayut and Deputy President Judge Uzi Vogelman.

64 As expected, those who approached the recruitment office received sharp criticism both from the spiritual leaders of the Haredi community and, more so, from the extreme faction within it, "Bnei Torah" who are affiliated with the "Jerusalem Faction." One of the representatives of this stream, the chairman of the "Bnei Torah" faction in the Jerusalem municipality, Rabbi Chaim Epstein, likened these recruits to "comrades who betrayed [them] in the midst of battle."

65 For example, the harsh words of Rabbi David Cohen, Rosh Yeshiva of the Hebron Yeshiva, were quoted against this phenomenon: "The heart bleeds for the talk heard from the margins of our camp, claiming that at this time of crisis, when all Israel is in danger, we should go help and should exit the walls of the yeshiva. Anyone who says such things has no knowledge of what Torah is, what the Jewish people is, or what yeshiva students are, nor of the concept 'The Torah, the Holy One, and Israel are one" (Zohar 3:73a)." This quote from Rabbi David Cohen was originally published in *Yated Ne'eman*, and discussed in Eliyahu Berkowitz, "Rising Wave of Haredi Enlistment in War May Spark Greater Integration," *Makor Rishon* (23 October 2023), available here (https://www.makorrishon.co.il/opinion/685921), and in an expanded annotated format, as published by the Israel Democracy Institute (https://www.idi.org.il/articles/51152). See also Yehoshua Pfeffer, "Haredi Israelis Are Joining the Army," *The Wall Street Journal* (14 November 2023). In response to this article, Aviad Hacohen and Menachem Butler submitted a Letter to *The Wall Street Journal* on 16 November 2023, though it has not yet been published:

Dear Editor:

Rabbi Yehoshua Pfeffer's recent opinion piece, "Ultra-Orthodox Israelis Are Joining the Army" (published on November 14), particularly during Israel's current war against Hamas in Operation Swords of Iron, presents an optimistic vision of societal integration. We also would like to wish so.

But notably, he mentions various expressions of mutual responsibility that are currently taking place in Israel. This principle demands that all year around and especially during times of national crisis, all community members, including the Ultra-Orthodox, should actively engage in addressing the situation. Such engagement is crucial, serving both as a national duty and a moral obligation to the collective well-being of society. However, this view contrasts sharply with the substantial and vocal opposition from many prominent leaders within the Ultra-Orthodox community itself. These dissenting voices, often overshadowed in public discourse, represent a significant segment of the community that firmly resists the idea of military service, underscoring a deep-seated conflict between modern integration and traditional values.

Rabbi Pfeffer, a member of the Ultra-Orthodox community in Israel, seems surprisingly unaware of the stated criticisms against this viewpoint from within his movement's leadership. Just for instance, Rabbi Dovid Cohen serves as the Rosh Yeshiva of Chevron Yeshiva in Givat Mordechai (a flagship institution of the Yeshiva world), in Jerusalem, and as a council member of Moetzes Gedolei HaTorah, the supreme rabbinical policy-making council of Degel HaTorah political party. Through his roles in these key religious and political circles, he significantly influences the Ultra-Orthodox community in Israel and abroad. Three weeks into the current war, the following remarks by Rabbi Dovid Cohen were reported by *Yated Ne'eman*, an official mouthpiece of the Israeli ultra-Orthodox community: "The heart bleeds for the talk heard from the margins of our camp, claiming that at this time of crisis, when all Israel is in danger, we should go help and should exit the walls of the yeshiva. Anyone who says such things has no knowledge of what Torah is, what the Jewish people is, or what yeshiva students are, nor of the concept 'The Torah, the Holy One, and Israel are one' (Zohar 3:73a)."

As academic observers of the Ultra-Orthodox community in Israel and globally, we have noticed a trend among prominent yeshiva leaders who, in contrast to well-intentioned activists like Rabbi Pfeffer, have publicly denounced the increasing number of Haredim joining the IDF. The impact of these denunciations, as well as the advocacy for more IDF integration, which could potentially lead to a "boomerang effect," remains unclear. However, these condemnations clearly reflect a firm opposition to military service and a commitment to the traditional value of uninterrupted Torah study.

Aviad Hacohen and Menachem Butler

Judah Halevi on War and Morality

Warren Zev Harvey

IN RABBI JUDAH HALEVI'S PHILOSOPHIC dialogue, *The Kuzari*, I, 113-114 (cf. I, 2-3), the Jewish scholar boasts to the King of the Khazars that the Christians and the Muslims are engaged in terrible wars, but we Jews are virtuous, meek, and do not kill anyone. The King immediately retorts: "Your humility is not by choice! As soon as you have a moment of triumph, you'll kill too [*idhā aṣabtum ẓafra, qataltum*]!" In other words, "Wait until you have your own State!"

In the soul-searching debates after the Qibya reprisal raid in 1953, Professor Ernst Simon cited this text from the *Kuzari* (*Beterem* 103, 1.1.54, p. 21). His point was that moral responsibility presupposes power. When the Jewish people lacked political power in the Exile, we did not have the opportunity to be morally responsible. It's easy to be virtuous when you don't have the power to harm others. Now, in our own independent Jewish State, our Jewish morality is finally being tested. Now that we have power, how will we use it? Will we choose war, like all the other nations, or will we choose peace? Simon's interpretation of *Kuzari*, I, 113-114, has been quoted often in subsequent Zionist literature. The State of Israel is an existential test of Jewish morality.

In the wake of the horrors of October 7th, when our army was caught unprepared by thousands of Hamas terrorists who breached our borders, murdered more than 1,200, wounded more than 3,600, tortured, raped, decimated communities, and took more than 240 captives into Gaza, I thought again about the Khazar King's reply to the Jewish scholar, and saw it in a different way.

The King is not a philosopher or moralist, but a political person. He presumably also had experience commanding his people on the battlefield. We shouldn't expect him to be a pacifist. His view was probably that of *Realpolitik*. He is saying to the Jewish scholar: When you have your own independent State, you will find that you too, like the Christians and the Muslims, will *have no choice* but to draft an army, and you will sometimes *be forced* to kill in order to defend yourselves. When you have power, you must learn not only when not to use it, but also when to use it. A State that cannot prevent the massacre of its citizens has failed morally.

The Israel Defense Force is now conducting a difficult military campaign against Hamas in Gaza. In the prayer for the soldiers of the IDF, we recite the words of Deuteronomy 20:4: "for the Lord your God is He that goeth with you [*ha-holekh 'immakhem*]." We pray that the Lord our God go with our soldiers, and grant them the knowledge of how and when to use power – in order to defend our people from terror, to achieve victory, and to secure peace.

Warren Zev Harvey is Professor Emeritus in the Department of Jewish Thought at the Hebrew University of Jerusalem where he has taught since 1977.

Protect Her with the Wings of Your Love

Warren Zev Harvey

This article, exploring the Prayer for the Peace of the State of Israel, was first published in Hebrew in Ha-Tzofe, an Israeli newspaper no longer in operation, on 24 November 1995, 20 days after Prime Minister Yitzhak Rabin's assassination. Originally released during a traumatic period for the State of Israel, this translation is presented nearly three decades later amidst another challenging time. The Prayer for the Peace of the State of Israel remains as pertinent now as it was then.

ONE WEEK BEFORE THE MURDER of Prime Minister Yitzhak Rabin, Professor David Tamar published an important article on the Prayer for the Peace of the State of Israel (*Ha-Tsofeh*, Sabbath issue, *Parashat Noaḥ*). The prayer, it emerges, was written in September 1948 by the first two Chief Rabbis of the State of Israel, Isaac Herzog and Ben-Zion Uziel, with the help of the celebrated author, S.Y. Agnon.

Praying for the Defenders of Our Faith

The Prayer for the Peace of the State of Israel is without doubt one of the most beautiful and moving Hebrew prayers composed in the modern era, and it is a classic document of Religious Zionism. It is also a wise prayer. It expresses with clarity the sublime messianic hope associated with the establishment of the State of Israel, but it is very-very careful not to engage in "calculating the End of Days" (*ḥishuv ha-ketz*) and not to give an unequivocal halakhic definition to the link between the State of Israel and the messianic era -- and certainly not to provide any support for the dangerous Hegelian-stychic conception according to which we are in the midst of a necessary and rational historical-messianic process whose direction and mystery we can understand. It does not, for example, describe the State of Israel as *atḥalta de-ge'ulah* ("the beginning of redemption"), for this concept is defined in Rabbinic literature (BT *Megillah* 17b, etc.), and its use could have possibly encouraged those who seek to "calculate the End of Days." Instead of this, it introduces a brand new phrase, *re'shit tzemiḥat ge'ulatenu* ("the beginning of the sprouting of our redemption").

Threefold Caution

In the phrase "*re'shit tzemiḥat ge'ulatenu*" there is a threefold caution:

1. The phrase is brand new, so it does not have an authoritative interpretation in either Scripture or Talmud. We are free to interpret it in different ways.
2. It does not speak of "redemption," but only of "the sprouting of redemption."
3. In fact, it does not even speak of "the sprouting of redemption," but only of "the *beginning* of the sprouting of redemption."

The phrase is brand new, but doesn't sound brand new. It recalls many and divers sources; for example, the fifteenth blessing in the Amidah ("Who makes sprout [*matzmiah*] the horn of redemption") or the dictum in the Jerusalem Talmud, *Berakhot* 1:1 ("the redemption of Israel in the beginning will be little by little"). Just like the State of Israel itself, the Prayer for the State is brand new but rooted deep in our tradition.

THE STATE NEEDS THE BLESSING

Throughout the years, the Prayer for the Peace of the State of Israel has become a kind of litmus test for the Zionist commitment of synagogues in both Israel and the Diaspora. In Zionist synagogues, it is recited. In non-Zionist ones it is not.

However, over the past two years the Prayer for the State has run into trouble also in Zionist synagogues. There are congregants who have argued that, given the peace policies of the Government, one ought not to ask of the Holy One, blessed be He: "Bless the State of Israel… Protect her with the wings of your love… Send Your light and Your truth to her leaders, ministers, and counselors. And perfect them with good advice from before You."

In the quiet synagogue where I pray in Jerusalem, there occurred a stormy incident about six months ago, when the cantor changed the words in the Prayer for the State, and proclaimed: "Protect her *from her leaders, ministers, and counselors.*" A very big uproar arose, and another congregant immediately approached the prayer stand and recited the Prayer for the State according to its original text. Others warned the cantor that even if he did not agree with the policies of the heads of state, he should have wanted God to send them "light and truth." Still others pointed out to him that the word "counselors" includes also the opposition.

Praying for the Defenders of Our Faith

Today, after the assassination of the Prime Minister of Israel by a Jewish citizen, the controversy over the Prayer for the Peace of the State of Israel looks different. It is now clear that our country needed the blessing more than we could have imagined, and today, sadly, it needs it even more.

Warren Zev Harvey is Professor Emeritus in the Department of Jewish Thought at the Hebrew University of Jerusalem where he has taught since 1977.

Faith, Vigilance, and Solidarity through Prayer

Basil Herring

I N MANY/MOST SYNAGOGUES IN OUR time, only a few minutes separate these two tefilot recited on most Shabbatot. But in historical time they are not only separated by a span of 925 years, they are also separated by a chasm of historical magnitude.

As is made painfully clear in the Av Harahamim, a prayer whose historical context is too often under-appreciated, when in 1096 our forebears in the Rhineland experienced the mass murder and suffering that the Crusaders inflicted on righteous, God-fearing Jews, the survivors could only beseech God, invoking the appropriate verses in Tanakh, imploring Him to avenge the death of the righteous, deter and defeat their enemies, and in the process ensure the continuity of His chosen people. For there was no Jewish army that could either come to their defense, or prevent those events from happening again. Hence, they composed the Av Harahamim, which we recite to this day.

Praying for the Defenders of Our Faith

Since 1948, however, the power of deterrence, and the mandate to safeguard the safety and sanctity of Jewish life, both physical and spiritual, are not only in the hands of Netzah Yisrael – the Eternal God of Israel – but also in the hands of Hayyalei Yisrael, the Holy Soldiers of Israel. Sadly, the horrors of the twentieth-century, and now the early decades of the twenty-first as well, have taught us that in addition to the necessary emunah (faith), bitahon (trust), and redemptive powers of Torah and tefilla, for us to survive and flourish in a cruel and demonic world where there is no shortage of Jew-haters, we must appreciate, support, and – yes – pray for the brave and righteous Jews who day in and day out, at the risk of life and limb, protect and safeguard not only the Jews of Israel but all of us, ba'asher hem sham, wherever we might be in the Jewish diaspora.

Rabbi Joseph B. Soloveitchik famously distinguished between tefilla be'tzibbur (prayer with the congregation), and tefillat ha-tzibbur (the prayer of the congregation, i.e., Klal Yisrael.) Perhaps it would not be too presumptuous to say that in our day there is a third category, i.e., tefilla la-tzibbur – a prayer for the Jewish people, to be protected and strengthened, guarded and defended against all its enemies, at home and abroad, not only by His providence, but by Jewish soldiers as well. And that is precisely the significance of the Mi Sheberach for the soldiers of Tzahal, "in the air, on the ground, and at sea." For which reason, it should be recited in every community, in one form or another.

Rabbi Dr. Basil Herring, a distinguished figure in the Orthodox Jewish rabbinate, has led several congregations throughout his career. He has served as past Executive Vice President of both the Orthodox Caucus and the Rabbinical Council of America. In addition, Rabbi Herring has made significant contributions in the area of Jewish liturgical research, and serves as the Editor-in-Chief of the RCA's "Siddur Avodat HaLev," soon-to-be-released in its 3rd edition.

Uniting In Prayer

Dov Huff

ONE OF THE FOUNDATIONAL PRINCIPLES of the Maimonides School is the idea of *tefillah b'tzibur*, communal prayer. Rabbi Joseph B. Soloveitchik zt"l explained in *The Lonely Man of Faith* that the entity that is the Jewish people is not merely a collection of individuals but also an organism in which each component, each individual, plays a unique and critical role, working in synchronous harmony with the other vital organs and breathing life into the unity that is the Jewish people. What emerges from this idea, of a system in which all components rely on and are responsible for one another, is a prayer community. A community in which your hopes are my hopes, your success is my success, and your prayers are my prayers. On October seventh the organism that is *Klal Yisrael* went into shock, and in the trauma centers of our *batei knasiyot* the emergency crisis response took the form of communal prayer.

At Maimonides our job is to teach students. How do we, as an institution built on the principle of the prayer community, speak to our students in a moment like this? How do we coherently frame this moment through the medium of prayer? The institution of, and messaging around, the recitation of the *tefillah l'chayalei tzahal* in our daily student *minyan* served to anchor our students in three fundamental ideas.

The first is an *halakhic* idea. We spoke to our students about *tefillah b'eiat tzarah*. The *tefillah* of our prayer community changed fundamentally on October seventh. From that moment, our *tefillah* was that of an *eit tzarah* – a moment of crisis in which prayer is mandated on a *Torah* level. Our addtion of the *tefillah l'chayalei tzahal*, along with *Avinu Malkeinu* and daily *Tehillim*, became symbols of this new meaning and purpose. It connected our own prayer to the *tefillah* detailed in the *mishnayos* of the second *perek* of *Masechet Taanit*, which until now had felt foreign and inaccessible, a relic of an unrelatable time. These added *tefillot* reinforced for our students that the activity we were engaged in for the first hour of the day had now fundamentally shifted as a reflection of the emergency crisis state of our people.

The second is a personal and interpersonal idea. The *tefillah* focuses our daily conversation with *Hakadosh Baruch Hu* by reminding us of our brothers and sisters, around the ages of our students, risking their lives in the defense of our people. As a school with many alumni who serve in the Israel Defense Forces, the *tefillah l'chayalei tzahal* anchors our *kavanah* in names and faces of people we know. It is a daily reminder to the teacher next to us whose child is at war and who they have not heard from in days, and to our friend whose older sibling is heroically fighting for our nation, that our thoughts are with our people in Israel and that we are doing our best to shoulder some of the burden they are carrying. This idea also finds expression in a new custom in which we dedicate the day's *Torah* learning at school to one of the soldiers who is part of the extended Maimonides family.

Finally, there is an *hashkafic* point. The Rav had a vision of not only *tefillah b'tzibur*, prayer with the community, but also *tefillat ha'tzibur*, prayer of the community – one prayer cried out by the singular organism of *Am Yisrael*. What greater expression could there be of this idea than to say a *tefillah* in unison with Jewish communites around the world, to cry out to *Hashem* in one unified voice to protect our protectors. Not only to speak the same words, but to express the same sentiment that all of *Am Yisrael* is carrying as a knot inside its collective chest. And in doing so, to remind our students that a seminal axiom of this unified *klal* was expressed to Avraham (Bereishit 17:8) in the first promise of its formation,"And I will give to you, and to your offspring after you, the land of your sojournings, all the land of Canaan, for an everlasting possession."

May *Hashem* grant us the continued realization of the covenant through which our *klal* is fundamentally linked to our land of Eretz Yisrael, and may our collective *tefillot* serve to protect our brothers and sisters in the Israel Defense Forces who are fighting for the promise that is Medinat Yisrael.

Rabbi Dov Huff is the Middle & Upper School Principal at The Maimonides School in Brookline, MA.

Prayer for the Peace of All the IDF's Soldiers

Ronit Irshai

THE PRAYER FOR THE WELFARE of the IDF soldiers always moved me. I felt that the soldiers who work day and night and are even willing to sacrifice their lives to protect us, deserve a special intention while praying for them. But ever since all five of my children enlisted in the army (including my daughter), the prayer has become very personal. The worry and anxiety for their well-being in military service, even on routine days, is not simple. On days of security tension, operations, or actual war, it is seven times harder, but it has become a norm for me and for many mothers and fathers in Israeli society.

In recent years, there has been a sharp debate in Israeli society about the enlistment of women in the army, especially in combat roles. Some believed that it weakens the army, that operational standards immediately dropped, and of course, rabbis who were concerned about modesty issues due to mixed-gender army service. Nevertheless, women were increasingly integrated into combat units. I believe that this debate has been settled after the terrible disaster that befell us on Simchat Torah, October 7, 2023. As the situation from the heroic battle in the south against Hamas terrorists becomes clearer, it turns out that the female fighters attacked like lionesses, saved many lives, and sometimes even paid with their own. There were tank fighters, paramedics, spotters, and many more who, without a moment's hesitation, exhibited the very valor and dedication we anticipate from soldiers of the Israel Defense Forces.

As described in the historical essays in this book, the prayer for the peace of the IDF soldiers is a relatively new prayer in the history of the Jewish people's prayers. Of course, it could not have been part of the prayer book for a people living in exile and dependent on others. This prayer reflects the new reality where we can defend ourselves with a strong army, an army of the people living in their independent state. Therefore, in order for the prayer to be authentic, it must also reflect the new reality where women fight alongside their male counterparts.

In the community where I pray, we have already changed the wording to "male and female soldiers of the Israel Defense Forces." I believe that for all the new female fighters and in memory of those soldiers who sacrificed their lives in the fight against Hamas, it is appropriate and even morally required to include them in the prayer. But that's not enough. I believe that another amendment is needed:

With the new feminist consciousness that has accompanied religious society for nearly fifty years, the time has come to also change the way our historical memory is shaped, which places only the patriarchs at the center. The matriarchs, the women, were undoubtedly a central part of Jewish history and our national narrative. They shaped it no less than the men, but the language of prayer has marginalized them. This fact is significant to me. Jews who pray three times a day with the standing prayer mentioning "Our fathers Abraham, Isaac, and Jacob," "Shield of Abraham," "Our God and the God of our fathers," and similar phrases,

Praying for the Defenders of Our Faith

solidify in their consciousness the marginalization of the nation's matriarchs. The fact that the prayer's language does not include them erases them from historical memory. With our return to our historical homeland and achieving state independence, we can no longer continue to sanctify this tradition. On the contrary, with the establishment of the State of Israel and the change of many diasporic patterns, we have an obligation to continue in this spirit of independence and correct what exile has distorted.

Therefore, it seems to me that justice will only be done to our matriarchs, the Jewish women who shaped the spirit of the nation no less than the men, and the Jewish women of today, who follow in the footsteps of Sarah, Rebecca, Rachel, and Leah, if their place is not omitted from this important prayer. Hence, we should pray:

מִי שֶׁבֵּרַךְ אֲבוֹתֵינוּ ואמותינו אַבְרָהָם יִצְחָק וְיַעֲקֹב, שרה, רבקה, רחל ולאה, הוּא יְבָרֵךְ אֶת חַיָּלֵי וחיילות צְבָא הַהֲגַנָּה לְיִשְׂרָאֵל..."

"May He who blessed our fathers and our mothers, Abraham, Isaac, and Jacob, Sarah, Rebecca, Rachel, and Leah, bless the male and female soldiers of the Israel Defense Forces..."

Professor Ronit Irshai is Associate Professor and the head of the gender studies department at Bar Ilan University.

Mi Sheberach: The Musical Aspect

Elli Jaffe

THE MI SHEBERACH PRAYER FOR IDF soldiers was composed and disseminated to the public by the one who was the first Chief Military Rabbi and later the Chief Rabbi of Israel, the esteemed Rabbi Shlomo Goren of blessed memory. In days past, it was customary for the community rabbi or the synagogue sexton to recite this prayer alongside the Prayer for the Welfare of the State of Israel.

The prayer for the peace of the state was graced with a musical adornment, particularly for the 40th anniversary celebrations of the state's rebirth, following the composition by Cantor Sol Zim that has become in our time one of the treasured jewels of religious music. To this, additional works were added, such as those by the late Cantor Moshe Stern, and Cantor Chaim Adler, among others. In contrast, the Mi Sheberach experienced a "musical drought." This changed when Dubi Zeltzer's renowned melody "Eretz Tzvi" was "adopted" to serve the Mi

Sheberach for IDF soldiers, incorporating the military and march-like essence that characterizes part of this tune.

Over the years, a number of melodies, arrangements, and performances have been added to this prayer, like the renditions by Cantor Yaakov Motzen (whose brother fell in the Lebanon War) and Cantor Yisrael Rand. Indeed, while the works of Zeltzer and Motzen are based on the military march character, Rand's creation carries a far more lyrical quality and includes a moving cantorial proclamation within it. Dubi Zeltzer's creation is also characterized by its 'Israeli-Sabra' essence, lending a spring-like freshness to the piece, which might well be the key to its enduring appeal.

This work has been successful not only in Israel but also among Jewish communities abroad.

Even in these days, when the soldiers of Israel stand at the forefront of our concerns and prayers, the Zeltzer melody is characterized by a special sensitivity, and whenever this prayer is heard in this tune, it evokes emotion in the listening audience.

This composition has achieved success not only in Israel but also in Jewish communities worldwide. In these times, when the soldiers of Israel are foremost in our thoughts and prayers, the Zeltzer melody resonates with a unique sensitivity. Whenever this prayer is played in this tune, it evokes deep emotion among the listeners.

Maestro Elli Jaffe is the founder, conductor, and Music Director of the Jerusalem Great Synagogue. He is a globally recognized conductor and composer of Jewish music.

The Use of the Word 'Avir' in the Prayer for the Israel Defense Forces

Yaakov Jaffe

LIKE ANY PRAYER WRITTEN IN the modern era, the prayer for the Israel Defense Forces can be evaluated as to the nuances of the formulation and text of the supplication. Some are general, such as which Biblical figures to cite at the start of the prayer,[1] and whether the prayer should include a promise for charity.[2] Others are specific, including which geographical boundaries should be referenced in the prayer and whether the prayer refers narrowly to the army or more expansively to other groups which protect Israel include police and the

1   Yaakov Jaffe, "The Rav's Siddur: Universalism, Particularism, and the Prayer Lives of Non-Jews," *Tradition: A Journal of Orthodox Jewish Thought*, vol. 55, no. 2 (Spring 2023): 93.
2   Hershel Schachter, *Nefesh ha-Rav* (Brooklyn, NY: Flatbush Beth Hamedrosh, 1994), 143 (Hebrew).

various clandestine services. This essay will focus on one short word in the prayer, *avir*, and the relatively mundane controversy around the recitation of this word, part of the vocabulary of Mishnaic Hebrew,[3] in the prayer and supplication.

In its core, the discussion of the word *avir* involves three separate topics, a general topic about prayers in the vernacular and any language other than Hebrew, a more specific one about prayers in Mishnaic Hebrew specifically, and then the very narrow question about the translation of the word *avir*, its origins, and the best word to refer to the air force within the prayer for the Israel Defense Forces.

Prayer in the Vernacular

Though technically Jewish Law permits prayer in any language (Sota 32a), a series of later limitations (see views cited in Orach Chaim 101:4) creates a preference, but probably not a requirement to pray in Hebrew, at least while praying with a group in synagogue. A Jew who does not speak Hebrew, and one imagines a Jew seeking to pray for something for which no word exists in Hebrew, may do so in any language (Magen Avraham 101:5).[4]

Following the decision of the early Reform movement to conduct services in the vernacular, later decisors became more adamant and

---

[3] The word appears more than two dozen times in the Mishnah, but always as the object of a preposition *le-avir*, or *be-avir*.

[4] It is noteworthy, that in Rambam's anthropological reconstruction of the impetus for the composition of the standard prayers, it is the lack of fluency in *any* language that motivates the composition of the standard corpus of the prayers, not the fact that the individuals did not have fluency in Hebrew (*Hilchot Tefilah* 1:4-5). Rambam does not say that prayer in the vernacular is prohibited. Rambam's view about the reasons for the composition of the prayer services can be disputed more generally, although it is outside the scope of this essay.

strident in the view that prayer in Hebrew is strongly preferred, if not absolutely required (See Mishnah Berurah 62:3, 101:13, Bei'ur Halacha to 101:4, Aruch Ha-Shulchan 62:4 [citing an 80 year-old precedent] and 185:1-8, for some evidence of the shift).[5] The Chatam Sofer authored multiple responsa devoted to this question in the early 19th century (6:84, 5:192-193, 6:84, 8:85), and he is often seen as the figure who was most vocal against prayer in the vernacular. Rabbi Moshe Sofer provides multiple rationales to forbid prayer in any language besides Hebrew, which are particularly germane to the question of *avir*.[6]

> **A linguistic argument**: that the precise meaning of each word in the authoritative Hebrew prayers cannot be captured correctly through translation,
>
> **A historical argument**: that Jews have always prayed in Hebrew, even when the language was challenging to them,
>
> **A public policy argument**: that prayer in the vernacular should be rejected as it was part of a larger series of changes proposed by the Reform movement, which were designed to change Judaism to match the Christian societies of the day,
>
> **A 'royal protocol' argument**: that one always speaks to a King using His own preferred language and

---

[5] Michael J. Broyde and Shlomo Pill, *Setting the Table: An Introduction to the Jurisprudence of Rabbi Yehiel Mikhel Epstein's Arukh Hashulhan* (Boston: Academic Studies Press, 2021), 282-283, 313-314.

[6] Many of these sentiments are also echoed by his contemporary and father-in-law Rabbi Akiva Eiger (Megilah 17a).

A mystical argument: that the world was created using Hebrew, that God speaks Hebrew, that prophecy is given in Hebrew and that the angels prefer to speak Hebrew.

Some of these factors are irrelevant to the use of a single non-Hebrew word in an otherwise Hebrew prayer. That one word may be a faithful translation of whatever concept the speaker wants to convey in Hebrew, and the use of one word is not likely to be seen as a broad support for the reform movement. However, the final two arguments offered by Chatam Sofer would indicate that, if possible, every word of every prayer should be in Hebrew. It is hard to know for certain whether Chatam Sofer indeed felt each of his arguments carried legal basis on its own; the overall polemical tone would advise caution in applying one or two of the arguments in a slightly different context. However, many modern authorities reference the notion that each word of each prayer should be in Hebrew for the mystical reasons, and this would encourage any composer of a prayer in the modern period to make sure to use exclusively Hebrew words.

Prayer in Post-Biblical Hebrew

Assuming prayer must be in Hebrew, one still wonders whether Mishnaic or Modern Hebrew can be used within the prayer service. By in large, the vocabulary of the prayers consists of words that are attested to in Biblical Hebrew, but the grammatical forms are often Rabbinic or Mishnaic. May one use a Hebrew word or Hebrew root that has its origins after the Biblical period? Jews have struggled with this question for over a thousand years. On one level, once a word has entered Mishnaic Hebrew, the word becomes part of the language. Boaz (to Pesachim 10:8) calls this process a conversion of sorts, as the word, even if borrowed from Greek or an Indo-European language is Judaicized and often a knowingly false etymology[7] is offered for the word to connect it to the already existing vocabulary of the Hebrew language.

The words of the mourner's Kaddish in Judaism are so ubiquitous, that most Jews reflexively assume that the words currently recited in the Kaddish have always been part of the Kaddish, ever since its origins in the Geonic era. Few realize that the word *yithalal*, is actually a later addition to Kaddish and not part of the original text, as it was later inserted as a Biblical Hebrew form to replace a form that only exists in Mishnaic Hebrew, *yitkales*.[8] Our Kaddish reflects a commitment to only use Biblical Hebrew vocabulary in prayers, not words in Mishnaic Hebrew.

The Hebrew root *k-l-s* means to mock or deride in all eight of the times it appears in the Bible (Kings 2:2:23, Jeremiah 20:8, Ezekiel 16:31, 22:4-5 Chabakuk 1:10, Psalms 44:14, 79:4). Yet, two major early prayers use this root in the context of praises of God: the kaddish, and the paragraphs preceding and following the Hallel at the seder.[9] The Mishnaic reading is likely the result of the borrowing of the word from the Greek, *kalos*, and were the word to remain in the prayers, it would be evidence of including words of Mishnaic Hebrew who have their origin outside of Biblical Hebrew within the prayer services. Both uses of the root *k-l-s* sparked controversy in the prayers, Ritva rejects the use of the word at the seder on account of its negative connotation in Biblical

---

7   For a discussion of false or folk etymology, see Winfred Lehman, *Historical Linguistics*, 3rd edition (New York: Routledge, 1992), 225.

8   The word *yithalal* is omitted in the prayer tradition of the Vilna Gaon (Maaseh Rav, #54).

9   The blessing following Hallel, the Nishmat prayer, is also recited on Shabbat morning. Though Nishmat is mentioned in the Gemara (Pesachim 118a), there is no way to know which portions of the current prayer of Nishmat were part of the prayer at the time of the Talmud.

Hebrew, and Rav Hai Gaon cites a controversy about whether the word should be included in Kaddish.[10]

Ultimately, Rav Hai Gaon argues that the word *yitkales* should remain in Kaddish and should be neither removed nor replaced with *yithalal*. Yet, he does not permit prayer in Mishnaic Hebrew, instead he re-interprets the word's meaning in Biblical Hebrew, such that the use of the word in the prayer conforms with Biblical Hebrew as well. Rav Hai Gaon felt the word underwent semantic shift and was not loan borrowing from a foreign language.[11] Modern practice is even more fraught, as the word has been removed from one prayer context, the Kaddish (Tur 56), and preserved in the other, the Seder.[12] Current practice resolves neither question: whether *k-l-s* has negative or positive connotations, and whether it is considered part of Biblical Hebrew or Mishnaic Hebrew.

One could argue that the objection against *k-l-s* is not primarily grounded in its origins as a loan word, but in the fact that its use in Mishnaic Hebrew runs counter to its use in Biblical Hebrew. Said

10 Louis Ginzberg, *Ginzei Schechter* (1927), vol. 2 (New York: Hermon Press, 1969), 161-164.

11 Rashi to Ezekiel (16:31) also attempts a translation for the word, "to speak," which might cover both the Mishnaic and the Biblical texts, but this translation is overly broad and overlaps with many other Hebrew words. It also fails to address why all eight of the Biblical references carry negative connotation, while the Mishnaic ones carry exclusively positive connotations. In contrast, Baer, *Siddur Avodat Yisrael* (1868), argues that presence of the word in Mishnaic Hebrew is sufficient to permit its recitation (130, 209); he makes no reference to Biblical Hebrew in justifying the use of the word.

12 Perhaps the use of the word in the seder is somewhat more excusable, as the Seder is an evening of storytelling, and not prayer. But the word is used in the two Hallel section of Maggid and Hallel, which is more prayer-like in nature. See Rema 473:6, describe the practice of Jacob of London to conduct the Seder in the vernacular.

differently, perhaps loan words could be used, just not loan words which compete with Hebrew words of the same root in meaning. Ritva appears willing to reject the word even were it part of Biblical Hebrew on account of its even partial or predominant negative connotation in Biblical Hebrew. The deletion of the word does not prove it considered an invalid loan word, and the recitation of the word does not prove it is considered a valid loan word; perhaps current practice just assumes the word to be Biblical Hebrew.[13]

Still, one adopting Chatam Sofer's mystical argument will object to the use of a word borrowed into Mishnaic Hebrew, given that the word was absent from the Biblical Hebrew which is the language of prophecy and the language of creation. Thought not associated with the halakhic or the mystical tradition, Ibn Ezra addresses this question strongly and directly in his commentary to Kohelet (5:1). Ibn Ezra argues firmly that prayers must be recited in Biblical Hebrew, and the later Rabbinic Hebrew is improper for prayer. He notes how Daniel's prayer (9:4-19) is written entirely in Biblical Hebrew, with no additions from Aramaic or Persian – though the book of Daniel on a whole is replete with such words, because prayer should use the words and forms of simple, Biblical Hebrew alone.

Before concluding that ideally, all prayer words should be only in Biblical Hebrew, we must note that there are a not insignificant number

---

13 Further complicating the problem is the fact that the Kaufman codex lacks this word in its version of the Mishnah (Pesachim 10:5) and it also does not appear in Rambam's formulation of the Mishnah (Chameitz U-Matzah 8:5), and therefore there is reason to argue that the decision to include this word in the prayers may be a later, Medieval decision and not one that has its origins in the time of the Mishnah. Ritva is aware of the version of the Hallel at the Hagadah which includes the word, but he argues that it is in error because the word has a negative connotation in Hebrew. Thus, if the word is used, it should not be understood as Mishnaic approbation of the use of loan words, as it may have been added only by later generations.

of examples of words who have their origins in Aramaic or in Rabbinic Hebrew that have found their way into central, major prayers, besides the unusual *k-l-s*. The word *chedvah* appears prominently in the wedding blessings (Ketubot 8a), despite the fact that the word is Biblical Aramaic and not Biblical Hebrew.[14] Use of this word is particularly striking as the Talmud singles out Aramaic as a language not to be used in prayer (Sota 33a)! Similarly, the daily blessing for atonement using the word *mehal* for forgiveness, despite the fact that the word is not extent in Biblical Hebrew.[15] The spring blessing for trees uses the Mishnaic Hebrew word, *ilan*, which has its origins in the Aramaic *ilan* (Daniel 4:7-23), in place of the Hebrew equivalent *eitz* (Brachot 43b).

One would be inclined to conclude, then, that even if prayer should be in Hebrew, one may pray using the vocabulary of Mishnaic Hebrew, even including words that were borrowed into Hebrew from another language. Still, borrowing of Aramaic words from another Semitic language, especially Aramaic words that appear in Biblical Aramaic might be more acceptable than borrowing words from an Indo-European language such as Greek.

---

14   This can be evidenced from the fact that: [1] the word only appears in the late Biblical books written when Aramaic was already the spoken language and where loan words are prevalent (Nehemiah 8:10, Chronicles 1:16:27), [2] the word appears in Biblical Aramaic (Ezra 6:16), [3] the word does not appear in parallel Biblical verses from the earlier period (Psalms 96:6), [4] the word is perfectly synonymous with a already existing early Hebrew word (*simcha*), [5] the word is used by the Aramaic Targum to translate that synonym into Aramaic (Targum to Genesis 21:6). See however Rashi and Ibn Ezra to Exodus 18:9.

15   The root *m-ch-h*, to wipe away or erase, does appear, and perhaps the root *m-ch-l* derives from that root, but the word *mehilah* does not appear, despite the fact that the words *selicha* and *kapara* do appear in Biblical Hebrew and could have been used instead in the prayer.

Origins of the Word Avir

No word resembling *avir* exists in Biblical Hebrew, although the word aer, ἀήρ, existed in Greek at the time of the Mishnah, and given the large number of Greek words borrowed into the Mishnah, it is not surprising that the word was transferred into it.[16] However, unlike many of the other Greek word borrowings, which are lengthier words, or which had sound combinations that were distinctively Greek and foreign to Hebrew such as initial "*ap-*" or final "*-os*" or "*-in*," *avir* is around the same size as a regular Hebrew word, and uses a similar vowel pattern to the word it replaced, *raki'a*`.[17] For that reason, modern readers of Hebrew might not even realize the foreign origins of the word.[18]

The Hebrew word *raki'a*` is used by Genesis 1:6 to describe the air space above the oceans and seas, and beneath the higher heavens, what would be called *avir* in Modern Hebrew. Indeed, Ibn Ezra, Radak, and Targum Yerushalmi all gloss the word *raki'a*` with avir in their commentaries. If so, why did the Jews of the time of the Mishnah find it necessary to use a new word in place of a pre-existing one? Two related answers present themselves. Most of the Mishnayot in question use the word *avir* to refer to air space along the same height as human beings; perhaps in search for a word to refer to the lower air space a new word was borrowed in from a foreign language.[19] *Avir* would refer to the air

---

16 "*Avir*" *Milon Even-Shoshan* (Israel, 2003), 28.

17 The patach ganuv that ends the word is not part of the original, core vowel pattern.

18 For some discussion, see "*Aviron u-Matos*" at hebrew-academy.org.il (11/08/2010).

19 Indeed, of the 17 times the word *raki'a*` in Tanach, many refer to air space well above where any human being could imagine to reach, see Genesis 1:14-17, Ezekiel 1:20-26, et al. This is also the way the word is used in the

around us, the troposphere, while *raki'a`* would refer to the rest of the atmosphere. Moreover, the noun *raki'a`* derives from the verb *r-k-`* which means to beat or to stretch (see Exodus 39:3, Numbers 17:4, Psalms 136:6),[20] a word that relates fittingly to an invisible heavenly barrier, but which would not fit with the air space in which human beings, arrows, catapult stones, and birds travel. True, Genesis 1:20 is explicit that *raki'a`* is the correct technical term for the location where birds travel,[21] but later generations of Hebrew speakers sought to differentiated between the two terms, leaving *raki'a`* for the higher heavens, and *avir* for the lower ones. Thus, we have here semantic change to the word *raki'a`* as a result of a partial loss of some of the original reference or referent followed by a loanword entering the language taking the place of the lost reference or referent.[22]

As noted above, a folk etymology concluded the process of the borrowing of the word into the Hebrew language, such that speakers of the language no longer associated it with its Greek origins, and instead believed the word had come from a Hebrew root all along. The Jewish mystical tradition is replete with reference to the notion that the word *avir* is derived from the word for *ohr*, light, with the addition of the letter *yud*.[23] The word is firmly ensconced in Mishnaic Hebrew, and it could be used just like any other word in Mishnaic Hebrew.

> first blessing of the evening prayer, where the stars are said to reside in the *raki'a`*.

20   See Rashi Exodus 39:3, Ezekiel 6:11, Psalms 144:2.

21   See also Radak and Chizkuni, loc. Cit., who identifies the term in the verse with *avir*. Shadal to Genesis 1:20 says that *raki'a`* refers to a lower part of the air than *shamayim*.

22   For a discussion of these phenomena see Lehman, 260-266.

23   See for example the Bible commentary of 13th century Menachem Recanati to Genesis 1:3, citing the Zohar. For further discussion of the relationship

Alternative Possibilities

In Biblical Hebrew, *raki'a*` and possibly *shamayim*, are suitable words which may refer to the air space above the heads of human beings, where the birds fly and possibly above the birds where the Israeli air force flies. However, these words have undergone sematic shift, such that the average Hebrew speaker today associated with these words with the higher heavens, or even the spiritual and metaphysical heavens, and not the airspace of the atmosphere. True, birds reside in the *raki'a*` and the *shamayim* (there are more than 30 examples of 'birds of the *shamayim*' in the Tanach), but Modern Hebrew is a different language than Biblical Hebrew, and even if prayer goers recite the words of Biblical Hebrew, they still think in Modern Hebrew. Indeed, when the word *raki'a*` appears in the memorial prayer, few are probably thinking of the luster of the sky; most are thinking of a supernatural luster of the highest metaphorical heavens instead. Similarly, when the Jew recites the prayer for the state of Israel, beginning with the words *Avinu she-ba-Shamayim*, the Jew envisions a Divine force in the spiritual heights, not a God who lives in the same space where the Israeli air force operates. If Rav Hai Gaon argued that semantic shift was reason to allow a word that formerly could not be used, is it a valid argument for excluding a word that formerly might have worked?

To the extent that one is greatly concerned with the use of Mishnaic Hebrew, loan words, or for that matter any language besides Biblical Hebrew, one would err on the side of using an alternative to *avir*. To the extent that one is less concerned about these factors, and instead argues, as Ibn Ezra quotes them, that "God cares about the heart," then words

---

between the word *avir* and *ohr* in Rabbinic literature, see David Shabtai and Yaakov Jaffe, "Morgue Construction and *Tum'at Kohanim*," *Journal of Halacha and Contemporary Society*, no. 58 (2009): 75n16.

Praying for the Defenders of Our Faith

that are clearer to the listener should be used; the word *avir* reminds one of the air force, the *cheil avir*, more than the word *raki'a`* does.

I would propose, however, that though *shamayim* would feel awkward or uncomfortable to modern listeners following the semantic shift, the word *raki'a`* is rare enough for the Modern Hebrew speaker that it still retains more of its original meaning. It meets the standard of prayer in Biblical Hebrew, without confusing the listener or creating a prayer that is unintelligible to the modern prayer goer. Still, the word *avir* is the one predominantly used, and is thus probably the most famous Greek word in the siddur of today.

Rabbi Dr. Yaakov Jaffe is the Rabbi of the Maimonides Kehillah, and the Dean of Judaic Studies at Maimonides School.

A Jewish Soldier in Prayer, His Rifle Bearing Petitions

Maoz Kahana

Israel's Independence Day, which falls on the 5th of Iyar, is preceded by Memorial Day for the Fallen Soldiers of the IDF, which occurs one day earlier. Quiet pervades the streets of the land. Cafes and entertainment venues are closed. Crowds ascend to the graves of the soldiers all over the country, especially at the military cemetery on Mount Herzl in Jerusalem. Many of the residents of the Land of Israel experience on this day emotions that are difficult to put into words. Memorial ceremonies are held in every school, neighborhood, and military base. The country's radio stations switch to playing nostalgic tunes – "Songs of the Land of Israel" as they are dubbed, some of them dating back to the 1960s and 70s. These songs capture the scents and feelings that bind people and the nation to their home, their land, and their country. The melodies and lyrics resonate with longing, comradeship and sacrifice. On Memorial Day, even the roads appear different: the typically assertive Israeli driving style changes slightly. There are no sirens, no shouts.

Praying for the Defenders of Our Faith

All of these are but expressions of a deeper and more fundamental movement. What changes on this day is found in the very essence of the soul. Sorrow, ever so palpable in these moments, is soaked in a certain tenderness, a tenderness and sensitivity that alter for a single day the fabric of life. It's about the connection between one person and another. It's about the gaze and the soul's interaction among passersby. The faceless stranger, walking in the street in front of you, ceases to be a threat for a moment, and is experienced as a companion and partner. Yet even the essence of one's lived experience transforms, that intimate interplay within oneself. The tone of speech softens, human openness and consideration become a lived and tangible reality. A different sensation envelops the individual – solidarity emerges from the depths of the soul into the public space, and pain accompanies the feeling of strength and understanding: these are our lives, and we must be worthy of the great sacrifices made for them..

There is no one who doesn't recognize someone among the fallen, or who feels as if they do – from family stories or from hearing on the radio. A strong yearning is present – a yearning for those who are no longer here. For young lives cut short in the shadow of wars. Sometimes I feel that this longing silently harbors another, more profound one: it's a yearning for what we dreamed we would become when we grew up, for what we wanted to be, as individuals and as a nation, and that has not yet come to pass. The pain of the void is also a direction of the soul: from the absence and from the yearning, I feel, emerges a deeper and more focused zest for life. A passion that is more profound and directed towards the essence. The national anthem – "Hatikvah" – which is heard all year as a vision of return to the land and the realization of dreams, is heard on this day as a memorial and as a longing, like the sound of a shofar that awakens the renewal of the covenant. I allow myself to say that on this Memorial Day, in the streets of the city, I feel a kind of a "Shekhinah" revelation.. I feel that in this collective experience that crosses "religious" and "secular" together, there is something of the high intentions of the High Priest on Yom Kippur in the Temple: giving of the heart and surrender of the soul; the depth of the heartbeat of life. This is the tremor that envelops the Israeli street on this day.

Who are the participants in this covenant, which is renewed, and what is it based on? To this question, there is likely more than one answer. I will offer perhaps a somewhat pragmatic answer, drawn from my own real-life experience as a soldier and commander in the IDF. When I stand in reserve duty, I encounter my jeep driver – who may often be an Arab from the Galilee. The Scout, who will accompany me in the field and track footprints, may be Bedouin. In the technical workshop, I might hear a Russian accent. The fighters will be a mix of secular and religious, Ashkenazi and Sephardic, Ethiopian, Russian, Druze, and everything else you can imagine. Among them, there will always be an idealist, a "new immigrant" not so long ago, with a heavy Anglo-Saxon accent. These are the participants in the army; these are also the ones who fall in the line of military duty and in Israel's wars. The Israeli army does not tend to echo "the dawn of our redemption" according to a preconceived formula. Instead, it is a reflection of the immigrant and minorities society, the real human mosaic from which the State of Israel is composed.

Does this negate the Jewish character of the military, its religious essence? In my eyes, quite the opposite is true. The Jewish people have established their place in the Land of Israel. Here, a covenant is being forged. At the core of this partnership is the arc of life, the goodness, faith, and a propound commitment of the Jewish people to its existence, values, and life. To this tapestry of life, others join with open hands and good hearts, contributing greatly to it. The Israeli mosaic is highlighted more prominently in the army than in day-to-day life, where everyone is closer to their own boundaries and families. Much of the transformative dimension in the spiritual openness I described, that collective experience common on Memorial Day for IDF soldiers – the connection between one person and another, is part of daily life and essential, even if somewhat hidden in the grueling military routine, especially in the reserve army: people of diverse beliefs, backgrounds, and origins, connected by their actions and deeds, for the sake of a higher purpose.

Something of this sort is already recorded in the Talmud. "The sailors are mostly pious," says the Talmud (Kiddushin 81a), and Rashi explains that since they are always at sea, in a place of danger, "They confront a perpetual trepidation and a celestial dread." The Israeli existence is perched upon tumultuous waters without respite. In a place of danger, there is always trepidation. The place where things are so unstable is where prayer continually surges; close and near to the threshold of consciousness. Action is accompanied by the tremor of prayer. This is the place of true piety. There is no end to the forms of prayer for the people of Israel: A prayerful thought. A melody's plea. A hidden silent prayer, knowing naught but the path of deed. . "A Jewish soldier prays with his rifle," wrote Uri Zvi Greenberg, and his words can also be interpreted as an expression of one of those forms of prayer – a physical deed stemming from devotion and surrender, which is itself a prayer; an act that resonates.

Few enjoy army life: far from family, without sleep, with no time for books. The camaraderie of friends and a sense of duty serve as a substitute for all that is usual and dear to a person in their life. But therein lies much of both the height and the lowliness. Something lofty is achieved by holding onto the tangible reality, which seems that even fervent devotion, as passionate as it may be, cannot attain. In the practice of wearing the uniform, there is a palpable inner transition – from the individual to the soldier. From one's own life and goals to those who march forward, one step ahead, leaning, as stated by Maimonides (kings,

Chap.7), upon the hope of Israel. In this matter, all soldiers are equal – combat soldiers and non-combatants alike. In the very belonging to an action "for its own sake," in the very act of wearing the uniform, it carries with it a sense of self-sacrifice. It is within this understanding that the uniform adorns its bearer.- so that if required, they are ready to give everything.

This experience is not spoken of in the words of the prophets; it is not written about in the Kabbalistic texts. But it is the one that emerges and ascends. Whoever partakes in it lives his life, for moments, within another human dimension, another one. He enters through a gate that no individual Jew can enter, as holy, pure, and clean as they may be. This gate is the gate of self-sacrifice. Not as a metaphor and not as a phrase. This gate is the gate of "nothingness."

In the prayer for the well-being of the soldiers, we briefly encircle the edge of this gate, standing at its border. We gaze upon the radiance shining above it, extend our hearts and hands towards this great endeavor, and pray for its welfare. Hand touches hand, and heart touches heart. The spark continues to burn. Am Yisrael Chai.

Maoz Kahana is an associate Professor in the Jewish History Department at Tel Aviv University.

A New Thirst for Life: Bereavement and Death in Israeli Society[*]

Maoz Kahana

I

IN THE ASHKENAZI COMMUNITY (Ashkenaz = Central Europe) of the Middle Ages, the dead held a very central place. In a somewhat surprising statement, one of the great sages of Ashkenazi (Germany) Jewry in the fourteenth century said that the cemetery is a "holy and pure place, a resting place of the righteous."[1] In the religious instinct

---

[*] This article is based on a speech that was delivered on Memorial Day for the Fallen IDF Soldiers in 2017 at Tel Aviv University. I want to express my gratitude to the dean, Professor Leo Corry for extending the invitation and for his friendship.
[1] Jacob Moellin, *Sefer Maharil: The Laws of Fasting*, #18 (Hebrew).

of many cultures, including Judaism, death is associated with impurity and destruction, and this expression sounds, even today, sharp and very strange.

The deep connection of Ashkenaz to its dead is certainly linked to one of the foundational experiences of Ashkenazi Jewry – the disturbances that accompanied the Crusades that began in 1096, whose memory did not fade even centuries later. The dead in the disturbances for the sanctification of God were called Kedoshim, or martyrs, in Ashkenazi terminology, and the communities named themselves after these Kedoshim – Kehillot HaKodesh or Kehilat Kodesh – a term familiar to us to this day. Many ceremonies were created in Ashkenaz, such as the Mourner's Kaddish recited in the synagogue in the year following death, and Yizkor – a ceremony of remembering souls on holidays and festivals, where the names of the deceased are read from the Memorbuch – a thick leather-bound book, centuries old. These are all typical Ashkenazi innovations created in the specific cultural existence of Ashkenaz, where life is lived in proximity to the dead. Similarly, there are lesser-known traditions like weddings in the cemetery, among others. Ashkenaz deeply experienced its dead. In Sefer Hasidim, created in the Rhineland in the twelfth century, there is a story about a small urban community that seemed to be forced to migrate from its place due to economic constraints and security threats: "One congregation wanted to go to another place. A dead person came to one in a dream and said to him, 'Do not abandon us.'"[2] The dead (in the dream) explained that leaving the city is abandoning the dead, who would no longer be visited.

---

2   Judah ben Samuel, *Sefer Hasidim*, ed. Jehuda Wistinetzki, with additions by Jacob Freimann (Frankfurt am Main: Wahrmann, 1924), 86 [no. 269] (Hebrew). See also Elliott Horowitz, "Speaking to the Dead: Cemetery Prayer in Medieval and Early Modern Jewry," *Journal of Jewish Thought and Philosophy*, no. 8 (1999): 303-317.

Maintaining this ongoing, living connection between the world of the living and the dead was perceived as an important and vital ideal.

This close accessibility appears very different, for example, from the place of Hades in Greek mythology, where the Styx – the river of death, separates Hades and the world, and Hades – the god of the underworld, dispatches Thanatos and Chronos to guard the souls of the dead lest they wander into the world and come into contact with the living.[3]

The record of a synagogue sexton named Juspa, from the 17th-century Jewish community of Worms, Germany, may illustrate for us how the cemetery functioned within the daily life of the Jewish community of the time. On the eve of the new year, Rosh Hashanah, Juspa describes how the community concludes the morning prayer and from the synagogue, the entire community together turns towards the cemetery. And so he wrote: "And afterwards [at the end of the prayer] they go to the house of life (the cemetery), and they encircle it. And there at the entrance of the house of life sit the poor, [and everyone distributes charity to them]. When reaching the graves of the holy ones, they say supplications and requests,"… "and it is customary to walk over the graves of the twelve community leaders."[4]

The "holy ones" mentioned here are the community members who died during the Crusades, and like them also the community leaders – The communal leaders of that era, whose tale of collective martyrdom has been preserved as a vivid memory across the centuries. The reality described here is most impressive – even many centuries after the Crusades, the community continues to visit its dead on the eves of

---

3   Thank you to my daughter Zion Chemda for suggesting this idea.

4   See *Wormser Minhagbuch des R. Jousep (Juspa) Schammes*, eds. Benjamin Solomon Hamburger and Eric Zimmer (Jerusalem: Machon Yerushalayim, 1988), 143, 173 (Hebrew).

Rosh Hashanah and Yom Kippur and to encircle their graves in a fixed community ceremony.

The ceremony preserves the exact location of the graves of people who died more than six hundred and seven hundred years before the events, even though no one is clearly counted among their descendants. The practice of circling the cemetery continued in European communities until the Holocaust, on days of fasting and distress, and it can be seen, in a certain respect, as the cultural "ancestor" of Israel's Memorial Day for the Fallen of the IDF, practiced in the State of Israel: a communal-collective ceremony, in which the entire Israeli community marks, in melody and deed, parts of its existential space and depths of its memories.

The practice of circling the cemetery may also surprisingly connect with a literary genre that at first glance seems quite distant, and I specifically refer to ancient travel literature: Many of the geographical documents of the Land of Israel, such as "The Travels of Rabbi Petachiah" of Regensburg, were created from "circles" of such European Jews, who left their community to circle older memorial sites: these were journeys to a new landscape, the Land of Israel, to which the emotional connection was like a great reservoir of memory that needed to be "circled" and collected.[5]

The "circling" reminds us also of the circular shape of the mandala, which in Sanskrit means "circle," and it appears in many cultures around the world – in America and in South Asia. The mandala is a symbol of inner wholeness, or enlightenment, and also in the communal space – more than "ascending" to a specific place, the circular motion outlines the nature of a cyclical movement, in which life and death are integrated into one whole existence, momentarily present together. Similarly, in the annual cycle. On Yom Kippur, each year, the living give charity also for the

---

5   See Elchanan Reiner, "Pilgrims and Pilgrimage to Eretz Yisrael, 1099-1517," (PhD Dissertation, Hebrew University of Jerusalem, 1988; Hebrew).

dead: they too, in their way, visit the members of the living community on the peak day of the year.[6]

These brief glimpses into the life of the community help explain the expression of Maharil, a great sage of Ashkenaz, mentioned earlier, that the cemetery is a "holy and pure place" – a provocative, sharp, and surprising expression that culminates the sense of inner completeness that the Ashkenazim found in the living contact with the resting place of the dead. We learn from this: frequent contact with death also offers an opportunity for life; richer and more fulfilling.

Juspa's ledger presents the cemetery as a place for human sorrow, but also for concern for the poor and needy – through giving charity, for continuing historical memory, and for personal and collective preparation towards sacred days. The living carry their dead in their hearts towards the days of festivals, judgment, and joy, where fullness and absence intertwine. Many Talmudic commentators note the importance for a person to walk "on the graves" even if they do not know anyone buried there. The personal purpose of the collective ceremony, they suggest, is heartbreak, which opens the door to compassion. Frequent contact with death can be the gateway to sensitivity and generosity towards others.

II

From the heartbreak, I shall seek to move to its joy, and from the world of the ceremonial community, we will make a sharp transition to a fantastical story taken from the world of the individual. The story I am now about to tell deals with an extraordinary extreme experience. It is taken from the book "*Reshit Hokhmah*" – a moral book by a

---

6   *Shulan Arukh, Orah Hayyim* 604:6. There are also various sources that describe customs related to wrapping the deceased in communal prayer shawls on Yom Kippur.

Safed Kabbalist from the 16th-century named Rabbi Elijah de Vidas. In his book, a whole section called "Shaar Ahava" (The Gate of Love) is dedicated. Contained within is the peculiar narrative I shall peruse, concerning an ostensibly unseemly passion, a frantic pilgrimage to the necropolis, culminating in an astonishing denouement:

> One day, as the king's daughter emerged from the bathhouse, a man from the dwellers of the city saw her and sighed a great sigh, saying, "If only she were mine to do with as I please."
>
> The king's daughter replied to him, "That can only happen in the cemetery, not here."
>
> Hearing these words, he rejoiced, thinking she had told him to go to the cemetery and wait for her there, and that she would come to him and he could do as he pleased with her.
>
> But she did not mean this; rather, she meant to say that only there, in the cemetery, are the small and the great, the young and the old, the despised and the honored (Job 3:19) equal – "small and great are there," where all are equal, but not here, in the real, living world. For it is impossible for a king's daughter to be approached by one of the common folk.

The rejection, full of scorn, is unequivocal, but the common man's carnal desire, and the educational gaps between him and the king's daughter, cause him to misunderstand the sarcasm, and he follows her instruction literally:

> The man rose and went to the cemetery, sat there, and constantly focused his thoughts on her, always contemplating her form. Due to his intense longing

for her, he detached his thoughts from all feelings, placing them entirely on the image of that woman and her beauty. Day and night, he continuously sat in the cemetery, eating, drinking, and sleeping there, for he thought, "If she does not come today, she will come tomorrow." He did so for many days.

Due to his extreme detachment from all feelings, constantly focusing his thoughts on one thing, his solitude and complete longing, his soul became detached from the senses and clung to higher thoughts until he was entirely free of all feelings, even from the woman, and attached to the Divine. After a few days, he shed all feelings and his desire was in the Divine intellect, becoming a complete servant of God, a holy man, such that his prayers were heard and his blessings effective for all passersby… Merchants, riders, and pedestrians who passed by there would turn to him and receive his blessing, until his name became known far and wide.

Therefore, the man surprisingly became a "holy man," a sort of Jewish dervish, whose blessing everyone traveling the road sought. The process of solitude profoundly transformed him. In modern terms, one might say that the beggar became a guru. To this tale, the Kabbalist from Safed adds sharp moral instruction, about the earthly desire that led the man to the cemetery and from there back – to the depths of his soul:

"One who does not desire a woman is like a donkey, and even less than it, and the reason is that from the sensual, one must discern the divine service… And attachment depends only on the desire and love of the Torah, until one desires it as the object of his passion."[7]

Let's refine the nature of the story a bit:

Gaps in status, language, and desire separate the two: The princess does not take the common man seriously. In her world, he is in no way her equal. To her, the cemetery symbolizes the inversion of normative life, the impossible. There, in a metaphorical and sarcastic manner, she sends the coarse man. The common man, in his desire, does not distinguish between metaphor and reality, and fails to recognize the strangeness and distinctiveness of the heterotopic space to which he is led. Thus, he finds himself alone in the cemetery, waiting in embarrassment for a woman who never arrives.

Yet here a profound reversal occurs – the cemetery is the meeting place of life and death, or, if you will, of the finite and the infinite. Isolated from the sounds of this normative world, the man sinks into his loneliness, allowing his wild desire to lead his imagination without interruption. According to the story, the unique nature of the place he inhabits acts upon him. The physical desire transforms into a spiritual one. The man clings to wisdom, to the Shekhinah, and becomes a different person. At the beginning of the story, it would be unthinkable that the princess would marry a common man, but at its end, the social gaps are reversed: the common man is graced with another princess – higher and more spiritual than the first – the common man is graced with the Shekhinah.

If we want to translate this Safed story from the 16th-century into the context of 21st-century Israeli society, we can recognize in it the understanding that continued proximity to the realms of bereavement and death can be a gateway for both the individual and the community

---

7   Shaar Ahava, Chapter Four.

to a metamorphosis: to the discovery of a radically different and even transformative perspective on life. From the viewpoint of the cemetery, the everyday appears in a different light. The urgent and the superficial lose their charm and their stunning, blinding power when measured against eternity, against the essence of life, its core. Then, the essential and the principal emerge. A new, more delicate and precise desire for life appears.

Often, the Israeli community in which we live, in all its parts, appears as an unconscious reincarnation of such a medieval Ashkenazi holy congregation as I described. Brown signs along the roads direct us to battle sites and monuments of various units, to collective memories and the stories accompanying them. Memorial signs and memory runs raise the names of the fallen. Through sports events, news editions, and memorial days, the memory and rationale of the fallen are brought into the common space we share. There is a great intensity in Israeli bereavement culture, difficult to find parallels elsewhere. Frequent contact with death may lead us as individuals and as a society to different paths – some anxious or aggressive, retreating from life or lightening its weight. It seems that this is not a cult of the dead. At the heart of the intensive memory culture developed in the State of Israel is the deep feeling that the lives that were taken have a message and value that can be distilled and applied, to illuminate our lives and to receive inspiration and purpose from it. From the connection between the world of the dead in "Ashkenaz" and the Safed story we dealt with, to the reality of Israeli bereavement, emerge paths with depth and significance: the profound presence in our lives of those close to us and those we remember – from our personal passage and also from pieces of our collective memory, brings with it a different view of life: painful and chastised yet alert and substantial. This essence can fill our lives with sensitivity and purity, with deep spirituality, solidarity, and great compassion, compassion for all. Perhaps in this way, we may merit the princess, to behold the Shekhinah.

Maoz Kahana is an associate Professor in the Jewish History Department at Tel Aviv University.

'They Are All Holy': Rabbi Yisroel Zev Gustman on the Sanctity of IDF Soldiers

Ari D. Kahn[1]

THE FOLLOWING ESSAY WAS WRITTEN many years ago. At the time, my children were young, and the thought of them serving in the army loomed far in the distance. In a subsequent postscript, I wrote about two of my sons who were then serving in combat units. As the years

1   This article draws from direct experience and reconstructed events relayed to me. It first appeared in an initial form on my blog 'Explorations' and at Aish.com, and since then, it has been republished and referenced in numerous books and articles.

have gone by, more sons, and our only son-in-law, have served in combat units. As I write these lines, some of them are in Gaza, protecting our People, defending our Land. Our prayers are with these brave, dedicated, idealistic Jewish soldiers, with our own sons, our nephews and nieces and cousins, the children of our neighbors and of the immediate and extended family of Israel. May they all return to their families in perfect physical, spiritual and emotional health. In the merit of our righteous ancestors and our righteous children, may the people of Israel be granted peace and tranquility in the Land promised to us by God.

Many years ago when I was a relatively young yeshiva student I had the opportunity to study with one of the great rabbis of the previous generation. His name was Rabbi Yisroel Zev Gustman (1908-1991) and he may have been one of the greatest rabbis of the 20th century. He was certainly the greatest "unknown" rabbi: While he fastidiously avoided the limelight and was therefore unfamiliar to the general public, he was well known to connoisseurs of Torah learning.

His meteoric rise from child prodigy to the exalted position of religious judge in the Rabbinical Court of Rabbi Chaim Ozer Grodzinski (1863-1940) at around the age of twenty was the stuff of legend – but nonetheless fact. Many years later, I heard Rav Gustman's own modest version of the events leading to this appointment: A singular (brilliant) insight which he shared with his fellow students was later repeated to the visiting Rav Chaim Ozer, who invited the young student to repeat this same insight the following day in his office in Vilna. Unbeknownst to Rav Gustman, the insight clinched an argument in a complex case that had been debated among the judges in Rav Chaim Ozer's court – and allowed a woman to remarry.

One of the judges presiding over the case, Rabbi Meir Bassin (1872-1931), took an interest in a certain young man and subsequently arranged for him to marry his daughter, Sarah (1905-1978). Unfortunately, Rabbi

Praying for the Defenders of Our Faith

Bassin passed away before the wedding could take place. Consequently, Rabbi Gustman was chosen to succeed him as the rabbi of Shnipishok and to assume his position on the rabbinical court. While Rabbi Gustman modestly attributed his selection to being "in the right place at the right time," it was evident that both Rabbi Bassin and Rabbi Chaim Ozer had recognized greatness in him.

While a long, productive career on the outskirts of Vilna could have been anticipated, Jewish life in and around Vilna was obliterated by World War II. Rav Gustman escaped, though not unscathed. He hid among corpses. He hid in caves. He hid in a pig pen. Somehow, he survived.

Rav Gustman served as my personal connection to the pre-war Jewish world that was decimated by the Nazis. I didn't have to imagine what a rabbi in pre-war Vilna might have been like; I had the privilege of seeing Rav Gustman, still embodying that era, 35 years after the war had ended. At the head of a small yeshiva in the Rechavia section of Jerusalem, Rav Gustman taught a small group of loyal students six days a week. But on Thursdays at noon, the study hall would fill to capacity: Rabbis, intellectuals, religious court judges, a Supreme Court justice and various professors would join along with any and all who sought a high-level Talmud *shiur* that offered a taste of what had been nearly destroyed. When Rav Gustman gave *shiur*, Vilna was once again alive and vibrant.

One of the regular participants was a professor at the Hebrew University, Robert J. (Yisrael) Aumann (b. 1930). Once a promising yeshiva student, he had eventually decided to pursue a career in academia, but made his weekly participation in Rav Gustman's *shiur* part of his schedule, along with many other more or less illustrious residents of Rechavia and Jerusalem.

The year was 1982. Once again, Israel was at war. Soldiers were mobilized, reserve units activated. Among those called to duty was a Reserves soldier, a university student and a Talmudic scholar, who made his living as a high school teacher: Shlomo Aumann (1957-1982), Professor Yisrael Aumann's son. On the eve of the 19th of Sivan, in particularly fierce combat, Shlomo fell in battle.

Rav Gustman mobilized his yeshiva: All of his students joined him in performing the mitzvah of burying the dead. At the cemetery, Rav Gustman was agitated: He surveyed the rows of graves of the young men, soldiers who died defending the Land. On the way back from the cemetery, Rav Gustman turned to another passenger in the car and said, "They are all holy." Another passenger questioned the rabbi: "Even the non-religious soldiers?" Rav Gustman replied: "Every single one of them." He then turned to the driver and said, "Take me to Professor Aumann's home."

The family had just returned from the cemetery and would now begin the week of *shiv'a* – mourning for their son, brother, husband, and father. (Shlomo was married and had one child. His widow, Shlomit, gave birth to their second daughter shortly after he was killed.)

Rav Gustman entered and asked to sit next to Professor Aumann, who said: "Rabbi, I so appreciate your coming to the cemetery, but now is time for you to return to your Yeshiva."

Rav Gustman spoke, first in Yiddish and then in Hebrew, so that all those assembled would understand:

> "I am sure that you don't know this, but I had a son named Meir. He was a beautiful child. He was taken from my arms and executed. I escaped. I later bartered my child's shoes so that we would have food, but I was never able to eat the food – I gave it away to others. My Meir is a *kadosh* – he is holy – he and all the six million who perished are holy."

Praying for the Defenders of Our Faith

Rav Gustman then added:

"I will tell you what is transpiring now in the World of Truth in *Gan Eden* – in Heaven. My Meir is welcoming your Shlomo into the *minyan* and is saying to him 'I died because I am a Jew – but I wasn't able to save anyone else. But you – Shlomo, you died defending the Jewish People and the Land of Israel'. My Meir is a *kadosh*, he is holy – but your Shlomo is a *Shaliach Zibbur* – in that holy, heavenly minyan."

Rav Gustman continued:

"I never had the opportunity to sit *shiv'a* for my Meir; let me sit here with you just a little longer." Professor Aumann replied, "I thought I could never be comforted, but Rebbi, you have comforted me."

Rav Gustman did not allow his painful memories to control his life. He found solace in his students, his daughter his grandchildren, and in every Jewish child. He and his wife would attend an annual parade (on *Yom Yerushalayim*) where children would march on Jerusalem in song and dance. A rabbi who happened upon them one year asked the Rabbi why he spent his valuable time in such a frivolous activity. Rav Gustman explained, "We who saw a generation of children die, will take pleasure in a generation of children who sing and dance in these streets."

A student once implored Rav Gustman to share his memories of the ghetto and the war more publicly and more frequently. He asked him to tell people about his son, about his son's shoes, to which the Rav replied, "I can't, but I think about those shoes every day of my life. I see them every night before I go to sleep."

On the 28th of Sivan 5751 (1991), Rav Gustman passed away. Thousands marched through the streets of Jerusalem accompanying

Rav Gustman on his final journey. As night fell on the 29th of Sivan, nine years after Shlomo Aumann fell in battle, Rav Gustman was buried on the Mount of Olives. I am sure that upon entering Heaven he was reunited with his wife, his teachers, and his son Meir. I am also sure that Shlomo Aumann and all the other holy soldiers who died defending the People and the Land of Israel were there to greet this extraordinary Rabbi.

On December 10th 2005, Professor Robert J. Aumann was awarded the Nobel Prize in Economics, and in an autobiographical statement several months later,[2] Professor Aumann reflected:

> Jews have been yearning for the land of Israel, and for Jerusalem, for close to 2000 years – ever since the destruction of the Temple by the Romans in the year 70, and the ensuing exile of the Jewish people. In our central prayer, which we recite three times a day, we ask the Lord to "return to Jerusalem Your city in mercy, and rebuild it and dwell therein." Jerusalem is mentioned many thousands of times in the scriptures, in our other prayers, in the Talmud, and indeed in all our sources. So when the state of Israel was established in 1948, my brother and I made a determination eventually to make our lives there. My brother fulfilled this ambition shortly thereafter, in 1950, but I decided first to complete my education. In 1953 I met an Israeli girl, Esther Schlesinger, who was visiting the United States; we were married in Brooklyn in April of 1955. In the fall of 1956 I took up a position as instructor of mathematics at the Hebrew University

---

2 See Robert J. Aumann, "Biographical," NobelPrize.org (2006), available here (https://www.nobelprize.org/prizes/economic-sciences/2005/aumann/biographical).

of Jerusalem, and have been there ever since. Esther and I had five beautiful children; the oldest, Shlomo, was killed in action in 1982, while serving in the Israeli Army in "Operation Peace for Galilee."

… For me, life has been – and still is – one tremendous joyride, one magnificent tapestry. There have been bad – very bad – times, like when my son Shlomo was killed and when my wife Esther died. But even these somehow integrate into the magnificent tapestry. In one of his beautiful letters, Shlomo wrote that there can be no good without bad. Both Shlomo and Esther led beautiful, meaningful lives, affected many people, each in his own way."

I suspect, as well, that he also took memories of his Rabbi, Rav Gustman.

The last time I saw Rav Gustman, I was walking in the Meah Sharim/Geulah section of Jerusalem with my wife and oldest son who was being pushed in a stroller. It was Friday morning and we saw the Rosh Yeshiva, we said hello, wished him "Good Shabbes." Then, I did something I rarely do: I asked him to bless my son. Rav Gustman looked at the toddler, smiled and said "May he be a boy like all the other boys." At first, my wife and I were stunned; what kind of blessing was this? We expected a blessing that the boy grow to be a *zaddik* – a righteous man – or that he be a *Talmid Chacham* – a Torah scholar. But no, he blessed him that he should be "like all the boys."

It took many years for this beautiful blessing to make sense to us. The blessing was that he should have a normal childhood, that he have a normal life, that he have his health… Looking back, I realize what a tremendous blessing Rav Gustman gave, and why.

Today, that son – Matityahu, and our second son Hillel, are soldiers in combat units in the Israeli Defense Forces. Brave, strong, motivated and idealistic, they are wonderful soldiers, wonderful Jews. I pray that they return home safely along with all their comrades, and live normal lives – "just like all the boys."

May it be the will of God that the People of Israel sanctify His Name by living lives of holiness which will serve as a light to the nations – and may no more children, soldiers or yeshiva students ever need to join that holy *minyan* in Heaven.

Addendum:

Over the years much more has been written about Rav Gustman. I would like to share a little more about him, specifically relating to the Land of Israel and the soldiers who protect her.

Rav Gustman had a student, Dr. Simcha Finegold, who was also his personal dentist and occasionally served as his driver; one such occasion was the drive to the funeral of Shlomo Auman. Dr Finegold recalled that once when Rav Gustman had come for treatment, while the Rosh Yeshiva was still sitting in the chair, Dr. Finegold asked the Rabbi's permission to pose a question. He said that his two sons would soon be finishing high school and he wanted to know if there was an obligation to join the Israeli army. He added that this was a personal question, and he would not quote Rav Gustman. Rav Gustman asked him to wait; he stood up, put on his rabbinic frock and his hat. Rav Gustman wanted to answer as a rabbi, and not as a patient sitting in the dentist's chair. He understood that this was an important question. When he was fully dressed, Rav Gustman asked Dr. Finegold to repeat the question. "What does the Torah, given to us by Moshe Rabbenu, say about this situation?" Dr. Finegold asked.

Rav Gustman replied, "What does the Torah say?! It says "Shall your brothers go to war, and you remain here?" (Bamidbar 32:6) He repeated the verse over and over as he paced the office, and then Rav Gustman

Praying for the Defenders of Our Faith

added: "You can quote me – that is what I say to whoever asks me," and as his voice trailed off, he added "but no one asks me."[3]

During the Peace for the Galilee War, Rav Gustman was quoted as saying that had he been a bit younger, he would have joined the army to help in the battle. He instructed his staff at the Yeshiva to interrupt him, no matter what he was doing, if soldiers came with questions. When some of the Yeshiva students complained that these soldiers were interrupting the shiur, Rav Gustman remonstrated them: "What they are doing is more important than what you are doing."

Another student recalled one particular morning in 1982, during the Lebanon War, when the atmosphere in the Yeshiva was light, even whimsical.

In the middle of delivering a lecture, Rav Gustman sensed the feeling in the room. He stood up abruptly, pounded the desk with his hand, and roared like a lion: "Your brothers went to war, and you remain here?" With tears rolling down his cheeks, Rav Gustman cried, "Jewish men – boys, are endangering their lives and you are sitting here!" he added "Do not stand on your brother's blood," and he lectured the yeshiva students from the depth of his soul for many minutes. Everyone present sat in stunned silence. After he calmed down a bit, Rav Gustman said, "If anyone here has merit or permission not to be in the battlefield, it is only if now in yeshiva –you understand that you are on the battlefield. You are soldiers in a time of war, which means there are no luxuries or comfort. Anyone who does not abide by these conditions, for even one moment, is guilty of spilling blood. Only someone who not only believes

---

3   See Eliezer Melamed, "The Last Gaon from Vilna," Besheva, no. 109 (13 November 1987), and see Uriel Banner, "Rav Israel Zev Gustman: Sparks of Light from His Personality," Asif, vol. 4 (2017): 537-616 (Hebrew).

but behaves as if they are in battle to save lives, and their learning is saving lives, can stay. Anyone who doesn't believe that can leave now."[4]

All those who were eligible to go and fight were encouraged to do so.

Rabbi Ari D. Kahn is Director of the Foreign Student Program, and a senior lecturer in Jewish Studies, at Bar-Ilan University.

---

[4] Uriel Banner, pp. 589-590, citing Rabbi Reuven Oriyah. The article by Banner explores different positions which Rav Gustman may have expressed at different times to different people regarding serving in the army.

Avenging Episodes of Persecution: A Note on the Text and Origin of Av ha-Rahamim

Ephraim Kanarfogel

THE CONSENSUS OF MODERN SCHOLARSHIP is that the brief yet poignant *Av ha-Rahamim* prayer, which typically follows *Yequm Purqan* in the morning liturgy for the Sabbath day,[1] was composed in an Ashkenazic milieu, to laud and lament those who died '*Al Kiddush*

---

1 See Ephraim Kanarfogel, "On the Text and Origin of Av ha-Rahamim," *Yeshurun*, vol. 27 (2012): 871-878 (Hebrew). The present work is an English translation of that article and the references have not been updated; note, e.g., Joseph Isaac Lifshitz, "Av ha-Rahamim: On the 'Father of Mercy' Prayer," in Stefan C. Reif, Andreas Lehnardt, and Avriel Bar-Levav, eds., *Death in Jewish Life: Burial and Mourning Customs Among Jews of Europe and Nearby Communities* (Berlin: de Gruyter, 2014), 141-154. In light of the horrific and tragic events that occurred in Israel on October 7, 2023 (and beyond), the relevance of this *tefillah* has unfortunately never been greater. This article is dedicated to the memories of all the *Kedoshim*, ה' ינקום דמם.

Hashem during the period of the First Crusade. One of the more recent attempts (and perhaps the most authoritative) to verify this identification was offered by Ephraim E. Urbach, in the introductory volume to his edition of the extensive *piyyut* commentary composed *circa* 1235 by Abraham b. Azri'el of Bohemia, and entitled '*Arugat ha-Bosem*. Urbach focuses on the fact that the German *dayyan* and prolific *payyetan*, R. Ephraim of Bonn (d. 1197), who was also an important commentator on liturgical poetry, is aware of the place of *Av ha-Rahamim* in the Sabbath prayers and offers interpretations of it, a clear indication that this composition was extant by his day. At the same time, R. Ephraim of Bonn also provides instruction for its recitation, suggesting perhaps that its presence was relatively recent and not yet universal. Both of these factors would make abundant sense if indeed this prayer was composed at some point after the First Crusade, in the early or mid-twelfth century.

Based on a passage in ms. Parma (de Rossi) 655 that he attributes to R. Ephraim, Urbach writes the following:[2]

> On the origins of *Yequm Purqan*, see e.g., Charles Duschinsky, "The Yekum Purkan," *Sefer Zikkaron Likvod ha-Dr. Shmuel Avraham Poznanski* (Warsaw, 1927; repr. Jerusalem, 1969), 182-198; and Neil Danzig, "Two Insights from a Ninth-Century Liturgical Handbook: The Origins of *Yequm Purqan* and *Qaddish de-Hadata*," in Stefan C. Reif, ed., *The Cambridge Genizah Collections: Their Contents and Significance* (Cambridge: Cambridge University Press, 2002), 74-122. My thanks to Mr. Menachem Butler for providing me with copies of these (and so many other) studies.

2 See *Sefer 'Arugat ha-Bosem le-R. Avraham b. Azri'el*, vol. 4, ed. Ephraim E. Urbach (Jerusalem: Meqitze Nirdamim, 1963), 49, based on ms. Parma 655, fols. 153c-153d. Urbach, in n. 53, lists the folios on which this passage is found as 144f-145a. However, these folios actually mark the beginning of the collection of commentaries to the *zulatot* between Passover and *Shavuot* rather than the end of this collection (which is Urbach's intended reference in his citation). It should also be noted that there is a one-folio discrepancy in the numbering of the pages in this manuscript. See Benjamin Richler, ed. *Hebrew Manuscripts in the Biblioteca Palatina in Parma: Catalogue*

> "R. Ephraim is the first person known to me to mention the *Av ha-Rahamim* prayer and to interpret it. At the end of the commentaries to the *zulatot* between Passover and *Shavuot* it is stated that after listing the names of the martyrs, the *hazzan* recites *Ashrei*. He then recites אב הרחמים שוכן במרומים in a loud voice."

This instructional passage continues with a midrashic source for the public mentioning of the martyrs, which is extended to include asking for His merciful protection of those individuals who gave their lives *'Al Kiddush Hashem* (who were beloved in life and are not separated from His love in death), as is reflected in the text of the *Av ha-Rahamim* prayer as well.[3] Urbach also cites several earlier scholars of *piyyut* who assigned

---

(Jerusalem: Jewish National and University Library, 2001), 299, and cf. the electronic catalogue of the Institute of Microfilmed Hebrew Manuscripts (hereafter IMHM) at the National Library of Israel in Jerusalem, in its description of film #13920. Urbach appears to have had the pagination that is used in Richler's work, while I will list all pagination from this manuscript according to the IMHM catalogue.

3 ר' אפרים [מבונא] הוא, עד כמה שידוע לי, הראשון המזכיר אמירת תפלת "אב הרחמים" ומפרשה. בסוף פירושם של הזולתות שבין פסח לעצרת נאמר: לאחר זכרון נשמות הקדשים או' החזן אשרי ולאחר אמירתו יתחיל בקול רם ויאמר אב הרחמים שוכן במרומים. תיקנו חכמ(י)' ישר' להזכיר בשבתות שבין פסח לעצרת נשמות הקדושים שקידשו השם ולא על חנם וסמכו המדרש [שה"ש א:ג] עלמות אהבוך ודרשי' על מות אוהבים להקב"ה עד שמשלימים נפש לו. ד"א עלמות אהבוך זה דור השמד...ועל דרש זה סמכו רבו' נ"ע להזכיר כל אותן שקידשו השם וכן אנו מבקשים פני אב הרחמים שיפקוד ברחמיו אותם הקדושים שמסרו עצמם על קידוש השם הנאהבים ונעימים בחייהם להק' ובמותם לא נפרדו מאהבתו וזהו עלמות אהיבוך. Subsequently, some additional comments on the text of *Av ha-Rahamim* are offered: ופסוק...מנשרים קלו ומאריות גברו, פס' בשמואל על שאול ויהונתן. נקמה מזכירין כמו הרנינו גוים עמו כלומר לאותו זמן ישבחו אומות העולם את ישר' ראו מה שבחו אומה זו שדבקה בהקב"ה בכל התלאות שעברו עליהם ולא עזבוהו. כי דם עבדיו יקום ונקם ישיב לצריו שלם להם על הגזל ועל החרם וכפר לשון פיוס... וכן דמם לא נקיתי אע"פ שינקו אותם משאר עבירות שפיכות דם ישרא' לא ינקה להם ואימתי תהיה זאת כשהקב"ה [דף קנג ע"ה] שוכן בציון ידין בגוים מלא גויות

this prayer to the period of the First Crusade and concludes that "from the words of R. Ephraim, it emerges that this prayer was instituted during the period of the First Crusade, and was meant to be recited on the Sabbaths between Passover and *Shavuot*."[4]

The passage in question was attributed by Urbach to R. Ephraim of Bonn in the course of his lengthy treatment of Ephraim's *piyyut* commentaries, which occupies five of the eight sections (and more than two thirds of the pages) of the second chapter of his introductory volume to the *'Arugat ha-Bosem* commentary. Throughout his study, Urbach assumes that Ephraim of Bonn was the major interpreter of

כמו שעשה במצרים שדנם במלאתם על הים. מחץ ראש פרעה שהיה שר על ארץ רבה וחשובה וכן בימי סנחריב שנפלו פגרים מתים וכן סנחריב עצמו שהיה ראשו של מטה, כן יעשה לאומות העולם שיעשו אותם חללים מגויותיהם וימחץ ראשיהם על הארץ לרוב. מנחל בדרך ישתה כלומ' נחלים ילכו הדמים ויתרוה הארץ מדמיהם אתחיל: 'על כן שינצחו אויביו ידום וכו. The *piyyut* commentary then resumes: זולתות לג' שבתות שבין י"ז בתמוז לתשעה באב.

4 See *'Arugat ha-Bosem*, ed. Urbach, 4:49, n. 51: מדברי ר' אפרים יוצא שהתפלה תוקנה בימי מסע הצלב הראשון ושנהגו לאומרה "בכל השבתות שבין פסח לעצרת", and cf. Ismar Elbogen, *Jewish Liturgy: A Comprehensive History*, trans. Raymond P. Scheindlin (Philadelphia, 1993), 162. See also Avraham David, "Historical Records of the Persecution during the First Crusade in Hebrew Printed Works and Hebrew Manuscripts," in Yom Tov Assis, et al., eds., *Facing the Cross: The Persecutions of 1096 in History and Historiography* (Jerusalem: Magnes Press, 2000), 197 (Hebrew). David lists *Av ha-Rahamim* among the *qinot* that commemorate the First Crusade on the basis of Urbach's identification (and specifically its association with R. Ephraim of Bonn).

piyyutim in ms. Parma 655 (and in several related manuscripts, including ms. Hamburg 152, and ms. Budapest Kaufmann 399), even though Ephraim's name does not often appear explicitly.[5]

In the nearly fifty years, however, since the publication of Urbach's introductory volume, scholars have argued that other Ashkenazic rabbinic figures, whose names are also mentioned only fleetingly in these manuscripts, composed quite a few of the *piyyut* commentaries that are unattributed in these large collections, and that their share and impact was much more significant than that of Ephraim of Bonn. Two of these rabbinic scholars, R. Shemayah and R. Yosef Qara, were students of Rashi who predated R. Ephraim by two generations. Their methods of *piyyut* interpretation within these collections are rather consistent, and it is possible to attribute quite a number of specific (albeit unnamed) comments to them.[6]

At the same time, however, the section of the extensive *piyyut* commentary in ms. Parma 655 in which the *Av ha-Rahamim* passage is found (fols. 130r-172v, which consists largely of interpretations of *yozerot*), appears to have been composed by a figure named Orsherago (אורשרגו, perhaps Ursheraga) b. Asher. Orsherago's identity as the composer of this section of commentaries, and the names of some of his teachers, emerge in a number of places. On fol. 161v of ms. Parma 655, the composer writes אני הכותב שמעתי, while a parallel passage

---

5 See *Arugat ha-Bosem*, 39-72. Ephraim's role in these various manuscripts is highlighted on pp. 39-43, 51-53, 68-69.

6 See, e.g., Avraham Grossman, *Hakhmei Zarefat ha-Rishonim* (Jerusalem, 1995), 328, 338-39, 355-56, 384-87, 516-21; Elisabeth Hollender, *Piyyut Commentary in Medieval Ashkenaz* (Berlin: Walter de Gruyter, 2008), 41-45; and the IMHM catalogue description of ms. Parma 655: א"א של לדעתו אורבך, ערוגת הבשם, ח"ד, ירושלים תשכ"ג, הפרוש שבכתב-היד הוא ברובו הגדול של ר' אפרים בן יעקב מבונא (ראה בפרט עמ' 39 הערה 84). אך באמת חלקו של ר' אפרים בפירוש הוא מצומצם מאד, ורובו הוא מאת מחברים אחרים.

found in both ms. Bodl. 1128 (fol. 32v) and ms. Bodl. 1148 (fol. 160v) reads: שמעתי אני הכותב אורשרגו ב"ר אשר. Fol. 145r in ms. Parma 655 mentions "my teacher R. Yaqar *ha-Levi*," (מורי ר' יקר הלוי), and R. Yaqar is mentioned again on fols. 151v and 158v. Fol. 158r records, ואני הכותב שמעתי מפי ר' יחיאל מפריש ("I the composer heard from the mouth of R. Yehi'el of Paris"). On fol. 152r, the phrase שמעתי מפי ר' אלעזר בן רבינו יב"ק ז"ל ("I heard from the mouth of R. Eleazar b. Judah b. Qalonymus of Worms") is found.[7]

Whether Orsherago actually sat before R. Yehi'el of Paris (d. c. 1260) and R. Eleazar of Worms (d. 1237, as the phrase שמעתי מפי suggests), or whether he received their teachings (directly) from others, he would appear to be a mid-thirteenth century figure, which is further supported by the fact that he studied with R. Yaqar of Cologne. Indeed, like R. Isaac b. Moses *Or Zaru'a* (d. 1250) and R. Meir b. Barukh of Rothenburg (d. 1293), Orsherago seems to have been a German rabbinic scholar who spent some time studying in northern France as well.[8] If Orsherago b. Asher is indeed responsible for the remarks in ms. Parma 655 about

[7] See the IMHM catalogue and Benjamin Richler, ed. *Hebrew Manuscripts in the Biblioteca Palatina in Parma: Catalogue*. See also Ephraim Kanarfogel, *The Intellectual History and Rabbinic Culture of Medieval Ashkenaz* (Detroit: Wayne State University Press, 2012), chapter 5, n. 321. n. 321. Simcha Emanuel, "Chronology and Eschatology: A Jewish-Christian Debate, France 1100," *Zion* 63:2 (1998): 152, n. 41 (Hebrew). My thanks to Dr. Pinchas Roth for this last reference.

[8] An elegy for the martyrs of Frankfurt in 1241, אשא בכי ונהי ואומר אויה, is attributed to an Orsherago in ms. Parma 1104, fol. 52v (and in ms. Jerusalem, private collection C [#41225], fol. 52v, and ms. Cremona [State Archives] 32-66 [#34136]). See also Israel Davidson, *Thesaurus of Mediaeval Hebrew Poetry*, vol. 1 (New York: Jewish Theological Seminary of America, 1970), 7741א; although cf. Efraim Kupfer, *Teshuvot u-Pesaqim* (Jerusalem: Meqitze Nirdamim, 1973), for a responsum authored by R. Orsherago b. Samuel.

Av ha-Rahamim, it becomes a bit more difficult to argue that *Av ha-Rahamim* reflects only the events of the First Crusade. Orsherago lived a century and a half later (and he lived a half century after the period of the Third Crusade, when there were also numerous incidents of Jewish martyrdom), although there is nothing that categorically rules out the First Crusade as his point of focus.

Indeed, some of the phrases found in *Av ha-Rahamim* closely resemble the Crusade chronicle attributed to Solomon b. Samson. In describing how two Jews, Abraham b. R. Asher and Samuel b. R. Tamar, were slaughtered *'Al Kiddush Hashem* in the forest near Mainz, the chronicler writes: ויכו את מר אברהם ויפול ארצה וימות. וגם מר שמואל נהרג שם עמו. וישימו בטחונם בקדוש ישראל ונכנסו שניהם יחד לאוצר מכללו [=היכלו של הקב"ה] עד יום פקודת דם השפוך ואז ידין בגוים מלא גויות וגו'. ונאמר הרנינו גוים עמו כי דם עבדיו יקום וגו'.[9] The final part of this passage consists of a partial paraphrase of the end of Psalms 79:10 (יודע בגוים לעינינו נקמת דם עבדיך השפוך), and citations of Psalms 110:6, and Deut. 32:43. The very same three verses also appear in the second part of the *Av ha-Rahamim* prayer. This Crusade chronicle was composed in 1140 (and perhaps reflects an account that was composed even closer to the events themselves), and was embedded in a communal chronicle composed in

---

9   See A.M. Habermann, *Gezerot Ashkenaz ve-Zarefat* (Jerusalem: Sifre Tarshish 1945), 42. An annotated English translation of this passage is found in Robert Chazan, *European Jewry and the First Crusade* (Berkeley: University of California Press, 1987), 271 (although Chazan, 346, does not note the paraphrase of Psalms 79:10).

Speyer in the 1170's.[10] The chronicle ends with themes of vengeance as well, although other verses and biblical phrases are cited in support.[11]

However, if we look closely at some of the early manuscript versions of the *Av ha-Rahamim* prayer itself, events that occurred after the First Crusade are perhaps intimated as well:[12]

אב הרחמים שוכן מרומים ברחמיו העצומים הוא יפקוד ברחמים
החסידים והישרים והתמימים קהילות הקודש שמסרו נפשם
על קדושת השם הנאהבים והנעימים בחייהם וכו'...וינקום נקמתו
ונקמת עמו ונקמת תורתו ונקמת דם עבדיו השפוך ככת' בת'
משה איש הא-להים הרנינו גוים עמו וכו'.[13] This formulation

10 See Robert Chazan, *European Jewry and the First Crusade*, 42-34; and cf. Robert Chazan, "The Hebrew First Crusade Chronicles: Further Reflections," *AJS Review* 3 (1978): 79-90.

11 See Habermann, *Gezerot Ashkenaz ve-Zarefat*, 58-59 (=Chazan, *European Jewry*, 296-97): ולמחרת [עשו] כמו כן עד שהרגו את כולם אותם ההולכים עם פידרון הכומר. ונקם הקב"ה נקמת דם עבדיו מהם ולא נותר מהם אפילו איש אחד... עד שדרכו על גבם כמו שדרכו על היבשה והפליטה באה. ושימעה ושמח לבנו כי הראנו ה' נקמה באויבינו. ובימים ההם לקתה החמה וביום ההוא שיבר ה' גאון אויבינו ונעקר שמם...ותשיב להם גמול ה' כמעשה ידיהם תן להם מגינת לב תאלתך להם וגו' תרדוף באף ותשמידם מתחת שמי ה' כי יום נקם לה' שנת שילומים לריב ציון וגו'.

12 See ms. Vatican 326 (IMHM #373; a western Ashkenazic rite, fourteenth century), fol. 32v.

13 See also ms. Leipzig (University), B. H. 36 (#74935; a western Ashkenazic rite, fifteenth century), fol. 75 (according to the newer system of pagination), in which the phrase at the end of the first line reads שמסרו עצמם על קדושת השם rather than שמסרו נפשם; and ms. Cluny (Museum) 12290 (#14772, a Worms rite, fourteenth century), fol. 114b. Israel Jacob Yuval, *Two Nations in Your Womb: Perceptions of Jews and Christians in Late Antiquity and the Middle Ages* (Berkeley: University of California Press, 2006), 136, records a version of this formulation from a private prayer for redemption by R. Simeon b. Samuel in his *Hadrat ha-Qodesh* (Regensburg, 1400), which is not found in the printed edition of this work (Thiengen, 1560), but is

is striking in that it petitions for several additional and distinct Divine vengeances beyond avenging the 'spilled blood of the servants' (a phrase found in Ps. 79:10), the lone such request in the standard text of the *Av ha-Rahamim* prayer.[14]

Although נקמתו and נקמת עמו can refer to the events of the First Crusade, and נקמת תורתו can refer to the Torah that had been previously studied and acquired by these martyrs, if this prayer was in fact composed in the mid-thirteenth century, it is possible to suggest that the 'revenge of the His Torah' in *Av ha-Rahamim* was intended to relate to the burning of the Talmud in Paris in 1242. Orsherago, who had contact with R. Yehi'el of Paris and his teachings, would likely have been well aware of the implications of this event, even though he is only an interpreter of *Av ha-Rahamim* and not its author. Another possibility is that the initial impetus for the composition of *Av ha-Rahamim* was indeed the First

---

preserved in ms. Moscow-Guenzberg 482, fol. 25r: קנא לשמך הגדול ונקום לעינינו נקמת תורתך ונקמת דם עבדיך השפוך על קדוש שמך. On R. Simeon and his work, cf. Israel Jacob Yuval, *Scholars in Their Time: The Religious Leadership of German Jewry in the Late Middle Ages* (Jerusalem: Magnes Press, 1989), 295-300 (Hebrew).

14 Cf. Israel Jacob Yuval, *Two Nations in Your Womb*, 136-137, who stresses the theme of Divine vengeance enunciated in the standard version of *Av ha-Rahamim*, noting also the parallel phrase found in the *Avinu Malkenu* prayer, אבינו מלכנו נקום לעינינו נקמת דם עבדיך השפוך. See the comment of *Mezudat David* to Ps. 79:10 (which is included toward the end of *Av ha-Rahamim*), that the phrase יודע בגוים in that verse connotes the initiation of vengeance. On the blood of the martyrs as a particular stimulus for Divine retribution, see e.g., *Sefer Hasidim* (Parma) 1533-34 (cited by Israel Jacob Yuval, *Two Nations in Your Womb*, 136n2). On the immediacy factor, note the textual variant in the *Av ha-Rahamim* prayer found in ms. St. Petersburg EVR IV 1 (#69479, a *siddur* of the eastern Ashkenazic rite, 1489), fol. 39r, וינקום בימינו לעינינו נקמת דם עבדיך השפוך, although a more common variant is simply דם וכו' וינקום בימינו נקמת.

Crusade, a development that is perhaps supported by the recitation of this prayer only during the period of *Sefirat ha-'Omer* according to several works of Ashkenazic custom.[15] The reference to the burning of the Talmud (נקמת תורתו) could then have been a subsequent addition, as part of an expansion of the various forms of vengeance that were being sought, as occasioned by other persecutions and disruptions during the twelfth and thirteenth centuries.[16]

Shmuel Glick has asserted that the earliest dated manuscript which mandates the recitation of *Av ha-Rahamim* is *Mahzor Nurenberg* (1331).[17]

15 See *Sefer Maharil: Minhagim shel Rabbenu Yaakov Molin*, ed. Shlomo Spitzer (Jerusalem: Machon Yerushalayim, 1989), 152-53; and see also Daniel Sperber, *Minhagei Yisra'el*, vol. 1 (Jerusalem: Mosad ha-Rav Kook, 1989), 107-111. Cf. *Minhagei R. Hayyim Palti'el* in Daniel Goldschmidt, *On Jewish Liturgy: Essays on Prayer and Religious Poetry* (Jerusalem: Magnes Press, 1980), 44 (Hebrew).

16 See e.g, R. Ephraim b. Jacob of Bonn, *Sefer Zekhirah*, ed. A. M. Habermann (Jerusalem: Mosad Bialik, 1970), 17-44. R. Ephraim recounts the persecutions of the Second Crusade in 1146-1147 in northern France, as well as a lengthy series of persecutions that occurred between 1171 and 1196 in both northern France and Germany, which included events associated with the period of the Third Crusade in England as well. See, e.g., Robert Chazan, "Ephraim b. Jacob's Compilation of Twelfth-Century Persecution," *Jewish Quarterly Review*, vol. 84, no. 4 (April 1994): 397-416; and Robert Chazan, *Medieval Stereotypes and Modern Antisemistism* (Berkeley and Los Angeles: University of California Press, 1997), 54-57; and Robert Chazan, "Emperor Frederick I, the Third Crusade and the Jews," *Viator*, vol. 8 (1977): 83-93.

17 See Shmuel Glick, *Or le-Avel* (Jerusalem: Schocken, 1991), 138n39. Glick further suggests (138-142) that the Ashkenazic custom of mentioning names of the deceased (הזכרת נשמות) at this same point in the Sabbath morning service also began in earnest only during the second half of the twelfth century. Even then, however, Yom Kippur remained the occasion on which the names of the departed souls were especially showcased. In this connection, note the instruction before the Av ha-Rahamim prayer in

Praying for the Defenders of Our Faith

Although several of the *siddurim* or *mahzorim* in manuscript that have been noted here predate that manuscript by at least a few decades, and Israel Davidson cites a note by I. M. Jost that he had located it in a manuscript dated 1290,[18] it does not appear that there are any references to this prayer in Ashkenaz prior to the mid-thirteenth century, the period of the burning of the Talmud. Even though *Av ha-Rahamim* was not recited on most Sabbaths according to at least one strain of Ashkenazic custom, it is nonetheless striking that there is no reference to this prayer, for example, in the extensive liturgical commentary and prayer order of R. Eleazar of Worms (d. c. 1230), or in related works.[19]

---

ms. Parma de Rossi 1030 (#12999; a western Ashkenazic siddur, fifteenth century), fol. 96r, which extends the recitation of Av ha-Rahamim from Sabbaths prior to Shavuot and Tishah B'Av to Shabbat Shuvah as well. See also Solomon B. Freehof, "Hazkarath Neshamot," *Hebrew Union College Annual* 51 (1980): 179-184. Cf. Yitzhak (Eric) Zimmer, "The Customs of Matanat Yad and Yizkor," in Joseph R. Hacker and Yaron Harel, eds., *'The Scepter Shall Not Depart from Judah': Leadership, Rabbinate and Community in Jewish History – Studies Presented to Professor Simon Schwarzfuchs* (Jerusalem: Mosad Bialik, 2011), 71-74 (Hebrew).

18 See Israel Davidson, *Thesaurus of Mediaeval Hebrew Poetry* (New York: Jewish Theological Seminary of America, 1924), 1:3 (40א).

19 See *Perushei Siddur ha-Tefillah la-Roqeah*, vol. 2, ed. Moshe Hershler (Jerusalem: Machon ha-Rav Hershler, 1992), 560-562; and see also *Siddur Rabbenu Shelomoh mi-Germaiza ve-Siddur Hasidei Ashkenaz*, ed. Moshe Hershler (Jerusalem: [s.n.] 1972), 173-174. There was apparently a *harahaman* request recited at the end of the grace after meals at this time in at least some Ashkenazic areas, which contained a phrase that calls for the avenging of "the spilled blood of Your servants" (Ps. 79:10). See *Perushei Siddur ha-Tefillah la-Roqeah*, 2:742 (הרחמן הוא...ימלא כל משאלות לבנו לטובה הוא ירום קרננו למעלה...וישפיל כל שונאינו למטה למטה ואתה על במותימו תדרוך [דברים לג:כח] הוא ינקום לעינינו נקמת דם עבדיך השפוך); and *Sefer Or Zarua*, part 2, sec. 89 (Jerusalem: Machon Yerushalayim, 2010), 2:132 (אם יש להרבות בשבת בהרחמן יצילנו מדקדוקי עניות וינקום נקמת דם עבדיו וכו').

Moreover, the fuller listing of the various objects of Divine vengeance, formulated in exactly the same way as in the *Av ha-Rahamim* manuscripts that have been noted, appears in an addendum to a supplication that was recited toward the end of the standard Ashkenazic *selihot* regimen on the eve of *Rosh ha-Shanah*. This lengthy supplication, a *baqqashah la-viddui* composed by R. Sa'adyah Gaon, was recited after the main *pizmon* by Rabbenu Gershom (זכור ברית אברהם), and was interspersed with the three *viddui* sequences that followed. In the final section of this composition, which represents an Ashkenazic addendum to Sa'adyah's *baqqashah*,[20] a listing appears of the many types or categories of innocent blood that was shed *Al Kiddush Hashem* (וקדשו שמך הגדול ולא חללוהו) during times of unspecified persecution, including דמי אבות ובנים, דמי רחמניות וילדיהן, דמי אחים ואחיות, דמי חתנים וכלות, דמי חכמים וחכמות, דמי הגונים והגונות, דמי חסידים וחסידות, דמי זקנים וזקינות, דמי בחורים ובתולות, דמי פרנסים וחזנים, דמי דיינים וסופריהם, דמי מלמדים ותלמידיהם, ודמי אנשים ונשותיהם. ונהרגו כולם יחד על קדוש שמך המיוחד. The earth is bidden not to cover their blood until God looks down from heaven and exacts His revenge, which is described in precisely the same terms as in the *Av ha-Rahamim* passage: וינקום נקמתו ונקמת עמו ונקמת תורתו ונקמת דם עבדיו אשר שפכו דמם כמים.[21]

The descriptions of the various groups of martyrs in this Ashkenazic portion of the *baqqashah* call to mind parallel phrases in the *qinah* for the ninth of Av by R. Qalonymus b. Judah to commemorate the First

20 See the introductory comment to the *baqqashah* by Saadyah Gaon, in *Seder ha-Selihot ke-Minhag Lita*, ed. Daniel Goldschmidt (Jerusalem: Mosad ha-Rav Kook, 1965), 123. I wish to thank my colleague Professor David Berger for initially drawing my attention to this passage. On the presence and impact of Sa'adyah's *selihot* in both Italy and Ashkenaz, see, e.g., *Piyyutei R. Yehi'el b. Avraham mi-Roma*, ed. Avraham Fraenkel (Jerusalem: Meqitze Nirdamim, 2007), editor's introduction, 26-31.

21 See *Seder ha-Selihot*, ed. Goldschmidt, 129-30.

Crusade (and composed shortly after the events of 1096), אמרתי שעו מני בבכי אמרר, which also seeks Divine retribution.[22] At the same time, however, the earliest manuscript of the three from which the *baqqashah* has been published (ms. Vatican 315, IMHM #365) is dated 1320, while the latest (ms. Goettingen UB hebr. 4 [IMHM #2121G]; an eastern German rite) was copied in the late fourteenth or early fifteenth century.[23]

As noted with regard to *Av ha-Rahamim*, the dating of these manuscripts allows for this part of the *baqqashah* as well to refer to additional, unspecified episodes of *Kiddush Hashem* that took place much later than the First Crusade. Although in its narrowest context, the phrase נקמת תורתו in this *baqqashah* may have been focused on the Torah that was studied and internalized by the various groups of learned martyrs that had been mentioned, it is quite possible that this

---

22 See e.g., *Qinot Mesorat ha-Rav*, ed. Simon Posner (Jerusalem: Koren, 2010), 497-503, and the digest of Rabbi Joseph B. Soloveitchik's comments, 504-06.

23 See *Seder ha-Selihot*, ed. Goldschmidt, in nn. 20-22, and see also the editor's introduction, 20. The third manuscript is that of *Mahzor Nuerenberg*; on its dating, see above, at n. 17. The passage in ms. Goettingen addresses the Almighty in the second person rather than the third, וינקום נקמתך ונקמת עמך ונקמת תורתך ונקמת דם עבדיך; cf. above, nn. 13-14. According to at least one manuscript version, a poignant responsum by R. Meir of Rothenburg (d. 1293), to a father who had slaughtered his family during a pogrom in Koblenz *circa* 1260, concludes with the phrase, וצור ישראל ינקום את נקמתינו ונקמת תורתו ונקמת דם עבדיו השפוך במהרה בימינו, although it is possible that this line was added by a later copyist. See *Maharam mi-Rothenburg: Teshuvot, Minhagim u-Pesaqim*, ed. Y. Z. Kahana, vol. 2 (Jerusalem, 1960), 54 (sec. 59); and cf. Y. Z. Kahana, "The Responsa of the Or Zarua and Maharam b. R. Baruch," *Sinai* 13 (1943-1944): 294. See also I. A. Agus, ed., *Teshuvot Ba'alei ha-Tosafot* (New York: Talpiyot, 1954), 189 (no. 101); and see now Simcha Emanuel, *Responsa of Rabbi Meir of Rothenburg and his Colleagues* (Jerusalem: World Union of Jewish Studies, 2012), 996, 1010, 1046

formulation also takes the burning of the Talmud into account.²⁴ This may depend to some extent on whether the *baqqashah* passage borrowed the phrase from the *Av ha-Rahamim* text or whether the reverse occurred. Most interestingly, however, ms. Goettingen adds a phrase not found in the other manuscripts of the *baqqashah*, which appears after the listing of the categories of martyrs (that concludes with the phrase וגם התורה הקדושה הנשרפה באש :(as above), ודמי אנשים ונשותיהם כמה וכמה פעמים.²⁵ This manuscript version refers explicitly then to the burning of the Talmud and to other related events, suggesting that the *baqqashah* was indeed intended to refer to a range of persecutions that occurred in Ashkenazic lands during the high Middle Ages, and not only to instances of martyrdom.

In similar fashion, the lost Torah that must be avenged according to the more detailed versions of the *Av ha-Rahamim* prayer which have been presented can refer to the Torah that had been studied by any of the learned martyrs who had perished 'Al Kiddush Hashem throughout the turbulent eleventh, twelfth and thirteenth centuries. But the prominent and distinct way that these versions highlight the loss of the Torah may also point to the burning of the Talmud as a point of focus. Ashkenazic *piyyut* contains laments for a number of the specific

---

24 Much has been written about the trial of the Talmud in 1240 that led to its burning. See e.g., Robert Chazan, "The Hebrew Report on the Trial of the Talmud: Information and Consolation," in Gilbert Dahan, ed., *Le Brûlement du Talmud à Paris (1242-1244)* (Paris: Les Editions du Cerf, 1999), 79-93; Paul Rose, "When Was the Talmud Burned at Paris? A Critical Examination of the Jewish and Christian Sources and a Suggested New Dating: June 1241," *Journal of Jewish Studies* 62 (2011): 324-339; and Judah Galinsky, "The Different Hebrew Versions of the 'Talmud Trial' of 1240 in Paris," in Elisheva Carlebach and Jacob Schacter, eds., *New Perspectives on Jewish-Christian Relations - In Honor of David Berger* (Leiden: Brill, 2012), 109-140.

25 See *Sefer ha-Selihot*, ed. Goldschmidt, 130.

persecutions that occurred in various locales during the first half of the thirteenth century.²⁶ There is particular sensitivity expressed already in early twelfth-century laments toward the loss of Torah scrolls and texts, especially through burning, a powerful sentiment that culminates in R. Meir of Rothenburg's full-length *qinah* about the burning of the Talmud (which Meir witnessed as a student of R. Yehi'el of Paris), שאלי שרופה באש.²⁷ Although the extent to which the burning of the Talmud and related rabbinic volumes caused a significant shortage of talmudic texts in northern France and beyond during the second half of the thirteenth century is a matter that still requires clarification,²⁸ the spiritual and societal impact that this event had on Torah teachers and students, and on the entire Jewish community, is unmistakable.²⁹

26 See e.g., Susan Einbinder, *Beautiful Death: Jewish Poetry and Martyrdom in Medieval France* (Princeton: Princeton University Press, 2002), 32, 73, 112-113; and Ephraim Kanarfogel, *The Intellectual History and Rabbinic Culture of Medieval Ashkenaz* (Detroit: Wayne State University Press, 2013), chapter 5.

27 See Einbinder, *Beautiful Death: Jewish Poetry and Martyrdom in Medieval France*, 27-31, 75-84, 163-164. See also Ezra Fleischer, *The Yozer: Its Emergence and Development* (Jerusalem: Magnes Press, 1984), 681 (n. 19).

28 See Ephraim Kanarfogel, *Jewish Education and Society in the High Middle Ages* (Detroit: Wayne State University Press, 1992), 74-75; Aryeh Grabois, "Une consequence du brulement du Talmud a Paris: le developpement de l'ecole talmudique d'Acre," 47-56, and Colette Sirat, "Le manuscrits du Talmud en France du Nord au XIIIe siècle, 121-27, in Gilbert Dahan, ed., *Le Brûlement du Talmud à Paris (1242-1244)*.

29 See, e.g., *Shibbolei ha-Leqet le-R. Zedekiah b. Abraham ha-Rofe*, ed. Solomon Buber (Vilna, 1886), fol. 126b:

וגם מן הרבנים שהיו שם שמענו שעשו שאלת חלום לדעת אם גזירה היא מן הבורא והשיבו להם ודא גזירת אורייתא...ומאותו היום ואילך קבעוהו יחידים להתענות בו בכל שנה ושנה...תהא אפרה עלינו לכפרה; Ephraim Kanarfogel, "Dreams as a Determinant of Jewish Law and Practice in Europe during the High Middle Ages," in David Engel, Lawrence Schiffman, and Elliot

In light of the fact that the *Av ha-Rahamim* prayer (and related liturgical formulations) cannot be documented until the mid-thirteenth century, the origins and focus (or foci) of *Av ha-Rahamim* remain a bit elusive. Nonetheless, it is hoped that additional manuscript research can shed further light on the issues and questions that have been raised here, which will lead to a firmer grasp on the historical development of this quintessential Ashkenazic prayer.

Professor Ephraim Kanarfogel is the E. Billi Ivry University Professor of Jewish History, Literature, and Law at Yeshiva University.

Wolfson, eds., *Studies in Medieval Jewish Intellectual and Social History - Festschrift in Honor of Robert Chazan* (Leiden: Brill, 2012), 137-138; and Simon Shwarzfuchs, *A History of the Jews in Medieval France* (Tel Aviv: Hakibbutz Hameuchad, 2001), 216-218 (Hebrew). From the fact that the full *Shibbolei ha-Leqet* passage dates the burning of the Talmud to 1244 (rather than 1242), and that it refers to the location of the burning as *Zarefat* (rather than Paris), Shwarzfuchs cogently theorizes that there were actually two (or more) burnings of the Talmud, the second of which (and beyond) consigned Jewish texts in other regions of northern France to the flames. See also Andre Tuilier, "La condemnation du Talmud par les maitres universitaires parisiens," in Gilbert Dahan, ed., *Le Brûlement du Talmud à Paris (1242-1244)*, 59-78.

On the Prayer for the Success of the IDF Soldiers and Policemen

Yoel Katan

DEUTERONOMY CHAPTER 23:

"An Ammonite or Moabite shall not enter the assembly of the Lord; even to the tenth generation none of his descendants shall enter the assembly of the Lord forever, because… they hired against you Balaam the son of Beor from Pethor of Mesopotamia, to curse you. Nevertheless, the Lord your God would not listen to Balaam, but the Lord your God turned the curse into a blessing for you, because the Lord your God loves you. You shall not seek their peace nor their prosperity all your days forever."

The Torah describes a terrible and dreadful act of malice performed by the Moabite nation (and the Ammonite people were in league with them), in which they hired a sorcerer and magician to curse us. Because of this, the members of this nation deserve that we should never seek their peace or their prosperity, and that we should also restrict and burden their immigration. The Torah emphasizes that a great miracle occurred to us: God decided in that event that He does not agree for Balaam to curse the people of Israel, and therefore He turned the curse into a blessing, a sign of the special love with which the Lord loves the people of Israel.

And here, everyone should ask: God, the Creator of heaven and earth and all their hosts, is the one supposed to carry out the curse that the curser pronounced, to put it into action. So, what's the problem? What's the great miracle? If a wicked person curses a righteous one, and God doesn't act upon the words of the curser, doesn't carry them out, then the story ends! How can the Torah regard this as an extraordinary miracle? Does every fool or wicked person who curses someone oblige, so to speak, God to carry out his plot?

The answer is straightforward: God has established rules governing the cosmos. Some of these rules, like the laws of physics and chemistry, are evident through the routine workings of the world. Yet, there also exist spiritual edicts, less visible but just as real. A curse can inflict harm; a malevolent wish might come to fruition, its potency depending on the one who curses and the one cursed — and this principle holds true. Balaam, who was attuned to the moments and manners of the Divine's ire as depicted by our sages, naturally bore a curse that was poised to manifest and wreak havoc. It wasn't for nothing that the Moabite king compensated him with 'a house full of silver and gold'; he possessed a unique power. To prevent Balaam's curse from taking root, the Divine, in a manner of speaking, had to overstep the usual boundaries, enact a

Praying for the Defenders of Our Faith

divine intervention, alter the very fabric of reality, and transform Balaam's maledictions into blessings — profound blessings, such as 'How lovely are your tents, O Jacob', and so forth. This was nothing short of a miracle.

From curse to blessing: A blessing too has its effect. There exists a natural law that at the right moment, when uttered by the right person, a blessing can manifest itself. Not always, and not in every circumstance, but blessings given by esteemed individuals at opportune times indeed come to fruition. This is a fact. It's a law of nature.

In essence, a blessing is a prayer, a request to God to bring about a certain outcome, as wished by the one bestowing the blessing. Every prayer is a petition to God to fulfill the desires of the supplicant, and God heeds these prayers. Not always, and not every time, but many prayers are indeed answered. This is a fact. It's a law of nature.

One of the prayers established in our times, shortly after the establishment of the state, is the prayer for the welfare of the IDF soldiers. These soldiers guard the existence of the state and its citizens, a state surrounded by enemies and haters. They often risk their lives to protect, guard, and save their brethren. It is fitting that we pray to the Almighty to watch over them, strengthen their hands, and help them succeed in their mission. This prayer should be genuine, properly phrased, and heartfelt. A few years ago, the Chief Rabbi of the Police, Rabbi Rami Berachyahu, proposed, and the Chief Rabbinate Council agreed, to include the police alongside the IDF soldiers already mentioned in the prayer's title. This isn't self-evident - in the eyes of many, the primary roles of the police are societal order (traffic, criminal matters, etc.) and not necessarily warfare and security. Is it fitting? And moreover, is it advisable to alter a prayer that has already been accepted by the community?

However, as mentioned, Rabbi Rami Berachyahu, the Chief Rabbi of the Police, was adamant. The Chief Rabbinate Council approved, and it seemed the matter was settled. But, in reality, it wasn't. The change wasn't embraced by most communities that recite the Mi Sheberach prayer for the IDF soldiers, especially those in the National Religious community. Thus, it remained in a state akin to 'halakhah ve-ein morin ken' – a law acknowledged but not actively practiced or taught.

Until the events of Simchat Torah 5784. As more details about the tragedy emerged, it was evident that many on the front lines, those who stepped in to mitigate the harm and confront the malevolent, were the police officers. Regrettably, many of them paid with their lives. Do they not deserve recognition and our gratitude? Shouldn't the community pray for their well-being and success? After all, prayer is a profound act, and it does have an impact; it's a law of nature…

Indeed, spurred by a grassroots push, numerous communities began to incorporate a revised blessing every Sabbath after the Torah reading. In these tumultuous times, after each communal recitation of Psalms due to the prevailing circumstances, they intoned an updated Mi Sheberach prayer:

'מי שברך אברהם יצחק ויעקב הוא יברך את חיילי צבא הגנה לישראל ואת השוטרים ואת אנשי הביטחון העומדים על משמר ארצנו וערי אלוקינו...'

> "May He who blessed Abraham, Isaac, and Jacob, bless the soldiers of the Israel Defense Forces, the police, and the security personnel who stand guard over our land and the cities of our God…"

May our prayers be accepted.

Rabbi Yoel Katan is the Director of the Shlomo Aumann Institute at Yeshivat Sha'alvim, and editor of ha-Ma'ayan.

Expressing Gratitude to IDF Soldiers through the Mi Sheberach Prayer

Aaron R. Katz

Growing up in Los Angeles as the grandchild of Holocaust survivors and attending mainstream Modern Orthodox shuls and schools, I can safely say that the Mi Sheberach for the IDF soldiers was a prayer that always deeply inspired and moved me. During the second intifada, I spent two years at Yeshivat Kerem B'Yavneh, which is considered the pioneering Hesder yeshiva, as it was the first institution to combine army service and yeshiva study.[1] It was during my time there

---

1   See "In Memoriam: Rabbi Chaim Yaakov Goldvicht," *ha-Tsofeh* (8 February 1995): 1-2 (Hebrew); David Weiss, "Letter: The Founder of Hesder Yeshivot," *The Jewish Press* (9 February 1996): 69; and *Yikra DeChaim*:

that I had roommates actively serving in the Israel Defense Forces, which made the prayer even more personal and meaningful.

Fast forward to today, as we've just celebrated our nine-year aliyahversary, and the tefillah is now evoking both pangs of guilt and an unprecedented sense of urgency within me. I can't help but reflect on my decision not to serve in the army. While as an overseas student at Yeshivat Kerem B'Yavneh, there was no obligation for me to join the Machal program, through which overseas students could enlist. In fact, only a small number of my peers chose to do so, in a completely voluntary but highly commendable manner. Furthermore, when I made Aliyah, I was exempted from mandatory service due to my age and family situation. At that time, I was the parent of two young children.

Especially in these challenging days following Hamas' attack on October 7th, and during Israel's war against Hamas, with numerous friends, neighbors, and work acquaintances risking their lives day and night, I find myself questioning the appropriateness of being at home during these times. I'm aware that I'm not alone in grappling with this dilemma. Many of my close friends have confided in me that they, too, wrestle with this profoundly emotional issue. It's likely that we will continue to confront this question in the months and years to come, hopefully during times of peace.

While I am blessed to stay at home physically with my family, I am deeply aware that this is only possible because of the dedication of the IDF soldiers serving on the front lines. I have found myself profoundly connected and inspired by the bravery of our soldiers, to the extent that a sense of awe now overcomes me as the Chazan recites the Mi Sheberach. And yet, during this time of war, to quote Rav Abraham Isaac Kook zt"l in *Orot Ha-Milhamah*:

> "the spirit of a complete Name is in her midst, and it is impossible for a man whose soul pounds within him

to be silent at this hour, without summoning all the powers that lie dormant in the nation: Awake, arise to your task!"[2]

We all must arise to our own task. This ranges from operating on the frontlines to supporting our own families and communities both physically and emotionally. There is also an urgent sense of an increase in Torah learning and prayers. Notwithstanding that, we must never for a moment lose sight of the tremendous sacrifice of our beloved soldiers.

I recently revisited the powerful essay by Rav Aharon Lichtenstein zt"l on "The Ideology of Hesder."[3] I found particular inspiration in a passage where he clearly highlights that support for the Hesder model is based on two fundamental principles:

"(a) the simple need for physical survival and (b) the fact that military service is often the fullest manifestation

Memorial Volume in Honor and in Memory of Rabbi Chaim Yaakov Goldvicht, Founder and Rosh Yeshiva of Yeshivat Kerem B'Yavneh, eds. Daniel Z. Feldman and Yisroel Kaminetsky (New York: American Friends of Yeshivat Kerem B'Yavneh, 1996; Hebrew).

For some scholarly writing on the Hesder movement, see Stuart A. Cohen, "The Hesder Yeshivot in Israel: A Church-State Military Arrangement," *Journal of Church and State*, vol. 35, no. 1 (Winter 1993): 113-130; Elisheva Rosman-Stollman, *For God and Country? Religious Student-Soldiers in the Israel Defense Forces* (Austin: University of Texas Press, 2015); and for a contemporary academic perspective representing a counterpoint, see Elisheva Rosman, "Haredim and Conscription to the IDF: Perspectives, Perceptions, Prospects," in Kimmy Caplan and Nissim Leon, eds., *Contemporary Israeli Haredi Society: Profiles, Trends, and Challenges* (London and New York: Routledge, 2023), 90-109.

2   *Orot Ha-Milhamah* (Hebrew), chapter nine, with translation from *Rav Kook's Orot*, trans. Bezalel Naor (Jerusalem: Maggid, 2015), 140-141.

3   See Aharon Lichtenstein, "The Ideology of Hesder," *Tradition: A Journal of Orthodox Jewish Thought*, vol. 19, no. 3 (Fall 1981): 199-217.

of a far broader value: gemilut hasadim, the empathetic concern for others and action on their behalf.[4]

Drawing inspiration from Rav Aharon's profound insights, we can infuse the Mi Sheberach prayer with a genuine sense of gratitude. This gratitude is directed towards the soldiers who, in their unwavering commitment to acts of selflessness and kindness, have undertaken extraordinary risks. We extend our heartfelt thanks to them for temporarily setting aside their personal lives and willingly facing danger to safeguard our homeland and our nation. We, those who remain at home, hold a deep and lasting sense of appreciation in our hearts, and we earnestly long for a swift reunion with our courageous protectors.

Aaron R. Katz, an ordained rabbi from RIETS and a graduate of the University of Chicago Law School, serves as a senior associate within the corporate and securities practice at Greenberg Traurig's Tel Aviv office. He resides in Israel with his wife and five children.

---

[4] Ibid., 207.

Personal Reflections on the Prayer for the Israel Defense Forces

Haim (Howard) Kreisel

WHEN ASKED TO WRITE THIS essay numerous thoughts came to mind. One of my first thoughts was, strangely enough, a story I heard many years ago. I was teaching medieval Jewish studies at the Reconstructionist Rabbinical College at the time. A notable Reconstructionist rabbi (from a very traditional background) came to speak to the students. I was both struck and surprised by one of his remarks in passing (much of his talk consisted of personal reflections). He talked of some of the problems that at times emerge in revising the prayerbook, and that what is left out is at certain times of crisis sorely missed. The example he gave was that at the outbreak of the Yom Kippur War, out of great concern and distress for what was happening in Israel, he opened the Reconstructionist prayerbook hoping to find some comfort in reciting Psalm 118 from the *Hallel - Min ha-Metzar* (*In* *distress I called upon the Lord*), particularly the verses, "*All the nations have beset me; by the name of the Lord I will cut them down. They beset me, they surround me; by the name of the Lord I will surely cut them down. They have beset me like bees; they shall be extinguished like burning thorns; by the name of the Lord I will surely cut them down.*" But the verses were not there (too militaristic?), and he felt at that moment his prayerbook had failed him.

I do not know if God hears our prayers, but I do know the need I feel in reciting them. The prayer for the Israeli Defense Forces has certainly taken on a greater poignancy for me in the last few weeks. The war has turned Israel into one big family. Ideological differences between us have been largely set aside (at least temporarily). Hardly anyone here does not know some of the victims (whether the murdered or kidnapped) or at least members of their immediate families. Few people I know have not been to one of the funerals or had not made a *shiva* call. The shared sense of shock, outrage, and desire to help those displaced from the border settlements and in some way also contribute to the war effort is palpable. Hundreds of volunteer groups sprung up overnight. In the Zionist camp, hardly any families do not have members who are either serving in the army or have been called up for reserve duty and rushed to their units (or who volunteered to do guard duty in their settlements if they were past the age of military service). The Israel Defense Forces as the army of the people (and not simply a professional military force), has again become the central institution in our lives. Despite all our various and conflicting utopian dreams, we are again reminded that our physical survival depends primarily on our family members and friends (or children and grandchildren of friends), who make up this unique fighting force. For me, at least, our hopes for them, that is to say, for us, are so aptly captured in the prayer that we recite on their/our behalf

As in most Zionist-Orthodox synagogues in Israel, we recite in my synagogue the prayer for the Israel Defense Forces every Sabbath,

Praying for the Defenders of Our Faith

following the prayer for the State of Israel. The prayerbooks we use (Rinat Yisrael and Koren), include both prayers. What has always made the prayer for the Israel Defense Forces special to me is the custom of the congregation to recite "amen" after every phrase. "He Who has blessed our fathers Abraham Isaac and Jacob, will bless the soldiers of the Israel Defense Forces [...] Our enemies who rise up against us may God give over to be routed by them. Amen. God will protect and save our soldiers from every trouble and distress. Amen. From every affliction and disease. Amen. And will send a blessing and success in all that they do. Amen. May our enemies be vanquished by them. Adorn them with a crown of salvation and a garland of victory. Amen [...]." The constant repetition of amen highlights the meaning of every phrase and makes us reflect upon it. I confess that at times in reciting this prayer I even felt a little guilty in not tempering in some manner what I wish will happen to our enemies (and I know of a few synagogues who for this reason changed the wording of the prayer). Does this prayer in some way reflect also my dark side? My attitude that it is them against us, and I want them to be totally routed by us.

Living in the South of Israel, I ended up praying this Simhat Torah without a minyan during the day. A few of us were already in the synagogue when someone came with the message that there was a directive to remain home. We also heard that Hamas broke through our impenetrable border and there was a battle raging in the border settlements (the extent of the slaughter we will only begin to learn that evening). In the following days we were able to maintain our daily morning minyan. On Mondays and Thursdays, and not only on Saturdays, we began reciting the prayer for the Israel Defense Forces, as well as a prayer for the hostages (also included in both prayerbooks we use), and a prayer for the wounded. I normally recite the prayer for the Israel Defense Forces on behalf of the congregation. I cannot remember when I have felt such emotion in reciting this or any prayer. Every word of the prayer has its place, its meaning, that God should protect our protectors and aid them to crush our enemies and emerge completely victorious. I no longer feel even a modicum of guilt in my desire. There are evil people and they must be completely vanquished. To me this is not only imperative for my own survival and that of my loved ones but also a moral imperative. I am grateful that the prayerbook I use has this prayer (too many prayerbooks even in Israel let alone in Diaspora do not include it), has not attempted to "tone it down," and that I do not not find myself in the position in which my prayerbook has failed me in this time of need.

Prof. Haim (Howard) Kreisel is professor emeritus in the Department of Jewish Thought, Ben-Gurion University of the Negev.

The Prayer for the Welfare of the Soldiers of the IDF and the Security Forces

Chief Rabbi David Lau

THE TORAH ENCOMPASSES THE ENTIRETY of human experience. The book of Deuteronomy devotes multiple chapters to the prosecution of war: which kind of war is obligatory and which optional, who must join the ranks and who is exempt. It tells us the rules of war: when to make overtures of peace, when to lay siege, when to fight, when to take spoils. We are told how to properly conduct ourselves as an army, like not cutting down fruit trees during a siege (because man is likened to the tree of the field), and how to behave as individual soldiers, by maintaining purity and cleanliness and avoiding anything unseemly (because Satan takes advantage of perilous situations).[1]

Rabbi Moses Nahmanides writes:

> Moses and the princes needed to know the number of soldiers fit for battle, and the number of each tribe, and [to know] what to command those arrayed for battle at the Plains of Moab, because the Torah does not rely on the miracle of one chasing a thousand. This is the meaning of "everyone in Israel who was able to go forth to war" (Num. 1:45), because the count was for the army of war.[2]

Leaders are obligated to know and keep an accounting of their soldiers so that they can be prepared for battle.

Notably, even those completely exempt from going into battle must still leave their homes initially, and only return after the Kohen anointed for war questions his troops:

> Has any man built a new house and not dedicated it? [...]
>
> Has any man planted a vineyard and not enjoyed its fruit? [...]
>
> Has any man betrothed a wife and not married here? [...]
>
> Is any man fearful and fainthearted? [...][3]

And regarding the final exemption:

> Rabbi Akiva says, It is as it sounds: he cannot stay in formation upon seeing a brandished sword.

---

1 Jerusalem Talmud, *Shabbat*, 2:6.
2 Commentary to Numbers 1:45.
3 Deuteronomy 20:5–8.

> Rabbi Yosei ha-Gelili says, One who is fearful on account of his sins.[4]

There is no rational explanation for the fulfilled vision of a nation exiled from its devastated land returning to it millennia later. No one can deny this reality, nor can one fail to see the hand of providence in it. The present war—Swords of Iron—in which the Jewish people fight fiercely against a cruel enemy, shows that we are still living in a fateful period. We face grave danger, encircled by enemies from within and without. The ray of light piercing this darkness is the Jewish people, who possess an indomitable spirit and capacity for self-sacrifice. Many are those who jeopardize their lives in the struggle against evil. This is not just another war in the annals of the Jewish people, but a war of human history. Every Jew burns with a sacred fire to accomplish this noble mission, and we see the great sacrifices made and the displays of love between our Jewish brothers and sisters. Whenever I visit the soldiers, I witness faith and unity pulsing through them.

The Sages said long ago about the verse, "For it is the Lord your God who goes with you to fight for you against your enemy, to bring you victory" (Deut. 20:4): "They come relying on the strength of flesh and blood, but we come relying on the strength of the Omnipresent."[5] Whoever fights the Jewish people raises their fist not only against them, but against God Himself. The existence of the Jewish people is assured, but it must march on the right path, that of the Torah.

Any student of Jewish history, who knows its boundless suffering and countless victims, grasps the importance of the Jewish people living in their own land.

---

4   Rashi on Deuteronomy 20:8.

5   Mishnah, *Sotah*, 8:1.

The blessing we make for the welfare of the soldiers of the IDF and the security forces is more than a plea for their success. It is an expression of the deep connection that these warriors have with their Creator.

The Torah outlines how we are to view this relationship. Victory comes amidst the knowledge that "it is the Lord your God who goes with you to fight for you against your enemy, to bring you victory" (Deut. 20:4). This prayer also articulates our right to the Land of Israel. When we bless those who stand watch over our borders, we affirm the borders of our Land—from the Lebanese border to the Egyptian desert, from the Mediterranean Sea to the approach of the Arabah.

The war for the Land of Israel is an obligatory war, as is any war intended to save the Jewish people from their enemies. When we recite this prayer for the soldiers in harm's way, who walk through the inferno, we profess our appreciation for them and declare that the heart of our people remains steadfast and courageous to march onward. We are the last generation of the oppression, and the first of the glimmerings of redemption. We pray for the Holy One to protect and deliver our soldiers from all trouble and distress, and to make our enemies be struck down before them.

We wait to see with our own eyes the fulfillment of the prophet's words, "Nation shall not raise sword against nation, nor shall they learn war anymore" (Isa. 2:4), and "They shall do no evil nor cause destruction in all My holy mountain" (11:9).

Rabbi David Lau is the Ashkenazi Chief Rabbi of Israel.

David Lau
Chief Rabbi of Israel
President of the Chief Rabbinic Council

דוד לאו
הרב הראשי לישראל
נשיא מועצת הרבנות הראשית

בס"ד, כ"ג חשון, תשפ"ד
7 נובמבר, 2023

תפילה לשלום חיילי צבא הגנה לישראל ואנשי בטחון

תורת ישראל מקיפה את כל מעגל החיים. פרקים שלמים נכתבו על מלחמה, יש מלחמת מצוה ויש מלחמת רשות, ישנה התייחסות מי חייב בעריכת מלחמה ולמי ניתן פטור ממנה. התורה קובעת כיצד יש לצור על עיר מתי "וקראת אליה לשלום", מתי יש להלחם ומתי "כל שללה תבז לך". בשעת מצור "לא תכרת" את עצי המאכל "כי האדם הוא עץ השדה", עד ירידה לפרטים של התנהגות אישית של קדושה טהרה ונקיות "ונשמרת מכל דבר רע" כי השטן מקטרג בשעת סכנה (ירושלמי שבת פ"ב).

כתב הרמב"ן (במדבר א מה) "והיו משה והנשיאים צריכים לדעת מספר חלוצי צבא המלחמה, וכן מספר כל שבט ושבט, ומה יפקוד עליו בערבות מואב במערכות המלחמה, כי התורה לא תסמוך על הנס שירדוף אחד אלף, וזה טעם 'כל יוצא צבא בישראל' כי המנין מפני צבא המלחמה" עכ"ל. קיימת חובה על מנהיגים לדעת ולספור את אנשי הצבא כדי להיות מוכנים אלי קרב.

מעניין להוסיף שגם אותם אלו שפטורים לגמרי מלצאת למלחמה, בשלב ראשון יוצאים, אלא חוזרים לביתם לאחר הכרזת משוח מלחמה שעומד ומכריז: "מי האיש אשר בנה בית חדש ולא חנכו" "ומי האיש אשר נטע כרם ולא חללו" "ומי האיש אשר ארש אשה ולא לקחה" "ומי האיש הירא ורך הלבב" "רבי עקיבא אומר כמשמעו, שאינו יכול לעמוד בקשרי המלחמה וראות חרב שלופה. רבי יוסי הגלילי אומר הירא מעבירות שבידו" (רש"י)

אין הסבר הגיוני לבאר תפיסת חזון ההתגשמות של אומה שגלתה מארצה שנחרבה ושבה אליה לאחר אלפי שנים. אין מי שיכול להתכחש למציאות זו ולא לראות בה יד השגחה. ימים אלו ימי מלחמת "חרבות ברזל" מלחמה בה עם ישראל נלחם במלא עוזו כנגד אויב אכזר, מראים שגם במציאות העכשווית אנו עדיין חיים בתקופה הרת גורל, בימים אלו נשקפת לנו סכנה גדולה, אנו מוקפים שונאים מבפנים ומבחוץ. קרן אורה מוצאים אנו כיום בעם ישראל, הרוח הבלתי נכנעת וההרגשה של מסירות נפש. רבים שמים נפשם בכפם במאבק כנגד הרוע. זו אינה מלחמה נוספת בתולדות ישראל זו מלחמה בתולדות הקיום האנושי. כל אחד מעם ישראל חדור אש קודש למען מטרה נעלה, ורואים מידה גבוהה של מסירות נפש ואהבת ישראל. בכל ביקורי בכינוסי חיילים בימים אלו ראיתי את רוח האמונה והאחדות מפעמת בהם.

כבר אמרו חז"ל (סוטה פ"ח) על הפסוק "כי ה' אלוקיכם, ההולך עמכם להלחם לכם עם אויבכם להושיע אתכם" "הם באין בנצחונו של בשר ודם, ואתם באים בנצחונו של מקום..." מי שנלחם בעם ישראל מרים ידו לא רק כנגד העם אלא נלחם נגד ה'. קיומו של עם ישראל מובטח אולם בדרך הנכונה לצעוד היא רק על פי תורת ישראל.

כל מי שנהירים לו ההיסטוריה של האומה היהודית, סבלותיה וקרבנותיה שעברו כל גבול אנושי, מבין את חשיבות הקיום של עם ישראל בארצו.

הברכה שאנו נושאים לשלום חיילי צה"ל ואנשי הבטחון אינה רק בקשה להצלחה אלא היא מבטאת גם את עומק הקשר שיש ללוחמים עם מי שאמר והיה העולם.

התורה מתווה לנו הדרך שיש לראות מעורבות זו. התשועה תבא תוך ידיעה "כי ה' אלקיכם ההולך עמכם להלחם לכם עם אויבכם להושיע אתכם" (דברים כ, ד). בתפילה זו באה לידי ביטוי גם זכותינו על ארץ ישראל. כשאנו מברכים את חיילי צבא הגנה ואנשי כוחות הבטחון העומדים על משמר ארצנו, אנו משרטטים את גבולות ארץ ישראל. מגבול הלבנון – עד מדבר מצרים מן הים הגדול עד לבא הערבה.

המלחמה על ארץ ישראל היא בגדר מלחמת מצוה, וכן מלחמה שהיא להצלת ישראל מיד צר. כשאנו נושאים תפילה עבור הלוחמים הנמצאים במצב סכנה, שרגליהם דורכות על הר געש, אנו מבטאים את הערכתנו

כלפיהם ואת העובדה שלב האומה לא חת ולא נרתע ואנו צועדים קדימה. דורנו דור אחרון לשעבוד וראשון לאתחלתא דגאולה והוא מתפלל שהקב"ה ישמור ויציל את חיילנו מכל צרה וצוקה ויתן את אויבינו נגפים לפניהם.

מצפים אנו לקיום דברי הנביאים "לא ישא גוי אל גוי חרב ולא ילמדו עוד מלחמה" ו"לא ירעו ולא ישחיתו בכל הר קדשי" שיתגלו לעינינו.

Prayer for IDF Soldiers in Ultra-Orthodox Mizrahi Prayer Books

Nissim Leon

In studies of Israeli society, the military frequently emerges as a linchpin, deeply entrenched in the lives of its citizens and shaping the contours of 'good' or 'republican' citizenship. This is a society anchored by a mandatory standing army, an expansive reserve service, and a political elite dominated by veteran military officers. Furthermore, for the vast majority of the Jewish populace, the military stands as a symbol of national consensus.[1] Some might argue that the prayer for the peace

---

1   See, for example, Baruch Kimmerling, *The Invention and Decline of Israeliness: State, Society and the Military* (Berkeley: University of California Press, 2001); Yoram Peri, *Generals in the Cabinet Room: How the Military Shapes Israeli Policy* (Washington, D.C.: United States Institute of Peace Press, 2006); Yagil Levi, *From "People's Army" to "Army of the Peripheries"* (Jerusalem: Carmel, 2007; Hebrew).

of the Israeli Defense Forces serves as yet another reflection of the fluid dynamics between the military and society in Israel. However, in the same vein, this prayer might also spotlight the boundaries of such fluidity, especially when viewed against a contrasting backdrop: the Ultra-Orthodox (or, Haredi) ideology.

The establishment of the State of Israel led the country's national rabbinical institutions to introduce new liturgical pieces, addressing this historical event, into the traditional prayer book. Two of these pieces are especially prominent: the prayer for the welfare of the State of Israel, which was composed by Nobel Prize-winning author S.Y. Agnon, and a prayer for the welfare of the soldiers of the Israel Defense Forces, apparently composed by Rabbi Shlomo Goren,[2] who served as the first Chief Rabbi of the Military Rabbinate, and as such was a key figure in the establishment and organization of the military chaplaincy. (He later served as Chief Rabbi of Israel.) The inclusion of the national prayer chapters in the prayer books in Israel over the years has been a source of distinction between the two religious factions involved in the editing of prayer books, their printing, and their publication. On one hand, there are the religious-Zionist circles and on the other, the ultra-Orthodox (ultra-Orthodoxy) circles. The religious-Zionist circles saw in the national prayer chapters a solid expression of the ideological integration they sought between religion and nationalism. Conversely, the ultra-Orthodox, ultra-Orthodoxy circles viewed these chapters as a "new tradition" which in their eyes continued the modern attempts to reform the traditional prayer, and certainly opposed, in essence, their initially skeptical historical approach towards Zionism and its symbolic

---

2   Reuven Gafni, "Houses of Prayer and Nationality: The Shaping of Hebrew Nationalism in Eretz Israel Synagogues during the British Mandate Period," (PhD Dissertation, Hebrew University of Jerusalem, 2013; Hebrew).

expressions.³ However, a close look at the ultra-Orthodox circles shows that at least one prayer chapter was adapted – the prayer for the peace of the IDF soldiers.

Gradually, the prayer for the State of Israel and the prayer for the welfare of the soldiers were integrated into the prayer service in many synagogues in Israel, on Sabbath mornings and on national holidays such as the Day of Commemoration for Fallen Soldiers and on Israeli Independence Day.⁴ While national-religious prayer books and those used in Mizrahi synagogues tended to include the prayer for the soldiers' peace, it is not incorporated in prayer books published by Ashkenazi ultra-Orthodox printers and editors. It is also not recited in their synagogues. On the other hand, it is incorporated in prayer books published by ultra-Orthodox Sephardic printers and editors, and it is recited in full or in various forms in synagogues managed by Mizrahi ultra-Orthodox rabbis or communities. This, of course, raises questions: What is the source of the difference? How do the editors of the prayer books from the ultra-Orthodox Mizrahi sector overcome the ideological obstacles that prevent the Ashkenazi ultra-Orthodox from including the prayer in their prayer books? And in general, what actually happens in the life of the synagogue among the praying community?

---

3   Aviezer Ravitzky, *Messianism, Zionism, and Jewish Religious Radicalism* (London & Chicago: The University of Chicago Press, 1996). Regarding the complexity of the relationship between Zionism and the Ultra-Orthodox, see Yosef Fund, "Into the Circle: Attempts by Agudat Israel to Join Forces with the Jewish Agency," *Yisrael*, vol. 21 (2013): 149-178 (Hebrew).

4   Aaron Ahrend, *Israel's Independence Day – Research Studies* (Ramat-Gan: Bar-Ilan University Press, 1998), 176-200 (Hebrew).

Ethnic Division in the Ultra-Orthodox Society

The ultra-Orthodox society in Israel is divided between two major ethnic factions. On one hand, there are the Ashkenazi ultra-Orthodox, whose family origins lie in Eastern and Central European Jewry, and on the other hand, the Sephardic/Mizrahi ultra-Orthodox, whose family origins are in Arab countries and North Africa. The ethnic distinction between Ashkenazi and Sephardic/Mizrahi ultra-Orthodox can be summarized in three prominent aspects[5]:

Historical Background: Ultra-Orthodoxy emerged as a reactionary religious ideology that progressively became organized and institutionalized in Central and Eastern Europe towards the end of the 19th-century and throughout the 20th-century.[6] This ideology sought to vigorously confront the national and societal changes within the observant Jewish community in Central and Eastern Europe. Like other modern Jewish ideologies, ultra-Orthodoxy also inspired a conservative response within the Jewish diaspora in Muslim countries. Initially, there were tradition rabbis in Morocco who sought help from the experience of East European Orthodoxy in the face of secularization and modernization processes. Later, the organization of strict rabbis from Baghdad and Aleppo who settled in Israel became prominent, building their religious world around the student community in the Porat Yosef yeshiva.[7] However, these developments were relatively marginal.

---

5   For an extended view for the ethnic and religious definitions, see Nissim Leon, "The Ethnic Structuring of 'Sefardim' in Haredi Society in Israel," *Jewish Social Studies*, vol. 22, no. 1 (Fall 2016): 130-160.

6   Menachem Friedman, *Haredi Society: Sources, Trends, and Processes* (Jerusalem: Jerusalem Institute for Israel Studies, 1991; Hebrew).

7   Neri Horowitz, "Shas and Zionism: A Historical Analysis," *Kivunim Hadashim*, no. 2 (2000): 30-60 (Hebrew).

The processes of becoming ultra-Orthodox in Mizrahi Jewry became more significant with the educational involvement of the Lithuanian yeshiva's rescue committee in Morocco after World War II. This activity continued and expanded in the young state of Israel, effectively laying the groundwork for hundreds of Mizrahi boys and girls who acquired their Torah education in ultra-Orthodox Ashkenazi-sponsored or managed educational institutions.[8] This ultra-Orthodox version found fertile ground among immigrants from Muslim countries due to many of them facing social distress, poverty, and attempts to erase their ethnic and traditional identity.[9] Recruitment by ultra-Orthodox educational systems in Israel and the return to religious observance movement strengthened the connection between the Sephardic/Mizrahi world of yeshivas and provided both favorable economic conditions for education and answers to questions of ethnic identity and consciousness that did not find a solution in the competing Orthodox version – religious Zionism.[10] The pinnacle of this development is the establishment of the Shas party as a political home for the growing sector of Sephardic/Mizrahi yeshiva students.[11]

Social Distance: As mentioned, the Ashkenazi ultra-Orthodox factions played a prominent role in the process of Mizrahi Jewry

8   Ibid.

9   Anat Feldman, "Ethnicity, Politics, and Education: The First Decade of Hachinuch Ha'atzmai, 1953-1963," *Dor le-Dor*, vol. 31 (2007): 117-150 (Hebrew).

10 See, in this context, the public positions of Avi Picard, "Religious Zionism and the Easterners: From Then Until Now," *De'ot*, no. 49 (2001): 4-7 (Hebrew); Chezi Cohen, "I am in the West (a) and my heart Is In the East: Religious Zionist Education – Could it Be Different?" *De'ot*, no. 49 (2001): 8 (Hebrew).

11 Shlomo Deshen, "The Emergence of the Israeli Sephardi Ultra-Orthodox Movement," *Jewish Social Studies*, vol. 11, no. 2 (Winter 2005): 77-101.

becoming ultra-Orthodox. They saw themselves as the spiritual saviors of Mizrahi Jews.[12] Ultra-Orthodox educational institutions managed by Ashkenazi ultra-Orthodox were often the place where hundreds of boys and girls from Mizrahi families were trained for an ultra-Orthodox lifestyle. However, this view of spiritual salvation also gave rise to what historian Yaakov Lupo termed "Torah colonialism."[13] This process led to ethnic segregation, with a limited number of Mizrahim admitted to Ashkenazi ultra-Orthodox educational institutions and the establishment of separate educational institutions. It gave rise to the development of social and cultural norms within the Ashkenazi ultra-Orthodox community, as well as a separation in marital relationships within ultra-Orthodox society. This has created a notable paradox within Mizrahi ultra-Orthodox society in Israel. On one hand, they see themselves committed to the ultra-Orthodox ideology and lifestyle in which they believe and were educated, and on the other hand, they know that in that reality dominant forces push them away and mark them as separate ethnic category – "Sephardim."[14]

Community Structure: To these two aspects, we must add the significant sociological difference between the two ethnic categories. While Ashkenazi ultra-Orthodox are organized into homogenous communities that try to differentiate themselves from those different from them and conduct a sectarian and class-based politics, the communities of the Mizrahi ultra-Orthodox can be described as more porous and conduct politics that is more attentive to the diverse religious

---

12 Jacob Lupo, *Shas de-Lita: The Lithuanian Take-Over of Moroccan Torah Scholars* (Tel Aviv: Hakibbutz Hameuchad, 2001; Hebrew).

13 Jacob Lupo, *Can Shas Restore Past Glory?* (Jerusalem: Floersheimer Institute, 2004), 11 (Hebrew).

14 Nissim Leon, "The Mizrahi Situation in Israel"s Ultra-Orthodox Society and Reactions to It," *Democratic Culture*, no. 14 (2013): 165-195 (Hebrew)

and social environment in which they operate daily.[15] This complex reality is not without conflicts. These can and do arise against the backdrop of disputes over the proper religious way of life. The ultra-Orthodox (Haredim) will call for stricter observance of religious commandments; the traditionalists will seek to moderate the radicalism and search for more leniency. Within this space, alongside boundary-setting works that aim to sharpen the Haredi identity,[16] there are also unifying works that encourage the imaginary continuity between the Haredi community and the traditionalist public.[17]

The attempt to break free from Ashkenazi ultra-Orthodox patronage, as well as maintaining a direct connection with the non-ultra-Orthodox Mizrahi public, has turned the Mizrahi ultra-Orthodox from a marginal factor in Orthodox Judaism into one of the most prominent forces in it. These factors manifested in a powerful political project in the form of the Shas party and in the religious renewal work in Mizrahi communities outside the enclaves of ultra-Orthodox society. A prominent place in the religious renewal work was taken by the revival of the prayer order practiced in Mizrahi synagogues.

---

15 Shlomo Fisher and Zvi Beckerman, "Church or Cult?" in Aviezer Ravitzky, ed., *Shas: Cultural and Ideological Perspectives* (Tel Aviv: Am Oved, 2006), 321-342 (Hebrew).

16 Asaf Sharabi, "Boundary Work in the Teshuvah Movement in Israel," (PhD Dissertation, Bar-Ilan University, 2005; Hebrew).

17 Nissim Leon, *Harediyut Rakah (Soft Ultra-Orthodoxy): Religious Renewal in Oriental Jewry in Israel* (Jerusalem: Ben-Zvi Institute, 2010; Hebrew).

Renewal of the Mizrahi Prayer Book and the Prayer for the Well-being of Soldiers

Anyone who has entered Mizrahi synagogues in recent years cannot ignore the influx of renewed printings of prayer books and various editions. Among the renewed prayer books, the following stand out: prayer books organized and edited in the mid-1980s by the family of Rabbi Ovadia Yosef, the spiritual leader of the Shas party; prayer books arranged in the 1990s by students of the Kisei Rahamim Yeshiva based on the traditions of the Jews of Djerba; and prayer books arranged and edited by small halakhic institutes and local rabbis, such as the Shira Hadasha institute of Rabbi Doron Ronen. The renewal of the Mizrahi prayer book included the use of a modern font, the insertion of halakhic instructions, a Hebrew explanation of the prayer words, a focus on aligning the printed prayer sequence with the actual practiced sequence, and adapting the prayer book to the various ethnic halakhic schools that developed in the last fifty years in Israel. Initially, it seemed that the renewal of the Mizrahi prayer book mainly involved rabbis and institutions. They sought, through their halakhic approach, to actively participate in reshaping the order of prayers and Mizrahi synagogue customs (hereinafter: the rabbinical prayer books). For example, the prayer books published by Rabbi Ovadia Yosef's family stood out. These prayer books played a part in promoting Rabbi Ovadia Yosef's halakhic method and in transforming it from a topic among halakhic books to a practice embedded in the life of the Mizrahi synagogue.[18] On the other hand, it seems that in the last decade, we are talking about a real industry that uses rabbinic approvals to sell as many prayer books as possible, when in fact it is a standard copy of the rabbinical prayer books.

---

18 Benjamin Lau, *From 'Maran' to "Maran": The Halakhic Philosophy of Rav Ovadia Yosef* (Tel-Aviv: Yediot Aharonot, 2005), 119-121 (Hebrew).

As part of the prayer book renewal project there was a need to address the status of the prayer for the welfare of the soldiers, which is recited regularly in many Mizrahi synagogues. With the exception of a single prayer book whose publisher is affiliated with Ashkenazi haredi circles, Mizrahi prayer books include the prayer. This is not self-evident: firstly, even among these circles, an anti-Zionist stance has been evident – sometimes even becoming strident and zealous, with Zionist ideology accused of attempting to secularize Mizrahi Jewish immigrants.[19] Secondly, the prayer for the welfare of the soldiers did not originally appear in Mizrahi haredi prayer books. For example, it is absent from the *Tefillat Yesharim* edition, published by Yaakov Salah Mansour in 1978.[20] This prayer book is among the oldest used in the traditional Mizrahi synagogue in Israel, and it also served as one of the primary ones before the new printings influenced by the ultra-Orthodox-Mizrahi circles. In the Saturday morning prayer sequence, the prayer for the soldiers' well-being is absent (there, pages 206-208).[21] A competing prayer book published by the Jerusalem printer, Yitzhak Ezra Bakal, boasts in its 1978 introduction that "since the establishment of the State, additional prayers and requests for the peace of the State of Israel, a prayer for IDF soldiers, and a prayer for Independence Day have been added [...] and these too were added according to the discretion of the publishers or were not printed at all."[22] Meaning, the inclusion of the prayer was innovative, and it did not find a place in the earlier printings of the prayer

---

19 Benjamin Brown, "Sephardi Rabbis and Religious Radicalism: Toward a Revision," *Akdamot*, vol. 10 (2001): 289-324 (Hebrew).

20 Yaakov Salah Mansour, *Siddur Tefilat Yesharim* (Jerusalem, 1978; Hebrew).

21 Ibid., 296-297.

22 Yitzhak Ezra Bakal, *Siddur Beit David ve-Shlomo* (Jerusalem, 1978), 5 (Hebrew).

books. The implication is that apparently, there was no need to print the prayer in the renewed prayer books since it does not align with the Haredi worldview, and it isn't a traditional written part of the prayer book. If so, why did they associate themselves with a modern liturgical tradition, which is fundamentally Zionist? Why didn't they continue the tradition of reciting the prayer orally, without the need for a guiding, seemingly "binding" text embedded in the prayer book? Why did they distance themselves from the Haredi opposition to national liturgy?

These questions will be examined through a short summary of interviews with the editors of four different prayer books that are popular among Mizrahi Haredi circles. These men are intimately familiar with the market, the texts, and the dilemmas involved. In addition, we present some of the results of a comparative analysis of different versions of the prayer for the soldiers' welfare as it appears among the various Mizrahi Haredi publishers.

Functional Reasons for Integrating the Prayer

Reasons for the inclusion of the prayer in some of the more popular editions of the prayer book arose in my interviews with some of the editors involved. The first reason they mentioned was their awareness that they are active in a competitive field. The prayer book industry operates within a market that includes many private and institutional clients who are not Haredi, and who generally want their prayer book to fulfil three main criteria: it must include the range of prayers as recited on a regular basis in Mizrahi synagogues; its print must be easy to read; and it must be reasonably priced. The editors explained that the prayer for the soldiers' welfare has, over the years, become an integral part of the Sabbath morning prayer service in Mizrahi synagogues. Prayer leaders and congregants alike therefore want the prayer to appear in the prayer book, for convenient reference.

A second reason pertains to the social context within which Mizrahi Haredi communities exist. Prayer book editors acknowledge that the question of including the prayer for soldiers is an integral part of an ideological stance. However, they argue that the issue is more a statement of Jewish solidarity than a question of Haredi affiliation. "The prayer book," one editor told me, "is a tool in the service of the great goal of restoring the old glory [of the Mizrahi tradition]; to imbue Mizrahim with religious pride." More than once the editors repeated what they view as a social fact: the world of Mizrahi Haredi yeshivas is very different from the world of their Ashkenazi counterparts. The Mizrahi yeshivas maintain a living connection with their non-Haredi environment. "Among us, every family has a soldier." "The army isn't something that we aren't familiar with. Many of the newly observant Mizrahim, or those on the path to full observance, are familiar with the army and hold it in esteem." "We are not Ashkenazim," one editor told me. "We don't cut ourselves off from our brothers. The state is a state, but our brothers are our brothers. The prayer is for them, not for the state.'"

Apparently, editors view the prayer as possessing national significance in the social rather than the political sense. To their understanding, the collective at the heart of the prayer is not the state but rather the people. This underlines the discrepancy between the ideological component of the prayer as originally composed (Zionism) and the desired component of solidarity in their version of it (Jewish peoplehood). What is interesting about this approach is that this fine distinction, proposed by a group that operates within the reality of the State of Israel, its representatives even playing an active role on the national political scene, closely resembles the way in which the bond of religious connection and solidarity between Israeli Jews and Diaspora Jews is often presented.[23]

23 Alexander Yakobson, "Jewish Peoplehood and the Jewish State, How Unique? – Comparative Survey," *Israel Studies*, vol. 13, no. 2 (Summer

Praying for the Defenders of Our Faith

Another reason for inclusion of the prayer that was raised in the interviews relates to the dominant influence of Rabbi Ovadia Yosef (1920-2013), the late founder and spiritual leader of the Shas party, and a personality who was perceived by many as a religious authority who transcended ethnic boundaries. Firstly, his sons have initiated several editions of the prayer book that seek to disseminate their father's religious approach. In addition, Rabbi Yosef headed a political movement that commanded influence in government ministries and various other public positions which were in a position to help disseminate these prayer books among institutions including schools, synagogues, and yeshivas, in Israel and outside of it. Therefore, many of the prayer books carry Rabbi Yosef's written approbation, representing a sort of stamp of approval and increasing the market value. What this has to do with the prayer for the soldiers' welfare is that Rabbi Yosef's associates have asserted that he would award his approbation only to prayer books that included the prayer, and explained this policy as arising from the rabbi's concern for the soldiers. While he did not recommend army enlistment, viewing Torah study as a more significant value, Rabbi Ovadia Yosef did not reject the army and its soldiers. On the contrary, research on Rabbi Yosef's religious approach points to a complex stance in relation to state institutions. On one hand, he was vehemently critical of the Supreme Court; on the other hand, he passionately defended the soldiers of the IDF. The background to this complexity may lie in the fact that during the years 1973–1983, Rabbi Yosef was the Sephardi Chief Rabbi of Israel. In his first year in this position, in October 1973, Israel found itself at war with Egypt and Syria. The Yom Kippur War is considered one of the most traumatic events in Israel's history, because of the surprise attack launched in the midst of the holiest day of the Jewish

2008): 1-27.

year, because of the difficult battles that were waged, and because of the large number of casualties. Rabbi Yosef was required to solve complicated halakhic problems that arose in view of the many missing soldiers. His direct involvement in these matters appears to have left in him a legacy of special concern for soldiers, expressed, inter alia, in his insistence that the prayer for the welfare of the soldiers be included in those prayer books that followed his teachings, or those seeking his approbation.

Adjustments to the National Liturgy in the Renewed Prayer Books

The interviews with the prayer book editors explained, therefore, why the prayer for the well-being of the soldiers is embedded in most of the prayer books published by the Mizrahi Haredi circles. Nevertheless, these prints are not made without modifications to the text of the prayer. It seems that these modifications slightly tone down the nationalistic hue of the prayer and connect it more to the Haredi perspective regarding the relationship between the army and society in Israel. Firstly, I will present the most noticeable modifications, and afterward, I will explain how they serve the Haredi worldview.

The official version of the prayer describes the Israel Defense Forces as the protector of the State of Israel. The prayer asks God to guard the army and its soldiers and help them achieve victory over the state's enemies. The following is the full official version of the prayer:

> He Who blessed our forefathers, Abraham, Isaac and Jacob - may He bless the soldiers of the Israel Defense Forces, who stand guard over our land and the cities of our God, from the border of Lebanon to the desert of Egypt, and from the Great Sea to the approach of the Arava, on the land, in the air, and on the sea. May the

> Almighty cause the enemies who rise up against us to be struck down before them. May the Holy One, Blessed be He, guard and deliver our soldiers from every trouble and distress and from every plague and illness, and may He grant blessing and success to all their endeavors. May He cause them to overpower our enemies and may He grant them salvation and crown them with victory. And may they embody the fulfilment of the verse: 'For it is the Lord your God Who goes with you, to wage battle for you against your enemies, to save you.' And let us say, Amen.[24]

The examination of several tens of prayer book prints in Mizrahi synagogues published by the Mizrahi Haredi circles reveals two prominent types of modifications to the prayer for the well-being of the soldiers. The first is in the form of added comments and introductions to the prayer chapter itself, and the second is an intervention in the wording of the prayer itself.

An examination of several dozen editions of the prayer book used in Mizrahi synagogues and published by Mizrahi haredi bodies reveals two types of changes to the prayer for the welfare of the soldiers. One type consists of prefaces to and comments on the prayer; the other involves amendments to the prayer text itself. As an example of the first type we might cite the Hazon Ovadia prayer book, published by Rabbi Yitzhak Yosef, son of Rabbi Ovadia Yosef. The prayer for the welfare of the soldiers appears, introduced by the words: 'When the Ark is opened,

---

24 Shlomo Tal, *Siddur Rinat Yisrael, Nusaf Sefarad*, 4th edition (Jerusalem: Moreshet, 1998), 277 (Hebrew).

some recite [the following]:"[25] In other words, recital of the prayer is a matter of personal or congregational discretion. There is no binding imperative with regard to its inclusion, its formula, or the manner in which it is to be recited.[26]

In my search for a more explicit stance, I found only one candidate amongst the selection of prayer books that I reviewed. This was the Ner Refael edition, published by a small *kollel* (yeshiva for married men) in Jerusalem. It is printed in limited numbers, but its editor, Rabbi Yosef Haim Mizrahi, is considered an authority among Mizrahi Haredi society. Most of the prayer books that he has produced include an amended version of the prayer for the welfare of the soldiers, which we shall address below. In the Ner Refael edition, along with the amendments, the following explanation appears:

> "It is well-known that the text of the prayer [for soldiers] commonly found in prayer books was written in cooperation with the 'poets of the nation' ... We therefore present an amended version, with the guidance of the 'luminaries of the nation.'"[27]

This forthright explanation alludes to the circumstances and secular authorship of the official text, presenting it as inseparable from the secular national liturgy whose content is foreign to haredi discourse, and therefore in need of mediation.

---

25 Yitzhak Yosef, *Siddur Hazon Ovadia* (Jerusalem: Yeshivat Hazon Ovadia, 1988), 458 (Hebrew).

26 Aaron Ahrend, *Israel's Independence Day – Research Studies* (Ramat-Gan: Bar-Ilan University Press, 1998), 196 (Hebrew).

27 Yosef Haim Mizrahi, *Siddur Ner Refael ha-Shalem, Od Yosef Hai* (Jerusalem: Kollel Ner Refael Tzedakka, 2007), 509 (Hebrew).

Praying for the Defenders of Our Faith

Alongside comments expressing overt or covert reservations with regard to the prayer, there are also amendments to the prayer text itself. These amendments seek to adapt the prayer to conform with the haredi worldview. An example is the replacement of the phrase "soldiers of the Israel Defense Forces," as it appears in the original text, with the abbreviated 'Israel's (or "Jewish") soldiers'. This change appears in several different editions.[28] The expression 'Israel's soldiers' is not specific: it might be understood as a reference to the soldiers of the IDF; it might include security personnel who are not soldiers. Alternatively, the phrase refers to yeshiva students, who – according to the haredi worldview – also protect the inhabitants of the State of Israel through their study.

In research on the responses of the Haredi society in Israel to the Six-Day War, Yair Halevi focuses on the term "Soldiers of Israel." Halevi shows how the Haredi press used the term "Soldiers of Israel" with a positive attitude towards the Israeli army for its military achievements. "The very term 'Soldiers of Israel' (and not 'Soldiers of the State' and not even 'IDF soldiers')," Halevi argues, "expresses a psychological relationship of closeness and affection, a relationship that is not taken for granted."[29] However, this is Halevi's interpretation. There could also be the opposite possibility, suggesting that this term attempts to push away the notion that the army, as a state institution, is the protector of the state. Instead, it offers a more general category that moves away from the Zionist wording to a vaguer one. For example, in the *Od Avinu Hai* prayer book, the words "soldiers" or "IDF soldiers" or even "soldiers of

---

28 For example, see Yaakov Yosef, *Siddur Tefilat Yaakov ha-Shalem* (Jerusalem, 1988), 384 (Hebrew), David Yosef, *Siddur Yehave Da'at* (Jerusalem, 1997), 326 (Hebrew).

29 Yair Halevy, "Sephardic Haredi Responses to the Six-Day War," (MA thesis, Hebrew University of Jerusalem, 2001), 37 (Hebrew).

Israel" are replaced with a more general statement: "He will bless all his people Israel who stand guard over our land."[30]

An explicit critical implication regarding the term "Soldiers of the Israel Defense Forces" is found in the *Ner Refael* prayer book edition: "He who blessed our holy and pure ancestors will bless, guard, protect, and help the soldiers of Israel, the yeshiva students, and the young children of our rabbi who stand guard over our land and the cities of our God, wherever they are."[31] The *Ner Refael* prayer book edition, as mentioned, is distributed in a limited manner, but it allows itself to significantly modify the prayer for the soldiers' well-being and to include explicit ideological meanings rather than implied ones. Thus, the prayer does not only include the soldiers of the physical army but also the soldiers of the spiritual army, the yeshiva students. Here the soldiers of the spiritual army – the yeshiva students – are placed on an equal footing with the soldiers of the physical army. To this view, yeshiva students also sacrifice themselves; they, too, do all that they can to protect the Jews living in Israel, and as such are partners in the national (although not necessarily 'Zionist') endeavor. Both the soldier on the battlefield and the soldier in the study hall are worthy of God's blessing, by virtue of their contribution to the collective. In the view of the *Ner Refael* editors, organized, widespread Torah study is not only a religious activity; it is a national heroic activity. It contributes to the security of the state and to the security of its soldiers. This argument occupies a prominent place in the discourse that negotiates the place of haredi society in Israel and also serves to urge yeshiva students to maintain conscientious study, in view of their vital role in protecting the country, its soldiers, and its citizens.

---

30 Nahem Levi, *Siddur Od Avinu Hai* (Jerusalem, 1998), 461 (Hebrew).
31 Yosef Haim Mizrahi, *Siddur Ner Refael ha-Shalem, Od Yosef Hai* (Jerusalem: Kollel Ner Refael Tzedakka, 2007), 509-510 (Hebrew).

Another example of intervention in the original prayer text can be found in one of the most popular prayer books in recent years in the Mizrahi community – the *Kavanat HaLev* prayer book, which was published in the late nineties. The publisher and editor of the prayer book is Rabbi Ronen Doron, a former student of the veteran Netivot Olam Yeshiva for Ba'alei Teshuva in Bnei Brak. The prayer mostly matches the official version. Similar to the *Avodat Hashem* prayer book, it also prefers the term "Soldiers of Israel" over "Soldiers of the Israel Defense Forces." Nevertheless, there is one interesting addition. Between the words "and with a crown of victory" and the words "and it will be fulfilled in them," the words "(and bring them back in complete repentance)" have been added in parentheses.[32] This addition clearly expresses both the initial ideological discomfort with the prayer and the desire to modify it, but this time in the spirit of the Mizrahi-Haredi project of returning to repentance. In this context, the concept of repentance as an idea and as a way of looking at reality has a significant place.[33]

Another significantly amended version can be found in the *Tefilat Rafael* prayer book. This prayer book is published by the Kabbalistic yeshiva Ahavat Shalom in Jerusalem. At the head of the yeshiva stands Rabbi Yaakov Moshe Hillel, who belongs to the circles of Haredi-Mizrahi that are more influenced by the Ashkenazi yeshiva world. In this prayer book, the accepted version of the prayer is notably absent. Instead, there is another prayer version entitled "Prayer for the Peace of the People of Israel." Here are parts of the prayer text:

---

32 Ronen Doron, *Siddur Kavanat ha-Lev* (Petah Tikva, 2006), 542 (Hebrew).

33 Nissim Leon, *Harediyut Rakah (Soft Ultra-Orthodoxy): Religious Renewal in Oriental Jewry in Israel* (Jerusalem: Ben-Zvi Institute, 2010), 161-164 (Hebrew).

> "May it be Your will [...] that You have compassion on all our brothers, the House of Israel, scattered in the four corners of the earth, and especially on the inhabitants of the Land of Israel, and have mercy on us and them, and save us from all kinds of harsh and evil decrees, and remove from us the enemy's blow [...] and strengthen, support, and empower the hands of all those who help and assist us, and those who protect us, and the hands of all those who do [...] for Your people Israel [...] and return the hearts of the misled to Your service and to Your fear, and send us soon Your servant David, Your righteous Messiah, to redeem those waiting for Your salvation [...] Blessed is He who hears prayer."[34]

In this prayer, various motifs familiar from the prayer for the soldiers' peace are embedded, but the word "soldiers" and its familiar derivatives no longer appear in this prayer book. It is also worth noting that the prayer does not deal with the State of Israel but with the inhabitants of the Land of Israel, and in fact omits any reference to IDF soldiers. This prayer version is very different from the original prayer. However, it is placed where the blessing prayer for the IDF soldiers is often recited.

Most of the amendments in the Mizrahi-Haredi prayer books indicate discomfort with the original "Zionist" version of the prayer. It seems that the prayer editors are attentive to the importance of ideological principles, but also to the heterogeneous environment to which the prayer books are addressed. Therefore, the amendments themselves are mostly minor, allusive, and subtle. Except for one or two versions, things aren't clear enough but hinted at in small but meaningful textual

---

34 Reuven Amar, *Siddur Tefilat Refael* (Jerusalem, 2004), 454-455 (Hebrew).

changes, especially in a society where a large part of its culture is devoted to grammar and studying the meanings derived from the written word.[35]

The reflective strategy employed here might be referred to as a "wink." As Geertz argues, the wink - i.e. a system of social allusions - is the basis upon which social contact is often conducted within a given culture.[36] A wink can be interpreted only from within a cultural system, by someone who belongs to that system or is familiar with it. The wink finds expression in plays on words and meaning, and these become manifest only where the parties to the social situation are familiar with each other and their respective views. The mutually recognized gap of perception, sensitive to slight nuances, creates a sort of complicity in the signifying of separate circles of social belonging.[37]

This is clearly apparent in the replacement of the expression "soldiers of the Israel Defense Force" with the expression "Israel's soldiers," as discussed above. The term "Israel's soldiers" is in fact, to borrow Geertz's terminology, a "thin" description of the "soldiers of the Israel Defense Forces." It supplies a convenient obscurity by means of which the editors of the prayer identify themselves as being loyal to both the haredi worldview and the Zionist state – i.e. both to those who view prayer as a patriotic duty and to those who view it as a liturgical option. In adopting the term "Israel's soldiers" instead of "the soldiers of the Israel Defense Forces," the editors attempt to translate the prayer from the language of

---

35 Haym Soloveitchik, "Rupture and Reconstruction: The Transformation of Contemporary Orthodoxy," *Tradition: A Journal of Orthodox Jewish Thought*, vol. 28, no. 4 (Summer 1994): 64-130.

36 Clifford Geertz, *The Interpretation of Cultures: Selected Essays* (New York: Basic Books, 1973), 17-19.

37 See, for example, Michal Kravel-Tovi, *When the State Winks: The Performance of Jewish Conversion in Israel* (New York: Columbia University Press, 2017).

Zionist nationalism to the language of haredi nationalism. The result is a reflective transition from national liturgy to the liturgy of Jewish peoplehood, and the creation of a variable, open prayer that removes the key to the wording from the hands of the state. Thus, the national prayer remains, while at the same time, through word play, it loses its national formality in favor of the nurturing of a popular, emotional connection.

From Text to Practice

Do these fragmented versions find a place in reality itself, namely in the non-Haredi Mizrahi praying communities on one hand and in the world of Haredi Mizrahi yeshiva communities on the other? The prayer for the soldiers' peace is almost nonexistent in Haredi-Mizrahi praying communities. It is also not found in Haredi-Mizrahi yeshivas. In some places, an interesting situation has arisen where the prayer book does not actually match the order of the prayer. While the prayer books include the prayer for the soldiers' peace, in the actual prayer order it is omitted. This issue has been resolved in Haredi-Mizrahi yeshivas that are close to the Ashkenazi-Haredi stream. Students are allowed to pray in the Mizrahi prayer version, but in the *Beit Tefilah* prayer book, there is no prayer for the soldiers' peace. The prevalent claim is that the format of the *Beit Tefilah* prayer book is very similar to Ashkenazi prayer books, but in a conversation with one of the supervisors in a Haredi-Mizrahi yeshiva, it was explicitly stated that the *Beit Tefilah* prayer book also aligns with the pure Haredi view and doesn't contain "new prayers," an alternative term for national liturgical sections. In one of the communities defined as a Mizrahi synagogue for Torah scholars, that is, a synagogue intended for families of rabbis and students from Haredi yeshivas of Mizrahi origin, it was found that the prayer for the soldiers' peace is recited during the morning Shabbat prayer when opening the Ark of the Torah scrolls, but in a soft tone and very succinctly.

On the other hand, in the non-Haredi Mizrahi praying communities, it is found that the prayer for the soldiers' peace continues to be one of the highlights of the Shabbat prayer in synagogues. This is the moment when the Holy Ark containing the sacred Torah scrolls is opened. The congregation tends to gather around the open Ark. After reciting a short chapter from the Zohar, the prayer leader, cantor, or rabbi usually recites a series of personal and general prayers for health, livelihood, and solutions to various problems. The prevailing belief is that "since now – when a Torah scroll is open – it's a time when the gates of heavenly mercy are open."[38] Among the general requests, the prayer for the soldiers' peace stands out. The commitment to this prayer in the synagogues of the non-Haredi Mizrahim in Israel is unequivocal. It teaches quite a bit about what we already know from sociological research on Mizrahim in Israel. Most of them hold nationalist and patriotic positions and tend to vote for right-wing parties.[39] The fervor with which the prayer is recited teaches about this quite a bit. It is usually said loudly, with intonation, and in a slow melody. These help to emphasize the words of the prayer. It is a somewhat serious moment. One can certainly see how the congregation identifies with the words. They tend to respond with a passionate "Amen" after each request or supplication included in the prayer.

Observations in non-Haredi Mizrahi synagogues taught me that the praying congregation also knows how to address the gap between the version in the prayer book and the official version, which is the original version of the prayer. The attempt to introduce Haredi versions can often lead to the following case described on the popular Israeli news site ynet:

---

38 Yosef Haim Mizrahi, *Siddur Od Yosef Hai ha-Shalem* (Jerusalem: Kollel Ner Refael Tzedakka, 2001), 480 (Hebrew).

39 Ephraim Yuchtman-Yaar and Tamar Hermann, "Shas: The Haredi-Dovish Image in a Changing Reality," *Israel Studies*, vol. 5, no. 2 (Fall 2000): 32-77.

> "Last Simchat Torah, a cantor in the synagogue was 'forced' by the congregants to recite the blessing for the peace of the IDF soldiers during the opening of the Ark. Cleverly, he used the phrase 'Soldiers of Israel' instead of the original 'Soldiers of the Israel Defense Forces'. When I asked him to correct it, he erupted at me in front of everyone, and the prayer was disrupted. Just like that. In fact, this is not only a religious struggle but also a national one, so we must not succumb to their demands, as it concerns the character and future of Israel, no less. If we lose Beit Shemesh, God forbid, we will lose the entire country."

In fact, there is a significant gap between the collective effort demonstrated in prayer revisions and the reactionary approach expressed in its actual recitation or non-recitation. The nuances and complexities are often replaced by decisiveness, which serves as a source for redefining the boundaries of ideology, and with it, reality. The place of soft Orthodoxy is taken by a more rigid tradition. The place of compromise is taken by a scrutinizing look at anyone who deviates from what should be. It's an interesting point worth pausing on, considering our regular understanding of the position of "the text" in the world of Orthodox religious communities.

Generally, one of the images accompanying religious Orthodoxy is its commitment to the holy text. By "text," it refers to organized and supervised compositions reflecting in Orthodox eyes the correct belief/practice. Holding on to the text is a fundamental approach to constructing an Orthodox religious culture. The text symbolizes the constant and continuous, as opposed to the transient and fluid. The Orthodox commitment to the written, organized word is expressed in attempts to be as precise as possible, relying less on personal creation. Conversely, the community holds a more fluid perception, knowing when to embrace or reject changes in reality, deliberately weighing them. However, the case of national liturgy we examined in this article indicates a reverse trend. The text itself knows how to adapt dynamically to definitions of reality; it knows how to deal with the symbolic components of the opposing ideology, in this case, nationalism expressed in civil religion and national liturgy. And in contrast, it's precisely the community that exhibits a rigid Orthodox approach. In Jewish studies, this is explained by distinguishing between custom and halakha (Jewish law). "Halakha" is the official instruction, anchored in a text based on the written instructions of the rabbinical leadership. Conversely, "custom" is the actual behavior formed based on local tradition and passed down orally from generation to generation. Interestingly, while halakha – the text – is always subject to changes resulting from ongoing debates among the leading authorities on the matter, custom can turn out to be rigid and meticulous, with fears of deviating from it precisely because there's no written instruction. It seems that we could observe something of this pattern in the case of national liturgy in Haredi-Mizrahi editions. The printed prayer emerges as a dynamic and reflective text, always subject to changes tailored to the target audience. In contrast, the actual conduct, meaning the recitation of the prayer, appears to rely on local custom, proving to be rigid and even reactionary.

Conclusion:

Contrary to the Ashkenazi Haredi circles, the Mizrahi Haredi circles include the prayer for the soldiers' well-being in their prayer books. However, they demonstrate unease regarding this prayer. A comparative analysis of the various versions of the prayer for the well-being of the Israel Defense Forces soldiers, published by printers and editors from the Mizrahi-Haredi stream, indicates a range of versions that obscure the state-based foundation of the prayer, emphasizing the principle of ethnic-national partnership. From this, it can be deduced that national liturgy, like any other type of liturgy, does not stand on its own. It operates within a reality full of social connections. As such, it can indeed be a source of significant tension between conservative circles and national circles. Yet, through reflective processing, it can serve as a source of healing the tension between the nation-state and the Orthodox circles.

Dr. Nissim Leon is a senior lecturer in the Sociology and Anthropology Department at Bar-Ilan University.

On the Recitation of the Prayer for the Israel Defense Forces During Operation Iron Sword

Zvi Leshem

THE STANDARD CUSTOM OF COMMUNITIES in Israel that recite the Prayer for the Israel Defense Forces is to do so after the Prayer for the State of Israel on Sabbath days and Holidays. It is usually recited standing, after the Torah reading, although some do so during the Torah reading as it is officially a "Misheberach" [May He Who Blessed] prayer.

To be honest, it is often recited without a great deal of attention or intention. Congregants do usually look up from their learning (or conversations) to answer Amen, but it is hardly one of the more intense parts of the service. It is as though we are well aware of our soldiers (often our own children or grandchildren), but in classic Israeli form, we take it for granted that they will continue to guard the country, and with God's help, everything will turn out all right.

Today however, nothing is all right. In light of the horrific massacre in the South and the subsequent war in Gaza, the prayer seems to have been redeemed from its usual state of quasi-apathy. In many Israeli synagogues it is currently being recited during or after every service, two or three times daily. This is often done in conjunction with the Prayer for the State of Israel (usually a weekly event) and the prayer for the healing of the sick (often also a weekly, or at most thrice weekly). These days, the phrase "the wounded" is added, or actually used instead of "the sick."

The prayer most often recited together with that for the IDF is one that many synagogues don't generally bother with at all; that for the safe return of missing and captured soldiers, today usually augmented with a phase referring to "the kidnapped hostages" as well.

We are all aware that in "normal" times, prayers that are recited frequently generally receive less attention and intention than those that, due to their rarity, are perceived as being more "special." Yet this is hardly the case. These two prayers, that for our soldiers and that for the safe return of well over two hundred hostages being held captive in Gaza, are graced with full silence and attention. Often coupled with the recitation of "Avinu Malkenu" and special Psalms, no one in the congregation is indifferent. Everyone stands, listens with full attention to the cantor and responds "Amen" with great passion. One senses the tension in the air. Brows are knit, and smiles, if there were, momentarily disappear. People are transported elsewhere. Some to the front(s), where friends, siblings, children and grandchildren are facing off against Hamas and Hizballah terrorists. Others imagine the unimaginable situation of those held captive in the tunnels of Gaza. And some minds cannot help but to return to the unthinkable horrors of the infamous Seventh of October.

In addition, it is a moment of profound unity and solidarity. We are all in this together, and everyone knows it. Glancing around the synagogue, taking in the pained and mournful faces of the congregants, we are thankful that we are not alone. There is strength in numbers and there is strength in faith. There is much strength in communal faith.

What will be the fate for the prayer for the IDF in the long run, after, with God's help, our victory over Hamas? Perhaps the answer breaks down in a similar manner to that regarding unity itself. The optimists among us are hopeful that even after the war ends, our society will remain united, and not return to the extreme divisiveness that characterized Israel in the months leading up to the invasion. The pessimists are convinced that nothing will change, and that as soon as we feel safe enough, we will return to our national pastime of internal bickering.

Similarly, after the war has been won and the hostages hopefully freed, will we go back to a perfunctory "Amen" at the end for the prayer for the IDF? I would like to think not. I hope that we will have internalized that there are some things that we cannot, and must not, take for granted. Among them are some that today seem self-apparent, including both unity and the Israel Defense Forces. The former requires our constant vigilance. The latter, at least our full attention when we pray for it.

Rabbi Dr. Zvi Leshem holds a PhD in Jewish Philosophy from Bar-Ilan University and received ordination from the Chief Rabbinate of Israel. He has three decades of experience in Israeli Torah education, including almost twenty years as Associate Dean at Nishmat and is the Rabbi Emeritus of Congregation Shirat Shlomo in Efrat. Additionally, he has been directing the Gershom Scholem Collection for Kabbalah and Hasidism at the National Library of Israel since 2011.

The Word חַיִל and its Significance

Aharon Lichtenstein

Rav Dr. Aharon Lichtenstein (1933-2015) had a longstanding tradition of studying Mishnayot in memory of those dear to him on their yahrzeits. This practice extended to the Memorial Day for the IDF's fallen soldiers, where he would dedicate time to study in their honor as well. Rav Lichtenstein was deliberate in his choice of Mishnayot to study. He would delve into them deeply, teach them with thoroughness, and always endeavored to relate their content to the memory and character of the fallen. Before us is a summary of things he said on the Memorial Day for the IDF's fallen soldiers, the 4th of Iyar 1987, and published in *Daf Kesher*: Newsletter for Yeshivat Har Etzion's Students in the IDF, no. 87 (26 May 1987): 3-4 [355-356] (Hebrew). For another example of 'in-depth Mishna study' like this, see Aharon Lichtenstein, "Mishnayot spelling the name 'Yitzhak' [In Memory of Yitzhak Levi]," in Yehuda Shaviv, ed., *Siah Yitzhak: Collection of Essays on Prayer in Memory of Yitzhak Lavi* (Jerusalem: Lavi Family, 1980), 321-327 (Hebrew). – Aviad Hacohen

The Word חַיִל and its Significance

IN OUR CONSCIOUSNESS, THE TERM חיל is associated with the army, and many times in the Tanakh (Bible) we read about "גיבורי חיל" which can be translated as "mighty men of valor."

Indeed, the term 'חיל' has a wide range of meanings. Among other things, it has a unique connection to the process of redemption, as the words of Balaam state: "A star shall come out of Jacob... and it shall crush the forehead of Moab and shall strike down all the sons of Sheth, and Edom shall be a possession... and Israel shall be strong" (Numbers 24:17-18).

Doing חַיִל is part of the redemption process. According to one opinion in the Talmud [Berakhot 34b], the opinion of Shmuel, the subjugation by kingdoms is the only external difference between this world and the days of the Messiah.

For those who look beyond just yesterday and the day before, this insight is simple and clear. Indeed, at times it seems that 'smashing the forehead of Moab and striking down all the sons of Sheth' - eludes even the wise and understanding. All this comes from the desire not to be caught up in the mindset of "my power and the might of my hand have gotten me this wealth," and from the fear of forgetting that "for it is the Lord your God who gives you the power to get wealth (חיל)" (Deuteronomy 8:17-18).

In light of all this, they sometimes forget the term 'חיל', in its most basic meaning.

I am reminded of words I heard thirty years ago from our revered teacher Rav Aharon Soloveichik. He spoke about the halakhah according to which on the 15th of Av we do not say the Tahanun prayer. According to one opinion in the Talmud (Bava Batra 121b), this was the day on which those who died in the incident at Beitar were given burial. Rav

Aharon continued: On a day that symbolizes not only the burial of Israel's slain but also a day on which all those who were nearly among the dead, broken vessels, were not brought to be buried in the Holy Land but to live in it, to build and be built up, is it conceivable that on such a day we would say Tahanun?

Indeed, at times, "even the wisdom of its wise men shall perish." In the face of overwhelming spirituality, the essence of the framework that ensures both the physical and spiritual well-being of the people of Israel becomes obscured and diminishes.

From overemphasizing the phrase "not by might (חיל) nor by power, but by my spirit," we forget that the intention of the verse is not to avoid relying on power and strength altogether, but to emphasize that that this is not sufficient (Zechariah 4:6).

Could it be that such basic things would be forgotten from our consciousness, like there's no significance to shaking off the yoke of foreign rule from our necks and walking upright in our land, within our land?

The term חיל speaks both of blossoming and growth, of social and economic flourishing, and here too, it is frequently referred to in the context of "my power and the strength of my hand."

Indeed, the ability to operate holistically and establish a spiritual-social-political-economic framework is tied to the state. There are entire domains in which Israel began to flourish as a "people" in the modern era only from the establishment of the state and onwards, with divine assistance.

The term חיל also has a halakhic meaning, even though this is not derived from the simple reading of the verse.

In the tractate Makkot (12a), there is a halakhah based on the verse "Bless, O Lord, his substance" (Deuteronomy 33:11), interpreting "his substance" (חילו) to mean "even the blemished among him" (אפילו

The Word חַיִל and its Significance

חללים שבו), stating: A priest who performed [his duties] while he was blemished - his service is valid.

According to most of the Rishonim, this applies only when the priest who served was unaware that he was blemished. However, according to Maimonides, even if the priest knew he was blemished and still served, his service is retroactively valid.

Certainly, Hazal saw the ability to achieve חיל (valor or substance) as also connected to the "profaned," to those debilitated. Even for those living in a world of secularism, who have not yet merited to reach a world of holiness - we should also pray on their behalf, "May You accept his substance and the work of his hands."

It goes without saying that we pray for them to merit reaching a world of sanctity, but in the meantime – when the shared responsibility rests on our shoulders – we pray for the entire Congregation of Israel, even for the "substance" (חיל) made by the "blemished" (חללים), through those who think they are engaged in mundane work, but the Holy One, Blessed be He, knows that they too are engaged in sacred work.

Of course, the true חיל (substance or force) is the one where even its mundane elements are grounded in foundations of holiness. Then, the sacred also rises up through their strength.

אנשי חיל יראי אלקים (Men of valor who fear God) – for those "men of valor" who understand life and know how to navigate it, to also be "God-fearing," so that their valorous actions will lead to the fear of Heaven and stem from its strength.

On this day, when we commemorate the חיל (valor), we pause and thank the Almighty for blessing us to achieve all that we have attained, and pray that just as we've reached partial accomplishments in the realms of the material and the spirit, so may we merit a complete redemption, in which the חיל will become part of the spirit, "and the earth shall be full of the knowledge of the Lord."

Out of gratitude for the past and the present, and with anticipation for the future, we ask, plead, and pray:

"ילכו מחיל אל חיל, יראה אל אלקים בציון"

"They go from strength to strength; every one of them in Zion appears before God" (Psalms 84:8).

Rav Dr. Aharon Lichtenstein (1933-2015), a disciple of Rabbi Joseph B. Soloveitchik, received his rabbinic ordination from Yeshiva University and earned a PhD in English Literature from Harvard University. He initially served as a Rosh Yeshiva at Yeshiva University. In 1971, he relocated to Israel and assumed the role of Rosh Yeshiva at Yeshivat Har Etzion, a hesder yeshiva founded by Rabbi Yehuda Amital in Alon Shvut, where he served alongside Rabbi Amital.

Professor Aviad Hacohen serves as the President of Sha'arei Mishpat Academic College and previously held the position of Dean at its Law School. His extensive academic research encompasses Mishpat Ivri, human rights, criminal law, civil law, and their intersections with Jewish law.

"Is it time for you to come home yet?"

Phillip I. Lieberman

On the desk in my office sits a laminated piece of paper reading "You are not totally the worst. Is it time for you to come home yet?" This missive reached me when I was on deployment with the US Navy to Camp Lemonnier, Djibouti, in the Horn of Africa, from June 2021 through January 2022. My wife Yedida's plaintive reflection arrived in a package that had come from Nashville to Djibouti via Bahrain, probably accompanying some sort of quotidian item like a tax form that required my signature or a pair of socks. The accompanying item is long forgotten, but the hopes and prayers of my family that I might return home—and soon—have stayed with me.

When I tell acquaintances or colleagues that I serve in the military, many of them presume that I serve the State of Israel, since the number of Jews in the American military is few. Travel on any highway in Israel on a Thursday afternoon and you will see soldiers heading home for Shabbat, but America's military includes outposts across the globe, and so the experience of American soldiers and sailors often involves traveling far away from our families, at times for long periods. While FaceTime and WhatsApp have made it possible for us to keep in touch, the distance and the sense of absence remains.

Knowing that my family and friends were praying for my safe return made the time remaining until the end of my deployment move more swiftly. That I could look into the sky and see the same moon that my family would see some nine hours later helped me count down the *rashei ḥodashim* (new moons) before I would return to them. That Jews around the world—including me—pray for their Israeli brethren serving in harm's way should remind them that we all yearn for the time they, too, will come home. Safe. And soon.

Phillip I. Lieberman is associate professor of Jewish Studies and Law, and chair of Classical and Mediterranean Studies, at Vanderbilt University. He is the author or editor of four books, including The Cambridge History of Judaism, volume 5: Jews in the Medieval Islamic World. At present, he is on military leave from Vanderbilt and serves the Department of History at the United States Naval Academy. Phil serves as a chaplain in the US Navy Reserve and currently holds the rank of captain.

Prayer as Adjudication

Berachyahu Lifshitz

Every Shabbat we offer a prayer to God to protect the State of Israel, and we ask Him to send His light and salvation to its leaders, ministers, and their legal and military advisors, and to guide them with good counsel. Even if the prayer is accepted, we do not know the depths of God's will, sometimes a person's choice repels the light and the good counsel sent to him from heaven, for God made man upright, but they have gone in search of many schemes.

Sometimes this rejection causes the heads, the ministers, and the advisors to be unable to thwart our enemies' counsel and to nullify our foes' thoughts. Their eyes are blinded, their ears are heavy, and their hearts are fat. And it was at such a critical time that our enemies carried out their evil plot, launching an onslaught upon us to destroy the State of Israel and to stop the process of our salvation.

Then the army of the Israel Defense Forces is called into service, and the soldiers go out bravely, risking their lives into battle to thwart the enemy's plot. Their thoughts are straight, and all the many calculations they make are only to defeat the cruel enemy, to repay him double for his bloodshed, to strike him hip and thigh, and to protect our soldiers as much as possible from any harm and not to endanger their lives needlessly.

The prayer, which is then raised from the mouths of us all for the peace of the soldiers, from a place of deep intention and from an awareness of absolute presence in times of distress, carries in such a case a dual character, and it has two faces.

One aspect is the prayer as supplication, and in this, it is not distinguished from all the prayers in which we ask of the Sovereign of the Universe, each about the trouble of his own soul that oppresses him, and for which he feels a deficit in his physical and spiritual completeness. Indeed, this prayer is different from the prayer of the individual in that it raises the needs of the community and the distress of the many above all our prayers. However, during the war, these are not a trace of comfort, but rather a great concern for all our soldiers, who then all become our relatives, our sons and brothers, since we have all united at the time we stand in such a supplicatory prayer. The horrors of war are today seen by our eyes in pictures and films and in immediate descriptions, and our hearts go out in dread and trembling and in hope and prayer for the soldiers. So we beg and cry for them.

Yet, after we have feared lest the enemy approach the camp and strike it, and we have prepared ourselves for prayer, supplication, and the giving of charity, we are also prepared for war. Here the other aspect of prayer comes to expression, the prayer as a form of litigation and adjudicating. We engage in a legal process (Isaiah 16:3), as did Pinchas in his time, of whom it is said, "Then stood up Pinchas, and executed judgment: and the plague ended" (Psalms 106:30), and "Rabbi Elazar said: it does not say 'and he prayed' but 'and he executed verdict.' This teaches that he engaged in legal argument with his Creator: he came and laid them (Zimri and Cozby) before the Almighty, saying: 'Master of the Universe, shall these cause twenty-four thousand from Israel to fall?!'" (Sanhedrin 44a). And

Praying for the Defenders of Our Faith

it is the same Rabbi Elazar who said (Berakhot 30b), "Hannah threw words upwards, as it is said, 'and prayed on the Lord' – teaching that she threw words upwards."

We come before the Divine, advocating on behalf of the soldiers, issuing a verdict and give an order: Defeat our enemies before us! Watch over and rescue our soldiers from every distress and strait! Bestow blessings and success upon all their actions! Contend on their behalf against their enemies, for they are Your enemies as well! And send forth Your light and Your truth to our leaders and their advisors, and rectify them with good counsel, that perhaps it shall not be spurned. Will they fall because of this?

And the plague ended.

Professor Berachyahu Lifshitz is Professor (emeritus) and former Dean, The Faculty of Law, The Hebrew University of Jerusalem, and the E.M.T. Prize laureate in Jewish Law.

Why, How and When We Recite מי שברך לחיילי צה"ל The Prayer for the Soldiers of Israel

Haskel Lookstein

I

We began to say this prayer at Congregation Kehilath Jeshurun after the Six Day War, a war which demonstrated the extraordinary bravery, skill and power of the Israel Defense Forces. Following that war, the bumper stickers in Israel featured the words

כל הכבוד לצה"ל, "Glory to the IDF."

Six years later, after the terrifying failures of Israel's leadership in the Yom Kippur War, and the glorious victory which overcame the failures, the bumper stickers in Israel read: ישראל בטח בה'" "O' Israel Trust in God."

Praying for the Defenders of Our Faith

The *Misheberach* for *Tzahal* had a different meaning to us, post Yom Kippur War, from its meaning post the Six Day War. We all understood that, ultimately, ה' איש מלחמה "God is the True Warrior." It was His Providence which enabled the IDF to triumph in both 1967 and in 1973. It will be His Providence which will lead Israel to victory after the terrifying pogrom of October 7th.

And, so, we must fervently pray to God to give the IDF כח לעשות חיל.

the strength, the power, the skill and the courage to defeat Hamas and the enemies of the State of Israel and the Jewish people.

II

We used to say the *Misheberach* at KJ every time we read the *Torah*: on *Shabbat*; on *Yom Tov*; and during the week, on Mondays and Thursdays and *Rosh Chodesh*, and on *Chanukah* and *Purim*. The Rabbi recited it immediately after the *kaddish* following *Torah* reading. We followed this practice until COVID. Regrettably, COVID adversely affected many things in *shul* life, including *davening*, even after we came back to *shul* in person. People expected the service to be shorter. Many meaningful prayers and practices were dropped and, among others, the recitation of the מי שברך לחיילי צה"ל was discontinued during the week.

It is unfortunate that an accelerated service brought about the partial elimination of this prayer. Let us analyze why this *Misheberach* is so important for us.

III

We recite the Prayer for the Israel Defense Forces for two reasons:

First, we recite it because Israel cannot survive without the power of the IDF and the fear that it instills in the enemies of the Jewish State. Israel lives in a very dangerous neighborhood of hateful murderers and beastly butchers. We always knew that, but, for some time, we didn't pay enough attention to it. After the pogrom of October 7th, we understand clearly that the only thing that stands between a secure and blessedly peaceful Israel and the Kishinev-like pogrom of October 7th, is the fear of a powerful IDF on the part of our enemies. We have to pray, fervently and tearfully, that *Tzahal* wins this war. We must pray at every possible opportunity, for the success and the safety of the soldiers of *Tzahal* and for God's support of the first line of defense for Israel and for us. The life of the Jewish State and our people depend upon it.

But, there is a second reason for reciting this prayer regularly, particularly for us as Diaspora Jews. Most of us have been reciting *Avinu Malkeinu* since October 7th on both weekdays and Shabbat. Rav Hershel Schachter made an Halakhic decision, right after October 7, that we should recite *Avinu Malkeinu* even on *Shabbat*. His basis was that when Yom Kippur falls on a *Shabbat*, we do not say *Avinu Malkeinu* because we do not petition God on a *Shabbat*. The exception, however, is at the closing prayer, *Ne'ila*, when the Gates of Repentance are closing and the Jewish people is in danger (Sakana). At *Ne'ila*, we pull out our entire liturgical arsenal and we recite and sing *Avinu Malkeinu* with heartfelt feelings, before we say *Shema Yisrael*.

This was an unprecedented *psak* by Rav Schachter. It was inspired by his clear understanding that we are in a שעת סכנה - a period of ultimate

Praying for the Defenders of Our Faith

danger to our lives. At such a time, we have to pray to our Father and our King with utmost fervor.

At KJ, we began reciting *Avinu Malkeinu* at every *Shacharit* and *Mincha*, on weekdays, and on Shabbat, starting the prayer with אבינו מלכנו שמע קולינו חוס ורחם עלינו, "Our Father, our King, hear our voices, pity us and have mercy upon us." The rabbi chants the verses and the congregation responds until the end of the *Avinu Malkeinu* passages when we all sing the last *Avinu Malkeinu* with a fervor that I have only heard at the closing of *Ne'ila*.

I understand that, in Israel, most do not add this prayer. But, even if that is so, we in the Diaspora should continue to say it. Israelis need no reminders that they are in an existential struggle. We do. They live, for the first time in a long time, in great vulnerability. They live it night and day, in many ways. We do not. They all have close relatives and friends who are risking their lives on the front lines. We do not. They experience rockets and missiles exploding around them. We do not. Their own lives are at stake in this war. Ours are not. They can add or subtract prayers as they wish, but we must change our liturgical routine in order to keep this struggle at the forefront of our minds for as long as the crisis lasts, until Israel destroys Hamas and wins this war. If our davening is elongated thereby by three minutes, so be it. Our prayers and our constant thoughts about Israel and its citizens make that necessary. This is our struggle too.

IV

Finally, how to recite the מי שברך לחיילי צה"ל. I have heard this prayer recited in any number of shuls. It is usually recited by someone – sometimes the rabbi – hastily and with very little feeling – like a routine prayer. We have never recited it that way at KJ. We recite it with utmost gravitas and *kavanna*, with an entire congregation standing in silence, at attention. We realize that we are praying for the lives of the soldiers of the IDF; we are praying for the survival of Israel which depends on the IDF. If we ever needed to be reminded about that, we surely understand it now. This prayer should be recited regularly and with the greatest possible feeling.

To paraphrase Rabbi Akiba's statement about *Shir HaShirim* – "If all the Books of Tanach are holy, *Shir HaShirim* is the holy of holies" – if all of the prayers in our *Siddur* are holy, מי שברך לחיילי צה"ל (the Prayer for the Soldiers of *Tzahal*) is קודש קדשים - the holiest of holies.

May God hear our prayers and bring victory to our soldiers and peace to our Land.

Rabbi Haskel Lookstein has been a Rabbi of Congregation Kehilath Jeshurun since 1958 and served as Principal of the Ramaz School from 1966 until 2016 when he became Principal Emeritus.

The Essence of the Prayer for Tzahal

Leonard Matanky

WHY DOES THE MISHEBERACH FOR Tzahal, the prayer for the soldiers of the IDF, resonate so profoundly within the Religious Zionist community? And why do people often stand in respect when this prayer is recited?

On one hand, the answers seem clear. The soldiers of Tzahal symbolize our newfound strength and pride as the Jewish people. They are living proof that we have a State capable of protecting itself.

But beyond that, this prayer connects the fate of Tzahal to the divine will. Consider its closing line, a verse from Devarim: "It is the Lord your God who goes with you to fight for you against your enemies, to deliver you."

As a result, this tefilla is more than just a prayer. It is a moment of profound significance, an opportunity for us to implore God's assistance in realizing the dreams of generations – to witness a nation that can hold its head high and is no longer reliant on the goodwill of others.

Consider these two stories from the past generation.

The first story centers around Yitzchak Zev Soloveichik, the grandson of HaRav Ahron Soloveichik zt"l,. Yitzchak Zev made history by becoming the first Soloveichik to enlist in the Israeli army, Tzahal. When this momentous occasion occurred, his grandfather, HaRav Soloveichik, couldn't contain his emotions. He proudly shared the news with everyone, expressing deep gratitude to God. To him, his grandson's service represented the fulfillment of the mitzvah of defending our land and our people—a mitzvah that had been unattainable just a few generations ago.

The second story, narrated by HaRav Yisrael Meir Lau, the former Chief Rabbi of Israel, revolves around a student at Jerusalem's renowned yeshiva Kol Torah. This student sought permission from his Rosh Yeshiva, HaRav Shlomo Zalman Auerbach zt"l, to leave the Beit Midrash and journey to the Galil to pray at the graves of tzadikim (righteous individuals). HaRav Auerbach's response was illuminating: "It's better to stay in yeshiva and engage in Torah study."

The student persisted, asking if there might be a suitable time for such a journey. HaRav Auerbach responded with wisdom: "To pray at the graves of tzadikim, you don't have to travel to the Galil. Whenever I feel the need to do so, I go to Mount Herzl to pray at the graves of the soldiers who died 'Al Kiddush Hashem.'"

These stories serve as poignant reminders of the sanctity of Tzahal, emanating from the soldiers' sacred mission to protect and defend our land. They exemplify the Jewish people's determination to be strong and proud rather than victims. Consequently, we should take immense pride in reciting the prayer for Tzahal and consider it an honor to do so.

However, there is another profound aspect that Tzahal represents, and this prayer serves to reinforce. HaRav Tzvi Hirsch Mecklenburg, in his commentary "HaKetav v'Hakabbalah" (Exodus 12:41), provides insight into the two Hebrew words used in the Torah to describe an army: חיל (chayil) and צבאות (tzva'ot).

HaRav Mecklenburg explains that חיל (chayil) signifies a collective bound together by strength and might, reflecting a physical unity. On the other hand, צבא (tzva'ot) conveys a deeper meaning—a unity of individuals who come together driven by a shared aspiration to participate in something greater than themselves. It represents a spiritual and purposeful unity that transcends mere physical strength.

Every time we recite the prayer for Tzahal, we celebrate the latter—the army that unites Jews of every background, socio-economic status, and academic standing. It is an army that goes beyond physical strength, as it is distinguished by its shared purpose and aspiration. Tzahal, the צבא הגנה לישראל, unites diverse individuals who come together to fight for something far greater than themselves. It stands as a beacon of security, pride, unity, and a testament to the Divine.

When we utter the Mi Sheberach prayer in our synagogues every Shabbat with intentionality and fervor, we invoke God's blessings upon them. We ask for God's protection, deliverance from trouble and affliction, and we beseech that they be crowned with deliverance and victory. This prayer encapsulates the profound significance of Tzahal, embodying the dreams of generations and safeguarding the future of our nation. Amen!

Rabbi Dr. Leonard A. Matanky serves as the head of school (Dean) of Ida Crown Jewish Academy and rabbi of Congregation K.I.N.S. of West Rogers Park. He received his ordination from Hebrew Theological College and PhD from New York University. He is a past president of Rabbinical Council of America, Chicago Rabbinical Council, and Religious Zionists of America.

Elef LaMateh, Elef LaMateh: Praying for IDF Soldiers

Dovid Miller

THE PRECEDENT FOR PRAYER ACCOMPANYING our soldiers as they go out to war is found in all three battles that our ancestors fought between the exodus from Egypt and their conquest of the promised land: the defensive battle against Amalek (Shemot 17;8-16); the battle to retrieve the captives taken by the King of Arad after the death of Aharon (Bamidbar 21;1-3); and the retributive war against Midyan that followed the sins of the cult of Pe'or (Bamidbar 31;1-11).

In the battle against Amalek, Moses lifted his hand, and it was held up until the sun set. This is understood by the Targumim (Yonatan ben Uziel and the Yerushalmi), the midrash Pirkei de-Rabbi Eliezer (chapter 44) and the Ibn Ezra as an act of prayer. Rav Avraham ben ha-Rambam compares this to the "raising of his palms skyward" (Divrei ha-Yamim II, 6:13) of King Solomon. Similarly, both Targum Onkelos and Rashi

Praying for the Defenders of Our Faith

interpret "his hands remained Emunah – a source of faith" (verse 12), as an expression of prayer. Our Sages in the Mishnah in Rosh HaShanah (3:8) understood that Moses inspired all the Jews to raise their eyes heavenwards in intense prayer!

In the battle to free the captives, the Torah tells us "And G-d heard Kol Yisrael – the voice of Israel" (verse 3). The targumim (Onkelos and Yonatan ben Uziel) interpret this voice as prayer, and the Netziv in his Haamek Davar explains that "Kol" means a prayer from the depths of one's heart (see also Haamek Davar to Bereishit 30:6).

In my humble opinion, we find the most meaningful expression of the twinning of battle and prayer in the war against Midyan. Here, the Torah states that there were to be one thousand soldiers from each tribe in the army. The Torah uses a redundant expression "Elef LaMateh, Elef LaMateh" (Bamidbar 31:4). Our Sages in the Midrash (Bamidbar Rabbah 22:3) infer that there were two thousand set aside from each tribe – one thousand who would go out to battle and one thousand who were designated to pray for the soldiers – a one to one ratio!

We find in the Talmud (Niddah 70b-71a) that every serious endeavor (gathering knowledge, wealth, raising children) requires an investment of directed effort and prayer in order to succeed – neither alone is sufficient. Victory in war and the safe return of our soldiers certainly needs that dual approach.

Rav Chaim Shmulevitz, the late Rosh Yeshiva of the Mir Yeshiva in Yerushalayim, gave a series of lectures in his Yeshiva during the Yom Kippur War in 1973. The notes of these lectures were published at the end of the volume "Sichot Mussar." He compares the soldiers of the IDF to "Harugai Lod"- to the martyrs of Lod, who were willing to sacrifice their lives to save the Jewish people, regarding whom the Talmud (Baba Batra 10b) states – "No human being is worthy of being in their section in the World to Come."

Rav Chaim concludes – our obligation to pray for the welfare of the IDF soldiers knows no bounds.

Rabbi Dovid Miller is a Rosh Yeshiva at RIETS, Yeshiva University, and serves as the director of the YU Caroline and Joseph S. Gruss Institute in Jerusalem, and is the Rosh Kollel of the RIETS Israel Kollel.

Reflections on the Mi Sheberach for the IDF

Elazar Muskin

A HISTORIC EVENT OCCURRED IN ONE of the most prominent Haredi communities in Israel soon after the War in Gaza began against Hamas. With over 300,000 soldiers amassed on both the Gaza and Lebanon borders, it was reported that a great Chasidic Rebbe announced his endorsement of reciting the Mi Sheberach on behalf of the IDF soldiers in his Beit Midrash. This was historic because up until that moment the Haredi community overwhelmingly, not only shunned the prayer for the Welfare of the State of Israel, but also the Mi Sheberach for the IDF.

Years ago, I recall the late Rabbi Dr. Joseph Grunblatt, one of the leading and most respected Orthodox rabbis in America during the second half of the 20th century and who served for more than half a century as the rabbi of Queens Jewish Center, bemoaning the fact that the Haredi and Yeshivish communities did not recite the Mi Sheberach for the IDF. He remarked that although he could understand the Haredi community's reluctance in endorsing the prayer for the State of Israel that included the controversial Messianic words, "Reisheet Tzmichat Geulateinu," that the establishment of the State of Israel is "the beginning of the flowering of our redemption," such concerns are totally absent in the Mi Sheberach for the soldiers. The Mi Sheberach simply expresses our prayer that God bestow success upon the soldiers as they fight the enemies of the Jewish people and that all the soldiers should be spared any injury as they fulfill their duties in the army. He questioned, what could possibly be objectionable with this prayer?

Furthermore, he remarked that there is no Shul or Yeshiva in the world, that would refuse to say a Mi Sheberach for a Jew who is ill. The request would immediately be fulfilled without any investigation pertaining to the religious level of observance for the one in need of a cure. And yet, when it comes to praying for the welfare of the IDF soldiers there is reluctance in some segments of the Orthodox community about reciting Mi Sheberach prayer.

A prominent Chasidic Yeshiva from Israel recently sent its representative to Los Angeles to collect funds for their Yeshiva. When they came to see me for my annual support, I asked, "Are you saying the Mi Sheberach for the IDF soldiers as they fight to protect you and the entire Jewish people?" When hearing the question, the Yeshiva's representative noticeably became uncomfortable and immediately said, "we are constantly davening and saying Tehilim." I said, "That is very nice but are you saying the Mi Sheberach for the soldiers?" Recognizing my dissatisfaction, he quietly admitted that they don't recite the Mi Sheberach for the IDF. I continued by asking if they say a Mi Sheberach for the sick. He responded that of course they do. If so, I inquired, then why don't you say the Mi Sheberach for the soldiers? They certainly need your Tefilot now more than ever." He sheepishly responded, "I don't know why we don't."

Praying for the Defenders of Our Faith

As long as I can remember, the Mi sheberach for the IDF has been limited to being said on Shabbat and Yom Tov morning in Modern Orthodox Shuls. A number of years ago, the Orthodox Union decided to try to change this. They printed special pocket size cards with the Mi Sheberach for the IDF, hoping that people would incorporate this Tefilah into their daily davening. Although at the time it didn't catch on, now in the aftermath of October 7th the Mi Sheberach for both the IDF and the captives has become part of both Shacharit and Mincha services in many Shuls, including my own.

There is no doubt that the enormity of the massacre that occurred on October 7th and the united determination of the people of Israel to confront and eradicate Hamas, has made us realize that the stakes are higher than ever before, and constant prayers are therefore needed.

The Mi Sheberach for the IDF now resonates more than ever. It demonstrates that we believe that we must turn to Hashem for His help if we want the IDF to win this battle. This message certainly should be endorsed by all in the religious community.

Nothing occupies our thoughts more than what is happening in Israel. This preoccupies our days, and therefore we are grateful that we have a Tefilah that expresses our deepest concerns. Rarely have I felt so connected to a Tefilah as I am when I recite the words of these Tefilot. When one's reality is clearly delineated in a prayer the words become charged with profound meaning.

May God indeed protect the soldiers of the IDF and may the captives return home safely very soon.

Rabbi Elazar Muskin serves as Senior Rabbi of Young Israel of Century City in Los Angeles and is a past president of the Rabbinical Council of America.

'Master of Wars, Sower of Righteousness': The Impact of the Great War upon Rav Kook

Bezalel Naor

WORLD WAR ONE ("THE GREAT WAR"), which left Rav Abraham Isaac Hakohen Kook stranded in Europe, first in St. Gallen, Switzerland, and later in London, England, left a profound impact on the Rav's thought. An important cluster of writings from that period form the section "*Ha-Milḥamah*" (The War) in his seminal work *Orot*. In this essay, we will see Rav Kook active on three fronts during those war years: practical engagement with a Jewish fighting force (the first in millennia of exile); composition of a modern kabbalistic work; and finally, laying the theoretical halakhic groundwork for a democratic state of Israel.

Praying for the Defenders of Our Faith

Activist

In Rav Kook's seminal work, *Orot* (1920), we find this intriguing statement: "Nationalism grows strong; self-awareness increases. [Knesset Yisrael] already knows that she has a land, a language, a literature. *That she has an army, she began to recognize in this world war.*"[1]

The world war that the Rav referred to was clearly World War One, but to which "army" was he referring? Though not yet an independent fighting force, there emerged in World War One, under the auspices of the British Army, a contingent of Jewish volunteers known as the Jewish Legion (in Hebrew, "*Ha-Gedud ha-'Ivri*").[2] They were tasked with liberating Erets Yisrael from the Ottoman Turks. Their military chaplain, Reverend Leib Eizik Falk (1889-1957) was an erstwhile disciple of Rav Kook from the days that he served as Rabbi of Bausk, Latvia.

Rav Kook penned several letters to Falk, explaining urgent matters of Halakhah regarding *kashrut*, Shabbat, and shaving, and offering guidance concerning the future of this fighting force.[3] The Rav blessed the Legion, "bearers of the banner of the beginning of the sprouting of our salvation."[4] He visited the Legion's army base in Plymouth, England, accompanied by the Rebbetzin and his personal secretary, Rabbi Shimon

---

1   Abraham Isaac Hakohen Kook, *Orot*, *Ha-Milhamah* (The War), chap. 7. In the bilingual edition translated by Bezalel Naor (Maggid: Jerusalem, 2022), p. 139.

2   *Orot*, p. 465, n. 77. Officially, they were designated the 40th Royal Fusiliers. Colloquially, they were known as "The First Judeans." Prime movers in the formation of the Jewish Legion were Ze'ev Jabotinsky and Joseph Trumpeldor. Exiles from Erets Yisrael, David Ben Gurion and Yitzhak Ben Zvi fought in the 40th.

3   *Iggerot ha-Rayah* (Jerusalem: Mossad Harav Kook, 1965), vol. 3, pp. 136-138 (Letter 859).

4   Ibid., p. 134 (Letter 854).

Glitzenstein, a Ḥabad Ḥasid.⁵ The Rav's purpose in his visit was to extend words of encouragement. In a follow-up letter, the Rav inquired how many *ḥumashim* and *tallitot* the soldiers would require.⁶

Liturgist

Years later, on Hanukkah 5686 (December 17, 1925), the flag of the Jewish Legion would be placed for safekeeping in the historic Ḥurvah Synagogue in the Old City of Jerusalem. At the official presentation ceremony, Rav Kook offered both a prayer of his own composition and a sermon. Both have been preserved.⁷

The prayer reads:

> Rock of Israel, shield of our salvation forever and ever,
>
> with thanks we greet You,
>
> bearing with us the esteemed flag,
>
> a remembrance of the strength of the salvation of Your right hand,
>
> when the Holy Land was conquered by the British Army,
>
> accompanied by a legion of our sons,

---

5   Ibid., pp. 135-136 (Letter 857). See also Ari Yitzhak Shevat, "*Derashat Harav Kook zt"l 'al hashivut ha-degel ha-'Ivri/ha-Yisraeli,*" p. 14.

6   *Iggerot ha-Rayah*, vol. 3, pp. 141-142 (Letter 864).

7   Yael Levin-Katz, "*Tefillot ara'iyot le-RAYH Kook*" (Ephemeral Payers of Rav Kook), *Akdamut* 9 (Tammuz, 5760 [2000]), pp. 56-58 ("Prayer upon the Transfer of the Flag of the 40th Fusiliers to Jerusalem"); Ari Yitzhak Shvat, "*Derashat Harav Kook zt"l 'al hashivut ha-degel ha-'Ivri/ha-Yisraeli*" (The Sermon of Rav Kook on the Importance of the Hebrew/Israeli Flag), archived at *Asif*, pp. 1-15. (Includes facsimile of Rav Kook's manuscript on p. 2.)

who donned a spirit of courage

on the day of battle and war,

and Your right hand and Your arm fortified them,

to see victory and the majesty of might,

and their eyes saw in the distance the day of their people's salvation

and the redemption of their holy land,

their ancestral inheritance from eternity.

The memory of this flag is sacred to us,

bound as it is with holy thoughts

and the divine flame of pure souls,

those who fell in this holy war,

the seal of whose blood

will be engraved for eternity as a memory of the holy martyrs;

and their soul will be bound in the bond of life

with the Lord of hosts, Master of all souls.

And those living among us,

add days to their days,

O King who desires life;

and may all the straight-hearted see together

the Lord's salvation of His people and His inheritance,

and (with) the blessing of peace for all the kingdoms of the earth.

Amen and Amen.[8]

---

[8] Levin, pp. 57-58. The English translation is my own (BN).

Homilist

The prayer was followed by a *derashah* (sermon) in which the Rav expounded on the symbolism of the flags of the tribes of Israel in the Torah and Midrash.[9] The sermon was a delicate balancing act between the particularistic, nationalist aspirations of the Jewish People and a cosmopolitan, universalistic outlook whereby the various nations are likened to the bands of a spiritual spectrum.[10] One is tempted to attribute Rav Kook's universalism to the watchful eyes of the British mandatory officials present in the audience that day, but other writings of Rav Kook bear out that this was indeed the Rav's authentic outlook.[11]

Kabbalist

Provided with this historical context, we are now in a better position to unlock one of the mysteries of Rav Kook's kabbalistic work, *Resh Millin*, which appeared around this time (London, 1917). *Resh Millin* is Rav Kook's independent *midrash* on the letters of the Hebrew alphabet.

In the afterword, wherein the author justifies issuing an esoteric tract at this time of global calamity, Rav Kook waxes extremely poetic:

> When the world proceeds normally, when life is without pogroms and riots, one's lofty thought can subsist on observations of life's movements, on societal life, and on the theories associated with them—i.e. the contents of

---

9   Cf. Abraham Isaac Kook, *Midbar Shur* (Jerusalem: Makhon RZYH Kook, 5759 [1999]), *Ha-Derush ha-Shelishi*, pp. 24-30. The sermon (delivered in Zeimel, Lithuania) was adapted by Bezalel Naor, *In the Desert a Vision* (Spring Valley, NY; Orot, 2002), *Bamidbar*, pp. 119-124.

10 Shvat, p. 13.

11 See "The Universalism of Rav Kook" in Bezalel Naor, *Navigating Worlds* (New York, NY: Kodesh, 2021), pp. 341-349.

revealed wisdom and talent—and one is assured that this wealth will enrich one's inner resources.

This is not the case at a time when life falls into pits dark with evil and chaos. Then the revealed world reels; its orders are confounded. If one will derive spiritual sustenance only from the revealed side, terrible impoverishment awaits one, to rob one of all one's simple faith.

Then, in order to maintain one's stand, there will come the age of burning thirst for the hidden content, for the inner observations that transcend the revealed surface of life, that have not been touched by the world's upheaval. And from this source of life, one "will draw water with joy" [Isaiah 12:3], moistening the dry bones of the revealed spiritual world left in such a shaken state by the derangement of life.

For this reason, the present writer felt pressured to record his thoughts concerning the *midrash* of the letters at precisely this time.[12]

Throughout this enchanted work, the bellicose backdrop of London under bombardment is never far from the writer's consciousness. (There abound stories of the Rav's and Rebbetzin's acts of heroism in London's bomb shelters.) Thus, in connection with the letter *zayin*, which has the meaning of "arms" or "weaponry," the Rav quotes from the Morning Prayer, "Master of wars, sower of righteousness."[13]

---

12 *Resh Millin* (London, 1917), pp. 136-137.

13 Ibid., p. 43 (*Ha-Tagin*). Cf. the conclusion to *Orot, Ha-Milhamah*, chap. 1 (p. 131).

The impingement of war on the Rav's consciousness is the best explanation for the curious passage in the preamble to *Resh Millin*:

> "The thoughts which precede all the letters always hover within us internally. We must bare our true courage, the leonine (*arieliyut*) that is in our midst, in order to be constantly aware of the character of the inconceivable conceptions."[14]

In a letter to Rabbi Shemariah Menashe Hakohen Adler of London, who penned a lengthy commentary to *Resh Millin*, Rav Kook shared all of the kabbalistic teaching that informed his neologism of "*arieliyut*."[15]

The Rav takes us on a whirlwind tour of divine names and *gematriyot* (alphanumerical equivalences). *Aryeh* (lion) has the numerical value of 216, which it shares with *gevurah* (stern judgment). But 216 is also 3 times 72, the *gematria* of *ḥesed* (love).[16]

The upshot is that on high, there is a convergence of the two attributes of love (*ḥesed*) and stern judgment (*gevurah*).[17] "And man, being a copy

---

14 Ibid., p. 1.

15 *Iggerot ha-Rayah*, vol. 3, p. 207 (Letter 896).

16 Ibid. There is a divine name of seventy-two elements culled from the three verses of Exodus 14:19-21. As each of the seventy-two elements consists of three letters, this yields a grand total of two hundred and sixteen, the *gematria* of *aryeh*. See Rashi, *Sukkah* 45a, s.v. *Ani vahu*.

17 One is reminded of the teaching of the hidden righteous man, Rabbi Moshe Ya'akov Rabikov ("The Shoemaker"), an early adherent of Rav Kook in the Jaffa era. In a kabbalistic vein, Rabinkov wrote (concerning the *kohen mashu'aḥ milḥamah*, who addresses the troops before they go to battle), that at the time of war against the enemy, by his very presence, the *kohen*— an embodiment of the attribute of love (*ḥesed*)—communicates to us the overarching principles of love and peace. The manuscript leaf of Rabikov's commentary to *Parashat Shofetim* was recently offered at auction.

of the divine, his might resides in the mystery of his soul ... then he is 'righteous, secure as a young lion' [Proverbs 28:1]."[18]

HALAKHIST

Until now we have discussed Rav Kook's roles of homilist and kabbalist. It should be noted that in his capacity as halakhist, it was his landmark decision that serves as the basis for conferring upon the Prime Minister of Israel the status of a *"melekh"* (monarch)[19] with the power to declare a *milhemet mitsvah* (compulsory war) in national self-

---

18 *Iggerot ha-Rayah*, loc. cit.
The comment of Rabbi Menahem Mendel of Shklov to the verse in Proverbs is quite apropos, in *Mishlei 'im Be'ur ha-Gra*, ed. Moshe Phillip [Petah Tikvah, 1985], Proverbs 28:1 [p. 303, n. 1]):
"I heard from one of those who stood in the presence of my master, teacher and rabbi, the Gaon [of Vilna], of blessed memory: The *Zohar* (II, 143a) asks how the righteous can be sure of their righteousness. The *Zohar* responds that it is for this reason that the righteous are likened precisely to a *kefir*, a young lion. [The Gaon explained] that the righteous rely upon the merit of the forefathers (*zekhut avot*), just as the young lion trusts in the fact that he is of the lion species. For this reason, the other wild beasts, though they be stronger than him, fear him. So the righteous trusts in the merit of his fathers who were righteous."

19 Avraham Yitzhak Hakohen Kook, *Mishpat Kohen*, no. 144 (datelined "19 Tevet, 5676 [1916], St. Gallen"), responsum to Rabbi Zalman Pines, pp. 337-338; Shelomo Yosef Zevin, *Le-'Or ha-Halakhah*, "Ha-Milhamah," chap. 1, p. 16. Rabbi Zevin points out that Rav Kook was preceded in this approach by Nahmanides in his conclusion to his glosses to Maimonides' *Sefer ha-Mitsvot*. See *Sefer ha-Mitsvot le-ha-Rambam 'im Hasagot ha-Ramban*, ed. C.B. Chavel (Jerusalem: Mossad Harav Kook, 1981), p. 409. And see Eliezer Yehudah Waldenberg, *Hilkhot Medinah*, Part One (Jerusalem: Mossad Harav Kook, 1952), pp. 175-178.

defense.[20] Apropos of the present conflict, there is lively discussion in the halakhic literature whether the commandment of providing the enemy with an escape route is restricted to a *milhemet ha-reshut* (optional war) or extends as well to a *milhemet mitsvah*.[21]

We conclude (as did Rav Kook) with the words of the Morning Prayer:

> "Master of wars, sowing righteousness, sprouting salvation."

Rabbi Bezalel Naor, a devoted scholar of Rav Abraham Isaac Hakohen Kook, is renowned for translating Rav Kook's influential work, "Orot" and numerous other writings by Rav Kook. He is also an accomplished author, contributing original studies to Jewish Thought in both English and Hebrew.

---

20 Maimonides, *MT*, *Hil. Melakhim* 5:1; Zevin, pp. 12-13.

21 See Maimonides, *MT*, *Hil. Melakhim* 6:7; Nahmanides, Positive Commandment 5; anonymous, *Sefer ha-Hinukh*, commandment 527; Joseph Babad, *Minhat Hinukh* (at end of work, commenting on Nahmanides' positive commandment 5); Meir Simhah Kohen, *Meshekh Hokhmah*, Numbers 31:7, s.v. *Vayyitsbe'u*; Joseph Rosen of Rogatchov, glosses to Solomon ibn Gabirol, *Azharot*, ed. David Abraham (Jerusalem: Feldheim, 2004), *Zohar ha-Raki'a*, par. 73 (p. 277); Waldenberg, *Hilkhot Medinah*, Part Two (Jerusalem: Mossad Harav Kook, 1953), 5:7 ("Laying Siege"), pp. 179-182.

A Mother's Reflections to Our Father in Heaven: Balancing Silence, Serenity, and Prayer during War

CB Neugroschl

I CONSIDER IT A PRIVILEGE THAT among the highlights of my day are the moments when I step into the Beit Midrash or The Student Center at Ma'ayanot Yeshiva High School for Girls. Here, I am consistently enveloped in the inspiration radiating from my students' tefillot. In the silence, there is an intensity that I feel and that spreads from them to me, to each other, and to Hashem. This daily practice of prayer brings a profound serenity, as we engage in a conversation with Hashem. Our tefillot serve to ground our day in gratitude for our countless blessings, renew our consciousness of Hashem's generosity, and enhance our kavannah deepening our personal connection with the Divine. The late Rabbi Jonathan Sacks eloquently described tefillah as our means of speaking to God, while learning Torah is how God speaks to us. These dual pathways of tefillah and limmud haTorah not only keep us connected to the Divine but also sanctify our lives, fostering a profound relationship with Hashem.

Strangely, things have become both easier and more challenging lately. Following the Shemini Atzeret massacres, as our world tilts into disarray and after learning that my children in Israel serving as Chayalim were "called up" for army service, my days have been a whirlwind of activity. I've been immersed in listening to others, managing orders for the Chayalim, organizing donations, and dealing with a multitude of tasks involving duffles, travelers, flights, and customs documents. This constant busyness is exhausting — a relentless pace that leaves little room for rest, sleep, or a moment's pause. Busy is hard. Hard to keep up. Too busy to stop, too busy to sleep, and too busy to slow down. Yet, in this chaos, I find that silence is even more difficult. Welcoming quiet into my hectic, disordered life is a challenge, as silence becomes the abode for lurking fears, worries, and unsettling possibilities.

And, so my world of tefillah is disordered too. It is both harder to daven and harder not to daven, all at the same time. There is no comfort when my tears won't stop and when the words are searingly real. There is no serenity when the need is greater than I've ever felt before. I need to daven like I've never davened before. It's a need that is achingly present and still allusive. For me, it's nearly impossible to be present with such an aching need for long. I can only endure small doses. In those small doses of silence there is no serenity present - but rather a silence that fills up with need, with urgency, with an earnest and aching yearning.

Praying for the Defenders of Our Faith

This is where my prayers live now. In the space where I stop the frenetic activities, where I am not in control.

During this period of immense sadness and distress, I am confronted with my own deep sense of need. Through tefillah, I turn to Hashem, "the God beyond, who is also the Voice within," seeking the silence and serenity that only He can provide, my sole refuge and redemption. Rabbi Sacks insightfully noted, "It is not easy to create the silence in the soul where prayer begins." This eit tzara, unlike any we've faced before, plunges us into deep pain, emphasizing our need for tefillah. I am deeply grateful for my community, both at home and school, whose presence affords me moments of silence to connect with my soul and Hashem. Our prayers during this challenging time are a profound reckoning with our reality, offering potential for transformation. May our tefillot during this Eit Tzarah connect us to Avinu she'bashamayim and transform our reality from distress to relief, from captivity to freedom, from darkness to light.

הַמָּקוֹם יְרַחֵם עֲלֵיהֶם, וְיוֹצִיאֵם מִצָּרָה לִרְוָחָה, וּמֵאֲפֵלָה לְאוֹרָה, וּמִשִּׁעְבּוּד לִגְאֻלָּה, הַשְׁתָּא בַּעֲגָלָא וּבִזְמַן קָרִיב.

May God have mercy on them, and bring them from distress to relief, from darkness to light, and from subjugation to redemption, speedily and soon.

Mrs. CB Neugroschl is the Head of School at Ma'ayanot Yeshiva High School for Girls since 2020, marking her return to the institution where she previously served as Director of Admissions and taught Jewish History and Philosophy. With over 25 years in education, she has significant experience in both Judaic and General Studies. Mrs. Neugroschl's academic background includes studying at Michlala College for Women, earning a B.A. from Stern College for Women, an M.A. in Near Eastern Languages and Civilizations from Harvard University, and studying at Yeshiva University's Bernard Revel Graduate School, focusing on the History of Halakha and Medieval Ashkenaz.

Words for This Time

Elhanan Nir

> Two weeks to the slaughter of
> Simchat Torah 5784
> And to the breakthrough of the southern front

MORE THAN A CENTURY AGO, in early 1917 during World War I, Rabbi Abraham Isaac Kook wrote "Rosh Milin" while in London. He marked the year of the book as the year of "Ezrat" (help). He concealed the writing of this book from his son, Rabbi Zvi Yehuda Kook, who was always wary of publishing his father's writings, believing the generation was not yet ready for their widespread dissemination. When the son learned of the book's publication, he expressed his opposition to it. From that moment on, he ensured he was always involved in editing and publishing his father's writings—a responsibility he bore until his death.

This is the most profound and esoteric book the Rabbi wrote. Rabbi Kook saw the book as a mystical response to the terrible events unfolding in the world at the time. He wrote that "even the sealed language within it has the power to shed a divine light on all who study it with purity of thought" (Letters of Rabbi Kook, vol. 3, no. 609). Great Kabbalists of Jerusalem, such as Rabbi Menachem Halpern—who wrote annotations

Praying for the Defenders of Our Faith

and explanations for all writings of the Ari—were deeply impressed by it, stating it was "extremely awe-inspiring; who can extol its virtues?" Rabbi Yaakov Moshe Charlap wrote to the author, Rabbi Kook, "We can only say that from the Holy of Holies in the Temple to the residence of the esteemed genius in London, there is a space cleared from the impure atmosphere of foreign air, and a holy conduit of sanctified air continually flows upon him" (Hed Harim, Letter 32).

Above the Visible Surface

Similarly to the custom in Hasidic communities of providing the "Noam Elimelech" as a protective charm for easy childbirth, Rabbi Zvi Yehuda Kook had the habit of distributing "Rosh Milin." Now, many of our soldiers, may God protect their arrivals and departures, carry this sacred book with them in their tactical vests and body armor.

The book is composed of Rabbi Kook's freeform writing on the Hebrew letters, crowns (tagin), vowel points, and cantillation marks, and it concludes with five significant annotations. I want us to read the first annotation:

> "When the world follows its usual course, when there are no disruptions and tumults in life, even the noble ideals of humanity can derive their sustenance from observing life's movements, from societal living, and from the doctrines of associations within them, which is the entire content of all revealed wisdom and talent. From this wealth, one is assured of inner enrichment. The regular flow of life can sustain daily existence. There is wonder in life. There is beauty in it. A sensitive person can fulfill their noble essence from this routine, from the simple grace and kindness that exists in life and reality."

However, when life descends into abysses filled with the shadows of wickedness and chaos, the visible world shakes, its orders become confused. If a person draws their spiritual sustenance solely from the visible side of the spiritual treasury, a terrible diminishment is prepared to befall them, robbing them of all their steadfast essence. Then, to maintain their stance, comes the turn of the burning thirst for the hidden content, for the inner insights that rise above the visible surface of life, untouched by the global turmoil. From this source of life, a person will joyfully draw water to hydrate the parched bones of the exposed spiritual world, left so staggered by the challenges of life's disruptions.

But when there are abysses, when there is an encounter with evil and wickedness, the visible can no longer suffice. Real-political analysis doesn't capture the entirety of existence; we are required to delve inward, to the hidden content, to the beyond – which we haven't reached thus far, from which we've also been apprehensive and fearful.

Rabbi Kook concludes with personal remarks, touching on his individual inclination in writing this book: "For this very reason, the urge came upon the writer of these lines to record these thought sketches related to the interpretation of the letters, etc., specifically at this time."

The Father Knocked on the Table

In moments like these, we are obligated to delve inward. Facing wickedness and evil, a mere response to the externalities of the world is insufficient. We require a profound revelation, a kind of articulation that in our daily lives we cannot, do not know how to, and dare not express. We all now reflect on what we experienced two weeks ago. I say two weeks, but it feels more like two years. We gaze upon the pogrom, the massacre, the most horrific riots that have taken place in the Land of Israel since the destruction of the Second Temple, perhaps even since the Bar Kokhba revolt. The events remain incomprehensible. The best and most skilled army in the region, intelligence services that are aware of every vehicle transporting weapons in some remote village in northern Syria – how did this months-long organization involving thousands of terrorists not warrant proper attention and response? How can we come to terms with this grave failure?

This failure, of course, reflects the pervasive attitude that has spread here in recent decades, holding us captive to the concept sharply articulated by the Israeli singer-lyricist, Shalom Hanoch, in his song, Kamocha Bidiyuk:

> "A stranger, he's your enemy – just like you.
>
> Suddenly, he too wishes to be – exactly like you.
>
> Suddenly, he rises, stands against you,
>
> Insisting on living."

But it has become clear that our enemy is not exactly like us. He doesn't want to be like us and he's not similar to us. He doesn't insist on living, contrary to the naive words of Shalom Hanoch. He is pure evil. Utter wickedness. Absolute cruelty. There was a dream here, mixed with hubris, of normalization, of a new Middle East; a dream that we no longer need territory, soil, settlements, security belts - that technology and cameras would suffice; a dream that they were essentially already like us, just wanting to live comfortably and quietly, believing that the good life and relaxed bourgeoisie would prevail. Thus, nationalism receded, and the messianic-utopian universalism of a world that has reached "they shall not hurt nor destroy" took its place, a world without differences and tension between nations and peoples. And now, the illusion of decades was shattered in one horrific moment. Everything mercilessly exploded before our eyes on the joyful morning of Simchat Torah, 5784.

I don't want to delve deeply into this. It's not my role. There are plenty of security analysts and experts on the situation, and they are enough. I also don't think now is the time for it. And it seems that even when the time comes, after our decisive victory, there will never be satisfactory answers to these terrible questions, and even if there are, they won't have the power to bring any of our fallen back to life. But right now, we cannot speak in familiar and routine expressions. Those are suitable for a situation where, in the words of the Rav Kook, "the world goes in its usual course," but now "life falls into pits full of the darkness of wickedness and chaos." Therefore, we must agree to speak in a language that deviates from everything we've said so far; we cannot speak logically now, but only acknowledge that this is a mythical, biblical event, one that transcends reason and understanding, going beyond any natural course or comprehension.

And this event is a historical event, an event of divine concealment.

After a year of unceasing internal conflicts, brotherly divisions of an intensity previously unknown in the State of Israel, the protective shield surrounding the lamb amidst the seventy wolves was momentarily lifted. The divine presence, the "Shekhinah" that envelops the camp of Israel, abandoned us for a few hours on that dreadful morning. It was as if the Father knocking on the table, shaking the earth.

On Hosanna Rabbah morning, we cried out "For three hours. Save us!"

On the morning of Hoshana Rabbah, we cried out "For three hours, save us, please!" And behold, the pogrom took place over three hours (as expressed by Colonel Ofer Winter, who fought in the battles of Kibbutz Be'eri, telling Yair Ansbacher that the main horror occurred in the first three hours, "God made us blind and deaf for three hours"), and we were not saved. At the time we pleaded in the rain prayer, "For life and not for death" - death came to our window, and the verses of "Lamentations" transformed before our eyes during Simchat Torah into a reality more horrifying than ever.

Praying for the Defenders of Our Faith

Behold, immediately after the sealing of fate on Hosanna Rabbah, the terrible verses from the Torah portion Ki Tavo materialized before our eyes:

> "Had they been wise, they would have understood this, they would have discerned their end. How can one chase a thousand, and two put ten thousand to flight, unless their Rock had sold them, the Lord had given them up?" (Deuteronomy 32:29-30).

Rabbi Ovadia Sforno commented on this:

> "They should have understood that it's not natural... unless their Rock had sold them. He fought against them, removed their strength, hence their might was drained and they became like women."

Just before further quarrels, this time involving Torah scrolls, everything halted. The dancing ceased, our joy turned to mourning. And now - an awakening, and this rousing from the dream is painful. The most dreadful of horrors.

The holy Zohar speaks of the Divine Presence that dwells only in a space of wholeness:

> Rabbi Yosi said, the Shekhinah (Divine Presence) only dwells in a complete place, not in a deficient or flawed place, not in a sad place, but in a joyous place. Therefore, when the sons of Jacob separated from their father and Jacob was sad, the Shekhinah did not dwell with him. It is written (Psalms 100:2) "Serve the Lord with joy; come before Him with singing." The Divine Presence doesn't dwell in sadness (Zohar Part 1, 197b).

The past year was a deficient space, a flawed place, a sorrowful place. This year was one in which the Divine Presence seemed to retreat from us.

It matters not who is at fault, who initiated, for "we are guilty," all of us. And now, in the past week, with the reading of the portion of "Bereishit," we return to the beginning, to the genesis, to the first Rashi that explains our connection to this Holy Land, to the Temple site, to the soil where prophets, kings, and scholars once walked. We must recognize that we are one body, one essence, and understand the depth of "the uniqueness in each individual, the qualities and levels that his peer does not possess, and all need each other… and through this self-nullification, they unite in the inspiration of His singular holiness" (Likutei Torah, Nitzavim 44, based on). We need to return to the acknowledgment of the Lord dwelling among us, "and in recognizing that God is within her, she will understand how to reveal her life source, will know how to uphold her vision from its inherent foundation" (Lights of War, 9). And this Sabbath, we will read the portion of Noah, the earth filled with violence, and the realization that we need to create a new world, a world of repair, in place of the chaotic world that loses its right and justification for existence.

This war reminds us of the ultimate plea of this nation, the plea and cry we voice in the Shabbat morning prayer:

> "From Your place, our King, appear, and reign over us, for we await You. When will You reign in Zion? Soon, in our days, may You dwell there forever. Be exalted and sanctified within Jerusalem, Your city, from generation to generation, and for all eternity."

The tumultuous times we face force us to introspect and realize our core essence and mission in this world. The hope is that through unity, prayer, and action, we can usher in a time of peace, understanding, and the Divine Presence once again shining brightly among us.

The story of the Rebbe of Tzanz-Klausenburg, who lost his wife and eleven children during the Holocaust, is truly heart-wrenching. In the darkest moments, when all seemed lost, he would whisper prayers of hope, calling for God's presence and reign in Zion. This deep faith and resilience allowed him, after surviving the horrors of the Holocaust, to remarry, have two more children (who would become the present-day leaders of the Tzanz community), and establish the Laniado Hospital in Netanya, Israel, dedicated to providing medical care to all Jews in need.

This consciousness and unwavering faith are what should guide us during challenging times. We fight for the most fundamental and elevated aspects of our existence: the basic right of a Jew to live in their homeland, which in itself is the highest form of manifesting divine presence. This fight is not just territorial but is a battle between good and evil, morality and injustice.

The current understanding in Israel is that these terrorists are akin to ISIS or the Nazis. This realization may have come late, but it is our hope that it's not too late. In a way, the entire nation of Israel is now in a state of "Teshuva" (repentance). A repentant individual is required to work with extra vigor to mend their ways and correct past mistakes. This understanding, which permeates Israeli society, is crucial. It internalizes the fact that this is not merely a territorial dispute but a deeper struggle over the essence of humanity. The world watches, waiting to see how Israel confronts this evil – whether with complacency, thus accepting its existence, or with determination, signaling that such malevolence has no place on this Earth. We desire a moral world, one filled with grace and compassion, not one dominated by harsh judgments and cruel atrocities.

Elhanan Nir

The transition from the doctrine of Abel to the doctrine of Cain

The transition from thousands of years of exile to the return of Israel to their land is not simple. The Jew throughout the generations was the weak one, "the one who is killed for you. You are considered as sheep for slaughter," as we say during the Hosannas. And now, he is required to walk before the Lord in the land of the living, to be strong. Zionism tried to convince us that it learned to make this transition properly, but it seems it did not. It appears we still reside in a mindset of exile marked by weakness and frailty. Even if we have power, we still don't know how to use it appropriately.

In this regard, the Kabbalists reveal to us that the transition from exile, or the shift from the "doctrine of Abel" to the "doctrine of Cain," from a doctrine where everything is merely "a rule and not a deed," a constant engagement in hypotheticals, contentment with the four parts of the Shulchan Aruch, to transitioning to the Rambam, dealing with all aspects of reality, which also includes the existence of a state in all its implications. This transition is the shift from the submissive Abel to the dominating Cain. Only then can we talk about the prophecies of Isaiah, full of vibrancy and the utopian dream of peace.

In this context, I want to bring words from the holy Shla'h (Shnei Luchot HaBrit): "This is the secret of 'Vanity of vanities, said Kohelet, vanity of vanities; all is vanity.' Hinting that the entire conduct of the world is in the aspect of Abel. And also a hint that this Abel conduct is in comparison to the future governance, which is from the side of might. And this is what our sages said in the Midrash Kohelet (11,12), the Torah that a person learns in this world is vanity compared to the Torah of the Messiah. Meaning it is surely from the aspect of 'Abel,' but the Torah of the Messiah is from the might of Cain, and our eyes see that a man from the side of might is strong and brave, and one who is from the side of kindness is poor, soft, and weak (Torah Ohr, Va'etchanan, 3). The Torah of the Messiah is from the "aspect of the might of Cain." It cannot be a continuation of the exile Torah from Abel's study hall. And in this era, whether we like it or not, all of Israeli society needs to undergo this transition. We thought those next to us were like us, but it turns out they are not. Redemption depends on understanding the transition from Abel to Cain, from weakness to strength; from a doctrine of redemption to a doctrine of redemption.

Revelation of the Singular

Part of understanding the transition from Abel to Cain also necessitates the realization that we are required to be one, "a single nation in the land." Even if belatedly and painfully, we now remember that there is no longer a pure right or a pure left, only together; that our existence here, and everywhere, defies logic, is always in daily existential danger, and always miraculous. In every generation, they stand against us – this eternal nation thousands of years old - to annihilate us. Now, we must decisively confront an enemy who prefers death to life, unparalleled in cruelty and wickedness; do our utmost, and ask the Almighty to finish for us, to plead that "In the greatness of Your excellence - You overthrow those who rise against You" (Exodus 15:7).

In Kabbalah, it is explained that there are moments when the highest stature of a person and a nation is revealed: the stature of the "yechidah of the soul", the Messianic level, the most exalted in existence. Yechidah, as explained by the Ari (Rabbi Isaac Luria), is "a very small spark that is of the essence of divinity drawn from the last level of the Creator, and this is the spark that is clothed in the power of a single created spark... called Yechidah" (Etz Chaim, 42, Chapter 1). This is the created spark that is fully connected with the spark of the Creator.

The Yechidah is revealed on three occasions:

1. On Yom Kippur. Hence there is a commandment to pray with the sinners, with the offenders of Israel, for on this day the singular aspect of their souls is revealed, illuminating them openly.

2. In the covenant of love between two lovers, where they commit to a shared life journey.

3. In self-sacrifice. When a Jew sacrifices himself for the sanctification of God's name, feeling that it is not a choice but the only conceivable path, it arises from the illumination of the singular aspect of his soul.

This is a revelation, beyond all conscious awareness, of the unique quality of a nation that came into the world to bring humanity blessings, morality, and rectification. The path of this nation is woven with pain and death, due to its mission to introduce life, grace, kindness, and compassion to existence. Indeed, the revelation of this "Yechidah" came to us from deep pain that reminds us that we are a nation of lions; from the midst of the flame, the angel of the Lord appears to us. As said by the Kabbalist-healer, Rabbi Moshe David Valle, a close associate of the Ramchal (Rabbi Moshe Chaim Luzzatto):

> "For this nation, a nation of lions – both by their nature and because of the Divine Presence that dwells upon them. And what is the nature of lions? At times they bow down and lie down, appearing weak, but in the end, they suddenly rise and tear apart their adversaries."

No one can predict the future, but it seems evident that things will never revert to how they once were. In the coming decades, we will need to roll up our sleeves and forge something new here. The military, political, social, and cultural structures that have faltered and collapsed will need to be reshaped and reinvented.

We will also need to craft a new religious-theological language to comprehend the events befalling us. We cannot continue to lean solely on traditional religious teachings and scholarly interpretations as we did leading up to this dire situation. Everything is transitioning from the teachings of Abel to those of Cain, and we must endeavor to understand this shift.

We will undertake this challenge with prayer and humility, with compassion and by recognizing the worth of others, and with an unceasing memory of these harrowing days. Together, we will move forward.

Elhanan Nir is an Israeli poet and writer. He teaches at Yeshivat Siakh Yitskhak and is the editor of the Shabbat supplement of Makor Rishon newspaper.

'He Who Blessed Our Ancestors... May He Bless the Soldiers of the IDF', 'Like Fiery Beings... They Flew Far to Restore Human Dignity'

Malka Puterkovsky

On the evening of Monday, October 29, 1956, the Sinai War, also known as Operation Kadesh, broke out. Approximately four days later, on November 2, 1956, the ha-Tsofeh newspaper published a notice. It announced, "A special Mi Sheberach prayer for the welfare of IDF soldiers has been composed by the Chief Rabbi of the IDF, Lieutenant Colonel Shlomo Goren, to be recited in all synagogues on the Sabbath following the Torah reading." The notice included the text of the prayer.

The prayer composed by Rabbi Shlomo Goren follows the pattern of blessings traditionally recited when individuals are called to the Torah during Saturday morning services, specifically upon the completion of their aliyah. This unique prayer contains a specific request addressed to the Holy Blessed One, asking for the protection of the lives and the success of the IDF soldiers' mission. It draws upon various forms of prayers and traditions.[1]

When examining the prayer texts, one should inquire: What are the Jewish values that underlie the congregation's recitation of this prayer in the synagogue, as they beseech the Almighty to protect our soldiers and grant them victory? The basis for addressing this question can be found in Rabbi Eliezer Melamed's response to a young woman's inquiry: "I struggle to comprehend the necessity of reciting blessings before and after consuming all types of food... Why is such meticulousness required in this matter?" Rabbi Melamed chooses to begin his response by discussing the "value of gratitude between individuals." He explains:

> "Firstly, blessings express the important moral value of gratitude. To properly understand this value, let's first address the importance of acknowledging the good between individuals. A person who knows how to express gratitude is someone who can step out of their egocentric bubble and connect to the world around

---

1 See the chapters by Aaron Ahrend, Nissim Leon, Yoel Rappel in this volume.

them, seeing it in a positive light. From this, they will be able to humbly relate to those around them and appreciate them for all the good they provide. ... But it's not enough to recognize their goodness in one's heart; one must also express it in words of thanks, which will bring joy to them, and the love between them will grow. The desire of both to do good deeds will be strengthened, and goodness will spread from them to all those around them."

At the beginning of his remarks, Rabbi Melamed emphasizes the importance of expressing gratitude towards others. When we pray for the well-being, benefit, and success of individuals, it reflects a profound sense of gratitude from the person offering the prayer. We owe a deep debt of gratitude to the soldiers of the IDF and the security forces, a debt that has existed for generations, even before the establishment of the state of Israel. This debt continues to this day as they enable us to live in peace, despite the security challenges we face both internally and externally. In the later part of his response, Rabbi Melamed underscores the significance of recognizing goodness and expressing gratitude to God, as reflected in the blessings recited before enjoying various aspects of life.

Yet, in addition to recognizing gratitude for the women and men of the security forces – in each member of the community's prayer for their well-being and welfare, there is woven the tradition we learned from Rava in the Talmud (Babylonian Talmud, Bava Kamma 92a): "Whoever requests mercy for his friend [who is in need of a specific salvation] and he [the one praying] himself needs [salvation and mercy in] that same thing – he is answered first." If a person in need of a certain deliverance prays and supplicates to God to grant this deliverance to his friend, who is also in need of it – it is precisely the petitioner who will first merit the deliverance. This is because God, as it were, is moved by the petitioner's display of mutual responsibility for his friend, and therefore, He grants the praying individual deliverance from his distress first.

The act of prayer requires a genuine and authentic appeal to God on behalf of one's friend, as stressed by the Chida (Rabbi Yosef Chaim David Azulai) in his commentary on 'Mussar HaShelah': "One must specifically intend [the prayer] for his friend, and not with the intention that it should also benefit himself."[2]

Indeed, when a person genuinely and profoundly wishes for the well-being of their friend, as in the case of our prayers for the soldiers and the entire community, this heartfelt prayer can be the catalyst that "arouses in God the will" to respond favorably to the petitioner's request first. Perhaps this is the essence of what Rivka Amitai meant in her song: "Every person needs another to pray on their behalf." She recognized the immense value in wholeheartedly empathizing with another's suffering and having a profound desire to do good for them.

> "Every person needs another to pray on their behalf,
>
> Someone to utter their name with lips
>
> Of faith, and hope, and life, to revive someone else.
>
> And every person needs a heart to lay upon them hands
>
> Of faith, and of blessing..."

Certainly, one should not simplistically interpret the tradition that "whoever prays for another is answered first" in relation to "praying for the peace of the IDF soldiers," since not all who pray are themselves soldiers "standing guard over our land," and in need of the promise that

---

[2] It is included in the Chumash "Torah Or," specifically in connection with the cities of refuge and ancient inheritance, at the conclusion of Parashat Vayera.

"the Lord will deliver our enemies who rise against us defeated before us… and will crown them with a diadem of salvation and a crown of victory."

However, one can point to an indirect yet strong connection between the Talmudic tradition and the special Mi Sheberach prayer for the security forces. After all, some of the soldiers of the Israel Defense Forces are sons, brothers, uncles, friends, loved ones, etc., of those among the praying congregation, so that the one who prays for their well-being, hopes and wishes that their loved ones will not be harmed and that they will see blessing in their endeavors.

This moreover—in praying for the protection of our soldiers and for their success in their mission, we are essentially praying for our own peace, our security, and the tranquility of our lives in this land. Who among us does not need protection, salvation, blessing in our endeavors, and the subduing of our enemies who rise up to destroy us?!

The idea of the faithful offering blessings to the heroic soldiers, praying for their mission's success, and recognizing that this victory would also bring goodness to the faithful themselves is beautifully expressed in the heartfelt renditions of many cantors and singers.[3] The tune that many use for singing the Mi Sheberach is the same one originally composed for El Eretz Tzvi (lyrics by Talma Alyagon-Rose and music by Dubi Zeltzer. This song was written in memory of the Entebbe hostage rescue operation by the IDF, whose words:

בַּחֲצִי הַלַּיְלָה הֵם קָמוּ	*Bechatzi halailah hem kamu*
וְהִכּוּ בִּקְצֵה הָעוֹלָם	*vehiku bik'tzeh ha'olam*

---

3   For a video of Chief Cantor of the Israel Defense Forces, Lt. Col. Shai Abramson, sing the Mi Sheberach for the IDF soldiers, to the tune of El Eretz Tzvi, see here (https://www.youtube.com/watch?v=hOErXxk2-fo).

Praying for the Defenders of Our Faith

כִּבְנֵי רֶשֶׁף חָשׁוּ הִרְחִיקוּ עוּף	kiv'nei reshef chashu hir'chiku of
לְהָשִׁיב אֶת כְּבוֹד הָאָדָם	lehashiv et k'vod ha'adam
אֶל אֶרֶץ צְבִי	El eretz tz'vi
אֶל דְּבַשׁ שְׂדוֹתֶיהָ	el dvash s'doteiha
אֶל הַכַּרְמֶל וְהַמִּדְבָּר	el hakarmel vehamidbar
אֶל עַם אֲשֶׁר לֹא יֶחֱשֶׁה	el am asher lo yechesheh
שְׂאֵת בָּנָיו לֹא יַפְקִיר לְזָר,	she'et banav lo yaf'kir lezar
אֶל אֶרֶץ צְבִי שֶׁבְּהָרֶיהָ	el eretz tz'vi shebehareiha
פּוֹעֶמֶת עִיר מִדּוֹר לְדוֹר	po'emet ir midor ledor
אֶל אֶרֶץ אֵם לִטְבוּרָהּ	el eretz em bit'vurah
קְשׁוּרִים בָּנֶיהָ בְּטוֹב וּבְרַע.	k'shurim baneiha batov uvara.

At midnight they arose

and struck at the edge of the world

like sons of ghosts they hurried to take flight

to return the honor of humanity

To the land of the deer (Israel)

to the honey of her fields

to the Carmel and the desert

to a nation who will not be silent/still

who will not abandon its sons to a foreigner

to the land of deer, in whose mountains

a city beats from generation to generation

> to the motherland to whose navel
>
> her children are bound in good and in bad

In the song El Eretz Tzvi, there is an expression of the deep mutual responsibility that exists between the army of the people and the entire Jewish people.[4] May it be His will that the tradition of "He who seeks mercy for his friend while he himself is in need of the same… is answered first" will be fulfilled in us. Thus, we – who pray for the welfare and benefit of our soldiers – will be blessed with peace, tranquility, health, blessing, and success, just as we have asked of the Almighty for all the men and women of security who stand guard over our land, in the hope that the Almighty "will send blessing and success in all the work of their hands… May God give our enemies, who rise against us, to be struck down before them! … And crown them with a crown of salvation and a crown of victory."

Lu Yehi, Let it be so!

Malka Puterkovsky has been teaching Talmud and Halakhah in Israel for over thirty years. She served as a torch lighter during Israel's 2015 Independence Day ceremony. She resides with her family in Tekoa.

---

[4] Consider the insightful commentary of Elhanan Samuel in his article "They Struck at the Edge of the World: When Israel's Soldiers Serve in the Army of the Lord," Makor Rishon (21 January 2021), and available online here (https://www.makorrishon.co.il/opinion/306621), stating, "Eretz Tzvi transcends being a song for just one operation or a single soldier. It's a significant anthem of our era's Divine guidance and the celestial messengers through whom He chooses to save us from our foes' grasp. This protection occurs constantly and persistently, at every border, across land, air, and sea, and in every locale where they stand guard—even at the farthest reaches of the earth."

On the Evolution and Significance of the Prayer for the Welfare of IDF Soldiers

Yoel Rappel

PRAYERS FOR THE WELFARE OF our soldiers were composed even before the establishment of the State of Israel, but it was specifically the Mi Sheberach by Rabbi Shlomo Goren that has been accepted and continues to be recited every Sabbath and holiday in synagogues in Israel and around the world. An investigation of its origins and developments reveals that rabbis made changes to it in accordance with the evolving reality.

On the evening of October 29, 1956, the IDF, along with the British and French armies, initiated a military campaign known as the Sinai War (Operation Kadesh) by attacking Egypt. Newspaper headlines on November 2, 1956, reported the surrender of Gaza to IDF forces, the capture of El-Arish by an IDF armored brigade, and the destruction of 50 Egyptian planes by the air forces of England and France.

On that day, when there was also a report about the entry of Soviet tanks into Budapest, the capital of Hungary, a brief notice was published on the last page of the ha-Tsofeh newspaper, stating: A special Mi Sheberach prayer for the welfare of the IDF soldiers was composed by the Chief Rabbi of the IDF, Lieutenant Colonel Shlomo Goren, to be said in all synagogues on Shabbat after the Torah reading. Here is the full text of the prayer:

> "May He who blessed our fathers Abraham, Isaac, and Jacob, bless the soldiers of the Israel Defense Forces, who stand guard over our land and the cities of our God, from the border of Lebanon to the desert of Egypt and from the great sea to the approach of the Arava, on land, in the air, and at sea. May the Lord cause our enemies who rise against us to be struck down before them, may the Holy One, blessed be He, protect them and save them from all distress and hardship, from every plague and illness, and send blessing and success in all the works of their hands, place our enemies under their feet, and crown them with a crown of salvation and a diadem of victory, and fulfill in them the verse, 'For the Lord your God is the one who goes with you to fight for you against your enemies to save you,' and let us say, Amen."

Eight years after the establishment of the Israel Defense Forces, in the midst of the days of battle in the first war after the War of Independence, the Chief Military Rabbi, Rabbi Shlomo Goren, published the prayer he composed for the welfare of the IDF soldiers. The prayer, its text and content, were directly derived, as can be immediately identified, from

Praying for the Defenders of Our Faith

the Mi Sheberach prayer that is blessed by everyone who ascends to the Torah on Shabbat or on a holiday. The original central sentences in the prayer written by Rabbi Goren are "who stand guard over our land and the cities of our God, from the border of Lebanon to the desert of Egypt and from the great sea to the approach of the Arava, on land, in the air, and at sea. May the Lord cause our enemies to be struck down before them… place our enemies under their feet, and crown them with a crown of salvation and a diadem of victory." As we shall see, these sentences stirred many to dip their pen and add or change the original text.

While the Chief Military Rabbi was bustling in the IDF's combat zones in the Sinai Desert and the Gaza Strip, the Chief Rabbi of Israel, Rabbi Yitzhak HaLevi Herzog, sat in Jerusalem and also wrote a Mi Sheberach for the soldiers of the IDF. A first reading immediately highlights the similarities and differences between the two prayers. And thus wrote Rabbi Herzog, in a prayer that was unpublished but found by Rabbi Shmuel Katz, a researcher of the history of the Chief Rabbinate:

> "May He who blessed our fathers Abraham, Isaac, and Jacob, bless the soldiers of the Israel Defense Forces, standing guard over the land, to protect Zion, the home of our life. May He strengthen their hands and crown them with an everlasting crown, and in His mercy, may He soon grant us to see the complete redemption of Israel, and the fulfillment of the prophecies of the prophets of Israel in the days of old, for the peace of the entire world. Amen, Amen."

Without delving into the specific differences between the two prayers, one significant difference is evident from a first reading. The prayer written by Rabbi Goren is phrased in a way that expresses a personal connection between the writer and those being blessed, between the Chief Military Rabbi and the soldiers of the IDF. The prayer written by Rabbi Herzog (who may have even preceded in writing it, but there is no source for this and it was found attached to the Yizkor prayer for the fallen soldiers of the IDF in the Sinai War) does not, indeed, indicate estrangement, but it contains a significant faith component in the complete redemption. It deals with a future, intangible matter, unlike Rabbi Goren, who focuses on a concrete description of the reality for which the IDF soldiers need blessing. The identity of the writer – Rabbi Herzog – is evident from the linguistic connection between the prayer for the state's peace and this prayer. In the prayer for the state's peace, Rabbi Herzog wrote about the IDF soldiers "and a diadem of victory shall crown them," whereas in the prayer for the soldiers' welfare he wrote "and an eternal crown shall crown them."

Both prayers, those of Rabbi Herzog and Rabbi Goren, were not the first of their kind and continued a very long Jewish tradition of writing prayers for the welfare of Jewish soldiers, and also for non-Jewish soldiers. The space is too limited to describe and detail all the dozens – and probably hundreds – of prayers composed in all the Jewish diasporas following various wars, only a very small part of which have been researched and published.

Four main rationales were given for prayers for the welfare of soldiers, similar to the rationales for prayers for the peace of the kingdom. These rationales reflect the viewpoints prevalent among the sages of Israel on one hand, and the reality of Jewish life in the diaspora on the other. The four are:

Love – love of the land, love of the government. Fear – fear of the government. Duty – explicit instruction from the government. Closeness to the government – a need of Jewish life.

Moshe A. Shulvass in his article "Hebrew Prayers for the Success of Italy's Wars of Liberation" presents a Jewish prayer from 1859 for the success of the Italian fighters against Austria. The prayer is relatively

Praying for the Defenders of Our Faith

short and simple, and its content reveals the reasons for its composition and recitation:

> "Therefore, you who are great in counsel and mighty in deed, now that a spirit of wisdom and valor has been stirred in their hearts (of the Italians. Y.R.) to shake off the yoke of their oppressors and they have sent out the vanguard of their army to meet them, to drive them from the land and proclaim freedom to all its inhabitants, be with them to restore it to its former glory, as in ancient days and former years. ...Bless, O Lord, their army and deliver them from the hands of the tyrants for there is no restraint for you to save...be for them a refuge and a hiding place... And both, the kings Napoleon III, Emperor of the French and Vittorio Emanuele (as in the original. Y.R.), King of Piedmont, who in their good will sent heavily armed battalions to assist Italy, may rise like lions and prevail like young lions to subdue their enemies."

The Jews of Romania composed a completely different version. The prayer "For the Victory of Our Armies, the Armies of the Romanian Forces, on the Battlefield," was composed during the reign of Ferdinand I (1865-1927), King of Romania from 1914 until his death. Despite his family ties with Germany, during the years of the First World War, Ferdinand led Romania into cooperation with the Allies. Against this background, the prayer should be read, in which it is said, among other things:

> "O Lord of hosts! Teach our soldiers warfare and their arm for battle; give us your shield of salvation and your right hand shall support us; the armies of our land will

increase their valor on the field of slaughter, and you will give them the strength of your salvation and crown them with a crown of victory."

An earlier prayer was written in honor of Emperor Francis II, the last of the emperors of the Holy Roman Empire, who reigned from 1792 to 1806. Following the dissolution of the empire, he relinquished the title of "Emperor of the Holy Roman Empire" and retained the title of "Emperor of Austria" until his death in 1835.

A multitude of Jewish prayers for soldiers, not necessarily Jewish ones, can be found in the USA. It seems that only a few of these prayers have been collected to date. The multitude of wars involving the U.S. Army over the last century and the fact that Jewish soldiers serve in most units led to the continuous writing of new prayers. Thus, prayers were written in the last fifty years for fighters in Vietnam, the Gulf War, Afghanistan, and so on. Almost everywhere an American Jewish soldier set foot, a prayer was written. Nearly a quarter-century ago, Prof. Jonathan Dr. Sarna compiled some of these prayers that have been composed since the American War of Independence. An American military rabbi who participated on behalf of the U.S. Army in the Gulf War (1991) told me at a rabbis' conference in the USA held a few weeks ago that during the war he wrote a prayer for the Jewish soldiers in the unit he served in. We shall therefore suffice with one sentence from the prayer printed in the prayer books (not the special ones published by the U.S. Army):

> "Bless the soldiers of the United States Army, who risk their lives to bring peace to the land. Be for them a refuge and fortress, do not let their foot slip, strengthen their hands and fortify their spirit to thwart the counsel of the enemy and overthrow the government of arrogance."

Praying for the Defenders of Our Faith

At first glance, the question arises why Rabbi Goren felt the need to compose a prayer for the welfare of the IDF soldiers when they are included in the content of the prayer for the peace of the state:

> "Strengthen the hands of the defenders of our holy land and grant them, our God, salvation and crown them with a diadem of victory, and grant peace in the land and everlasting joy to its inhabitants."

In response to this, at least four main reasons can be identified that led the Chief Military Rabbi to write the prayer. The first reason was undoubtedly related to the non-acceptance (at least in those days) of the prayer for the peace of the state. An examination of the prayer books printed in the State of Israel in the first two decades of its existence reveals that the prayer for the peace of the state is very rare and was only printed in a few of them. In cases where it was printed, it was added as an appendix at the end of the prayer book and not as an organic part of the order of prayers. Thus, for example, until 1967, as far as I have checked, the prayer for the peace of the state was not printed in the IDF prayer book, including in the editions of the unified version edited by Rabbi Goren. Hence, the author had a reason to believe or estimate that a prayer for the welfare of the IDF soldiers would at least be accepted by the IDF soldiers.

The second reason is related to the Sinai War itself. The eight years from the War of Independence to 1956 were characterized by two main processes: mass immigration and economic austerity. The Sinai War, which continued the series of retaliatory actions in which small and elite units took part, brought back to the public consciousness in the small country with a population of no more than two and a half million, that security is of paramount importance, and that the IDF is the people's army. The mass mobilization of reservists and the blackout nights across the country certainly proved this. The prayer for the welfare of the IDF soldiers was thus a pure expression of faith in the major shift in public consciousness.

The third reason links the writing of the prayer to the Jewish tradition in the centuries before the establishment of the state. We have already shown how deeply rooted in Jewish communities was the consciousness, the need, the desire, and even the duty to express loyalty to the kingdom, the empire, or the state through prayer for the welfare of the fighting soldiers, in addition to the "Hanoten Teshuah" prayer that was said, and is still said, for the peace of the authorities and the rulers themselves: the king, the queen, the emperor, the president, and the prime minister.

A fourth, historical reason, relates to the days of the national struggle for the establishment of the State of Israel. It is worth elaborating on this a bit. Yechiel Eliash, the founder of the religious platoons in the Haganah, who established the Bnei Akiva movement and the Elitzur Sports Association, recounts in his book "A Vision Brought to Action," a document of great historical importance for the history of religious Zionism, about the days when the underground movement against the British rule was formed. In those days, he testifies, the question arose, "What is this war, and is it permissible for a Jew to endanger himself in this struggle?"

There were lengthy and comprehensive discussions about this, until it was decided by the rabbis that the questions related to the Jewish rebellion were political questions, and therefore it was agreed that they would be discussed between Rabbi Herzog, the Chief Rabbi of Israel, and Moshe Shapira, a member of the Jewish Agency's executive. "A few days later," writes Eliash, "I was summoned to Rabbi Herzog, who announced the halakhic decision that the war against the White Paper is a mitzvah war." Following this ruling, it was possible to provide answers to all the halakhic questions raised by those enlisted in the underground movement. Eliash later recounts that "with the increase

Praying for the Defenders of Our Faith

in enlistments in 1947, the Chief Rabbi Herzog wrote a letter to the Rabbinical Committee, and the Chief Rabbis composed a special prayer for the defenders":

> "Our Father in Heaven, protect us, awaken your might before the defenders of Israel and go out for our salvation, send us your help from the sanctuary and support us from Zion. Strengthen us and give us courage and make us successful in our war for the honor of Your name, for our people, and our land. Command Your angels for us to keep us from all harm, so that no soul shall be afflicted. Please, Lord, save us. Please, Lord, make us successful. Return us all to our places healthy, whole, and joyful in Your salvation. Return us, our Father, to Your Torah and bring us close, our King, to Your service, and bring us back in complete repentance before You. Please forgive, pardon, for the sins, iniquities, and transgressions that I have sinned, transgressed, and committed before You. Make us worthy of the complete redemption of Israel quickly, speedily, soon. Hear, O Israel, the Lord our God, the Lord is One. Blessed be the name of His glorious kingdom forever and ever. For Your salvation, I hope, O Lord."

This prayer, composed according to Eliash's testimony in 1947, apparently served the recruits for military service until the 21st of Sivan, when IDF soldiers first swore allegiance to the State of Israel. The day after, ha-Tsofeh newspaper reported on its front page that the recruits to the IDF in Tel Aviv were privileged to have the city's Chief Rabbi, Rabbi Isser Yehuda Unterman, who later became the Chief Rabbi of Israel, recite a Mi Sheberach prayer composed by the Chief Rabbinate for the enlisted for the peace of the conscripts:

"May He who blessed our fathers Abraham, Isaac, and Jacob, Moses and Aaron, David and Solomon, bless all our brothers and sisters who have enlisted for defense service in our holy land, who stand guard day and night to defend our people and the cities of our God with their lives, and fight bravely to prevent the destroyer from harming the settlements and points of habitation - because we pray for their welfare, the Holy One, blessed be He, will protect them from all trouble and distress and from every harm and disaster and will spread the canopy of our peace over them along with all their brethren, the house of Israel, and they shall merit to see the consolation of Zion and the ingathering of the exiles and the complete redemption, and may soon in our days be fulfilled the promise of the Lord written in our holy Torah 'And I will give peace in the land, and ye shall lie down, and none shall make you afraid', so may it be His will, and let us say Amen."

Rabbi Goren was undoubtedly aware of the two prayers that emerged from the beit midrash of the Chief Rabbinate, and he sought to establish the fact that the prayer for the welfare of the IDF soldiers is written by the Chief Military Rabbi, responsible for all religious affairs in the IDF, and he neither accepts nor seeks or expects the Chief Rabbinate to do the work of formulating the prayer for him.

To delve into Rabbi Goren's creative process in composing prayers (fourteen different prayers including a prayer before going to battle, a traveler's prayer for flying, a Nachem prayer for Tisha B'Av, etc.), one must turn to his article "The Traveler's Prayer for a Paratrooper in Light of Halakhah," in which he details the halakhic issues he faced while writing the prayer. This important article lays out a halakhic-thought

Praying for the Defenders of Our Faith

pattern that seeks to anchor the new prayer in prayers that have long been an integral part of the prayer book.

Rabbi Goren testifies that "it was clear from the outset that it was not possible to establish a new framework for this prayer (for the paratrooper) that had never existed before, since, since the sealing of the Talmud, we do not have the authority to innovate a formula for blessings to be said in the name and kingdom, which were not established by the Men of the Great Assembly, nor to change the formula of the blessings of our sages of blessed memory." Therefore, "we needed to find an old prayer framework sanctified from generation to generation that was established by the sages of the Talmud, and to fully express the dangers (of the various jumps)." The solution found was to adopt the prayer format of "Tefilat ha-Derekh" (The Traveler's Prayer) and adapt it to a renewed text for the paratrooper's prayer. This clarifies the decision to adopt the formula of Mi Sheberach for those who ascend to the Torah as a textual foundation for the prayer for the welfare of the IDF soldiers.

To the best of my knowledge, one change was made with the knowledge of Rabbi Goren in the prayer for the welfare of the IDF soldiers. The words "May the Holy One, blessed be He, protect them and save them from all trouble and distress…" were replaced during his tenure as Chief Rabbi of Israel, apparently with his knowledge, with the words "May the Holy One, blessed be He, protect and save our soldiers." Any other correction or change that was introduced, some by the Chief Rabbis at different times, was made, as far as I know, without his knowledge or even without his consent.

In January 1988, Rabbi Zalman Koitner, personal assistant to then-Ashkenazi Chief Rabbi Avraham Shapira, replied that "one should not 'polish' (as in the original) prayers that were established by genius rabbis," in response to a question asked about how the prayer for the welfare of the IDF soldiers can ignore the fact that IDF soldiers, following the

Lebanon War, are in Lebanese territory, risking their lives daily. Rabbi Koitner concludes his response by saying, "The words 'from the border of Lebanon' have a broader meaning than just a geographical one and are not referring only to a state border."

In 1993, the question of amending the prayer "from the border of Lebanon" was raised once again. Aharon Mezia wrote a letter to the Chief Rabbis, and in response, Rabbi Eitan Eisman, advisor to the Chief Rabbinate, replied on behalf of Chief Rabbis, suggested that after the words "to the approach of the Arava," the prayer should include the phrase "and in every place they are found."

Another attempt to make a change in the text of the prayer for the welfare of the IDF soldiers was sought by Rabbi Moshe Tzvi Neria, head of the Bnei Akiva yeshivot. During the Gulf War (1991), he wrote to Rabbi Eitan Eisman requesting that after the words "on land, in the air, and at sea" in the prayer for the welfare of the IDF soldiers, the words "and all the forces of the nations standing in the battles against our enemies" should be added. This was obviously referring to the coalition forces led by the U.S. that attacked Saddam Hussein's Iraq. In his letter, Rabbi Neria suggested that instead of the words "and save our soldiers," it should read "and save all soldiers."

Rabbi Neria's letter was annotated by hand that Rabbi Eliyahu agreed to the changes, but the changes were not incorporated into the prayer, and even if made by different worshippers, they were one-time and did not become part of the prayer text. Rabbi Neria's request should be seen in a broader context. The request itself suggests that the text of the prayer should be adapted to the current reality. This is probably the background for the changes Rabbi Neria sought to introduce in the prayer for the peace of the state, which were all rejected.

Five years later, in December, the issue of "From the Border of Lebanon" arose again. Chief Rabbi Eliyahu Bakshi-Doron responded to Rafi Dehan, a member of the Petah Tikva City Council, stating, "The proposed amended version should bless the soldiers of the Israel Defense Forces who stand guard over our land and the cities of our God, wherever they may be, on land, in the air, and at sea." Rabbi Bakshi-Doron's reasoning for the proposed amendment was that "there are soldiers serving in various places around the world who also deserve blessing."

The proposed amendment was not accepted as written. According to the letter, it was necessary to omit from the prayer the words "from the border of Lebanon to the desert of Egypt, and from the great sea to the approach of the Arava," which, as is well known, were not omitted. From the words of Rabbi Bakshi-Doron's response, it emerges that he was the one who added the words "wherever they may be," which have since, in many cases, become part of the text of the prayer.

A particularly sharp article against the introduction of changes in the prayer text was written by Rabbi Hillel Unsdorfer, rabbi of Kibbutz Beit Rimon, who gained fame during the Yom Kippur War when he was captured by the Egyptians along with other fighters of the Mezach stronghold and left the position with a Torah scroll in his hand. Rabbi Unsdorfer, who died in a road accident in the week he wrote his article, testifies that some changed the prayer text on their own accord and removed the word 'border': "Thus, they included in their prayer the soldiers operating within Lebanon and beyond the border." However, Rabbi Unsdorfer does not accept this approach of changing the prayer text to suit the changing reality and writes:

> "...there is no need to change the prayer at all. Instead, we should return to the prayer written in the prayer books and cancel the change made by "the meticulous ones." Then we will realize that the prayer encompasses

all the IDF soldiers wherever they may be. We only need
to understand what we are saying."

These and other amendments demonstrate how close the connection is between prayer and politics, how much worshippers or their spiritual leaders seek to integrate their political views into the prayer text. Moreover, it is a testament to how much rabbis, especially Chief Rabbis, do not insist on preserving the original text that was accepted and find themselves the right to make new in the established prayer, something they dare not do in the prayer practiced from time immemorial.

Another amendment proposed in the early 2000s (the exact year is unknown) originated in the study house of the Religious Kibbutz Yeshiva. In the prayer text distributed by the yeshiva, two sentences of great significance were added after the words "on land, in the air, and at sea." The basis of the addition can already be seen in the title of the prayer, which is "For the welfare of IDF soldiers and civilians in danger." The first sentence is familiar, and the second gave expression to the addition introduced in the title of the prayer. It was written: "On land, in the air, and at sea, and in every place they are, and all the civilians who are in the line of fire and at risk of attacks."

According to the amendment proposed by Rabbi Mordechai Eliyahu and incorporated in the prayer book Kol Eliyahu, it is said as follows (the additions are emphasized):

> "May He who blessed our holy fathers Abraham, Isaac, and Jacob, Moses and Aaron, bless, guard, protect, and elevate above and above [from Hanoten Teshuah] all the soldiers of the Israel Defense Forces… may plagues always fall before them… may our enemies be always subdued under them and may He crown them with a crown of salvation and a diadem of victory always. And

wherever they turn, may they be insightful and successful [from Hanoten Teshuah] and fulfill in them the verse…"

To the short prayer formulated by Rabbi Goren during the days of battle, Rabbi Eliyahu added seventeen words that significantly changed the original meaning and intent. The new prayer has a purpose for achieving practical intentions and results.

Above the last version brought, the words "Short Version" are printed, and indeed, subsequently, a "Long Version" is brought, also the creation of Rabbi Eliyahu. This version appears more as an eclectic collection of verses that do not constitute the creation of a stylized, polished, and genuinely meaningful prayer. I do not intend to dwell on the long text but to note that as early as the early 1960s, prayer texts for the welfare of the IDF soldiers were published, much longer than the one written by Rabbi Goren.

The credit for composing a long version of the Mi Sheberach prayer belongs to Professor Ezra Zion Melamed, as presented in his book Pirkei Minhag ve-Halakhah published in 1960. Professor Melamed, who was one of the prominent Talmud scholars at the Hebrew University, wrote several prayers and compiled them in his book. Among them is the "Al Hanissim" prayer for Independence Day. In the version of the prayer he wrote, he mentions the fighting soldiers, the wounded of battle, and the entire congregation of Israel. To overcome the issue of borders, he writes, "May He who blessed… bless all the young men of Israel standing in battle wherever they are, who sacrifice their lives and dedicate their youth for the conquest of the Land of Israel and the protection of its borders." And further: "Healer of all flesh, send complete healing to all the sick of His people Israel, including all the wounded and injured wherever they are…" Professor Melamed's version is simple, not particularly inspiring, but addresses the concerns close to the heart of anyone concerned for the soldiers' welfare. It can be assumed that in the synagogue his father founded in Jerusalem, the congregation prayed the version he composed.

I wish to conclude this initial discussion of the history of the prayer for the welfare of IDF soldiers by presenting prayers written by Rabbi Ovadia Yosef. More than any other rabbi in Israel, Rabbi Ovadia insisted on not endorsing any prayer book that did not include a prayer for the welfare of IDF soldiers, just as he insisted on not endorsing any prayer book that included a prayer for the welfare of the state. This was a principle for him, which I heard directly from him, and he did not deviate from it throughout the years since he completed his tenure as the Chief Rabbi.

In the late 1960s and 1970s, I worked as a young editor at Kol Israel while Rabbi Ovadia Yosef was Chief Rabbi of Tel Aviv. I edited the 'Halacha Corner' program. We outlined the new program with Rabbi Ovadia Yosef and encouraged listeners to submit halachic questions, but strictly on postcards, not in envelopes. Within two days, we found ourselves inundated with postcards, adding the task of sorting and selecting 3-6 questions for each program to our recording and editing duties. Our primary criterion for selecting questions was their current relevance; we aimed to avoid addressing purely theoretical questions, a preference shared by Rabbi Yosef. Our goal was to showcase Rabbi Yosef's extensive knowledge and the program's success hinged on the timeliness of the questions and answers. As a result, the number of people seeking guidance from Rabbi Ovadia Yosef, then Chief Rabbi of Tel Aviv, increased weekly. (Many have asked about the fate of the hundreds of questions that were not broadcast. In consultation with Rabbi Yosef, we decided to retain all the postcards at Kol Israel. As for their current whereabouts, I have no knowledge.) We maintained a recording routine at Rabbi Ovadia Yosef's home. His son David often joined. Rabbi Ovadia insisted on not knowing questions in advance.

Praying for the Defenders of Our Faith

The recordings were precisely 29 minutes. We used signals to stick to the schedule. Rabbi Ovadia's program aimed to serve the people and provide halachic rulings. And here a small note. I am often asked why, in my opinion, Rabbi Ovadia Yosef insisted that in every prayer book, to which he gave his 'approval,' the prayer for the peace of the IDF soldiers should appear, and it does. The answer to this, based on things he said, is found in reading the painful cases of more than two hundred and sixty IDF soldiers, "the brave and the valiant" in the words of the Rabbi, who fell in the Yom Kippur War and left their wives as agunot. Rabbi Yosef dealt with the greatest pain but found a halachic solution to free each of the agunot from her chained state. The direct recognition of the spirit, courage, and bravery of the IDF soldiers is what underlies his demand to say a prayer for the peace of the IDF soldiers every Sabbath and holiday.

Against this backdrop of extraordinary sensitivity, one can understand the special prayers he wrote both during Operation Cast Lead (2008-9) and during Operation Pillar of Defense (2012). In the prayer during Operation Cast Lead, he wrote, "Please, Lord, guard and protect us and all the soldiers of the Israel Defense Forces," and during Operation Pillar of Defense, he wrote in the prayer, "And all their enemies and pursuers shall fall before them, their swords shall enter their own hearts, and their bows shall be broken." These prayers were an addition to the prayer written by Rabbi Goren, which was accepted by Rabbi Ovadia Yosef, who adopted it and required its printing by anyone seeking his endorsement for a prayer book.

Upon examining the prayer for the welfare of the IDF soldiers written by Rabbi Shlomo Goren during the Sinai War and comparing it to the prayer that appears today in prayer books and is recited in many synagogues every Sabbath, one will find that the differences are noticeable but not significant in terms of content and intention. The two additions, the mention of "security forces" and the presence of IDF soldiers "wherever they may be," have long been accepted and welcomed additions.

I have no doubt that I have not presented all the changes that were made to the prayer in a one-time manner. The recitation of the prayer for the welfare of the Israel Defense Forces (IDF) soldiers is today a unifying and consolidating factor in the prayer order in synagogues, and even more so in the battlefield to where the IDF soldiers have recently returned.

Dr. Yoel Rappel has over 40 years of experience as a journalist and senior program editor at the Israel Broadcasting Authority. He also served as the director of the Elie Wiesel Archive at Boston University from 2009 to 2015. Dr. Rappel is a prolific author with 34 books translated into 8 languages. His latest work, *Politics and Prayer: Jewish Prayers for the Government and State of Israel*, was published in 2023 and includes a Foreword by Israeli President Isaac Herzog.

Uniting Humanity's Mission Amidst Unprecedented Times

Robert S. Reichmann

THIS WAR FEELS DIFFERENT. It's almost as if we've all – from the far-left to far-right – transformed into Israeli's overnight. Hasidim are praying in the streets of Boro Park, Anti-government activists are on the front lines, Haredim hold BBQs on the border, some in an unprecedented move have even enlisted. Four hundred thousand reservists have flocked back to Israel from all over the world, many of them not even called up, but of their own accord. There's something deep at play. It seems that we are engaged in a fight of divine origin, one not simply of Jewish people, but that of humanity itself.

The Torah cycle began alongside this war, and its teachings resonate more vividly than ever. It begins with the eternal struggle between good and evil, the soul versus ego. Noah's story reflects humanity's first devolution towards evil, where corruption had taken over humanity.

Although man's idealized objective is to influence humanity to mend its ways, Noah feels he cannot. Instead he focuses inward, protecting himself from the influences and elements.

We witnessed evil's resurgence on October 7th, beyond imagination, yet what's even more disturbing is how it found acceptance within our culture and institutions. Instead of embracing an internal path towards meaning and purpose, we've shifted our focus outward, embracing victimhood, blame, cancel culture, and even violence; a reflection of a society in decline, echoing the generation Noah. As with Noah, we must instead find our strength inward and upward, within our soul and from the creator.

The introduction of Abraham, the first Jew, marked a significant shift. He believed in God's presence in this world and introduced a moral imperative to humanity. His actions, standing up for his beliefs and putting others first, reflected his kindness and truth. It is those who can stand against evil while focusing on humanity, not themselves, who carry forward God's message.

Yet, even Abraham couldn't save everyone. Sodom and Gomorrah's corruption led them to another extinction event. Notably, one of their distinguishing factors, as noted by Rashi, is that the young led the old astray. This is echoed today, in a world tearing down monuments and claiming superiority over leaders' past. Again, the world lacks history's moral compass.

Our story revolves around our connection to the Creator, the corruption of our egos, and the quest for reconciliation. Morality, left unchecked, descends into chaos, infecting anyone. We must maintain moral clarity and take responsibility for our world to survive.

In today's dark world, it's easy to feel helpless and hopeless. But as with Abraham, we must stand up for what's right and think beyond ourselves.

Praying for the Defenders of Our Faith

The late Rabbi Lord Jonathan Sacks said "to be a Jew is to know that over and above history is the task of memory." We must recall the past not simply as a matter of lineage, but as a living directive. Our mission is to recall our forefathers' memory, accept their responsibility, and perpetuate their legacy.

It is this same fight that is being waged on the front lines by the IDF and by the entire Jewish people around the world. Israel may be battling terrorists, but the war is for nothing less than for humanity's itself. We will survive, but our mission is to uphold our forefathers' memory, accept their responsibility, and perpetuate their legacy. In a world of chaos, we are to be a light in the darkness. As Jewish people, we fight not for ourselves but for the soul of humanity.

Robert S. Reichmann is the President of Reichmann Rothschild, a family office focused on investment and philanthropic activities. He serves on the boards of Lighthouse Credit Union, Canadian Friends of Jerusalem College of Technology (JCT), and Kama-Tech, an Ultra-Orthodox High-Tech Entrepreneur Acceleration Program. He holds an MBA from Bar-Ilan University. His late grandfathers, Albert Reichmann and Kurt Rothschild, were two of the leading Jewish philanthropists and supporters of Torah causes in the past generation.

Prayer for Our Heroic Soldiers

Yitzchak Avi Roness

As I sit and write these words my beloved son is fighting in Gaza alongside his comrades. He is there with cousins and close friends, other soldiers from our community and his yeshiva, his entire battalion and brigade.

My heart is filled with various emotions that intermingle and collide…

At times, my heart bursts with immense pride and admiration, and I am filled with optimism in the face of the soldiers' heroic spirit and sense of mission.

At other times, feelings of tension and anxiety prevail, and from my heart emerges a plea:

> May they return in peace…

As I try to collect my thoughts on the nature of this prayer, here are some that come to mind:

Praying for the Defenders of Our Faith

There is a prayer that bursts forth and ascends, emerging from the walls of a person's heart. This prayer breaks out from within, and rises straight to the heavens.

And there is an inverse prayer:

A prayer seeking to break through the heart's walls, originating outside of one's heart, trying to find a way in. A prayer that seeks to influence the heart, to reshape it anew.

There is a prayer in which the heart's emotions swell and rise, flooding and overflowing.

The purpose of the prayer is to serve as a mouthpiece for the heart.

To take these emotions and lift them heavenward.

'נשא לבבנו אל כפים אל אל בשמים' (איכה ג, מא)

"We lift our hearts with our hands to God in the heavens."

In this prayer, the mind serves the heart.

It patiently listens to emotion and tries to put the confused feelings into words.

The words of the prayer transport the painful and perplexed emotions.

They bring order to them and direct them towards the heavens.

And there are times when the mind seeks to guide and control the heart.

(What is appropriate to feel? Is it right to cry?)

The clear thought,

balanced and measured,

seeks to guide the heart,

to direct the emotions and determine their nature.

There is a prayer where the mouth is the heart's spokesperson.

A prayer that clarifies and defines, organizes the chaos, gives presence and place to fears and anxieties, to hopes and dreams.

And there is a prayer that is an inner, slow and difficult labor.

"A labor of the heart."

Not an attempt to express what already exists within me, but a desire to reshape myself anew, to change.

To improve and ascend.

"Create in me a clean heart, O God, and renew a right spirit within me."

So it is with prayer in general, and so it is with the prayer we say for the soldiers.

One cannot compare the prayer of a mother whose son is fighting on the front lines , who cannot sleep for fear, who has lost her appetite, and cannot concentrate to the prayer of the philosopher or of the head of the yeshiva, governed by intellect and ideas.

The mother's prayer comes from a tumultuous heart, she pours out what weighs on her heart, lays her pain and worries, her hopes and heart's desires before the One in the heavens.

She asks that her pure heart be accepted before Him as a sacrifice, perhaps He will show compassion and mercy.

But there is also an inverse prayer.

One that descends from above.

That emerges from a higher point – from clear knowledge and pure wisdom, and seeks to bring a new spirit, strength and valor, down into the heart.

A prayer that emanates from an understanding of the magnitude of the event,

of its importance,

its sanctity,

and from there seeks to establish new chambers,

Praying for the Defenders of Our Faith

new realms,
within one's heart.

✦ ✦ ✦ ✦ ✦

For those who seek to elevate their hearts and direct their feelings, let's dedicate a few words to more deeply appreciate the virtues of the IDF soldiers, and our duty of praying for their well-being:

"No one else in the world is worthy of standing in their midst."

The destruction arrived as a result of baseless hatred, and as such, it will be rectified, when the time comes, by baseless love.

V'Ahavta L'reiacha Kamocha

Love thy neighbor as yourself.

The love of one person for another,

of each person for their fellow.

The readiness of a person to give of themselves for the sake of others.

My own concern for the well-being of those beside me.

For their life and their welfare.

This type of selfless love, thank God, exists in various forms of kindness we see around us, but among these concrete acts of love, the soldiers of the IDF stand out uniquely as a shining concretization of selfless love. For the greatest gift one can give is the willingness to sacrifice one's life, to give one's very existence.

There is kindness that is given to an individual in need of help and support, and there is love and kindness from which the entire nation benefits, the community as a whole.

There is kindness in helping a person cope with life's difficulties, and there is kindness in granting the gift of life itself.

During the Yom Kippur War, the head of the Mir Yeshiva in Jerusalem, Rabbi Chaim Shmuelevitz spoke of the duty to pray to the Holy One, blessed be He.

The main message he developed was the need to strengthen oneself in Torah study and prayer, with the understanding that this fortification would provide the strength we need to with stand and overcome the enemy.

Towards the end of his talk, Rabbi Shmuelevitz began discussing another matter:

the virtue of the soldiers on the front lines, and our collective duty to recognize and appreciate their sacrifice.

Rabbi Shmuelevitz explained that since the soldiers are endangering their lives for the people of Israel, it would be appropriate to equate their virtue with that of *tzaddikim* known as *Harugei Malchut* the 'martyrs of the kingdom', whom the Talmud states are of an incomparably high stature. And so Rabbi Shmuelevitz continued: "I say of those who sacrifice their lives for our salvation, that no one in the world can stand in their midst; and our obligation to pray for them is boundless..." (Sichos Mussar, p. 157).

Similarly, the Pele Yoetz wrote that one who saves people from death is "as if he upheld the entire Torah." He further added, "There are many among the children of Israel who may appear outwardly as empty vessels, but they hold on to the commandment of saving Israel, and through this they surpass, and transcend, the sages and great ones of Israel" (Pele Yoetz, entry 'Rescue').

Exactly so...

And let us conclude with a prayer.

A prayer for the peace of our soldiers, and deep-seated faith that their self-sacrifice, and the profound unity among them, will serve as an example to the entire nation:

Of care and mission.

Of love and concern.

A grand message of selfless love, through which we shall be worthy of redemption!

Rabbi Dr. Yitzchak Avi Roness is a lecturer in various colleges (Michlala, Orot, Givat Washington) and a communal Rav in Beit Shemesh.

A Frontline Soldier's Reflection on the Mi Sheberach Prayer, One Month After October 7

Hananel Rosenberg

SIMCHAT TORAH ON OCTOBER 7ᵀᴴ 2023, in the morning hours at the synagogue. The distressing news begins to arrive, and one by one, friends leave the prayer: one to answer the phone he carries with him every Saturday and holiday, the second is called by his wife to answer the home phone, the third and fourth are friends in the same reserve unit and are updated together. Simultaneously, the sirens start. The prayer for the safety of the IDF soldiers, which had been said after the eagerly awaited Torah reading, takes on a special, poignant meaning.

Praying for the Defenders of Our Faith

In my case, the call arrived during the afternoon. I was asked to personally call every soldier in my platoon. Some of them don't respond due to the holiday, while others do respond and instantly grasp the gravity of the situation, with their spouses in the background, some of whom are crying.

This isn't my first emergency call up to reserve service. We were called urgently to the reserves during Operation Protective Edge in 2014, the Second Lebanon War in 2005, Operation Defensive Shield in 2002, and with the outbreak of the Second Intifada in September 2000. But this time, the atmosphere was different. The feeling that the home front has become a battlefield, that the home itself has turned into the front line. That the prayer for the well-being of the IDF soldiers is replaced by a prayer for the safety of civilians, for the well-being of the communities around Gaza. And the mobilization of the soldiers followed suit: fighters who had been released from active reserve duty almost a decade ago called and pleaded to be re-enlisted. The feeling that the home is burning, and no one can sit idly by.

The military purpose of our unit, the soldiers of the Givati Brigade, is to be a security battalion. This is how we operated during the first two weeks when we spread out in southern settlements, cities, and streets where the massacre took place. But afterward, we were transferred under the responsibility of the Home Front Command and called to a different type of work.

Among the attendees of the music festival, which turned into a massacre of violence and bloodshed, there are still several young individuals who remain missing, and despite our best efforts to identify them, their fates remain unknown. The participants at the festival scattered far and wide, both by car and on foot, and the terrorists followed them. Even as I write these lines a month later, my unit and I continue to engage in the intense and exhausting task of searching in the vicinity of the festival and for kilometers around it, from dawn until dusk. Our mission is to find any remnants or items that might assist in locating the missing individuals, provide identifications, or gather information that will help us understand their fate. At times, we find something and mark it for the identification teams following in our footsteps, concluding the day with the recitation of the Kaddish.

The morale is unwavering, despite the complex task at hand, and physical endurance intertwines with psychological resilience. Thus, the prayer for the well-being of the IDF soldiers returns to its place, but takes on a different meaning: "May the Almighty protect our soldiers from every hardship and adversity, and from any affliction and illness." Both physical challenges and psychological distress are encompassed, God forbid.

In the 1950s, the IDF (Israel Defense Forces) took on some of its roles in assisting with the development of the frontier and deploying soldiers for construction, agriculture, and settlement tasks. In the past two decades, as we have discovered, the IDF has been involved in establishing a new command. Alongside the existing regional commands – Northern, Central, and Southern – a new regional command has been established: the Home Front Command. Its role is to focus on supporting the civilian sector, rescuing and saving lives, and assisting in the rapid recovery of the home front after wartime conflict.

To conclude, I offer the following words of the Mi Sheberach for the IDF soldiers, "mi-gvul halevanon ve'ad midbar mitzrayim umin hayam hagadol at levo ha'aravah bayabasha ba'avir uvayam" / "From the Lebanon border to the Egyptian desert, from the Great Sea to the Aravah," but not only within these borders, but no less – what's in between them. "Bayabasha ba'avir uvayam" / "On land, in the air, and at sea," but also in cities, villages, settlements, and agricultural farms; in the communities surrounding Gaza, at the music festival, among the burning cars, and amidst piles of tents and the clothing they left behind. And thus, the scripture is fulfilled in them: "For the Lord your God, who goes with you to fight for you against your enemies," but not only against your enemies, but also to uplift, support, and strengthen your spirits and settlements, because "the entire land is Your domain." "le-Hoshiya Etchem, ve-Nomar Amen," To Save You, and Let Us Say Amen.

Dr. Hananel Rosenberg is a Senior Lecturer of Communication at Ariel University, where he focuses his research on the psychosocial consequences of smartphone usage among various age groups, with a particular emphasis on children and adolescents. He is also the son of the late Professor Shalom Rosenberg, who sadly passed away earlier this year.

The Prayers of the Mothers and Fathers of 'hayeladim' on Israel's Frontlines

Elisheva Rosman-Stollman

ONE OF THE MORE BIZARRE experiences of having a son in a combat unit in the IDF, is being part of WhatsApp groups with other parents. In some ways, its similar to being in the group we had for our youngest daughter when she was in kindergarten and to the groups we have had as parents of elementary and high school students. These groups are a platform for parents to discuss buying group gifts at the end of training phases, coordinating visits to bases, thinking out loud: can we also collect money for the soldier whose parents are not in Israel so that he will have the same gift as everyone else? What can be done regarding a derelict officer?

Praying for the Defenders of Our Faith

We did this before, when they were kids – just exchanging "officer" for "teacher"; "soldier" for "child."

But it is also different. Parents discuss them as 'hayeladim' – the children. But they are young men. Carrying rifles. Learning how to use hand grenades, mortars, explosives.

Since October 7th, both the group comprising parents of our son's reserve unit (a relic of their regular service resurrected in honor of the current war), as well as the group for parents of our son who is still in active service, have become a micro cosmos of what Israeli society is experiencing. Parents can worry together, instead of being alone with depressing thoughts. They can share information, ideas and speculations regarding 'hayeladim', who are very much not children at this point in time: where are they? What are they doing? Do they have their phones? Is everyone safe? Who is wounded?

Interestingly, besides the usual messages concerning practical issues (what about laundry? What is the food situation? How about supplies and military gear? Have we all paid for the gift sent to the injured at the hospital?), one of the main topics that arises again and again in the group is supplying protection for sons in uniform in the form of prayer: hafrashat challah, collective Tehillim, a Torah scroll being written with a letter for every soldier, finding tzitzit for soldiers who want them.

And individual prayer. For parents, it seems that prayer has become something to focus on. It is a way to "do something" when we can do little more than worry. It also seems that all parents – observant or secular – attach importance to prayer at this time. Specifically, to prayer naming soldiers by their given name(s) and the name of their mother, as done traditionally when one is in need of God's protection and help. Ilai David ben Naomi. Yinon Ben-Tzion ben Rachel. Shira bat Shimrit.

In this sense, the fact that a specific prayer for soldiers is said in synagogues on Shabbat since the war began, is significant. Both for parents, and for the soldiers themselves. It is seen as providing tangible protection for the soldiers in battle: there seem to be no atheist parents in foxholes.

The Mi Sheberach said in all synagogues for soldiers in the days since October 7th has also become an emotional crescendo every Shabbat. Over the years, since it is an accepted staple in Israeli Orthodox communities' prayer, the Mi Sheberach for soldiers of the IDF has naturally become rather routine; like other parts of the service we take for granted. In the current situation, it has evolved. Many congregations choose to sing the prayer together. In a congregation in the town of Efrat, where women read the prayer (not the chazzan), a mother of soldiers was asked read the Mi Sheberach on Simchat Torah itself, even before the full extent of the attack was known. Her son was called up during services and left for the front. When her voice broke reading the Mi Sheberach, the entire congregation began to cry.

This continues to happen every Shabbat in congregations all over Israel. The prayer becomes a focal point for everyone's anxiety, hopes and fears. Everyone has a family member, a friend, a neighbor, in uniform. The general feeling is one of sending collective protection to soldiers and that the power of the community is concrete.

The prayer for the release of hostages is usually said immediately after the Mi Sheberach for soldiers – adding to this feeling.

Dr. Elisheva Rosman-Stollman, PhD, is a senior lecturer and Deputy Chair of the Political Studies Department at Bar Ilan University. Her research focuses on civil-military relations in Israel, religious soldiers, and religious feminism. Her work has been published in notable academic journals, including Armed Forces & Society, Nations and Nationalism, Religions, and Israel Affairs

What Good is Communal Prayer?

Tamar Ross

In relating to the urgency and importance of communal prayer during the current military crisis, I prefer to begin with some philosophical reflections regarding the efficacy of prayer in general.

For starters, I will cite the confession of a former colleague who, several days before dying of cancer, declared: "I don't pray because I believe in God; I believe in God in order to pray." These words, that effectively divorce the significance of prayer from any guarantee that such activity will affect the outcome of our plea in any supernatural sense, obviously disassociate from a popular line of apologetics that is often invoked in response to failed appeals to divine mercy and justice, especially in cases of national calamity that appear so obviously undeserved. Such attempts at preserving the concept of divine beneficence rely on the notion that we cannot know God's ways, or – in a slightly different vein – that He is not in the position of a servant, duty-bound to carry out his boss's demands;

even though He hears our prayers, sometimes His answer is "no."¹ But my primary interest in quoting my friend's statement in this context is not merely to reject this variety of theodicy, but rather to relate to a far more radical implication that it bears: namely, that the very notion of prayer, along with all its accompanying theological baggage, is only a product of human need, rather than a supernatural means of alleviating it.²

In conceding that all our theistic God-talk and appeal to a transcendent Being controlling worldly affairs from without is a narrative that lacks factual grounding, I appear to be aligning fully with

1   Both these arguments gained currency as responses to the failure of mass prayers to prevent two heart-wrenching tragedies in Israel. The first instance was the murder of Nachshon Waxman in 1994, as detailed by Debbie Stone of NCSY, in "When God Says No: The Story of Nachshon Wachsman," available at the NCSY Website (https://staff.ncsy.org/education/material/Gq9X0SuNrI/when-god-says-no-the-story-of-nachshon-wachsman). The second event occurred in 2015, when Naftali Fraenkel, along with two other Israeli teenagers, were also tragically murdered, and reflected upon in "5 Years Ago, Naftali Fraenkel Was Killed By Terrorists. His Mother Looks Back On A Journey From Grief To Joy," as reported by the Jewish Telegraphic Agency (28 June 2019), available here (https://www.jta.org/2019/06/28/israel/5-years-ago-this-month-naftali-fraenkel-was-killed-by-terrorists-his-mother-marked-the-tragic-milestone-with-a-joyous-moment).

2   As Rabbi Menachem Froman, a contemporary and unconventional Israeli thinker, activist, and mystic who also died prematurely of cancer, provocatively put it: "Sometimes I believe that the entirety of theology, all religions, and every discourse on God are birthed from the need to rationalize the innate human act of prayer. An individual prays and seeks to understand to whom he's praying, why he's praying, and the essence of his actions. To contextualize this, he identifies it as 'God' and crafts an all-encompassing religious perspective around it. Yet, at its very core, everything is about prayer." See his collection of aphorisms in Menachem Froman, *Making Hasidim Laugh* (Jerusalem: Amutat Hai Shalom, 2016), 160 (my translation from the Hebrew).

reductionist of an atheistic bent. Members of that camp are quick to note that skepticism regarding the objective efficacy of prayer has already been amply confirmed by various scientific experiments carefully designed to eliminate the influence of random variables, such as age, sex, health, or differences between groups who are aware that others are praying for them and those who are not.[3] But when such hard-nosed views are voiced even by self-professed religious believers (myself included), sympathy for this more naturalist orientation might be taken to suggest that even when stripped of its commonly held expectations of heavenly intervention, prayer is nevertheless a crucial and powerful tool – albeit of a different sort.

When reciting Psalms or prayers geared more specifically towards the current crisis in Israel, we may ostensibly be engaged in seeking divine intervention after the fashion of earlier times. While such efforts often appear superstitious and outdated to the scientifically inclined, religious believers might argue otherwise. In turning to the sanctified vocabulary of the past, humbly acknowledging our vulnerability, or seeking the compassion of a heavenly Father in order to protect the state of Israel and its Defense Forces against their enemies on strength of His historic promise to our ancestors, religious advocates might contend that we are in effect declaring the moral justice of our cause, galvanizing the traditional forces of national unity in order to protect it and seizing the opportunity to publicly declare our indebtedness gratitude to the Israeli army for their unbelievable sacrifices on our behalf. The very collectivity of these acts fortifies a sense of community and strength. But beyond this naturalist, common-sense understanding, I would like to introduce a more esoteric view of the virtue of collectivity that might be worthy of consideration.

3   See, for example, Jonathan Jong, *Experimenting with Religion: The New Science of Belief* (Oxford: Oxford University Press, 2023), 4-8.

According to this view,[4] while the act of prayer ostensibly consists of appealing to a higher Other whose nature is inscrutable and whose methods of governance often appear to lack clear sense, the natural human impulse to pray reflects an inbuilt yearning of the soul to tap into a far more expansive view of the divine as all that exists. This vision of Ultimate Being as undifferentiated infinity is admittedly unattainable so long as we are bound by the prison of our imagination, which lends credence to the false view of ourselves as subjects, separate and distinct.[5] Understood in this light, the theistic picture of God as the all-powerful Other is a necessary stepping-stone in bridging the gap between our illusory sense of selfhood and the unattainable vision of God as all that there is.[6] So long as we retain the misleading view of our own particularity, we feel the need to speak and communicate our needs, wishes, hopes, fears, senses of gratitude, or wonder, to a divine Other.[7] Under such conditions, that infinite state of being in which the illusory borders between natural and supernatural visions of reality are virtually obliterated remains beyond our grasp. But the greater our willingness to

---

4   As articulated in various versions of modern Kabbalah but relying here primarily on the formulations of Rabbi A.I. Kook.

5   Rav Kook, *Orot hakodesh* II (Mosad Harav Kook, 1985), 399-401; *Shmoneh Kevatzim* I, Kovetz Aleph (Jerusalem: Mosad ha-Rav Kook, 1999), par.65 (Hebrew).

6   Ibid.

7   See, for example, Rav Kook's introduction to his commentary on the Hebrew prayerbook – *Olat Reayah* I (Mosad Harav Kook 1985), p.11, par. 2 where he poetically describes the human soul as "constantly engaged in prayer, incessantly flying and yearning for its lover," suggesting that such yearning is an inevitable feature of the human condition, whose constancy in the human soul is revealed during the time of actual prayer, "like a flower that opens its petals out to the dew."

move our prayers beyond the particular to the general, the greater our ability to merge between the two.[8]

As opposed to the more commonplace defense of communal prayer in times of stress, the mystic view presented here doesn't rely on rational argument. It rests rather on the willingness of the praying individual to open herself out to an existential moment of yearning to connect heaven and earth, ideal and real, in light of a vision of Ultimate Reality that defies any distinction between miracle and nature, because in that reality all that is possible already exists.[9] Despite the theistic vocabulary, the moment of opening outward itself is the true performance of faith and a step towards its realization. While secularists, religious Zionists of various stripes, and haredim may still differ regarding the concrete role of present-day Israel in realizing the Messianic dream, attaching our personal fears, hopes, and aspirations to the urgent real-world interests of our national collective necessarily broadens the scope of our self-perception, thereby arguably lending an added measure of force to our supplications.

I must confess that I personally feel ambivalent regarding this esoteric approach, which – amongst other features – offers a new channel for explaining the added power that Jewish tradition has attributed to giants of the spirit in times of crisis.[10] On the one hand,

---

8   See, for example, *Shmoneh Kevatzim* I, Kovetz 1, par. 674; kovetz 8, par. 87). In accordance with this line of thought, Rav Kook preferred to relate requests for individual blessings to matters more general concern. In a similar vein, Rav Kook's son explains the halakhic requirement to build synagogues with windows in light of the need to include the outside world in our prayers.

9   Rav Kook, *Orot hakodesh* III, 26, 27, 31.

10 For a contemporary example in this connection, see Smadar Cherlow, *The Tzaddiq is the Foundation of the World* (Ramat Gan: Bar Ilan University Press, 2012), 52-55 (Hebrew), and her account of the correspondence

the theological underpinning of this view (i.e., understanding that our theistic conceptions of God as Other are an inescapable consequence of our illusory sense of ourselves as individuated beings) appeals to me. On the other hand, I have yet to be convinced of any observable "homeostatic" connection between this-worldly well-being and the degree to which we, or our spiritual heroes, overcome any illusory sense of individuation. But I also am painfully aware of the fact that we humans have barely begun to scratch the surface of possible modes of existence and consciousness that recent discoveries of neuroscience, astrophysics, space technology and artificial intelligence are now opening, and boggle the mind in terms of their potential significance and ramifications.[11] In the last resort, like my friend whom I cited at the beginning, I pray because I need to; bound by the prison of my imagination, I instinctively address my thoughts,

> between R. Shalom Harlap and R. Kook (alluding to the former's bizarre visionary experience at the Western Wall and sense of lost opportunity to join forces with the expansive soul powers of his master), testifying to the secret belief animating R. Kook's and his circle of disciples regarding the power of select individuals to raise the welfare of their generation at large.

11 Worthy of note in this connection is pragmatist William James' observation of the extent to which telepathy (or similar challenges to currently regnant views of mind-matter relations) are ignored simply because under present conditions, taking such evidence seriously would severely undermine prevailing notions regarding the uniformity of nature and "all sorts of other things without which scientists cannot carry on their pursuits." As against this, James suggests that were we shown something that we as scientists might *do* with such evidence, we might not only have examined it, but "even have found it good enough," see William James, "The Will to Believe," in *Essays in Popular Philosophy* (New York: Dover Publications, 1956), 10-11. The writings of Rabbi A.I. Kook are similarly replete with references to the fluidity of scientific method, and his conviction that this fluidity is both a cause and effect of our varying self-conceptions as spiritual beings and agents. Of particular interest in the context of our discussion is his penchant for breaking down binaries between spirit and matter, and the role that his unique interpretation of Zionism plays in this context.

hopes, and wishes outward to some hypothetical Other. While the exact nusakh handed down to me by tradition doesn't always precisely match my inner feelings or convictions, this is the language of my community and – if only in terms of its declarative value, a shared sense of obligation to pray for this community can be an indispensable source of comfort and strength.

Professor Tamar Ross is Professor Emerita of the Department of Jewish philosophy at Bar-Ilan University.

A Personal Reflection on Faith, History, and the Prayer for the Peace of IDF Soldiers

Elyakim Rubinstein

A s I began writing these words, the prayer for the IDF soldiers' peace, performed by Lt. Col. Shai Abramson, Chief Cantor of the Israel Defense Forces, played in the background. In this book, my friend Dr. Yoel Rappel and other contributors note that the prayer was composed by Chief Military Rabbi Shlomo Goren. Rabbi Goren, who would later ascend to the rank of general and subsequently become the Ashkenazic Chief Rabbi of Israel, crafted this prayer following the Sinai Campaign in 1956. Over time, this prayer has become a staple of the Shabbat liturgy in synagogues in Israel and around the world. During times of war, the prayer is recited daily with fervor. Over the years, minor amendments were made to refine the text without changing its essence. Blessings were added for the security forces, who work hand in hand with the IDF day and night. Shai Abramson sings it in a melody composed by Dubi Zeltzer.

There are two recent prayers that constantly resonate within me: the prayer for the peace of the state, which Dr. Rappel researched and Professor Avraham Steinberg also wrote about, and the prayer for the welfare of IDF soldiers. I am the son of parents whose lives symbolize the history of the Jewish people during the Holocaust and our national rebirth. My father endured the loss of his family in the Holocaust: his parents, sisters, brother, nephew, aunts, uncles, and cousins, all of whom, along with their entire town's residents, were mercilessly executed and buried in a mass grave in Belarus in 1942. My mother was part of a delegation that brought to Israel in 1945 the exiles from Mauritius, whom the British had prevented from entering the country in 1940 and relocated to the tropical island where many of them died. My mother also volunteered for the IDF during the War of Independence as the first head nurse of the military hospital Tel HaShomer, now known as Sheba (named after its first commander). I was a baby of about a year old; both my parents were drafted, and I was left with an aunt and uncle. Our family, like many, was deeply intertwined with the IDF's foundation. Later on, my cousin Cpl. Avraham Alberson (Ben Porat) fell in action in the Navy in 1952, and he, along with his comrades, remains missing. 2nd Lt. Nimrod Harari, whose father, my cousin Yoske, fought in the Palmach, fell in action in Sinai in 1973. Friends and children of friends have fallen over the years. Now, even a grandchild of friends has fallen in this most recent war, a conflict suddenly thrust upon us. And conversely, our four daughters served in the IDF in the education corps and saw up-close the diverse Israeli society, mobilized side-by-side. Now our sons-in-law, many of our relatives and friends, their daughters and sons, are called up for the campaign.

There is, therefore, in my eyes a special significance, always and especially in these days, to the prayer for the peace of the IDF soldiers. The words "guarding our land and the cities of our God," and also "subdue our enemies beneath them and crown them with a crown of salvation and a diadem of victory," and the verse in Deuteronomy (20:4) "For the Lord your God is the one who goes with you to fight for you against your enemies to save you," which corresponds with the verse (Psalms 18:38) "I will pursue my enemies and overtake them; I will not turn back until they are destroyed" – all these resonate deeply with all of us.

On faith: The merciless slaughter of 1,200 Jews, simply for being Jews, in barbaric brutality without mercy for the old and young alike, naturally raises questions of faith. These questions echo the soul-searching that arose after the Holocaust, even if on a different scale. How can one return to the regular order of faith in light of these events? There are no easy answers. We are not privy to the divine ledger, neither here nor in other circumstances, and we remain without words when faced these questions. Some will call it "hidden countenance" (hester panim). Responding to those who question remains a challenge. Yet, maybe there's a glimmer of solace found in the annals of history, in that national and sacred memory etched into our very DNA. It's an enduring commitment to the Divine and the 'Shema Yisrael,' a strength that surpasses any one of us, not seeking the unknown — embodying the timeless spirit of Israel. The prayer for the welfare of IDF soldiers also carries encouragement in this space, because it connects a harsh earthly reality and heart's heaviness with an entanglement of hope, in the unity of the soldiers regardless of their worldview or background, and with it, the general moving unity of the broader community in these trying times.

Justice Prof. Elyakim Rubinstein was appointed to The Supreme Court of Israel in 2004, and held served as the Deputy President from 2015 until his retirement in 2017. He had previously served as the position of Attorney General of Israel from 1997 to 2004. Serving in a variety of capacities in the Ministry of Foreign Affairs, he played a pivotal role in crafting Israel's historic peace agreements with Egypt and Jordan.

Shake Off the Dust, Arise

Haim Sabato

A HARSH AND CRUEL BLOW FROM the enemy has struck us. Deep sorrow. Grief, pain, and distress pierce the heart, almost unbearably. Eyes filled with tears. Added to this is the anger and deep disappointment from the oversights, and the sadness that our prayers and pleas during the Days of Awe did not break the barriers of heaven, and the joy of the Torah turned to mourning.

But we must remember: sadness is not depression, and pain is not despair. Sadness and pain can be building blocks, while despair silences and depression destroys. A person must harbor deep pain and sorrow, coupled with the ability to shake off the dust, revealing immense spirit. Not a strength derived from foolish arrogance or the pride of physical power, but one that emerges from the inner spirit of our people. A strength stemming from deep faith.

Praying for the Defenders of Our Faith

Especially when facing evil forces, mental fortitude is essential for victory. Let our hearts not waver; we should not tremble or be disheartened.

I remember myself as a young tankist during the Yom Kippur War. When we reached the Suez Canal and faced the dire situation, though initially shocked, filled with anger, disappointment, and pain, we soon channeled these emotions, drawing immense inner strength. United, we resolved to fight with all our might, fearless and undeterred, to save our people and subdue our enemies. It was this strength that sustained us.

A person is tested in times of crisis, as is a nation. In challenging times, one can either sink into the depths of despair or rise like a lion from the dust, humbly drawing strength and vigor from our inner spirit, our morals, and our faith. In every generation, ruthless enemies have sought to destroy us, but the Rock of Israel and our Redeemer has delivered us from their hands.

A tearful eye weeps, and a courageous heart.

Our hearts are torn with the pain of our brothers in the south, but our spirit is resilient, ready to shake off the dust, to fight, to triumph, and together uplift our beloved nation in peace and serenity.

Shake off the dust and rise, wear your glorious garments, my people.

Rabbi Haim Sabato, an Israeli Rosh Yeshiva and author of Aleppan-Syrian descent, is a Yom Kippur War veteran and co-founder of the Hesder yeshiva in Ma'ale Adumim, Yeshivat Birkat Moshe.

Rabbi Haim Sabato delivered these remarks at Yeshivat Birkat Moshe, on October 10, 2023, and they are presented here in English translation with his permission.

The Mi Sheberach for IDF Soldiers: Division Turns to Unity

Dov Schwartz

THE PRAYER FOR THE WELL-BEING of IDF soldiers and security forces is mainly recited in synagogues of Modern Orthodoxy and Religious Zionism. Some suffice with its recitation, while others say it adjacent to the Prayer for the State of Israel. Paradoxically, the prayer for the well-being of IDF soldiers and security forces, which expresses concern, empathy, love, and responsibility towards fighters and combat support personnel risking their lives, highlights the religious divide of Jewish society. This prayer is not recited both by secular individuals who are not traditional, nor by many ultra-Orthodox communities. The former group simply is not a praying community, and the latter, while being a praying community, primarily omits the Mi Sheberach for IDF soldiers and security forces because this prayer indirectly mandates recognition of the democratic and liberal State of Israel. According to the moderate ultra-Orthodox view, the State of Israel is an entity no different from other countries, hence they are indifferent towards it and do not recognize it. According to the extreme ultra-Orthodox view, the State of Israel is an affront to Heaven, and therefore they oppose its very existence. I posit that the apparent paradox is indeed a beacon of hope. The prayer for the IDF soldiers and security forces symbolizes more than a plea for safety—it's a testament to our collective yearning for unity. To substantiate this claim, I will trace the ideological evolution of this prayer through the lenses of Modern Orthodoxy and Religious Zionism.

Religious Zionism emerged in 1902 as the 'Mizrachi' faction within the Zionist Organization, a response to the Zionist movement's expansion into the realm of culture and education.[1] Zionist leaders aimed to create a 'new man' by negating the 'Diaspora Jew,' with this Diaspora identity at the time encompassing religion. Observant Jews who supported the Zionist ideal recognized that the expansion of Zionism into education and culture would deepen its secular orientation. Thus, the members of 'Mizrachi' aligned with Herzl's approach, seeing the primary goal of Zionism as providing a 'safe haven'—essentially a solution to the issues of anti-Semitism and the persecution of Jews by consolidating them in the Land of Israel. According to "Mizrachi," Zionism was intended to save Jews and nothing more.[2] This can be seen as a pragmatic

---

1   See Shmuel Almog, "The Significance of Culture," in *Zionism and History: The Rise of a New Jewish Consciousness*, trans. Ina Freedman (New York: St. Martin's Press, 1987), 84-174; and Dov Schwartz, *Religious Zionism: History and Ideology* (Boston: Academic Studies Press, Boston 2009), 10-15.

2   See Eliezer Don-Yehiyah, "Ideology and Policy in Religious-Zionism: R. Yitzhak Ya'akov Reines' Conception of Zionism and the Policy of the Mizrahi under His Leadership," *Ha-Tzionut, vol.* 8 (1983): 103-146 (Hebrew).

division between Zionism and Religious Zionism. But the members of "Mizrachi" had a deeper motivation. They knew that in order to bring about the redemption of the nation, they needed to create unity. The divide between the secular and the religious was too deep to be resolved in 1902 (and perhaps even today). Therefore, "Mizrachi" turned to the lowest common denominator, which was the physical salvation of the Jews. Members of Religious Zionism knew that there was no dispute within the Zionist movement that its primary role was to save Jews. The debates were about how far to continue from there. Both Herzl and his faction, as well as members of Religious Zionism, hoped that the further realization of the Zionist idea would bridge the gap between the secular and religious camps.

National unity is thus the backbone of Religious Zionism. Rabbi Abraham Isaac Kook vehemently disagreed with 'Mizrachi,' believing that the focus should be on education and culture, and that the religious side should strive to dominate the movement. As a result, he never joined 'Mizrachi.' However, 'Mizrachi' had a different approach. They sought the unifying element and found it in the survival of the Jewish people.

The struggle for national unity characterized the political path of Religious Zionism. The movement's leaders prided themselves on the achievement of the National Unity Government following the Six-Day War. Indeed, they were a central force that compelled the members of the Labor Movement to incorporate "Gahal" led by Menachem Begin into the unity government. On numerous occasions, the National Religious Party (NRP) demanded a national unity government, even at the expense of the interests of the religious Zionist camp. Unity was not just an ideological backbone, but also an operative factor in the path of Religious Zionism.

Rabbi Joseph B. Soloveitchik, who served as the president of "Mizrachi" in America from 1946, offered a deep theological interpretation of the unifying perspective of Religious Zionism. In his work "Kol Dodi Dofek,"[3] which Rabbi Professor Isadore Twersky, his son-in-law, described as the "great manifesto of Religious Zionism,"[4] Rabbi Soloveitchik introduced the concepts of the "Covenant of Fate" and the "Covenant of Destiny. This distinction has sociological and philosophical roots (Ferdinand Tönnies, Martin Buber, and others), on which I will not elaborate here.[5] The meaning of the "Covenant of Fate" is precisely the lowest common denominator that makes a nation as such. When the anti-Semite does not differentiate between one Jew and another, he renders equality a national trait. When the existence of a nation is characterized by perpetual suffering, then mutual support and philanthropy define its existence. In the book Vision and Leadership, he followed the story of Joseph and his brothers, illustrating through the narrative's details how suffering transforms existence into brotherhood. The essence of the "Covenant of Destiny" is the notion that the "Covenant of Fate" is not the end of the story. There is a purpose beyond mere existential fate. Within existential fate, one can also discern a teleological dimension. That is, neglecting the "Covenant of Destiny" is a missed opportunity.

3   For further, see Dov Schwartz, *From Phenomenology to Existentialism: The Philosophy of Rabbi Joseph B. Soloveitchik*, vol. 2, trans. Batya Stein (Leiden: Brill, 2013), 193-226.

4   For further, see Isadore Twersky, "The Rov," *Tradition: A Journal of Orthodox Jewish Thought*, vol. 30, no. 4 (Summer 1996): 13-44, quote at 31, recently-reprinted in Isadore Twersky, *Perpetuating the Masorah: Halakhic, Ethical and Experiential Dimensions – Essays in Memory of Rabbi Joseph B. Soloveitchik*, eds. Carmi Horowitz and David Shapiro (Jerusalem: Maggid, 2023), 111-158, quote at 144.

5   For further, see Dov Schwartz, *Leadership, Literature, Nationality: The Philosophy of Rabbi Joseph B. Soloveitchik*, vol. 5 (Ramat-Gan: Bar-Ilan University Press, Forthcoming).

A recurring theme in Rabbi Soloveitchik's thought, both formally and substantively, is the fusion of existential polarities into individuality. The religious person (*homo religious*) and the cognitive man ultimately converge in the persona of the Halakhic man. Majestic man and man of faith represent two coexisting modes of existence within each person. Similarly, fate-driven and purpose-driven existences are two influential forces shaping us all. Individuals often navigate between these two, engaging in activities such as aiding soldiers, easing the hardships of security forces through entertainment, hosting communal gatherings, and similar endeavors. He can participate in activities of supplication to bring back the captives. These blessed activities are a clear expression of fate-driven existence. However, a person can miss out on purpose-driven existence, meaning they fail to understand the transcendent significance of fate-driven existence. There are values that go beyond fate-driven existence, and the important engagement in such existence should not overshadow them. Perhaps this is the essence of Rabbi Soloveitchik's message for today, but it is also the foundation for national unity.

Praying for the well-being of the IDF soldiers and security forces, in my view, is the key to national unity. There are Haredi communities that do not recognize the sanctity of the State of Israel but support and openly pray for the soldiers of the IDF and the security forces. A prominent example of such a large community is the Chabad Hasidic movement. A prayer for the well-being of IDF soldiers and security forces can serve as the minimal basis for national unity, especially in times like these. Are minor language adjustments needed to align it with different worldviews? If in the Declaration of Independence, the name of God could be replaced with "Tzur Yisrael," then linguistic adaptations should enable even secular individuals who are not traditional to identify with such a prayer.

Praying for the Defenders of Our Faith

This task now falls on the shoulders of the rabbinate, and the urgency of the moment is a factor that allows for such a decision and pushes for its realization.

Professor Dov Schwartz currently heads the Department of Philosophy at Bar-Ilan University and holds the Natalie and Isidore Friedman Chair for Teaching Rav Joseph B. Soloveitchik's Thought.

Psalms for a State of Vertigo

Bacol Serlui

THE FIRST NIGHT OF MY life when I heard a siren, I almost died of fright. I was eight years old and the Gulf War woke us up and out of bed. My mother placed gas masks on my brother and me, laid us down in our sealed room, and opened a small green book. I was in second grade and already knew how to read. A scrap of gray paper contained random numbers: 20, 121, 130. From the green book she read aloud verse by verse and we, small and frightened, answered after her. It was the first time I recited the Psalms.

I remember the words: ancient, strange, beautiful. I did not understand and yet I understood: "From the depths I called you, O Lord," "I will lift up my eyes to the mountains, from whence will my help come?" In my mind's eye I saw a man standing in the dark in front of towering mountains, his soul possessed by darkness and fear. I was still frightened, but I knew that in this book there was someone who was just as scared as I was. Months later at school we read Psalm 27: "The Lord

Praying for the Defenders of Our Faith

is the stronghold of my life, of whom shall I be afraid when evildoers draw near to devour my flesh?" I didn't understand the meaning of the word evildoer, but I felt the visceral terror of a person pursued by those coming to eat his flesh. I understood that *Tehillim* is a book written through great terror, communicating that fear and discussing it.

Poetry is a wonderful thing. From within a personal and private experience, a poet writes and his words reach the other side of the world, to another soul in another place and time. But the phenomenon called "*Tehillim*," written about 3,300 years ago, has no equal in literature. There is even older poetry than it; known to us from the ancient epics such as Gilgamesh in Mesopotamia, the Indian Ramayana, the Greek Iliad and Odyssey—all still read to this day as ancient, wonderful works that reveal important spiritual and psychological foundations of human existence. But the intimate phenomenon of reading age-old *mizmorim*, in which a person in distress reaches out to a book written thousands of years before he was born and finds in it a contemporary outlet for his soul is unique in human culture. And these wondrous words were written in our own spoken language, Hebrew. Language is a dynamic, rapidly changing space, and the language of poetry often becomes obsolete within decades. Most English speakers today have difficulty reading Shakespeare, distant from them by only about 500 years. Hebrew's resurrection as a spoken language, a miracle in itself, kept the Bible accessible and close. The Book of Psalms is accessible to us because we speak its language, Hebrew, which has changed but little.

But not only in Hebrew. When the Iron Curtain collapsed in Poland, the Nobel Prize-winning poet *Czesław Miłosz* translated the Psalms into Polish. In a short time, the book became an unprecedented bestseller and sold over a million copies. After the brutal desolation of the communist spiritual oppression, a tremendous thirst for simple religious speech arose. What is it in this ancient book that touches people like that?

Today, in the Autumn of 2023, as evening falls, darkness rises in the soul. I am afraid and worried about my people, my dear ones. I struggle with every breath. I feel as if my soul is in a state of vertigo—for a moment hopeful, for a moment sorrowful; a moment of trust, a moment of anxiety. Late at night, I open my *Tehillim* to Psalm 69:

> *For the lead player, on shoshanim, for David.*
>
> *Rescue me, God, for the waters have come up to my neck.*
>
> *I have sunk in the mire of the deep, and there is no place to stand.*
>
> *I have entered the watery depths, and the current has swept me away.*
>
> *I am exhausted from my calling out.*
>
> *My throat is hoarse.*
>
> *My eyes fail from hoping for my God.*

And King David reaches out to me, the hand of a drowning man who plucks me from my whirlwind. The psalmist is perhaps the most honest person who ever walked the earth, and no human emotion is alien to him. He is known as a man of war but first and foremost he is a man of truth, voicing the fear, the terrifying feeling of suffocation, the drowning. The helplessness and distress in the face of the force of the repeated and unanswered request, in the face of the enemy at the gate seeking to take his soul. I read and re-read of the drowning David. Unlike other psalms which stipulate a time or event—"He fled before Absalom his son" or "He altered his good sense before Abimelech"—it is not known when this psalm was written. What caused this distress? A time of war and persecution, or maybe just the turmoil of the soul, the persecution of his own soul? I don't know, but I feel he expresses the depth of my own distress.

Praying for the Defenders of Our Faith

Psalms are the weapon of the weak, of the powerless in the face of words. When I am full of gratitude, full of joy and doubt and sorrow, the ancient words come to me. They are such an intimate part of my inner language that I cannot imagine my life without them. They resonate with me and are relevant in ways I could not imagine. Reciting *Tehillim* at this time, during the current events in Israel, reveals to me how much of a warrior King David was, and how many of the psalms were written in the storm of battle. Towards the end of the book, *mizmor* 140 stuns me:

> *Free me, Lord, from evil folk, from a violent man (מאיש חמסים) preserve me.*
>
> *Who plot evil in their heart, each day stir up battles.*
>
> *They sharpen their tongue like a serpent, venom of spiders beneath their lip. Selah.*
>
> *Guard me, Lord, from the wicked man's hands, from the violent man preserve me, who plots to trip up my steps.*
>
> *The haughty laid down a trap for me, and with cords they spread out a net.*
>
> *Alongside the path they set snares for me. Selah.*
>
> *I said to the Lord, "My God and You. Hearken, O Lord, to the sound of my pleas."*
>
> *Lord, Master, my rescuing strength, You sheltered my head on the day of the fray.*
>
> *Do not grant, O Lord, the desires of the wicked, do not fulfill his devising.*
>
> *They would rise. Selah.*
>
> *May the mischief of their own lipes cover the heads of those who come round me.*

> *May He rain coals of fire upon them, make the violent evil man be trapped in pitfalls.*
>
> *I know that the Lord will take up the cause of the lowly, the case of the needy.*
>
> *Yes, the righteous will acclaim Your name, the upright will dwell in Your presence.*

This psalm, written thousands of years ago, seems to predict the horrors of these days. I find that the strongest expression of evil in the eyes of the poet is "People of Hamas" (the evil violent folk), and he repeats this throughout the book. But the images in this chapter are so intense that they are read as our reality: the people of Hamas *are* evil schemers who lay traps and mines to overthrow righteous people with their tricks. The poet begs God to save us from them, to put a shield over his head as protection. I think of Simhat Torah when this prayer took on an existential, terrible meaning. David begs that his enemies will fall into ravines—the obstacles and pits and tunnels that they themselves have dug. And in the midst of this terrible reality, King David sends me a beautiful verse of strengthening and justifying the judgment: "I know that the Lord will take up the cause of the lowly, the case of the needy." Even when the worst of all happens, God's judgments are justice, and He demands the favorable judgment of the righteous. And I think of King David as a warrior, as a poet, as a great believer, a man who does not place his trust only in his military might but in something greater and more powerful than him, even when He is not revealed and when His judgments seem unbearably difficult, just as they do at this moment. This is how King David gained eternal life—not only as a king and a warrior but as a poet. His most personal prayer is also my prayer.

I turn to another beloved psalm, chapter 13:

Praying for the Defenders of Our Faith

> *To the lead player, a David psalm.*
>
> *How long, O Lord, will You forget me forever? How long hide Your face from me?*
>
> *How long shall I cast about for counsel, sorrow in my heart all day? How long will my enemy loom over me?*
>
> *Look upon me, answer me, Lord, my God. Light up my eyes, lest I sleep death, lest my enemy say, "I have prevailed over him," lest my foes exult when I stumble.*
>
> *But I in Your kindness do trust, my heart exults in Your rescue.*
>
> *Let me sing to the Lord, for He has mercy on me.*

Poets search for words, but great believers have the ability to say unbelievable things. Only the most faithful can turn to God in this way, calling out the cry of abandonment and loneliness: "How long, O Lord, will You forget me forever?" I feel abandoned, abandoned forever, at a loss, troubled day and night, haunted. And the wonderful recurring phrase "How long?"—until when and where will he shout his loneliness, his despair, his loss of power? He writes his own soul: the wounded, the frightened, the trembling. Here comes the terrible cry for help, repeated countless times in the book: "Look upon me, answer me!" Look at me, look at my distress, *answer me!*— perhaps the most desperate human request of man to his Creator. And what a terrible darkness in the soul, facing the joy of his enemies, facing the danger of death.

And out of dark terror is also born a deep sense of security. This is one of the marvelous phenomena in the Psalms. The very same chapter contains a desperate cry of loneliness and despair, and a few verses later a complete reversal of feeling. "But I in Your kindness do trust, my heart exults in Your rescue. Let me sing to the Lord, for He has mercy on me." For years I have wondered about this turn-about that so characterizes the book—how is it that over four short verses the poet goes from the terror of death and a sense of abandonment to complete security in God's grace? It was only years later that I realized that the shouting out itself gives rise to the faith and trust and confidence. Like a baby whose mother brings him into the world with a terrible cry of pain, a terrible cry that leaves the soul clear and pure—the cry is part of the process of escaping the panic of the strait. After the praying poet gives a roaring voice to the depths of his soul, the awareness of salvation is born within him. This is how the Psalms teach us the work of prayer from that time to the present day—a personal cry in a private language for every pain to the exhaustion of the soul, from which we can exit the strait.

This escape from the strait is not only for the individual. Leo Tolstoy writes in one of his letters that the deeper one goes into the human soul, the more universal things he will discover. Sometimes it seems to me that the deeper we go into the human soul, the more we arrive at the Psalms, to the most primordial encounter between man and God in moments of joy and sorrow. David writes in Psalm 119: "I shall acclaim You with an honest heart as I learn Your righteous laws." Like all good poetry, Psalms is an amazing work of literary art that teaches inspired readers and writers how to create, or in other words, how to pray. To arrive with an honest heart and hence the path to thanksgiving and recognition of the Creator's righteous judgments.

And back to these days. At noon on that dark Shabbat of the holiday of Simhat Torah, one of our sons went off to war. I almost died of fear, trembling, and sorrow for the little we knew, from worrying about him and others. And what does a person do when he has no way out? He cries and screams his way through. And like my mother and all the other women, I sat with my *Tehillim*, reciting from beginning to end until the close of the holiday, until my tears dried up and the breaking news broke me once again. I recite the Psalms again and again and feel that

Praying for the Defenders of Our Faith

the *Tehillim* are reading me, dubbing my fear and sorrow, giving me a voice. Three millennia ago a Jew sat and poured out the agony of his soul in times of peace and war, and here he reaches out a hand of prayer and speaks to our own day, until we will be redeemed.

Bacol Serlui, an Israeli poet, literary critic, and teacher of Hebrew literature, is the recipient of the 2022 Yehuda Amichai Prize.

This essay is an expanded version of an article that was originally published in Makor Rishon on October 24, 2023. The translation was prepared by Jeffrey Saks and initially published on TraditionOnline.org. It is reprinted here with the kind permission of the author and Tradition: A Journal of Orthodox Jewish Thought.

The Text of Rav Ezra Zion Melamed's Mi Sheberach for IDF Soldiers

Daniel Sperber

Among the texts quoted in Avraham Yaari, "Supplements to The Mi Sheberach Prayers: Their Evolution, Customs, and Texts," *Kiryat Sefer*, vol. 36, no. 1 (December 1960): 116 [no. 88] (Hebrew) is one by Rav Ezra Zion Melamed's text of a Mi Sheberach for IDF Soldiers, as he published in *Pirkei Minhag ve-Halakhah* (Jerusalem: Kiryat Sefer, 1954), 194 (Hebrew), and whose text reads:

מי שבירך אבותינו הקדושים אברהם יצחק ויעקב משה אהרן דוד
ושלמה הוא יט יברך את כל בחורי ובנות ישראל העומדים במערכה
בכל מקום שהם, המוסרים את נפשם ומקדישים את נעוריהם
על [כיבוש ארץ ישראל ו] שמירת גבולותיה ועל הגנת העם.

Praying for the Defenders of Our Faith

יגן ה' עליהם בימין עזו ויפרוש סוכת שלומו עליהם. ובבוא עליהם אויב תקיים בהם תפילת משה "קומה ה' ויפוצו אויביך וינוסו משנאיך" (במדבר י, לה), וברדפם אחרי אויבינו תקיים בהם הברכה "ורדפתם את אויבכם ונפלו לפניכם לחרב" (ויקרא כו, ז) [ובצאתם לכיבוש והתיישבות תקיים לנו הבטחתך "כל המקום אשר תדרוך בו כף רגלכם לכם יהיה" (דברים יא, כד)]. ומכל פעולה ומכל קרב ישובו כולם בשלום ולא ייזנק איש מהם ולא ייפקד איש מהם. וישובו לבתיהם בריאים ושלמים. והוריהם ישמחו בהם שמחה שלמה ויזכו לראות בחופותיהם והם ישמחו בבניהם.

ורופא כל בשר ישלח רפואה שלמה לכל חולי עמו ישראל ובכללם לכל הפצועים והנפגעים בכל מקום שהם. הוא בחמלתו ישלח להם במהרה מרפא וארוכה למחלותיהם ומכותיהם וישובו לאיתנם. והחונן לאדם דעת יאיר את עיני כל המטפלים בהם, חובשים ורופאים, אחים ואחיות, ויחזקם במלאכתם הקדושה.

וכל הקהל הקדוש הזה יבורך מפי עליון בכל טוב. אלוקי ציון ימלא משאלות לב כל אחד ואחד לטובה ונזכה כולנו לגאולה שלמה ותחזינה עינינו בשוב ה' ציון ובקיבוץ נידחי ישראל מארבע כנפות הארץ לתוך ירושלים הבנויה, הוותיקה והחדשה, במהרה בימינו אמן.

May He who blessed our holy forefathers Abraham, Isaac, and Jacob, Moses, Aaron, David, and Solomon, bless all the young men and women of Israel standing in the battle wherever they are, who give their lives and dedicate their youth for [the conquest of the Land of Israel and] the protection of its borders and the defense of the people. May the Lord protect them with His mighty right hand and spread His canopy of peace over them. And when an enemy comes upon them, may the prayer of Moses "Arise, O LORD, and let Your enemies be scattered, and let those who hate You flee before You" (Numbers 10:35) be fulfilled in them, and in pursuing our enemies, may the blessing "You shall chase your enemies, and they shall fall before you by the sword" (Leviticus 26:7) [and when going out for conquest and settlement, may Your promise be fulfilled for us "Every place on which the sole of your foot treads shall be yours" (Deuteronomy 11:24)] be fulfilled. From every action and every battle, may all return in peace, and may none of them be harmed or missing. May they return to their homes healthy and whole. May their parents rejoice with complete joy, and may they merit to see their children's weddings, and may they rejoice in their children.

And the Healer of all flesh shall send a complete recovery to all the sick of His people Israel, and among them to all the injured and hurt wherever they are. In His mercy, He will swiftly send them a cure and relief for their illnesses and wounds, and they will return to their strength. And the One who grants wisdom will enlighten the eyes of all who care for them, paramedics and doctors, brothers and sisters, and strengthen them in their holy work.

And this entire holy congregation shall be blessed from the mouth of the Most High with all that is good. The God of Zion shall fulfill the desires of the heart of each and every one for good, and may we all merit a complete redemption and may our eyes behold the return of the Lord to Zion and the ingathering of the dispersed of Israel from the four corners of the earth into a built

Jerusalem, the ancient and the new, speedily in our days. Amen.

Rav Ezra Zion Melamed was a saintly person (whom I knew well),[1] and his words reverberate strongly in the current situation.

Prof. Daniel Sperber is the Milan Roven Professor of Talmudic Studies (emeritus) and former Dean of the Faculty of Jewish Studies, where he is currently President of the Ludwig and Erica Jesselson Institute of Advanced Torah Studies at Bar-Ilan University.

---

1 See Noah Aminoah, "The Man of Torah and Science: The Scientific Work of Ezra Zion Melamed," *Jewish Studies*, no. 35 (1995): 103-117 (Hebrew), and earlier in *Studies in Rabbinic Literature, Bible, and Jewish History: Ezra Zion Melamed Jubilee Volume*, eds. Yitzhak Gilat, et al. (Ramat-Gan: Bar-Ilan University Press, 1982; Hebrew).

Setting the Mi Seberach for IDF Soldiers to Music

Composed by Dubi Zeltzer
Transcribed by Yitzy Spinner

Thoughts on Praying for Israel's Soldiers

Joseph Tabory

I N Ashkenazi synagogues, between the public reading of the Torah on Shabbat and the Musaf prayer, there is a window of opportunity for public messages. The Yerushalmi states that the reason that the *shofar* is blown at this time, rather than first thing in the morning, is because that this is the time when everyone is in the synagogue. In modern times, the only public messages at this time are the two *yekum purkan* prayers in Aramaic (the first is a prayer for the leaders of the community and its Torah scholars and the second is a general prayer for the community) and a *mi sheberach* in Hebrew for the community with special emphasis on those who contribute materially to the community – such as by bringing fuel for lighting the synagogue, or bringing wine for *havdalah*, or by feeding guests or supporting the poor. Minhag Ashkenaz also includes here a memorial prayer for Jewish martyrs. On the Shabbat before *rosh chodesh*, there is included here also an announcement of which day(s) will be celebrated as *rosh chodesh* in the coming week. These prayers (or announcements) are just a few of those which have been composed and offered at this point in the communal service.

These prayers, while speaking to God (in the third person), are also addressing the community. The messages to the community may be roughly categorized as meant to encourage respect for the hierarchy of the community; to encourage people to contribute to the community, and to make general announcements formulated in the language of prayer.

With these considerations in mind, we will now turn to the prayer for the soldiers of Israel. There are those who refuse to recite the prayer for the soldiers while others recite a prayer for the soldiers, but at a different moment in the Shabbat service. The reasons for the refusal or for reciting the prayer in a different context are worthy of another discussion. But this discussion is limited to those synagogues in which the prayer for the soldiers is recited in conjunction with the prayer for the State of Israel.

It is clear to me that there is no need of an element of encouragement in this prayer. We have recently seen how motivated the soldiers are in this battle. But this motivation is not just because of the pogrom on *simchat torah*. It is well known that many soldiers are keen to do 'significant service', which is a code term for service which is demanding and dangerous.

Neither is there need to encourage the community to respect and cherish the soldiers. Any one who saw all sections of the populace volunteer to help the soldiers and their families in any way that they can, knows that these soldiers are among the most respected and admired section of the populace. What is meant at this junction of the synagogue service is a heartfelt prayer, not only for the safety of the soldiers but also for their success. When I hear this prayer I think of a talmudic discussion about the status of the Temple priests: are they agents of God

Praying for the Defenders of Our Faith

or are they agents of the people. The prayer for the soldiers reminds us that they are our agents – they are fighting for us. People who stand for this prayer are signifying, among other things, their identification with the soldiers who are fighting for us. But the closing verse of this prayer: because *Adonai* your God is going with you to fight for you' (Deu 20:4) points to another aspect: our soldiers are also the agents of God, fighting in His army to save His people.

May our prayer be fulfilled.

Rabbi Prof. Joseph Tabory is a professor of Talmud at Bar-Ilan University in Israel. He is also an ordained Orthodox rabbi. He received his PhD from Bar-Ilan University in 1978.

The Call to Return Home

Daniel Tropper

A FRIEND OF MINE TOLD ME that on that bleak Simchat Torah when Hamas terrorists attacked Israel and committed their unspeakable atrocities, his son was travelling in Nepal. The next morning, the Kathmandu airport was full of young Israelis clamoring frantically for tickets to return to Israel in order to join their army units. The Nepalese thought the Israelis had lost their minds completely: Why return to Israel? That's a war zone! Remain here safe and secure!

The clamoring Israelis included all types: men and women, religious and secular, leftists and rightists, Sefardim and Ashkenazim. These were people who, just days earlier, had confronted each other feverishly battling over an effort to make major changes in the Israeli legal system. They included reservists who announced they would not respond to a call to reserve duty! The shock of the Nepalese observers certainly calls for some explanation. What happened?

Praying for the Defenders of Our Faith

The underlying source of this "insane" spectacle is that we are not speaking of professional soldiers, but rather of Jews with a spark of kedusha. Every Jew, distant as he may be from Torah and Mitzvot, has that spark. Occasionally the spark may dim, it may seem to fade – but it is never extinguished. It may remain dormant for years and tragically never find expression. However, a crisis of the Jewish people elicits immediate regeneration. That very same young man who, a mere month ago, cursed the religious and ridiculed the Sabbath, is ready today to risk his life for the continuity of Am Yisrael.

It is for this IDF soldier and for his varied colleagues who all share that spark that we say a prayer for the success of the IDF.

Rabbi Daniel Tropper is the Founder and President Emeritus of Gesher.

Sociological Aspects of the Prayer on behalf of Soldiers in the Israel Defense Forces

Chaim I. Waxman

BY WAY OF INTRODUCTION – I have no idea how [or if] prayer works with God, and I certainly have no idea how God works. In fact, during the entire week of *Parashat Bereishit*, I kept asking "Why?" – "*Bereishit* God created the heaven(s) and earth' Why?" So far, I have found no satisfactory answer. For the purposes of the subject at hand, the *Mi Sheberach* prayer for the soldiers of the Israel Defense Forces (IDF) soldiers, as a Sociologist and I can only try to deal with the issue the subject within the context of relationship between people and prayer/prayer and people.

Praying for the Defenders of Our Faith

The Prayer for the Welfare of Israel's soldiers, *Mi Sheberach le-Chayalei Tzahal*,[1] is incorporated into most Ashkenazi non-haredi siddurim. The vast majority, if not all, Ashkenazi haredi siddurim do not include it, but it is now standard, though with some textual variations, in virtually all Sephardi siddurim.[2] As is typical of prayer,[3] it is recited as part of communal prayer services, with variations between Ashkenazim and Sephardim as to when within the services it is recited, and with variations within Israel and even more so in diaspora communities, as to how frequently (under normal conditions) it is recited. Amidst the ongoing conflict between Israel and Hamas, the prayer for the soldiers of the Israel Defense Forces is being recited daily across Israel after each prayer service—morning, afternoon, and evening. This invocation has also found a place in synagogue services around the globe, reflecting a global Jewish solidarity with those in harm's way.

Given its communal character, there are denominational differences in terms of who engages in the prayer. In Israel, according to the most recent data available, the overall percentage of Jews who attend synagogue service once a week or more is 27 percent. It is highest among Haredim (85%), followed by Datiim (74%), Masortim (32%), an Hilonim (1%). The overall percentage of Israeli Jews who never attend synagogue services and, presumably, never pray, is 33 percent. As for prayer, 21

---

1   See the chapters by Aaron Ahrend, Nissim Leon, Yoel Rappel, and Levi Cooper to this volume.

2   See the chapter by Nissim Leon in this volume.

3   Marces Mauss, *On Prayer: Text and Commentary*, ed. W.S.F. Pickering (New York: Berghahn, 2003), 33-34; Robert Wuthnow, "Prayer, Cognition, and Culture," *Poetics*, vol. 36, no. 5-6 (October 2008): 333-337.

percent of all Israeli Jews say they pray daily: Haredim, 76%; Datiim, 58%; Masortim, 21%; Hilonim, 1%.[4]

In the United States, the percentage of Jews who pray daily seems to be slightly higher. According to the Pew Research Center's "Religious Landscape Study" of 2007 and 2014, other than the Unaffiliated/Religious Nones, Jews have the lowest rates of prayer among all religious groups in America. For example. 29 percent of Jews, as compared to 27 percent of Israeli Jews, said they pray daily. The percentage among Catholics who said they pray daily was 59%; Mainline Protestants, 54%; Muslims, 69%.[5]

There are currently reports of many soldiers in haredi units actively fighting along their non-haredi fellow soldiers, and they claim that they receive very strong support from the major rabbis ("*gedolei harabbanim*")[6] The percentage of eligible haredim who enlisted still appears to be quite low; there is little empirical evidence of a change in the haredi leadership stance toward army service; and, although a minority recite a *tefilla* for those fighting in the current war, haredim do not recite the Mi Sheberach for the soldiers of the IDF despite its containing much less, if any, of the

---

[4] Data courtesy of the Pew Research Center, available here (https://www.pewresearch.org/religion/2016/03/08/religious-commitment).

[5] Data courtesy of the Pew Research Center, available here (https://www.pewresearch.org/religion/religious-landscape-study/frequency-of-prayer).

[6] See, for example, example, "Contributing Their Part: Numerous Haredi Soldiers Among Recruits in Various Units," *Makor Rishon* (13 October 2023; Hebrew); "Not Just Prayers: War Sparks Unprecedented Mobilization by Ultra-Orthodox Israelis," *Times of Israel* (22 October 2023); "150 Haredi Men Draft into IDF, Thousands Expected to Follow," *Times of Israel* (23 October 2023); and "Haredi Jews, Exempt from Israel's Military Service Mandate, Sign Up to Fight," *The Washington Post* (1 November 2023), among other articles.

Praying for the Defenders of Our Faith

political Zionist wording of, for example, the Prayer for the Welfare of the State / *Tefillah L'Shalom haMedinah*.[7]

While Israelis who recite the prayer have a personal relationship with the IDF and Security Forces, diaspora Jews, for the most part, do not and one might then ask why they recite the *Mi Sheberach*. As indicated, Orthodox Jews attend synagogue services and pray much more frequently than do the non-Orthodox, and Orthodox Jews have stronger attachments to Israel than do those who are not Orthodox.[8] Standing and reciting the *Mi Sheberach* gives it special status gives it and the defense forces of Israel special status, thereby strengthening the connection with Israel.

In the United States, as well as in other English-speaking nations, the inclusion in synagogue services of the prayer for the soldiers of the Israel Defense Forces (and the Prayer for the State of Israel) arrived, in 1986, with within the Rabbinical Council of America edition of the ArtScroll Siddur, which marked a significant departure from the RCA's previous editions of their Siddur.[9] This edition remains widely used in American synagogues, even though these prayers are appended to the

---

[7] Regarding this prayer, see Yoel Rappel, "The Identity of the Author of the Prayer for the Welfare of the State," in Shulamit Eliash, et al., eds., *Maasuah LeYitzhak: Rabbi Yitzhak Isaac ha-Levi Herzog Memorial Volume*, vol. (Jerusalem: Yad Ha-Rav Herzog, 2009), 594-620, esp. 620 (Hebrew), and more recently in Yoel Rappel, *Politics and Prayer: Jewish Prayers for the Government and the State of Israel* (New York: Ktav Publishing House, 2023

[8] Chaim I. Waxman, "Israel in Orthodox Identity: The American Experience," in Danny Ben-Moshe and Zohar Segev, eds., *Israel, the Diaspora and Jewish Identity* (Brighton: Sussex Academic Press, 2007), 52-61.

[9] There were, of course, synagogues that had previously recited the Mi Sheberach. The example of Congregation Kehilath Jeshurun on Manhattan's Upper East Side is discussed by Rabbi Haskel Lookstein in his chapter in this book.

back of the standard haredi ArtScroll Siddur, underscoring its broad acceptance within the community. Indeed, the RCA siddur solidified the Mi Sheberach prayer for IDF soldiers as a staple within Modern Orthodox synagogue services. Until the publication of ArtScroll's edition of the Rabbinical Council of America siddur,[10] far fewer Modern Orthodox synagogues included the Mi Sheberach in the regular weekly shabbat service. When they did, it was most frequently in due to the presence in the congregation of young men and women who had spent a year or two in Israel after high school, a phenomenon which became very popular since the late 1970s.[11]

Chaim I. Waxman, Professor Emeritus of Sociology and Jewish Studies at Rutgers University, served as a member of the Department of Sociology from 1975 to 2006.

---

10 Today, there is a completely new (non-Artscroll) edition of the RCA Siddur as well as the new, highly regarded Koren-Sacks Siddur for English-speaking Modern Orthodox communities. Both of these, of course, place the Prayer for the State of Israel and the Mi Sheberach for IDF soldiers after the prayers concluding the reading of the Torah and Maftir, and before the Torah in returned to the Aron Kodesh

11 Shalom Berger found that, by the middle of the 1990s, up to 90 percent of the graduates of Modern Orthodox high schools were studying in yeshivot and seminaries in "Year in Israel" programs. Shalom Z. Berger, "A Year of Study in an Israeli Yeshiva Program: Before and After," (PhD Dissertation, Yeshiva University, 1996); Shalom Z. Berger, Daniel Jacobson, and Chaim I. Waxman, Flipping Out? – Myth or Fact? The Impact of the 'Year in Israel' (New York: Yashar Books, 2007).

Praying for the Refuat Ha-Nefesh of the IDF

Jason Weiner

Following the horrific *Simchat Torah* massacres, I had the opportunity to visit Israel on a rabbinic solidarity mission. During that trip we went to the Shura military base in Ramla, where all the corpses of those who were murdered, and soldiers who fall in battle, are sent.[1] We meet with the IDF rabbis who are tasked with identifying these bodies, which is sometimes unfortunately a very difficult task. As they described how holy and challenging their work on this base is, one of the rabbis shared how this has been more gruesome and difficult than anything he'd ever done before.

The IDF was aware that they were asking a lot of these individuals, and thus appointed psychologists to debrief with them at the end of every shift. These soldiers welcomed the idea. Just 10 minutes into his

---

1   For a recent journalistic account of this IDF Chevre Kadisha at the Shura Military Base, see the news report by Yair Ettinger, about his visit there (https://twitter.com/kann_news/status/1722263620695011436).

first session, trying to describe the unspeakable things he had seen on this base, one IDF rabbi told us that the psychologist he was talking to broke down in tears and walked out, explaining that he was overwhelmed by what he was hearing, and that this rabbi would need to find someone else to talk to. The rabbi knew what he'd experienced was horrible, but once he realized that even seasoned mental health professionals couldn't handle the details, he knew it was very severe and would likely remain with him for his entire life. He then turned to all of us, and gently said, "I know you all pray for the IDF and for our soldiers to be safe. Whenever you say a *mi she'berach*, please have us here on this base in mind particularly when you pray for a *refuat ha-nefesh* (healing of soul)." Since then, I've thought of these brave soldiers every time I pray.

Indeed, whenever we pray for the sick, we typically have physical healing in mind. But this prayer always places "healing of soul" before mention of physical healing. Our rabbis knew that emotional well-being is conducive to healing of the body and that mental or emotional struggles are just as real and debilitating as physical ones. There are times when war is absolutely necessary, but it is horrific nonetheless, and we don't only want our soldiers only to survive these intense battles physically, but we also pray for them to be able to live productive and healthy lives when they return home.

The simple request of this dedicated rabbinic soldier is a crucial reminder and transformed the way I conceptualize all of my prayers for the IDF. I no longer have in mind just a large and mighty Army, but the very human individuals who are must experience some of the worst things that anyone can undergo, and will then have to spend the rest of their lives processing them. May the Almighty bring us victory over our enemies, and enable all of our soldiers to return home both in one piece *and* whole. Whole in spirit and in body.

Amen.

Praying for the Defenders of Our Faith

Rabbi Dr. Jason Weiner serves as the senior rabbi and director of the Spiritual Care Department at Cedars-Sinai in Los Angeles, where he is responsible for the chaplaincy team and all aspects of spiritual care.

The Holiest Jew

Avi Weiss

Over many years, I have had the opportunity to lead scores of rallies in support of Medinat Yisrael. At every opportunity, I emotionally cried out "Ashrei ha-'am she-yesh lo tzava – ve-tzava musari – ki-Tzva Haganah Le-Yisrael – Blessed be the nation that has its army the strongest per capita and the most moral army in the world – the Israeli Defense Forces."

For me, the holiest Jew is one who is a member of the IDF (Israel Defence Army). Born to a father who experienced being beaten up as a youngster in the town of Oscweicim which later became Auschwitz, I understand on a very familial level the dangers of powerlessness and the need for 'Am Yisrael to defend itself. Of course, power has its challenges. In Israel, our army is strong, and yet, it reflects an ethics of power – a ṭohar ha-neshek – that I believe has no equivalent in the world.

In more recent years my respect for Israel's army has become personal. Today, I am a military grandfather, as our daughter Elana and her husband Michael made 'aliyyah – and their children are in the IDF. It is one matter to speak in generalities about Tzahal. It is quite another when family members are serving.

Praying for the Defenders of Our Faith

Rabbi Avi Weiss is the founding rabbi of the Hebrew Institute of Riverdale, Bronx, N.Y., and founder of Yeshivat Chovevei Torah and Yeshivat Maharat rabbinical schools. He is a co-founder of the International Rabbinic Fellowship and longtime Jewish activist for Israel and human rights.

This text is a brief extract, with his permission, from a longer article in Avi Weiss, "Showing 'Am Yisrael the Way," in Yosef Yuval Tobi, Shmuel Glick, and Renée Levine Melammed, eds., Streams of Love, Yuvle Ahava: In Loving Memory of Yuval Haiman (Jerusalem: Haiman Family, 2017), ix-xiv, and which was reprinted in Avi Weiss, "The Holiness of IDF Soldiers," in Journey to Open Orthodoxy (Jerusalem: Ktav and Urim, 2019), 587-591.

The Noble Sacrifice of IDF Soldiers

David Yosef

הרב דוד יוסף, חבר מועצת חכמי התורה:

שואלים אותי מהי השקפת התורה כלפי המלחמה והחיילים בימים הללו, התשובה היא חד משמעית - החיילים הם האחים שלנו, אחים אהובים, שהיום הם מוסרים את נפשם למען כלל ישראל אשריהם ואשרי חלקם איזה כאב נורא מרגיש כל אחד מאתנו יום יום כשאנו שומעים על הריגתם של חיילים שלנו, על האחים היקרים שלנו, לכן אנחנו כולנו מחזקים את ידיהם כל הזמן, אנחנו מתפללים, אנחנו מוסיפים 'אבינו מלכנו' בתפילה, אנחנו לומדים תורה להצלחתם.

כבר מתחילת המלחמה קראתי שכל אברך שלומד תורה יאמץ חייל ויקדיש את לימוד התורה שלו להצלחתו ולהצלתו ולשמירתו של החייל. ובעזרת השם עם ישראל ינצח, החיילים שלנו, הקב"ה ישמור עליהם, הקב"ה שומר עליהם וימשיך לשמור עליהם, ובעזרת ה' ילכו מחיל אל חיל, וגבר ישראל.

אמן כן יהי רצון.

People ask me what is the Torah's perspective regarding the war and the soldiers in these days. The response is unambiguous - the soldiers are our brothers, beloved brothers, who today are sacrificing their lives for the sake of all Israel. Blessed are they, and blessed is their portion.

Praying for the Defenders of Our Faith

What terrible pain each one of us feels day by day when we hear about the killing of our soldiers, our dear brothers. Therefore, we all strengthen their hands all the time, we pray, we add 'Avinu Malkeinu' in prayer, we study Torah for their success.

Since the start of the war, I have advocated for every Torah student to adopt a soldier and dedicate his Torah study for his success, his rescue, and his protection. With God's help, the people of Israel will prevail, our soldiers, may the Almighty protect them, the Almighty watches over them and will continue to watch over them, and with the help of God, they will go from strength to strength, and the man of Israel will prevail.

Amen, may it be His will.

Rav David Yosef is a son of the late Maran Ovadiah Yosef, served as Chief Rabbi of Har Nof, Jerusalem, and is Head of Kollel Yechaveh Da'at, a rabbinic institute that trains Sephardic Dayanim in the State of Israel. He sits on the Moetzet Chachmei HaTorah (Shas Council of Torah Sages), the rabbinical body with the ultimate religious authority overseeing the Israeli Shas political party in the State of Israel.

Made in United States
North Haven, CT
08 December 2023

45351532R00320